PREACHING WITH AN ACCENT

 A catalogue record for this book is available from the National Library of Australia

PREACHING WITH AN ACCENT

Biblical Genres for Australian Congregations

Edited by Ian Hussey

Preaching with an Accent: Biblical genres for Australian congregations

© Ian Hussey 2019

Print ISBN: 978-0-9945726-6-0
E-Book ISBN: 978-0-9945726-7-7

First published in Australia in 2019

Morling Press
122 Herring Rd Macquarie Park NSW 2113 Australia
Phone: +61 2 9878 0201
Email: enquiries@morling.edu.au

www.morlingcollege.com/morlingpress

The publication is copyright. Other than for the purposes of study and subject to the conditions of the Copyright Act, no part of this book in any form or by any means (electronic, mechanical, micro-copying, photocopying or otherwise) may be reproduced, stored in a retrieval system, communicated or transmitted without prior written permission.

All Scripture quotations, unless otherwise indicated, are taken from the Holy Bible, New International Version® Anglicised (NIVUK), NIV®. Copyright ©1979, 1984, 2011 by Biblica, Inc.™ Used by permission. All rights reserved worldwide.

Scripture quotations marked 'NRSV-A' are from the New Revised Standard Version Bible: Anglicized Edition, copyright © 1989, 1995 National Council of the Churches of Christ in the United States of America. Used by permission. All rights reserved worldwide.

Designed by: Impressum

CONTENTS

Contributors vii

Introduction 1
   Ian Hussey

1
Describing Australians 9
   Ian Hussey

2
Preaching the Pentateuch to Australians 28
   Murray Capill

3
Preaching Old Testament Law to Australians 52
   Martin Pakula

4
Preaching Old Testament Narrative to Australians 69
   Christine Redwood

5
Preaching Wisdom to Australians 87
   Marc Rader

6
Preaching Psalms to Australians 103
   David J. Cohen and Erin Martine Sessions

7
Preaching the Prophets to Australians 125
   Kirk R. Patston

8
Preaching New Testament Narrative to Australians 146
Tim Patrick

9
Preaching Paul's Epistles to Australians 162
Tim MacBride

10
Preaching the Petrine Epistles to Australians 189
Mike Raiter

11
Preaching the Johannine Letters to Australians 213
Bill Salier

12
Preaching Hebrews, James and Jude to Australians 229
Brian Harris

13
Preaching Revelation to Australians 248
Ian Hussey

Endnotes 273

CONTRIBUTORS

Ian Hussey

Ian is a lecturer and director of Post-Graduate Studies at Malyon Theological College, Brisbane, an affiliated college of the Australian College of Theology. Between 1993 and 2010, he was solo/senior pastor of Nundah/North-East Baptist church in Brisbane. Ian has taught or co-taught (with John Sweetman) homiletics at Malyon since 1994 and is the director of the Malyon Preaching Centre. Ian researches local church vitality, including research into preaching. He recently published an article in the *Journal of the Evangelical Homiletical Society* on 'Vulnerability in Preaching: How Far is Not Enough?' with Allan Demond. He preaches in local churches most Sundays.

Murray Capill

Murray is principal of the Reformed Theological College in Melbourne, an affiliated college of the Australian College of Theology, where he also lectures in preaching and pastoral ministry. Originally from New Zealand, Murray was pastor of a church in Auckland for ten years, before moving to Australia in 2001 to become pastor of a church in Geelong and teach at the RTC. He is the author of *Preaching with Spiritual Vigour* (2004) and *The Heart is the Target* (2014).

Martin Pakula

Martin was brought up Jewish and converted to Christianity at university. He is an ordained Anglican minister who has been involved in parish ministry, university student ministry, Jewish mission and lecturing at Bible college. He is currently an adjunct lecturer in Hebrew and Old Testament at the Presbyterian Theological College in Melbourne.

Christine Redwood

Christine is the lead pastor at Seaforth Baptist Church and an adjunct lecturer at Morling College, Sydney, an affiliated college of the Australian College of Theology, where she is completing her PhD in Old Testament narrative. She was the Morling College preaching intern in 2010.

Marc Rader

Marc is the senior pastor at Gymea Baptist Church in the south of Sydney and a member of faculty (part-time) at Morling College, an affiliated college of the Australian College of Theology, where he lectures in biblical studies and preaching. In 2013 he completed a DMin exploring how preachers could obtain effective feedback. An engaging Bible teacher, Marc's preaching is featured on the Australian Christian Channel (New Horizons).

David J. Cohen

David has been head of biblical studies at Vose Seminary, an affiliated college of the Australian College of Theology, since 2004, teaching in the area of Hebrew Bible and language. His doctoral work explored how praying lament psalms may help people respond to personal distress. David is an internationally renowned author, theologian and pastor who preaches regularly and facilitates workshops focusing on the using the psalms in personal devotion and corporate worship.

Erin Sessions

Erin Martine Sessions is an academic, poet, speaker and writer. She lectures in integrative Studies at Excelsia, Sydney, and is a spokesperson for Common Grace's Domestic and Family Violence justice team. She is currently working towards her PhD on Song of Songs and violence.

Kirk R. Patston

Kirk has been in ministry for more than twenty years. He has pursued postgraduate study on the book of Isaiah and on the connections between the book of Job and the human experience of disability. His working week is a mix of three days of Old Testament lecturing at Sydney Missionary and Bible College, an affiliated college of the Australian College of Theology, and two days of preaching and pastoring.

Tim Patrick

Tim Patrick is principal of the Bible College of South Australia, an affiliated college of the Australian College of Theology, where he teaches systematic theology and practical ministry. He served in pastoral ministry for ten years before moving into theological education and ministry training. His research interests are at the intersection of biblical studies, theology and Anglican ministry. Tim is married to Catriona, and they have three children, Poppy, Jonty and Remy.

Tim MacBride

Tim MacBride has been on the faculty of Morling College, an affiliated college of the Australian College of Theology, since 2008, and commenced lecturing full time at the beginning of 2011. Prior to this, he spent twelve years on the pastoral team at Narwee Baptist Church in the areas of teaching and creative ministries. Tim's doctoral work was in the area of rhetorical approaches to the New Testament and how these can be used in preaching. His book, *Catching the Wave: Preaching the New Testament as Rhetoric*, was published in 2016.

Mike Raiter

Michael Raiter began his career as a high school teacher in Sydney and Pakistan. He studied at Moore Theological College in Sydney, becoming the head of the Department of Missions in 1997. From 2006 to 2011, Mike served as the principal of the Melbourne School of Theology. He is currently the director of the Centre for Biblical Preaching, an organisation that seeks to train and equip churches around the globe in expository preaching.

Bill Salier

Bill worked as a primary school teacher before studying at Moore Theological College and working at Liverpool Anglican. Bill returned to Moore in 1996 as a lecturer and became vice principal in 2007. He joined Youthworks College, an affiliated college of the Australian College of Theology, as principal in 2015, and lectures in biblical studies and Greek.

Brian Harris

Brian Harris is the principal of Vose Seminary, an affiliated college of the Australian College of Theology, and is pastor at large for the Carey Group, a church, school and community centre planting movement based in Perth, Australia, where he also chairs the board. In demand as a speaker, teacher and writer, Brian presents at conferences, theological colleges and churches around Australia and New Zealand, as well as in other parts of the world.

INTRODUCTION

Ian Hussey

Nobody likes to be pigeonholed. Australians especially, I suspect. Many would point to 'ethnic profiling' – viewing a person's race, ethnicity, religion or national origin as the basis for suspicion – as an undesirable endpoint of the practice of generalisation. However, categorisation is a useful tool in a number of realms. The government, for example, finds it useful to group people according to certain characteristics to tailor the delivery of resources in the most effectual way.

But does categorisation have a role in preaching? You may be aware of the concept of contextualisation, which suggests that gospel communicators should seek to understand the culture to which they are ministering in order to adapt their message to the context. This means that if you cannot accurately describe or understand the culture into which you are preaching, your sermon may be a very blunt instrument indeed. Contextualisation brings a sharpness and relevance to a sermon that may otherwise be missing. And in order to do contextualisation, some categorisation is necessary. You must make some generalisations about your audience in order to adapt the message to them.

This volume is based on categorisation – perhaps even ethnic profiling! It will endeavour to create a picture of the 'average' (I deliberately avoid the use of the word 'normal') Australian in order to better contextualise sermons. Of course, such an approach is a hazardous one, especially in a diverse nation like Australia. Not every Australian, by any stretch of the imagination, will demonstrate all of the characteristics described in the coming pages. Further, there are other cultural descriptors and nuances Australians may have that will not be described there.

However, even though generalisations should be treated with caution, they do have their value. In particular, they give us the language to begin to talk about the features of a cultural group. In doing so, the descriptors cause us to think more deeply about the characteristics of the culture or subculture to which we are called to minister.

Much of the analysis of Australian culture upon which this volume is based will be done by comparing statistics. However, Tim Foster speaks on behalf of many when he writes that, in trying to discern culture, 'statistics are superficial and tell us almost nothing of any importance'.[1] Statistical analysis can certainly be 'impersonal' and ignore cultural narratives, but it does help us to ask important questions and think more deeply about the people we are preaching to. When undertaking the difficult task of understanding cultures, there is a place for both the analysis of cultural narratives and statistical analysis.

And so, I ask you to set aside your justifiable hesitancy about the process of categorisation we are about to undertake in the hope that you will see the benefits for your preaching that come from this activity.

But before we look at these descriptors of Australian culture, we need to discuss a number of assumptions that underpin this volume.

The Tasks of the Preacher

There are, of course, many tasks that the preacher must undertake in preparing, delivering and reflecting upon a sermon. The process involves determining the meaning of a passage of Scripture in order to apply it to a particular context. This process may be called exegesis or the 'hermeneutical task'. This is a complex process, which may involve utilisation of 'biblical theology',[2] 'theological interpretation of Scripture'[3] or 'canonical criticism',[4] just to name a few possible approaches. However, whatever approach or approaches are taken, evangelical preachers will at some point be looking to make a grammatical and historical examination of the text. As part of that examination, they will be taking into account the particular genre of the ancient literature and the nuances that this genre brings to interpretation. Certainly, God's own authorship and intention should not be discounted and may, through the Spirit, exceed the grammatical-historical horizon of the human author. Still, attempting to discern the author's original intention will normally be a key focus in the sermon preparation process.

Many of the genres found in the biblical literature are unfamiliar to most twenty-first-century Australians. Their interpretation requires informed diligence on the part of the preacher. There has been much written on the interpretation of biblical genres down through the centuries. However, in this volume we hope to present a brief summary of the key principles of interpretation for the Australian preacher.

You will see that the term 'genre' is used to this volume in a broad sense as well as the narrower sense just described. You can certainly identify specific literary genres in the Scriptures (for example, poetry or narrative), but you can also classify groups of books into genres. For example, the Pauline epistles and the Petrine epistles are both the same literary genre, epistles, but we also use the term 'genre' to distinguish between these two groups of literature because they have distinct literary and theological features.

The contributors to this volume have been asked to identify the key hermeneutical issues that present for the particular group of books they have been allocated. Some of the questions they wrestle with include:

- What are the key introductory issues that influence the interpretation of these books?[5]
- What are the key literary issues associated with this genre? How do these literary and other features affect our interpretation of the texts?
- What grammatical and historical background to these books is crucial to their interpretation?
- How has the church historically interpreted these books?
- How should the literary form of these books influence the preaching of them?

The next task faced by preachers is the 'contextualisation task': the process of taking the message they have discerned from the text and making it relevant to their audience. This means preachers need to have some knowledge of the culture of the congregation they are preaching to. Yet Raymond Williams says the term 'culture' is one of the most complicated words in the English language.[6] To keep things simple, in this volume we will be using 'culture' to describe 'the ideas, customs, and social behaviour of a particular people or society'.[7]

Cultures exist at many levels, including family, school, community, organisation, ethnicity and nationality. People may be influenced by multiple cultures simultaneously. The people who exist in a culture are influenced by the expectations of that culture, but the culture, over time, is also shaped by the people who live in it. Some people will be shaped by a culture more strongly than others, but even those who are resistant to its power will be aware of the culture's expectations.

An assumption that underpins the approach of this volume is that human culture is fallen. This means that no human culture is perfect, but it also means that no culture is bereft of worthwhile features. From our own culture-shaped perspective, we may look at different cultures and consider one to be more godly than another, but we must concede that even though Australian culture has been shaped by its Judaeo-Christian heritage, there are some elements that are worthy of affirmation and others that are worthy of critique. The contributors to this volume have the challenge of affirming and critiquing the Australian culture, as it is described, in light of the biblical message contained in the genre they are analysing.

Another assumption of this volume is that the wider Australian culture influences the members of Australian church congregations. Of course, Christians aim to influence the world towards the values of the kingdom of God. Vanhoozer describes this as being 'cultural agents'.[8] But it would be naive to assume that it is not a two-way street. As much as we would hope that Christian values prevail, the reality is that our congregants will come to their pews each Sunday having already been influenced, to varying degrees, by the world they have been interacting with for the previous six days. And so, the authors of this volume will be working from the assumption that even though the listeners to the sermons will be Christian, they will also have been influenced by the 'non-Christian' features of Australian culture described in the next chapter of this volume.

Indeed, preachers need to recognise that 'Aussie culture' distorts even their own interpretation of the Scripture. 'There is no way in which we can step outside of ourselves and engage in some transcendental act of knowing which would lift us out of the creaturely conditions of knowing.'[9] Hence, local communities, and the preachers who inhabit them, have their own distinctive and nuanced 'local' theologies. This being so, even when given logical priority over social science, a local theology can be, and indeed should be, the subject of critical reflection and challenge from social science. The description of Australian culture in the next chapter will help highlight some distortions Australians, and even Australian preachers, may bring to interpreting Scripture, and so warn us of the hazards.

As with the hermeneutical task, there is considerable debate about how contextualisation should occur. I will just make two comments here. Firstly, contextualisation is inescapable. Even the process of translating a Greek word into English is an exercise in contextualisation, fraught with all the dangers that accompany any practice of contextualisation. The question is not whether to contextualise, but how far to contextualise. Secondly, contextualisation should not mean that the core message of the gospel is compromised. Both these comments can generate much discussion in themselves, but I beg your indulgence as I ask you to 'go with us' at this point.

As mentioned, to perform the contextualisation task, preachers must first understand the culture into which they are attempting to contextualise the message. This process of understanding culture is sometimes called 'cultural hermeneutics' or 'cultural exegesis'. Just as we exegete, or draw out meaning from, Scripture, we also want to exegete, or draw out meaning from, cultures.

It is difficult to exegete a culture from within it. It is often only as we travel overseas that we appreciate this. When we are in a different culture, it is easy to see its distinctives relative to our own. But when we return to our own culture, we also see it in a new light. We see our own system of meaning is no longer absolute and certain; flaws become visible and alternatives have a new credibility.[10]

Vanhoozer has developed a model of cultural hermeneutics based on examination of cultural 'texts', which he defines as intentional human actions that communicate meaning and call for interpretation.[11] These texts include literature, movies, buildings and even shaving cream. Foster says we must study the symbols, myths and rituals that together form cultural narratives. The various cultural narratives shape identity, provide meaning and direct behaviour.[12]

In this volume we are doing some cultural exegesis of Australians in a different way. By looking at survey data that compare Australians to the rest of the world, we are able to see some distinctives of the Australian culture. These findings are discussed in the opening chapter. The contributors to this volume have taken the rough description of Australians presented in this chapter and reflected on it theologically, drawing on the genre they have been assigned.

Sociologists distinguish between 'thin description' and 'thick description' of phenomena.[13] For example, a thin description of an incident might be 'the opening and closing of an eyelid'. A thick description of the same incident might be 'a wink'. In other words, a thick description is not just concerned with a superficial description of a phenomenon, but its interpretation. It is a movement from 'what' has happened or is happening to 'why' it happens. The theological interpretation of the cultural distinctives thinly described in the next chapter provides a thick description of Australian culture – perhaps even the thickest possible description.[14] It also then allows us to preach more effectively because of this deep understanding.

The answers to the following questions, provided by the contributors to this volume, will provide a 'thick description' of Australian culture:

- How does this collection of biblical books address the relationship Australians have to the natural environment?
- How do these books address Australia's individualistic tendencies?
- What do they have to say about Australia's obsession with egalitarianism?
- What does this collection of books teach about the rule-based approach of Australians, reflecting their desire for an ordered environment?
- How do these books address the strong Australian commitment to punctuality and timeframes?
- What does this collection of books say about Australia's secular philosophy?
- What does this group of books say about Australia's postmodern philosophy?
- What do they say about pluralism? About the institution of the church?
- What does this group of books have to say to Australia's multicultural society and multicultural churches?
- What does God say through these books to the wealthy and consumerist Australian?
- What message do these books have for the anxious and depressed in our communities?
- And finally, what do these books say to those Australians who consider themselves time poor?

Not only does the Scripture interrogate the sociology presented in the next chapter, but the sociology raises questions of the Scriptures. One feature of Practical Theology is its insistence on 'mutual critical correlation/conversation' between Scripture and the world.[15] This process may challenge traditional interpretations and resource new readings not envisaged by the original human author, albeit within the bounds of our orthodox theology and in line with the overall trajectory of God's mission as revealed in Scripture.[16]

On occasions, the contributors in this volume focus on specific verses or passages in some of the genres. However, they mostly look at the broader themes or methods of interpretation of the biblical genres they are addressing. The task of the reader will then be to take those general themes and hermeneutical and contextual insights and use them as they preach specific sections of the relevant biblical genre.

I offer a word of warning at this point. There are various metaphors to describe the role of preachers. One is that of prophet. Indeed, I think the eighth century prophets serve as the most helpful biblical model for the role of the contemporary preacher. These prophets took the texts of the ancient covenants and applied them to a new generation of Israelites. In the same way, the contemporary preacher takes the ancient texts and applies them to this generation. However, such a prophetic role is a dangerous one. One need look no further than the consequences of Jeremiah's ministry for his personal safety. The modern preacher needs to be similarly cautious in adopting this prophetic role. As we gain insights into the Australian culture, we will need to confront our congregations with the points of difference from God's ideal culture (the kingdom of God). But we need to do so carefully so as not to alienate the congregation before they listen to the biblical message that will follow.

To ensure that congregations do not reject the cultural diagnosis that is being presented to them, preachers need to be well prepared to back their suggestions with evidence. The material in the next chapter may serve that purpose to a degree, but stories and illustrations from contemporary Australian society will be more useful. As preachers, we need to learn to exegete the cultural narratives that are all around us. In addition, we must be careful to use the language of 'I' and 'we' rather than 'you' language with our listeners. This will help the congregation see that we are not just critiquing them but ourselves as well.

One final note. Contextualisation involves discerning not only what elements of the original message are particularly relevant for Australians, but also how the ancient genre can influence the delivery of the twenty-first-century sermon to an Australian congregation. Scholars of preaching sometimes talk of matching the form of the sermon to the form of the text. Our contributors will give us some guidance on this as well.

And so, each chapter in this volume will (for the most part) contain the following sections:

INTRODUCTION

1. **Introduction:** discussion of the general issues related to preaching this collection of books.
2. **The hermeneutical task:** insights into the interpretation of these books.
3. **The contextualisation task:** insights into the particular message of these books for Australian culture.
4. **A sample sermon:** an example of the type of sermon that can be preached to an Australian congregation, provided with some comments on the hermeneutical and contextualisation tasks that have influenced the shaping of this particular message.

Our hope is that this volume will help you in the impossibly difficult but incredibly valuable and sacred task of preaching.

It has been wonderful to draw upon the expertise of the contributors in the compilation of this volume. It has been pleasing to bring *some* ethnic and gender diversity to the task. However, many readers will have noticed the preponderance of older Anglo-Saxon men among the contributors. Let me say that this was in no way deliberate and is in fact, I consider, a weakness in the volume. Be assured that I did endeavour to have more women contribute to the volume, but the sad reality is that there are not many women preaching academics in Australia to drawn on. My prayer is that this situation will change and that a future edition of this volume will carry the voice of women and ethnic minorities more loudly.

1
DESCRIBING AUSTRALIANS
Ian Hussey

Introduction

At the Lausanne Younger Leaders Gathering in 2015, a group of young Australians were given the task of creating an Australian narrative based on the gospel narrative of creation, fall, redemption and restoration. Here's what the eastern state delegates put together as our 'national story':[1]

Creation: Setting

We are a nation who likes to see ourselves as the underdog who overcomes. We value individualism, which is often expressed in the need for personal space and materialistic pursuits. As a nation we are fairly secular, pragmatic and politically conservative. We expect a fair go and often rely on our government to provide that, especially around health and education. We love holidays, sport, being outdoors and hanging with friends and family. We are a multicultural people who are still trying to work out what it means to be an 'Australian'. We are blessed to live in a beautiful place in the world with lots of sunshine! There is a lot that is very good about Australia. At its best, this is a country where all nations can come together and learn to live in peace. It can be a nation that helps the most vulnerable through a very good welfare system and people who are prepared to help and volunteer.

Fall: Conflict

There is a dark side to our multiculturalism. We struggle at times to deal with the history of the English colonisation and how that continues to impact the Indigenous peoples of this land. There is also sometimes a fear of people from Asian and, more recently, Middle Eastern backgrounds. Our refugee policy has been criticised for a lack of compassion. There has also been a massive failure in our institutions, where people in power have abused their positions; this has resulted in a deep scepticism of authority (and has affected people's views of the church). Drought and floods continue to impact the wellbeing of families in our land. We are a nation of consumers, who worship gods of sport, time, money and sexual freedom. This leads to many casualties like broken families, workaholics, addiction etc. Even though Australians have so much, there is often a deep unhappiness and discontent. All of this, Christians would name as sin, though there seems to be an inability to acknowledge such things and work through brokenness.

Redemption: Climax

We celebrate authenticity and genuineness. Heroes tend to be unconventional, sport stars, the underdog, or comic. Our heroes are largely those who have overcome their circumstances and who demonstrate that anyone can get ahead. We long to move forward and embrace change but are cautious about what the result will be. We seek help from our peers, social media, the pub, as well as professionals, but are sporadic in our application of what we learn. Experiences are important to us. There are signs that people are desiring to work for the common good, to find reconciliation with Indigenous people. Christians are starting to speak up more for refugees and the vulnerable. There are glimpses of a spiritual reawakening, that something more is needed.

Restoration: Resolution

We are striving to be a people who are involved in our communities, making a difference for the common good. Most people want *shalom*, though we have different ideas of what that ultimately looks like and how to get there. Sport often unites as well as the physical beauty of our land – these things stir in us a spiritual longing. People are looking to be their authentic self (particularly around the issue of sexuality). Life is good here, but not as good as it could be.

I think this narrative will warmly resonate with many Australians. 'Yes, that is us!' But as discussed in the Introduction, it is difficult to accurately exegete your own culture. What we see from within our culture can be quite different to what someone from outside our culture sees. And so, in this volume we are using comparative statistics in order to objectively see some of our cultural distinctives.

Although Australia has a relatively ethnically diverse population, there are a number of cultural features that influence the thinking and behaviour of people, whether they were born into the Australian culture or whether they have migrated into it. The degree of influence that the cultural features have on individuals varies from person to person. However, the language I am about to introduce helps us to diagnose the nature of the people in our congregations and help us to better take the ancient message of the Scripture and apply it in a way that will be transformational for them.

The first five descriptors of Australians presented here emerged from the work of scholars who, during the twentieth century, sought to quantify the features of various cultures in order to better understand them. Their motives were not entirely pure, of course. Globalised business has a keen interest in being able to operate profitably in different cultures and discovered that simply taking a person from one culture and expecting them to lead effectively in another culture was a false premise. So, scholars like Gert Hofstede have pioneered the whole new science of 'cultural dimensions'. Business has been willing to invest large sums of money for empirical research designed to quantify ethnic cultures. The research has been widespread and exhaustive, utilising thousands upon thousands of participants, and we can be fairly confident about its conclusions.

In 2006, Luciara Nardon and Richard M. Steers[2] reviewed the most popular models of national culture developed by scholars such as Kluckhohn and Strodtbeck, Hofstede, Hall, Trompenaars and Schwartz, identifying the convergences and divergences among them. Instead of advocating one model over another, they assumed that all of the models had important insights to contribute to our understanding of culture. They therefore integrated the models, seeking common themes that collectively represented the principal differences between cultures. They then developed their own model based on their findings. As such, it represents the best summary of the models.

The culture models attempt to do two things: Firstly, each model offers a set of dimensions along which cultures can be compared. They offer a form of 'intellectual shorthand for cultural analysis',[3] allowing us to break down cultures into dimensions like power distance, uncertainty avoidance, and so forth, and thus create a language for what would otherwise be an impossible task. Secondly, four of the models offer numeric scores for rating various cultures. Even though the numbers are only approximate, they do provide some idea of the magnitude of how these cultures might vary.

Nardon and Steers identify the 'big five' cultural dimensions which can be used to classify different ethnic cultures. These are: 1) relationship with the environment; 2) social organisation; 3) power distribution; 4) rule orientation; and 5) time orientation. At first glance, these five themes seem to replicate Hofstede's five dimensions, but the other models serve to amplify, clarify and, in some cases, reposition dimensions so they are more relevant. Indeed, the commonality across these models reinforces their utility (and possible validity) in better understanding culture.

Here are the descriptions of the 'big five' cultural dimensions and the descriptors ('Scale Anchors') of each end of the continuums:[4]

Cultural Dimensions	Focus of Dimensions	Scale Anchors
Relationship with the Environment	Relationship with the natural and social environment: Extent to which people seek to change and control or live in harmony with their natural and social surroundings.	Mastery vs. Harmony
Social Organisation	Role of individuals and groups: Extent to which social relationships emphasise individual rights and responsibilities or group goals and collective action.	Individualism vs. Collectivism
Power Distribution	Power distribution in society: Extent to which power in a society is distributed hierarchically or in a more egalitarian or participative fashion.	Hierarchical vs. Egalitarian
Rule Orientation	Relative importance of rules: Extent to which behaviour is regulated by rules, laws, and formal procedures or by other factors such as unique circumstances and relationships.	Rule-based vs. Relationship-based
Time Orientation	Time perception and tasks: Extent to which people organise their time based on sequential attention to single tasks or simultaneous attention to multiple tasks.	Monochronic vs. Polychronic

These five dimensions of culture identified by Nardon and Steers will serve to give us the first five descriptors of Australian culture. The following draws heavily on their work.

Relationship with the Environment	Social Organisation	Power Distribution	Rule Orientation	Time Orientation
Mastery+	Individualist+	Egalitarian+	Rule-based	Monochronic

*The + signifies that this descriptor is especially prominent

Relationship with the Environment: Mastery

There are important variations across cultures in the degree to which each tries to control their environment or adapt to their surroundings. Here are the descriptors of the two ends of the continuum:

Mastery	Harmony
Focus on changing or controlling one's natural and social environment	Focus on living in harmony with nature and adjusting to one's natural and social environment
Achievement valued over relationships	Relationships valued over achievement
Emphasis on competition in the pursuit of personal or group goals	Emphasis on social progress, quality of life, and the welfare of others
Emphasis on material possessions as symbols of achievement	Emphasis on economy, harmony, and modesty
Emphasis on assertive, proactive, 'masculine' approach	Emphasis on passive, reactive, 'feminine' approach
Tendency towards the experimental; receptivity towards change	Tendency towards the cautious; scepticism towards change
Preference for performance-based extrinsic rewards	Preference for seniority-based intrinsic rewards

The synthesis of the research would suggest that many Australians tend to want to master their environment and value achievement over relationships. Given the harshness of the Australian continent, this has been no easy feat, but we have managed to eke out an existence and largely make ourselves immune, especially in the coastal cities, to the radical extremes of the sunburnt country. In the process we have become assertive and innovative.

In recent years theologians have begun to think more deeply about God's intended relationship between humanity and the environment. What did God mean when he said he intended for Adam and Eve to steward the creation? What do the different genres in the Bible say about humanity's relationship to creation? What does this mean for the more recent Australians, who seem bent on mastering the environment and less inclined to want to live in harmony with it than did the Indigenous custodians of the land?

The finding that many Australians value achievement over relationships also suggests that despite the popular emphasis on 'mateship', Australians are generally more concerned about personal success than personal relationships, at least compared to the rest of the world.[5] We are also competitive and value material possessions as a symbol of achievement. This description may cut across the Australian ideal of the Anzac spirit, but whether we like it or not, the research suggests this is the way we actually are.

The Bible talks a lot about the importance of personal relationships and the dangers of valuing ourselves by our achievements. What does God want to communicate to twenty-first-century Australians through the specific biblical genres discussed in this volume?

Social Organisation: Individualistic

The cultural dimension that has received the most attention in the research literature is individualism-collectivism, which Nardon and Steers refer to as *social organisation*. Some cultures are organised based on groups, while others are organised based on individuals. The most common terms used to describe these different cultures are *individualistic* and *collectivistic*.

Individualism	Collectivism
Person-centred approach valued; primary loyalty to oneself	Group-centred approach valued; primary loyalty to the group
Preference for preserving individual rights over social harmony	Preference for preserving social harmony over individual rights
Belief that people achieve self-identity through individual accomplishment	Belief that people achieve self-identity through group membership
Focus on accomplishing individual goals	Focus on accomplishing group goals
Sanctions reinforce independence and personal responsibility	Sanctions reinforce conformity to group norms
Contract-based agreements	Relationship-based agreements
Tendency towards low-context (direct, frank) communication	Tendency towards high-context (subtle, indirect) communication
Tendency towards individual decision making	Tendency towards group or participative decision making

Australians are fiercely individualistic. They are strongly focused on personal/individual self-actualisation rather than achieving identity through group membership and success. Related to this is the frankness of Australian communication, even compared to our Western cousins from Great Britain and the United States.

Aussies who have encountered the collectivist culture of different ethnic groups, either through international travel or engaging communities of migrants to Australia, are more likely to be aware of Australia's strong individualistic leaning. Individualistic Australians have often been surprised by the strong community ethos that exists in many ethnic groups they have encountered. Although the language of 'community' is very popular in Australia at the moment, and these collectivist migrant groups have some influence on the individualistic tendencies of Australian culture, it is possible that the predominant culture will prevail even in second and subsequent generation migrant families.

The challenge for our contributing authors in this volume is to find what the different biblical genres both affirm and critique about Australia's fiercely individualistic culture. It is worth remembering that there will be things to affirm and critique of both individualism and collectivism. It will be insufficient to simply conclude that Australian culture is 'wrong' because of its strong individualistic tendencies. God's message for Australians will be more subtle than that.

Power Distribution: Egalitarian

The third common theme running through the various models relates to how individuals within a society structure their power relationships. Is *power distribution* in a society based primarily on vertical or horizontal relationships? Is power allocated *hierarchically* or in a more *egalitarian* fashion?

Hierarchical	Egalitarian
Belief that power should be distributed hierarchically	Belief that power should be distributed relatively equally
Belief in ascribed or inherited power with ultimate authority residing in institutions	Belief in shared or elected power with ultimate authority residing in the people
Emphasis on organising vertically	Emphasis on organising horizontally
Preference for autocratic or centralised decision-making	Preference for participatory or decentralised decision-making
Emphasis on who is in charge	Emphasis on who is best qualified
Respect for authority; reluctance to question authority	Suspicious of authority; willingness to question authority

Many would trace the origins of Australia's fiercely egalitarian culture (or, at least, its lip service to equality) to our convict origins. The generally anti-establishment demeanour of the transported criminals created a desire for equality and the dismantlement of the traditional English class structures. It is likely that the famous 'tall poppy syndrome' – the tendency of Australians to cut down leaders to the same level as everybody else – is also a consequence of this strong historical influence.

Jesus of Nazareth and his followers transformed the world with their radical ideas. One such idea was that of human equality. The way that Jesus treated women, children, the sick, the Gentiles and even the demonised brought a profound change to the power structure of societies. Where Christianity spread, rich and poor, slave and master related to one another equally in the body of Christ. However, the Bible also recognises the role of leadership and the subsequent exercise of power, as long as it is used in the service of others. What would God affirm in our egalitarian culture? What is God's attitude to the 'tall poppy syndrome'? Is Australia's rejection of legitimate authority pleasing to God?

Rule Orientation: Rule-Based

The issue of rules as a means of reducing uncertainty in society is a recurring feature of the various models of culture. Rule-based cultures have a tendency to develop a multitude of laws, rules, regulations, bureaucratic procedures and strict social norms in an attempt to control as many unanticipated events or behaviours as possible. 'People tend to conform to officially-sanctioned constraints because of a belief in the virtue of the rule of law, and will often obey directives even if they know violations will not be detected.'[6] Waiting at a red light in the absence of any traffic is a good example of this.

By contrast, in relationship-based cultures control comes from parents, peers, superiors, supervisors, government officials and so forth. There is less record keeping and formality. There is also greater tolerance for noncompliance with rules, based on the assumption that formal rules cannot cover all contingencies and that flexibility is required.

These differences are summarised in the following table.

DESCRIBING AUSTRALIANS

Rule-based	Relationship-based
Individual behaviour largely regulated by rules, laws, formal policies, standard operating procedures, and social norms that are widely supported by societal members	While rules and laws are important, individual behaviour often regulated by unique circumstances or influential people, such as parents, peers, or superiors
Universalistic: Laws and rules designed to be applied uniformly to everyone	Particularistic: Individual circumstances often require modifications in rule enforcement
Emphasis on legal contracts and meticulous record keeping	Emphasis on interpersonal relationships and trust; less emphasis on record keeping
Rules and procedures spelled out clearly and published widely	Rules and procedures often ambiguous or not believed or accepted
Rules internalised and followed without question	Rules sometimes ignored or followed only when strictly enforced
Emphasis on doing things formally, by the book	Emphasis on doing things through informal networks
Low tolerance for rule breaking	Tolerance for rule breaking
Decisions based largely on objective criteria (e.g., rules, policies)	Decisions often based on subjective criteria (e.g., hunches, personal connections)

Personally, I find this descriptor of Australian culture more difficult to perceive. Aussies like to think they are 'laid-back'. However, we must accept, based on credible empirical research, that compared to other cultures Australians are rule-based. We like rules to take the uncertainty out of life. Australians who have travelled overseas often return home with a new appreciation of the 'orderliness' of Australian society, especially when it comes to driving on the roads. 'Being weak on crime' and 'going soft on criminals' are sticks that oppositions use to criticise governments. Perhaps these reflect our preference for rules and order.

The Bible contains many laws. Indeed, entire sections of the Scriptures are dedicated to their careful description. In several places, believers are instructed to observe the laws of the secular authorities. Yet at the same time there is an emphasis on relationship as the basis for order. Jesus was critical of the way that the religious leaders of his time interpreted and applied the laws. The challenge to the authors of this volume is to uncover what God thinks about Australians using laws to bring order and certainty to their environment.

Time Orientation: Monochronic

The key question to discern a society's time orientation is whether people approach their life one task at a time, in a linear fashion, or attempt to perform multiple tasks simultaneously. Do people pay close attention to time and tend to be punctual, or do they tend to be late? 'Do they separate work and family life or see them as an integrated whole? Do they take a linear or nonlinear approach to planning? And, finally, are they focused and impatient or unfocused and patient?'[7]

Monochronic	Polychronic
Sequential attention to individual tasks	Simultaneous attention to multiple tasks
Linear, single-minded approach to work, planning, and implementation	Nonlinear, interactive approach to work, planning, and implementation
Precise concept of time; punctual	Relative concept of time; often late
Approach is job-centred; commitment to the job and often to the organisation	Approach is people-centred; commitment to people and human relationships
Separation of work and personal life	Integration of work and personal life
Approach is focused but impatient	Approach is unfocused but patient

Many Australians who have travelled overseas return with stories of how they have been left waiting somewhere while a person from another culture has paid no attention to agreed timeframes. Australians are focused on their watch and more aware of time than many other cultures. This cultural feature also spills over into work, where Australians tend to be committed to the task and less so to the people involved. The separation between the work and personal life is sharper, while there is a tendency to be impatient with others.

While the Bible advocates for careful stewardship of the resources that have been entrusted to humanity, it also emphasises the importance of humans in God's economy. Is Australian's obsession with time and task consistent with the values of God's kingdom? What does God think about our tendency to break our lives up into segments (work, family, friends) and deal with them in a linear fashion? Here is another tough one for our contributors to wrestle with.

Secular

Having dealt with the 'big five' cultural dimensions described by Nardon and Steers, we move to some more descriptors of Australian culture that emerged from comparative research with other nations. The first is Australia's secular philosophy.

In his book *A Secular Age*, Charles Taylor identified three different forms of secularism.[8] The first type can be defined as the complete removal of God and religion from the public sphere. This does not necessarily mean the population is not religious, but that religion is confined to the private sphere. Australia cannot be defined as secular according to this definition of secularism.[9] The state *does* interact with religion in Australia. For example, the federal government funds schools run by religious organisations, funds religious school chaplains, prays in the parliament and recognises marriages conducted by religious celebrants.

Taylor's second form of secularism is defined as a population that is not religious, even where the state is. This is the case in much of Western Europe. In Britain, the Church of England is still the state church even though most of the population would not identify with a religion. Australia is not secular according to this definition either. Australia's population is still predominantly religious, although the number of people identifying as having no religion is growing. In the 2016 Census, over sixty percent still identified with a religion, although this percentage is dropping, especially among young people.[10]

In Taylor's third version of secularism, religion is not removed from the public sphere; rather, it is just one voice among many, including those with no religion. This would seem to be the best description of Australian secularism. Australia is secular, but it has a form of secularism where religion is allowed in the public sphere along with every other voice. This is in contrast with the situation in previous generations where Australian Christians could expect the voice of the church to be louder than that of other perspectives. The Australian church is now just one voice among many and must justify its perspective with a newfound vigour to compete with every other minority lobby group.

However, the voice of the Christian church may not always be welcome in the public sphere. Although just over 60 percent of the Australian population identify with a religion, a bigger share of Australians than respondents in most other countries consider religion potentially harmful, according to the polling carried out by the Ipsos

Social Research Institute.[11] The survey of more than 17,000 people across 23 countries showed 49 percent of respondents across all countries agreed with the statement, 'Religion does more harm in the world than good'. But the proportion of Australians agreeing with that statement was, at 63 percent, well above the international average. Only Belgium (68 percent) had a higher proportion of people than Australia who agreed religion does more harm than good, while Germany and Spain were on par with Australia. This suggests that even some Australians who identified as religious also maintain that religion does more harm than good. We are a complicated lot.

Lending weight to the suggestion of a growing secularisation of Australia, whatever definition you use, was the Ipsos finding that only 27 percent of Australians agreed with the statement 'my religion defines me as a person'. That was well below the American figure (49 percent) but higher than in Great Britain (23 percent). Japan had the lowest share (14 percent). Further, while half of those across the 23 countries surveyed agreed with the statement 'religious practices are an important factor in the moral life of my country's citizens', only about four in 10 Australians agreed with that statement, a much smaller share than the two-thirds of Americans who agreed. In Australia, 25 percent agreed that religious people make 'better citizens', a much lower share than in America (45 percent) and Russia (44 percent) and India (62 percent). The international average agreeing that the religious make better citizens was 32 percent. This suggests that Australians have drifted a long way from an appreciation of the value of their Judaeo-Christian heritage.

Although the majority of people in our churches will not have the same degree of secularisation reflected in the broader Australian population, it is to these secular thinkers that our congregations must relate. Much of the Old Testament emerges from the religious contexts of Israel (although the book of Daniel offers a superb example of living in a pagan, if not secular, environment), whereas most of the New Testament emerges from a secular world not unlike that which exists in Australia (akin to Taylor's third version of secularism). It provides a rich spring of resources for how Christians can relate to the secular world they live in. It falls to the preacher not only to help their listeners break down the sacred-secular divide, but also to equip them to understand and interact with a secular world from a religious predisposition.

Postmodern

Defining postmodernism is a difficult business because, as the name implies, it is a description of something that is not, rather than something that it is. Postmodernism is perhaps most simply defined as 'not modern'. The Oxford English Dictionary defines it as 'a late-twentieth-century style and concept in the arts, architecture, and criticism that represents a departure from modernism and has at its heart a general distrust of grand theories and ideologies'.[12] I think this will serve as a definition for our purposes.

I find one of the most enlightening manifestations of postmodernism is postmodern architecture: the seemingly impossible juxtaposition of a variety of incompatible construction materials (timber, masonry, corrugated iron, brick glass, panelling etc.) into a single structure with its implied rejection of traditional building practices. This is the spirit of postmodernism, a spirit that has not influenced just architecture but the very way that people think about their world.

Postmodernism, as it influences the thinking of Australians, is not in itself a negative thing. Indeed, some elements of postmodernism are more aligned with Christianity than modernism. For example, postmoderns are more likely to embrace the spiritual world than the scientifically-minded modern thinker. Two aspects of postmodernism are of particular importance for Christian preachers: pluralism and anti-institutionalism.

Pluralist

Pluralism is a condition or system in which two or more states, groups, principles or sources of authority coexist. It is form of society in which the members of minority groups maintain their independent cultural traditions. It is also a philosophical system that recognises more than one ultimate principle.[13]

'Pluralism', 'multiculturalism' and 'tolerance' are three related words with a great deal of currency in Australian culture. Voicing the understanding of many, the Canberra Times wrote in 2015:

> What prevents Australia from descending into destructive, hateful divides is tolerance. It works in two ways: we accept that other people hold different views but we also accept their right to share those views – even, and this is where it can be difficult, if their views show little tolerance for others. These two elements of tolerance do not always sit comfortably together. But pluralist countries rely on their citizens' ability to respect difference; it is what makes our society work.[14]

The pluralist orientation of Australians is also reflected in the Ipsos Global Poll mentioned earlier. Australia has an above-average share who felt 'completely comfortable' being around people with different religious beliefs to their own (84 percent).[15] While many Australians are not religious, this does not translate to fear or dislike of individuals who have different beliefs to our own. One in six worldwide said that they 'lose respect for people' after finding out that they are *not* religious. Only one in eight Australian respondents shared that sentiment, showing greater than average religious tolerance (or apathy).

Religious pluralism is both an opportunity and a vulnerability for Australian Christians. Despite an anti-Christian ethos in some quarters, the majority of Australians are likely to say to a Christian 'if it works for you, good'. However, religious pluralism also means that the claims of Christianity can simply be set aside alongside those of other religions. This is a particular problem for Christians who recognise the exclusivity of salvation through Christ.

On the whole, the Jewish Scriptures take a fairly dim view of religious pluralism. However, the New Testament emerges from the *Pax Romana*, which allowed for divergent religious belief as long as it did not disturb the profitable status quo for the Roman authorities. As such the New Testament serves as a rich resource for twenty-first-century Australian Christians, who now sit squarely in a pluralist society.

Anti-Institutional

Australians are losing trust in their institutions. Along with most Western nations, the general population's level of trust in four key institutions – NGOs, Business, Media and Government – is at the lowest recorded level since the Edelman Trust Barometer Annual Global Study started collecting general population data in 2012.[16] Australian's trust in government dropped eight points to 37 percent from 45 percent in 2016, 10 points in the case of media (from 42 percent to 32 percent), five points to 52 percent for NGOs and four points to 48 percent for business in general. Trust in media has suffered especially: 32 percent is one of the lowest levels globally, 11 points below the global average of 43 percent. The credibility of CEOs as spokespeople dropped significantly, reaching a lowly 26 percent in 2017 (compared to 39 percent in the previous year).

Hughes has demonstrated that the church has not escaped this trend, with just 21 percent indicating they had great or complete confidence in the church in 2009.[17] The Royal Commission into Institutional Responses to Child Sexual Abuse has highlighted the woeful response of the church to the child abuse that occurred under its auspices, and this will further reduce people's trust in the institution.

Roy Morgan Research conducts an annual survey of Australian attitudes to 30 professions.[18] The 'minister of religion' profession has been on a steady decline, coming in at sixteenth on the list (behind accountants, public servants and lawyers) with only 34 percent of Australians rating the profession as 'high' or 'very high' for ethics and honesty. This figure is down from 51 percent in 2011.[19]

In Australia's growing postmodern-influenced society, the church faces an ongoing challenge if it is identified as an 'intolerant institution'. The response to this phenomenon is ecclesiological. What do the Scriptures teach about the nature of the church and tolerance to those outside the church? Is the church an institution or is it something else? What would it mean for the church to move beyond being an institution?

How can it, or should it, 'deinstitutionalise'? The different genres of the Bible will have interesting things to say about this question.

Multicultural

According to the 2016 Census, Australians now come from nearly 200 countries and represent more than 300 ethnic ancestries.[20] One in four people in Australia (26 percent) were born overseas, a one percentage point rise from the figure recorded in the 2011 Census. That is higher than the United States (14 percent), Canada (22 percent), New Zealand (23 percent) and the United Kingdom (13 percent), making Australia one of the most multicultural nations in the world.

England is still the most common birthplace of migrants to Australia (15 percent), but the number of migrants from China (up from 6 percent to 8.3 percent since 2011) and India (up from 5.6 percent to 7.4 percent) is growing. The combined figure (15.7 percent) means that, for the first time, more Australians are of Chinese and Indian birth than of English birth. Christianity is the most practised religion among the overseas-born population (47 percent), while 31 percent are Buddhist, 28 percent are Islamic, 27 percent are Hindu, 7.6 percent are Sikh and 3.2 percent are Jewish. More than one in five Australians (21 percent) speak a language besides English at home. Mandarin remains the next most common language, spoken at home by one in every 40 Australians.

Not all Australians are comfortable with this diversity, though. According to the Challenging Racism Project (Western Sydney University), almost 50 percent of Australians think that overseas arrivals should assimilate into Australian culture.[21] Notably, 32 percent of survey respondents have 'negative' feelings towards Muslim Australians.

The ethnic diversity is even more apparent in the church. Of the 36 percent of church attenders who were born overseas in 2016, 27 percent were born in a non-English-speaking country (up from 18 percent in 2006) and 9 percent in another country where English is the main language.[22] Linguistic diversity is also more prevalent in the church, with a quarter of churchgoers (25 percent) speaking a language other than English at home. Some 22 percent of those people are bilingual or multilingual.

So not only is Australia a distinctively multicultural nation, the church in Australia is even more so. Even if your church is not multicultural, in all likelihood it will be soon. Either way, the members of your congregation live in an ethnically diverse context. Our preaching needs to take into account this distinct feature of Australian culture. Much has already been written about preaching in multicultural churches.[23] But, the different genres of the Bible say different things about ethnicity. Several genres may have very specific things to say to the multicultural churches of Australia.

Wealthy and Consumerist

Australia ranks as the second-best country in the world for its quality of life according to a United Nations index.[24] The score is calculated by combining data on life expectancy at birth, mean and expected years of schooling and standard of living, which is measured by gross national income per capita. Australians can expect to live to over 80 years, have on average 13 years of schooling and the gross national income per person is about $60,000. A Credit Suisse report shows Australia is the second-wealthiest country in the world, behind Sweden.[25] In Australia, median wealth stands at $213,000, far higher than the equivalent figure of $45,000 in the US. Although there are genuine poor in Australia, many who feel that they are not rich are, relative to the rest of the world, actually wealthy.

This great wealth and wellbeing allows, and perhaps even causes, Australians to be great consumers. This is no better demonstrated than by Australian obesity rates. Australia is the fifth most overweight and obese of the OECD countries, with 11.2 million adults (63 percent) with a Body Mass Index of 25 or higher in 2017.[26] Australians are also the world's second largest consumers of textiles, buying on average 27 kilograms of new clothing and other textiles each year.[27]

We also waste an incredible amount. Based on a national survey of 1644 respondents carried out by Roy Morgan Research, Australian households annually wasted $1226 on items purchased but unused in 2004.[28] This was approximately equal to one month's repayments on an average Australian home mortgage. Total wasteful consumption of goods and services that were never or hardly ever used was over $10.5 billion annually. By way of comparison, this amount exceeded spending by Australian governments on universities and roads. One can only speculate how much is wasted by Australian consumers now.

The addictive nature of consumerism is highlighted by the fact that despite Australians being wealthy, they are working longer hours in order to earn money to feed the consumerism. A study by the University of Melbourne sought to discover the reasons why people are increasingly compelled to work more than 50 hours a week.[29] The answer was consumerism. It was the 'work-and-spend' trap – an endless cycle characterised by the desire for higher living standards, linked with greater levels of debt that can only be managed by working longer and harder.

Despite our great wealth, we are more likely to take than give. Gershon Nimbalker, Advocacy Manager of Baptist World Aid, pointed out that Australian Christians currently give an average of 2.6 percent of their income to charity, which is lower than the 3 percent given by the broad Australian community during the Great Depression.[30] He also reported that Australian Bureau of Statistics figures from 2010 show we are spending 25 times more on recreation than on giving.

The Bible has a great deal to say about wealth. Indeed, it seemed to be one of Jesus' favourite topics of discussion. A wander through the carparks of most suburban churches in Australia would illustrate that consumerism is not just a problem for the broader community. We have here perhaps the most important, and threatening, features of Australian culture. We look to the authors of the various chapters of this volume to discern the particular message of each of the genres to our Australian community.

Anxious and Depressed

In 2014–15 there were 4 million Australians (17.5 percent) who reported having a mental or behavioural condition.[31] Anxiety-related conditions were most frequently reported (2.6 million people or 11.2 percent of the population) followed by mental health disorders, including depression (2.1 million people or 9.3 percent). Mental and behavioural conditions were more common among women (19.2 percent) than men (15.8 percent).

Eight Australians commit suicide each day, six of them men. For every person who succeeds, there are another thirty who attempt suicide, with around 85,000 people trying to take their own lives in any given year. Suicide is the most common cause of death in Australians aged 15–44, more likely to kill you than a motor vehicle accident or skin cancer.[32]

Some of this rampant anxiety is likely fuelled by fear. Another Ipsos poll found that 82 percent of Australians feel a 'real threat' of a terrorist attack in the next 12 months – 10 percentage points above the international average.[33] That proportion was the same as Turkey, which has recently suffered a series of major terrorism attacks. Australians are also more fearful of nuclear attacks (higher than South Korea!), armed conflict, computer hacks and health epidemics (the same as Mexico and higher than Argentina) than most other countries. The Lowy Institute has found that feelings of safety remain at their lowest point in the 13-year history of polling. While most Australians (79 percent) say they feel 'safe' overall, only 20 percent (down four points since 2015) feel 'very safe', and 21 percent feel unsafe overall.[34]

Although Australia's rates of suicide and mental illness are not abnormally high when compared internationally, about 10 percent of the community suffer from anxiety or depression despite the considerable resources devoted to mental health. Meanwhile, Australians would seem to have a greater sense of fear that many other countries.

When one considers depression and anxiety from a scriptural perspective, one's mind usually turns to the Psalms and wisdom literature. But what do other Bible genres tell us about God's attitude to human anxiety, depression and fear? Are the levels of anxiety and depression experienced by Australians a result of a fractured relationship with the Creator? What is God's message to those who suffer from depression and anxiety in our churches?

Time Poor

Compared with other OECD countries, Australia is below average in work-life balance. 'Australians are feeling time poor, with 45 percent of women and 36 percent of men saying they are always or often rushed or pressed for time, compared with 21 percent of women and 28 percent of men who were rarely or never rushed or pressed for time.'[35] Australia ranked fifth in the OECD countries in 2015 for the percentage of workers reporting that they worked more than 50 hours per week.[36] They were lowest in the OECD for reported time used for leisure and personal care.

A 2011 study found that just under a fifth of an Australian's days (17 percent) is spent on committed activities such as caring for children, and a similar (16.5 percent) time is spent on employment and education.[37] However, this varies depending on type of household. Parents with dependent children have the least amount of free time in a day (14.5 percent, or 3.5 hours). 'Men and women with a higher household income spend longer hours in employment-related activities and less on recreation and leisure. However, those in the lower household income spend a much larger proportion of their day on recreation and leisure.'[38]

The same study showed that Australians spent 4.4 hours a week, or 53 minutes a day for a five-day working week, travelling to and from work.[39] This has increased from 3.9 hours in 2002. Cox has estimated that Australia's workers are travelling for longer times to work than in nearly all similar, or larger-sized, metropolitan areas in Canada and the United States.[40] For example, the average one-way work trip travel time in Melbourne is about 36 minutes, which is longer than other major metropolitan areas in the US or Canada. Sydney's one-way work trip travel time is 34 minutes.

A final contributor to a sense of time poverty may be the amount of time we are looking at screens. Roy Morgan Research has reported that Australians (aged 14-plus) average over 18 hours of television and 13 on the internet at home each week. That is an average of almost 4.5 hours per day.[41]

The authors of this volume have a difficult task in taking the distinctive message of their genre and applying it to perceived time poverty of Australians.

A Cultural Narrative

As mentioned above, although statistics are less personal than listening to the life stories of Australians face-to-face, they do give us some insights into what life is like for Australians. At the risk of over-generalising, we can attempt to articulate an Australian narrative based on the distinctives of Australian culture compared to other cultures across the world.

The 'typical' Australian is an achievement-driven person who seeks to master their environment and their workplace in order to gain personal significance. Although they have had contact with collectivists and see some aspects of that life as appealing, they remain individualistic and private. The typical Aussie is also strongly egalitarian. They are suspicious of the 'tall poppies' and keen to see all people treated equally. They enjoy the order of life in Australia. People obey the road rules and violence is still a newsworthy item. They also enjoy the order that comes from punctuality and good driving. Although they are laid-back, they still like things to be done in a proper order and in a timely manner. Our Australian is an increasingly secular being. They have a respect for religious people, but they want the churches to recognise that they are only one voice among many in the Australian community. This is because of their largely pluralist and anti-institutional tendencies.

There is a good chance that our Australian has a non-English ethnic heritage. But even if they do not, they are increasingly engaged in a multicultural community. Although there is a great deal of harmony in multicultural Australia, there is also an undercurrent of tension, especially with some ethnicities. Our Australian is also likely to be quite wealthy and consumerist, although some are underemployed and struggle to achieve their aspirations. If they are fully employed, they have a sizable income, but even then, money is often tight because they have an expectation of nice clothes, nice cars, nice homes and overseas holidays. However, despite this high quality of life, our Australian may well be experiencing anxiety, depression and fear. There is a gnawing unpredictability to life, which has left them unsettled. This feeling is amplified by a sense of time poverty. Life seems so busy, especially for those with young families. However, despite this busyness they find time to relax most days with their screens.

So, there is our cultural exegesis – a roughly drawn picture for sure, but an objective point of reference when creating a thick description of our congregants. Now we turn to the Scriptures to extract from the beautiful complexity simple messages for God's loved people in Australia.

2

PREACHING THE PENTATEUCH TO AUSTRALIANS

Murray Capill

Introduction

Beginnings are significant. Whether the beginning of a person's life, a new year or the opening minutes of a football match, the start matters.

Australians have begun to recognise exactly this regarding our own nation. We have been far too slow to acknowledge that the beginnings of our nation were not in the eighteenth century, when convicts arrived from England. The Indigenous peoples of Australia have long lived on this land, explored its beauty and wealth, formed communities and developed languages and culture. Our beginnings as a nation matter.

Long before that, however, there was another beginning – the one recounted in Genesis and the four subsequent books of the Pentateuch. It is the beginning that lies behind every other beginning. Genesis means 'beginning', and it recounts the origin of the world, of human life and society, of God's covenant community and of the gospel itself. From the creation account to the devastating impact of the fall, from a universal flood to the choosing of one man to be the father of many nations, from the vast implications of the covenant promises to the often-scandalous lives of the patriarchal family, Genesis weaves together dozens of rich and compelling narratives.

The subsequent books of the Pentateuch build on those beginnings, charting the journey of God's people out of Egypt and to the edge of the promised land. Exodus is the story of redemption and the constitution of a nation chosen to live in covenant with the Lord. Leviticus is the story of a nation that was to be holy, set apart for the Lord. Numbers is the story of a forty-year detour as the Israelites wander in the wilderness, learning to trust the God they had disbelieved. Finally, Deuteronomy rehearses the story as they prepare to finally take possession of the land the Lord had promised their father Abraham hundreds of years earlier. Moses preaches a series of powerful sermons, reminding Israel of who they were, where they had come from, how they were to live in the land they were about to enter, what would become of them if they disobeyed, and what they would inherit if they lived in faithful covenant with their God.

These are the mighty beginnings recorded in the Pentateuch – beginnings not only of the nation of Israel, but of our world and human existence, of relationship with God and worship, of sin and redemption, of blessing and curse. The Christian perspective is that these books tell the true story of our world.[1] We will only understand ourselves, this world and God if we understand where it all began.

Needless to say, then, this is not only rich and fertile ground for preachers, but essential territory for God's people. While preaching from the Pentateuch may be relatively rare in the overall preaching diet of many churches, it is a strategic undertaking that we dare not ignore. Rich themes emerge from these books, many of which speak directly to the questions, tensions, fears, aspirations and challenges faced by Australians.

The Hermeneutical Task

Authorship

The historic Christian and Jewish conviction has been that the Pentateuch was written by Moses. This is the viewpoint adopted in the New Testament, with the Pentateuch variously called 'the law of Moses' (e.g., Luke 2:22) or simply 'Moses' (e.g., Luke 16:31; Acts 15:21).[2] Of course, as Longman and Dillard assert, 'In a strict sense, the Torah is anonymous. Nowhere do these five books explicitly or implicitly claim that Moses is their exclusive author', yet 'early Jewish and Christian tradition … is virtually unanimous in ascribing Genesis through Deuteronomy to him.'[3]

This consensus view was shattered by the impact of historical and source criticism, which, from the 1870s to the 1970s, widely accepted what is known as the Graf-Wellhausen Documentary Hypothesis.[4] According to the Documentary Hypothesis, the Pentateuch is a late composition comprising four main sources, differentiated by such things as their use of the divine name, the presence of doublets and repetition, and divergent styles and theologies.[5] 'It was held that J (Yahwist) dated from Israel's monarchy around 950 BCE, E (Elohist) from the time the divided kingdom around 850 BCE, D (Deuteronomist) from shortly before the exile around 620 BCE, and P (Priestly Code) from after the exile around 500 BCE.'[6]

More recently, however, this hypothesis has been shown to be just that: a hypothesis. Duane Garret argues, 'The time has long passed for scholars of every theological persuasion to recognise that the Graf-Wellhausen theory, as a starting point for continuing research, is dead. The Documentary Hypothesis and the arguments that support it have been effectively demolished by scholars from many different theological perspectives and areas of expertise.'[7]

Scholars on both sides of the debate have since moderated their views. 'The cutting edge of scholarship is devoting less and less energy ... to the question of sources and more and more to the final composition of the Pentateuch and the individual books within it.'[8] The newer literary approach to the biblical text has led to a fascination with the Pentateuchal narratives, especially those of Genesis, with a realisation that it has 'a literary unity that displays artistic brilliance when judged according to the canons of its own Semitic culture'.[9]

At the same time, 'the traditional evangelical position on the question of the composition of the Pentateuch is undergoing a subtle but important shift as well. Evangelical scholars recognize that the Pentateuch contains pre-Mosaic sources as well as post-Mosaic glosses'.[10] For example, it is not too hard for the most conservative of scholars to concede that Moses probably did not author the narrative of his own death in Deuteronomy 34, or the statement that 'Moses was very meek, more than all people who were on the face of the earth' (Numbers 12:3). So, 'Although a good case can be made that Moses authored the essential shape of Genesis and of the Pentateuch, he clearly did not author the extant text in our hands.'[11] Yet, 'it is possible to affirm the substantial Mosaic authorship of the Pentateuch in line with the occasional internal evidence and the strong external evidence, while allowing for earlier sources as well as later glosses and elaboration'.[12] Moses, it has been argued, was eminently suited to be the author of the Pentateuch, since his 'superb training, exceptional spiritual gifts and divine call uniquely qualified him to compose the essential content and shape of Genesis and the Pentateuch'.[13]

The fact that a strong case for substantial Mosaic authorship can be made is highly significant for preachers today, since it allows us to identify the original audience and to treat the Pentateuch, and each book within it, as a cohesive literary whole.

Audience and Emphasis

On the basis of Mosaic authorship, we can identify the intended audience as 'the generation of Israelites that was about to go into the Promised Land. All the events of the Exodus and the wilderness journey as well as the giving of the Law at Mount Sinai were cast as something that happened in the past ... The focus of the writer was on the future, the next generation'.[14] This must colour how we interpret the narratives.

Greidanus describes the 'history-writing of Genesis as ancient, kerygmatic historiography'.[15] The aim is not merely a factual, dispassionate account of what happened, but a proclamation of the significance of what happened historically for the people of Israel as they move into the promised land. That is not to say the narratives are not factual or historical. 'It is not enough to say that the biblical narratives are only "history-like" and to relegate them to the level of "realistic narrative [Frei]" ... The authors of the biblical narratives give every indication of intending their works to be taken as history rather than fiction ... There is reasonable evidence that the history recorded in these narratives corresponds to the events themselves.'[16]

Yet, as factual history, the narratives are essentially 'sermons addressed to ancient Israel; they seek to impart God's relevant message to Israel'.[17] They 'acquaint Israel with the God of their ancestors and his acts to preserve a people and to restore his kingdom on earth'.[18] The history of Genesis 'is theological in nature, since it is mainly interested in describing the relations of Yahweh, the covenant God, with his people'.[19]

This has implications for our preaching. As with all biblical literature, we will need to pay attention to authorial intent and note carefully wherever the narratives contain a narrator's comments. Furthermore, far from merely recounting the stories, we will need to align with the intent of the narratives and preach to our audience the message the text intended to preach to the original hearers.

Literary Structure

The overall structure of the Pentateuch is another field rife with controversy and change.[20] Taken as a whole, the Pentateuch has three main divisions: the introductory section of Genesis 1:1—11:26; the extended portion focusing on 'God's purposes achieved through people and events leading to, occurring at and ensuing from Sinai in Genesis 11:27—Numbers 36:13'; and the final rehearsing and interpretation of that journey in Deuteronomy.[21] The large middle section here can be further divided into the pre-Sinai narrative, where the people of blessing are chosen and preserved (Gen 11:27—Exod 18:27); the Sinai narratives where the covenant is defined and tabernacle worship established (Exod 19:1—Lev 27:34); and the post-Sinai narratives, describing the first and second generations that, respectively, forfeited the promised land through disobedience, and awaited entry into it during their forty years in the wilderness (Num 1:1—36:13).

While preaching entire books of the Pentateuch may be daunting for preachers and congregations alike, short, focused series from any of these sections can be both manageable and edifying. Endless options present themselves, including, for example, preaching on the foundations of the world (Genesis 1–11); on one of the patriarchs (Abraham, Genesis 12–25; Isaac and Jacob, Genesis 24–32; or Joseph, Genesis 37–52); on the deliverance from Egypt (Exod 1–19); on tabernacle worship (Ex 20–34); on the wilderness wanderings (Num 10:11–22:1); or on one of Moses' speeches in Deuteronomy (Deut 1:6—4:40; 5:1–29:19; 27:1—28:68; 29:1—30:20).

The Pentateuch as a whole is sometimes referred to as 'the law' or *torah* (e.g., Matt 5:17–18; Luke 2:22). For our hearers, that sounds like it is all about rules, statutes and legal considerations. However, as Selman points out, 'A survey of the 220 occurrences of *tôrâ* throughout the OT reveals three main aspects to the word. It involves (1) teaching or instruction to be learnt, (2) commands to be obeyed and (3) guidance about how to live in specific situations.'[22] *Torah* therefore incorporates both narrative and law.[23] Since both are quite distinct genres and cover vast amounts of material, the remainder of this chapter will focus particularly on preaching the narrative portions of the Pentateuch, and in particular the Genesis narratives. In the next chapter, Martin Pakula will examine how to preach law.

Preaching Narrative

It is significant that the Bible in general, and the Pentateuch in particular, contains so much narrative.[24] Thomas Long regards this as 'odd' because other religions do not tend to depend so heavily on narrative to convey their thought.[25] The oddity, however, is intentional. 'The prominence of the narrative genre in the Bible is related to the Bible's central message that God acts in *history*. No other genre can express that message as well as narrative.'[26]

It is essential that preachers work with the distinct literary features of Old Testament narrative. In the first place, this involves recognising the *plotline* of each narrative, from exposition, to crisis, to resolution, to denouement.[27] It also demands attention to how *characterisation* is developed. Jeffrey Arthurs identifies the significance of dialogue, action, titles and names, physical descriptions, authorial comment, the response of other characters, and foils, where there is a deliberate contrast to the protagonists (as, for example, Lot's choice of the well-watered land near Sodom in Genesis 13).[28] Attention should also be paid to the *rhetorical devices* used in Hebrew narrative, such as repetition, inclusion, chiasm, stereotyped patterns and varying structural levels.[29]

Preaching the Metanarrative

Every narrative we preach sits somewhere in the larger narrative of the entire Bible. 'The Bible as a whole is best understood as a story or drama'[30] that claims 'to tell the true story of our world's history'.[31] This grand story, or metanarrative, has an overarching structure into which each individual narrative must be placed. This overall plotline of the Bible is often described in four stages: Creation–Fall–Redemption–Consummation.[32] There is merit, however, in adopting a six-stage storyline. Christopher Wright describes this as Creation–Fall–Promise–Gospel–Mission–New Creation.[33] Similarly, but more fully, Bartholomew and Goheen outline the Bible's story as a drama in six Acts:[34]

Act 1: God Establishes His Kingdom: Creation

Act 2: Rebellion in the Kingdom: Fall

Act 3: The King Chooses Israel: Redemption Initiated

(Scene 1: A People for the King; Scene 2: A land for His People)

Act 4: The Coming of the King: Redemption Accomplished

Act 5: Spreading the News of the King: The Mission of the Church

(Scene 1: From Jerusalem to Rome; Scene 2: And into All the World)

Act 6: The Return of the King: Redemption Completed

The value of thinking in terms of a metanarrative is that every text we preach from can be seen to build on what has gone before and move towards what is to come. This helps us avoid atomising stories from which we merely lift moralistic lessons, rather than seeing each narrative as a step on the journey from the Garden to the City.

This metanarrative is essentially a missional story. It proclaims God as King over all who, when his subjects rebelled, enacted a plan to restore the kingdom. His plan is global and, while narrowed initially to one man and then one nation, was intended to bring blessing to all nations. Abraham and Israel were 'blessed to be a blessing'.[35]

As we preach, we need to remember we are preaching to people living in Act 5. We are preaching to people on mission, and we must help them see not only where the narrative we are preaching from fits into the story, but where they fit in as well.

Preaching Christ

In placing each narrative within this larger storyline of the Bible, we reduce the danger of moralising, allegorising or spiritualising it.[36] But a new danger emerges. We can end up flattening out the story, preaching a biblical-theology framework rather than the narrative itself. Our messages become predictable and boring as we take essentially the same route from every text to Jesus and preach a familiar gospel message no matter how intriguing, confronting or compelling the original narrative is.[37]

Timothy Keller, a strong advocate of preaching Christ every time, observes, 'You can't really preach any text … unless you show how its themes find their fulfillment in the person of Christ'.[38] However, he recognises that if we 'have not spent time in the text itself, the way Jesus is described will sound the same from week to week'. He then proposes the solution: 'If you go deeply enough into the original context, there will be as many different ways to preach Christ as there are themes and genres and messages in the Bible.'[39] This is the key to preaching Christ-centred messages without sameness: going deeply into the substance of each text.

The Pentateuchal narratives are brilliantly written stories. As preachers, we need to tease out the complex and compelling dynamics of each narrative that reveal so much about human nature, the tensions and ambiguities of human life and the complexities of 'living in the gap between promise and reality'.[40] At the same time, we must show that these narratives are the foundational stories of a people whose identity, sanctity and destiny would only be realised when, hundreds of years later, there arose from among them a redeemer. Likening the Old Testament to a journey, Wright asserts, 'The coming of Jesus was not just the end of the journey but the whole purpose of the journey. He was not only the destination but the *fulfilment*.'[41]

Summary

In view of these hermeneutical considerations, we may summarise our task as preachers:
- We will preach the Pentateuch as the foundational narrative of God's people, substantially written by Moses for the Israelites as they were poised on the cusp of taking the promised land.
- We will preach it as rooted in historical fact, yet intended not merely to recount those facts but to proclaim to God's people an essential message about who their God is: the Creator, Redeemer God who is holy and yet who has made a covenant with his people to be their God and they to be his people.
- We will place each narrative within the Bible's metanarrative, showing how it fits into the Bible's true story of the world.
- We will endeavour to unfold the brilliant artistry of each story, helping our hearers enjoy the narratives and understand their original message, while all the time driving towards where the narratives ultimately drive: the coming of the Messiah who, in his death and resurrection, secured for his people their true identity, sanctity and destiny.
- We will show that a central part of that true identity, sanctity and destiny was for them to be a source of blessing to the nations, and so we will preach a message that is essentially missional in its focus.
- We will also preach the text wanting to press the main message of each story on the hearts of our hearers, paying careful attention to how the message speaks not just about the gospel generally, but to the particular needs, idols and aspirations of Australians.

We turn, then, to the next major task of the preacher: the task of contextualisation.

The Contextualisation Task

The patriarchal narratives, covering the lives of the founding fathers of Israel (Abraham, Isaac, Jacob and his twelve sons), are gripping stories, replete with rich themes that speak pertinently to many of the characteristics of Australians observed in chapter 1. As preachers, we ought to relish the dynamics of narratives that could easily fit into many a TV mini-series on Netflix. Deception, greed, lust, adultery, murder, love, wealth, war, redemption, forgiveness and reconciliation are woven into the fabric of these stories. Part of effective contextualisation is to show just how remarkably contemporary the themes of these ancient narratives are. There is nothing new under the sun.

The more substantial challenge, however, is to unearth the robust theological themes that lie beneath these dynamics and unpack the ways in which they both challenge and affirm realties we face as Australians. We will consider here four themes of particular relevance.

Fixing a Broken World

The Abraham narrative begins at Genesis 11:27, where we have the start of the *toledot* (that is, the story, account, or generations) of Terah. Genesis is divided into ten such sections,[42] but 'contrary to what one might expect, the accounts are not essentially about the titular ancestor but about his descendants'.[43] Hence, the *toledot* of Terah is largely about Abraham, the *toledot* of Isaac is largely about Jacob, and the *toledot* of Jacob is largely about Joseph and his brothers.

The Abraham narrative is therefore part of the sixth of ten major narrative sections. Although we are only twelve chapters into Genesis, we are well into the Bible's story. In fact, the call of Abraham is essentially God starting over for the third time. He began first with Adam and Eve, created in his own image and placed in a world of pristine excellence. But the perfection of paradise was soon shattered, inviting God's immediate judgement and curse. From Genesis 3 to 5 there is a wretched downward spiral of sin, violence and human arrogance. So, a second judgement takes place, and God purges the world with the Noahic flood, starting again with one man and his family. But again, sin advances, and in Genesis 11 we encounter humankind's brazen attempt to ignore God and make a name for themselves as they band together to build a tower reaching to the heavens. This invites the third judgement; they are scattered across the face of the earth and their languages are confused.

It is against this dark backdrop that God makes vast promises to Abraham. Remarkably, as God had started first with Adam, and re-started with Noah, so he starts again with Abraham. He does so with a view to fixing a broken world: reversing the effects of the curse, overcoming sin and evil, reconciling his rebellious subjects to himself and redeeming creation from its bondage to decay.

God promises to make this one man into a great nation and to give him a great name (which is precisely what the people of Babel had wanted to achieve for themselves). Secondly, he promises to bless him so he will not live under God's curse, which has plagued humanity since the fall in Genesis 3, but with God's favour. God will watch over him, protect and prosper, restoring the fullness of life that God gave in Eden.[44] Thirdly, God promises to bring blessing to the ends of the earth through him, so that the nations he has just scattered because of their prideful rebellion will be gathered together into one universal people of God.

These promises reverberate throughout the Genesis narratives.[45] Indeed, 'they inspire the whole plot, not only of the Abraham narrative and the book of Genesis but of the Pentateuch, the rest of the Old Testament and, indeed, the whole Bible'.[46]

It is an audacious plan to fix a sin-torn world. How will it ever be achieved? A major spoiler is given in Genesis 12:7, with God's promise that 'to your offspring I will give this land'. In Galatians 3:16, Paul takes this singular collective noun to refer to one seed, Jesus Christ. It is through him that these promises will ultimately be fulfilled. God has made his name great; God has blessed him; and through him God is bringing blessing to the ends of the earth. In fact, the promise to Abraham was the promise of the gospel itself: 'And the Scripture, foreseeing that God would justify the Gentiles by faith, preached the gospel beforehand to Abraham, saying, "In you shall all the nations be blessed"' (Gal 3:8).

Christopher Wright observes that this single, grand storyline of the Bible 'answers the fundamental questions that all human beings ask:

- What is this world we live in?
- Who are we, and what does it mean to be human?
- What has gone wrong with everything, and why are we in the mess we are in?
- What is the solution to all the 'wrongness' in the world and ourselves?
- Where will it all end, and is there any hope for the future?'[47]

Australians have a range of answers to these worldview questions. Our pluralist society endorses multiple perspectives on who we are, what's wrong and what the solutions are. That something is wrong is without question. We have noted in the 'Describing Australians' chapter the prevalence of anxiety and fear; the latent racial tensions and unresolved injustices suffered by the Indigenous peoples of this land; the damage done to the vulnerable, as exposed by the Royal Commission into Institutional Responses to Child Sexual Abuse; the environmental issues that have developed due to our 'mastery' relationship to creation; and the negative impact of fierce individualism, where personal wellbeing can ride rough-shod over family and community values.

If you listen to our politicians, you would expect the solutions to be found in jobs and growth. Governments from both sides of the political divide focus primarily on the economy, health, education and infrastructure as the saviours of our broken world.

But Genesis proposes a radically different solution. God's plan to fix a broken world is neither political nor economic. His plan is the gospel. The greatest need of Australians is not better education, greater access to the NBN or lower taxation. The greatest need is reconciliation with the God we have rebelled against. We need forgiveness for our sins and a restored relationship with our God.

Similarly, our biggest problems are not the things that go wrong around us: floods, fires, crime, domestic violence. These are, of course, massive problems of deep concern to our society, but they are symptoms of a deeper problem that emergency services or the judicial system can never address. Our fundamental problem is the sinfulness of our hearts. We are rebels against our Maker, and we stand in need of forgiveness, reconciliation to God and heart change. That is the greatest need of every Australian, though we will never hear that diagnosis in the media or from our politicians.

It is also somewhat confronting to our Australian psyche to realise that God's plan is not primarily about Australia. Our national anthem leads us to celebrate that we are 'young and free', living in a land 'of golden soil and wealth for toil' that 'abounds in Nature's gifts, of beauty rich and rare'. So we cry out, 'Advance Australia fair!' Perhaps nowhere does our nationalism rise to the surface more than in sport, where we are fiercely devoted to our national teams' success and to Olympic and Commonwealth Games gold, and equally devastated when our national heroes let us down, particularly through unsportsmanlike behaviour. While there is nothing inherently wrong with such national pride, the gospel story is a story about many nations, not just ours. As such, it is a story that calls Australian Christians to have a global and missional mindset, reflecting God's grace not just for us but for the peoples of the world.

If as Australians we have a sense of being blessed, we will do well to remember that God intends those he blesses to be a blessing to others. Blessings are not to be hoarded but shared. The promises made to Abraham were not primarily individualistic. Sure, the blessings in time brought him wealth and prosperity, and his great name made him a leading and respected figure in the region of Canaan. But these blessings were not for his personal aggrandisement or pleasure but for the advance of God's plan to fix a broken world. His calling was essentially a call to join God's mission.

It is the same for us. As Australian Christians, we enjoy many rich blessings. The affluence of Australia has made for a wealthy church. Many churches are exceptionally well resourced, and as preachers we have access to resources that are the envy of many. Books, conferences, theological colleges, linguistic tools, major Bible software packages and new church buildings are par for the course. We also live with remarkable freedom. Although we experience increasing pressure around issues such as freedom of speech and biblical values, we can still preach and disciple without fear of recrimination.

Such blessings lay on us significant responsibility to advance the work of the gospel. These are gifts of God that are not to be used for selfish indulgence but for gospel ministry. Not that we should preach that message in a way that guilt-trips people into feeling they better give more, or share their faith with their neighbour, or go on an overseas mission trip. Guilt-motivation misses the point completely. Greater than the material and contextual blessings is the blessing of being drawn into God's mission to fix a broken world.

Personally, I find that enormously encouraging. I can barely fix a tap, a computer problem or a car, let alone the problems of world poverty and injustice. But by God's grace I have been drawn into God's mission. Through Christ and the work of the gospel he is fixing a broken world, and I am able to participate in his project. As I love my neighbour, or share my faith, or disciple a new believer, or participate in Christian community or represent the values of the kingdom of heaven in my workplace, I am joining a project of ultimate worth and eternal significance. This is the most significant way to maximise the wonderful blessings and opportunities we have as Australian Christians.

Living as Pilgrims

In Genesis, closely entwined with the promise of blessing is the promise of land. Yet occupation of the land was not to take place, in the biblical narrative, until after the five books of the Pentateuch. Only with Joshua would the Israelites take possession of the land promised to them. Until then they would live in Canaan as aliens and strangers.

When Abraham is first called to leave his home and go to a place God would show him (Gen 12:1) he is being called to the life of a pilgrim. 'In this attitude, Abram becomes a model of the true believer. The true believer is like him – a sojourner, a traveller, a wanderer, a pilgrim. The true believer has no fixed focus for his or her security, except in God and his word and purpose.'[48]

In the course of the Genesis narratives, only one small piece of the land of Canaan is ever procured. In an extended narrative in Genesis 23, Abraham negotiates to buy a burial site for his wife, Sarah. By that time, he had lived in Canaan for over sixty years, but he had not come into possession of one scrap of real estate. The fact was, he could not procure land because he was, as he says to the Hittites, an alien and stranger among them (Gen 23:4). An alien or sojourner (Heb. *ger*) was 'one who didn't enjoy the rights of a resident, one who had abandoned his homeland for political or economic reasons and sought refuge in another community'.[49] The situation was reasonably close to that of a refugee today. A stranger (Heb. *toshav*) was 'one who has no land of his own but is settled upon that of another, a sort of tenant'.[50]

In the fascinating narrative of Genesis 23, Abraham, the alien and stranger, wants to buy land. The Hittites say to him, 'Look, you're a mighty prince among us. Just use it.' But he doesn't want to just use it because then it won't be his. He wants to buy it, own it, take possession of it. So the land owner names what seems to be 'a fairly stiff price', and Abraham pays up without further negotiation.[51] He secures one field with a cave in it that will, in time, become the burial site not only for Sarah, but later for himself, Isaac, Rebekah and Jacob.

Why was he so keen to buy it, not just use it? Because this was the first small slice of the land God had promised to give him, and he viewed it as a down payment on the rest of the land. Abraham acquired this in faith, believing God would keep his promises and one day give his descendants the rest of the land.

For all his years in Canaan, Abraham was not 'living the dream' but 'living the promise'. Living the dream means living for now. In Australia it is the dream of owning your own house, and then having a bigger house, a better car, a larger salary, a more luxurious holiday, a greater number of gadgets, more friends, more fun. Ironically, though, the dream produces anxiety. British journalist Ruth Whippman, author of *The Pursuit of Happiness and Why It's Making Us Anxious*,[52] identifies two fundamental problems. Firstly, our happiness expectations are set on having a perfect life, perfect job, perfect kids, perfect everything; an Instagram life. There is an enormous gap between our expectations and reality, and that makes us anxious. Secondly, we are looking for happiness within. The message is to find yourself and be true to yourself. But happiness is only found in the context of relationships with others.

How wise, then, for Abraham to 'live the promise', not the dream. And interestingly, his descendants did too. Genesis makes much of the deaths of its protagonists, the book concluding with two more significant funerals. When Jacob finally died in Egypt, aged 147, there was but one place he wanted his embalmed body to be laid to rest: back in the one field they owned in Canaan. Similarly, over fifty years later, when Joseph died in Egypt, aged 110, he requested that his bones be taken back to the promised land when his people were eventually delivered from Egypt. He spoke in faith of a day when God would deliver them, foreseeing the Exodus and eventual possession of Canaan.

His faith was not groundless. God did visit them, and when the Lord delivered them from bondage to Egypt, Joseph's bones were taken to Canaan (see Ex 13:19; Josh 24:32). Presumably some noble soul had to carry them for forty years in the wilderness!

The point made by the burial plot and the return of bodies to Canaan is that, throughout Genesis, God's people are aliens and strangers, longing for a better country. They were clinging to the promise of a better city, and if they did not get to see it in their lifetime, they at least wanted to be buried there, believing God would give it to their descendants. But the patriarchs were looking for more than Canaan. They knew God's promise was greater than a piece of land. Hebrews 11:13–16 articulates their desire for a better country, a heavenly one. By faith, they had a sense of something beyond the grave and beyond Canaan.

Lot, however, is presented in Genesis 13 as a foil to this motif.[53] Due to the great increase of their flocks and herds, he and Abraham decide to part company. Lot looks up and sees the lush, fertile pasturelands of the Jordan plain. It is ominously described as being like Eden, towards Zoar, near Sodom and Gomorrah. The mention of Eden prompts memories of when Eve also pursued what was pleasing to the eye. And Sodom and Gomorrah are, infamously, the two cities the Lord would soon judge for their great wickedness.[54] Lot should presumably have said something like this: 'Uncle Abram, there's no way I'm moving from you and your land. God has promised to bless you and all those with you. I'd rather walk away from my possessions than walk away from the blessing.' But his choice was to settle in best of the land rather than to live as an alien and stranger.

It is not too long before all comes unstuck. In Genesis 13 he chooses to live near Sodom; in Genesis 14 he is living in Sodom; and in Genesis 19 we find him in the gates of Sodom, a metaphor for participating in the leadership of the city doomed to destruction.[55] There seems little doubt that Lot is intended to be a warning to us. And Jesus explicitly made that point regarding his wife (see Luke 17:32).

It is not only the founding fathers of the faith, however, who were called to live as aliens and strangers. '[T]he Bible wants all of God's people to realise that they are in an Abraham position.'[56] This is the language Peter uses to describe Christians in the world, and it is apt language for Christians in Australia. Despite the beauty and wealth of this land and the rich blessings we enjoy, we are not to view this country as our true home. We are to have our eyes set on the heavenly city, and must be content to live as strangers and aliens in Australia.

We could easily approach this theme in a confrontational way, challenging people to live more simply, shed some possessions, cling less to people and things in this world, change their budget to reflect heavenly investments, try less hard to fit in with the people around them, and perhaps forgo, for the sake of the gospel, some of those lengthy and expensive grey nomad holidays or overseas cruises. All are valid challenges.

But there is another reality that may register more deeply in people's hearts. Living the promise, not the dream, is surprisingly freeing. Living as an alien and stranger on earth means you don't have to have all the world's goodies to be happy. You don't have to fit in and have everyone love you and think you're amazing and have a perfect life. You can cope with dreams not being realised, because better is coming. You can cope with fewer possessions, because you know we're not taking them with us anyway. It is not only life-changing but life-freeing to have our hearts set on the eternal city.

Living as pilgrims might also have an impact on how we view ethnic 'aliens and strangers'. Australian governments have been plagued by the issue of refugees and border control. It is a complex issue that readily divides. But it is interesting that later in the Pentateuch, the Israelite experience of having been aliens in a foreign land is leveraged to teach them love, compassion and mercy for other aliens and strangers (e.g., Lev 19:34). The opening chapter noted the complexity of Australia's multiculturalism.

We are an ethnically diverse nation and, for the most part, we celebrate that. But few things have divided us more than our response to refugees and asylum seekers. While as preachers we will have to be careful not to preach a political agenda, we do need to bring perspective on the issue by addressing the remarkable grace, favour, mercy and compassion God has always shown to the alien and stranger, and the motif of sharing freely with others the abundance with which God has blessed us.

Accepting that Good Things (and God's Things) Take Time

Australians are time-conscious. While ostensibly laid-back, we dislike delays and live heavily scheduled lives. We often feel time poor, and we keep an eye on the clock. We value our time, including our private time, our viewing time, our family time, our 'me' time. We resent hold-ups, even if for only a few minutes. A computer page that doesn't load, a slow car in front of us or a queue in the fast food restaurant can be the cause of instant frustration.

When we enter the world of the patriarchs, things slow down dramatically. In the Genesis narratives God seems to have a remarkable disregard for what we would regard as timeliness. Abraham was called to leave his home when he was 75 years old, a late start to say the least. He was promised a child and then waited for 25 years before the promise was realised, by which time he was 'as good as dead' (Rom 4:9, Heb 11:12). Although he had been told he would be the father of many nations, by the time he died he has just two sons, one illegitimately conceived through his own desperate measures to get things moving (Genesis 16).

Along with the delayed promise of an heir, there is an even longer delay in the promise of land. In Genesis 15, God renews the promise but now also gives a timeframe. He is told his 'offspring will be sojourners in a land that is not theirs and will be servants there, and they will be afflicted for four hundred years' (15:13). Abraham himself will never see the land promised (15:15) and his descendants will not inherit it until 'the fourth generation, for the iniquity of the Amorites is not yet complete' (15:16).

We are given here one of the two main reasons for lengthy time delays in Genesis. Here, surprisingly, the reason is God's mercy to the unbelieving Canaanites. Although they are already deserving of God's judgement, he intends to delay it until their iniquity is complete. In the words of 2 Peter 3:9, 'The Lord is not slow to fulfil his promise as some count slowness, but is patient toward you, not wishing that any should perish, but that all should reach repentance.'

The second reason is that God uses the lengthy delays to teach the patriarchs faith, gradually disarming them of their independence, exposing the sinfulness of their hearts and working for their transformation not their gratification. The dysfunctionality of the patriarchal families almost beggars belief. Abraham twice shamefully mistreats his wife by passing her off as his sister, thereby letting her be taken by other men (Genesis 12 and 20). In desperation to produce an heir, he and Sarai hatch a disastrous plan for him to conceive a child via her handmaid, Hagar (Genesis 16). He repeatedly takes things into his owns hands instead of trusting the Lord. But over time his faith grows, and the climax of the narrative is the 'test' of faith in Genesis 22. Abraham now displays great faith in God, having learnt by long and painful experience that God can do the impossible. In fact, he now believes that, if necessary, God could even raise the dead (see Heb 11:19).

In the next generation, deep-seated disunity along with parental favouritism underlie the devious scheme hatched by Rachel to secure the blessing from Isaac for her favoured son, Jacob. He is another of the patriarchs who is refined by lengthy trails. He was by nature and by name a fighter, a wrestler, a heel grabber, a deceiver.[57] His life was marked by struggle with people: his father Isaac, his brother Esau, his uncle Laban. He wrestled with these men for decades until, on his return to the promised land after twenty years in exile, God wrestled him (Genesis 32). From that point on, the focus of Jacob's struggle and tenacity was to change. He would no longer be wrestling with men for blessing, but wrestling with God.

A similarly long, slow transformation is seen in his twelve sons. The final *toledot* of Genesis is that of Jacob's family. Ostensibly it is the story of Joseph, but it is in reality the story of the twelve brothers who would become the leaders of the tribes of Israel.[58] At the start of the narrative they look like anything but national leaders. Lies, envy, hatred and deception mark the early stages of the story. But God works with this dysfunctional family over many years, to humble and change them. First humbling and then exalting Joseph, he then works through him to humble and convict the brothers. Joseph's own journey of transformation is lengthy, with some thirteen years passing from when his brothers sell him into slavery to when he is exalted to the position of prime minister in Egypt. Similarly, the transformation of the brothers is slow, as several more years pass while they traipse up and down to Egypt, buying grain and encountering the most mysterious responses from the unknown Egyptian lord.

In time, we see a full and remarkable transformation, captured most strikingly by the speech of Judah in Genesis 44:18–34. His speech, contrary to his earlier actions, is marked by humility and grace, evidencing the deepest love for his father whom he had earlier deceived, pledging to be a man of his word, and offering to sacrifice himself for his brother.

Throughout these narratives, the writer is making clear that through lengthy trial and difficulty, God teaches his people faith and brings about transformation so that they become the people they are meant to be.

God's preparedness to take vast amounts of time to bring about his gospel plans and to work his transformation in our hearts is confronting to our time consciousness.

We will have to remind not only other people, but ourselves as well, that sanctification takes time and gospel work is often slow. Our culture wires us to demand rapid results. We want to see converts made quickly, disciples made quickly, leaders made quickly. This inclines us to put our confidence in programs and strategies. If we run this course or event, secure that resource, or work to these KPIs, we will see results. But that is not how God works. It takes years to take someone from immaturity to maturity; years to make a leader; years to work through issues of abuse or overcome the damage of a dysfunctional relationship or deal with deeply embedded sins in our lives. Faith never promises quick fixes.

Iain Duguid's concept of 'living in the gap between promise and reality' is helpful.[59] We've received gospel promises and are waiting for their fulfilment. But right now, we are living in the gap between the two. What does the gap look like? In Australia it looks like unemployment, infertility, stretched finances, church splits, children who go off the rails, cancer, chronic fatigue, and a thousand other trials. Yet it is in the gap that faith grows. It is here we learn to pray, to trust, to surrender. It is here we see God provide and surprise.

Finding Individual Worth in Community

We have noted in the description of Australians that ours is a fiercely individualistic culture. Our focus is on personal identify and success rather than collective wellbeing. It is an aspect of our contemporary narrative that the Genesis narratives address.

Articulating five narratives of the late modern (or postmodern) world, Timothy Keller notes that our Western storylines typically both arise out of and depart from the Christian tradition.[60] One of the five is 'the social narrative' concerning the place of the individual in society. Keller notes that to a significant degree, an emphasis on the rights, dignity and eternal worth of the individual is a unique contribution of Christianity. But divorced from belief in God it becomes a dangerous lie:

> Western secularism ... is radically and increasingly individualistic. The higher purpose of a social order, under this narrative, is not to further the interest of any one group nor to promote any particular values or virtues but rather to set all individuals free to live as they choose without hindrance, regardless of any communal relationships, as long as they don't harm someone else's freedom to live as he wishes. Choice becomes the one sacred value and discrimination the only moral evil.[61]

According to Australian pastor and cultural critic Mark Sayers, 'What we are experiencing is ... the enthroning of the self as the greatest authority. God is increasingly relegated to the role of servant, and massager of the personal will.'[62] We are taught to believe that 'the highest good is individual freedom, happiness, self-definition, and self-expression'.[63]

Consequently, 'traditions, religions, received wisdom, regulations, and social ties that restrict individual freedom, happiness, self-definition, and self-expression must be reshaped, deconstructed, or destroyed'.[64]

So how are we to navigate the relationship between the individual and the community? Genesis indicates a complex interplay of the two. The patriarchal narratives come from the fledgling days of the nation of Israel, long before the development of the pervasive institutions of the temple, the priesthood and the monarchy. They are, in many ways, the stories of individuals who travelled vast distances, married beautiful women, gathered many possessions, established households, negotiated with their neighbours and acted in both magnanimous and deplorable ways.

But these individuals were also part of the community God was forming. When God called Abraham, he was not just calling an individual but the father of a future family, a covenant community, a nation. Abraham himself is declared to be righteous on the basis of his personal faith in the promise of God (Gen 15:6). But he is, at the same time, the head of a community which carried the promises he believed. Indeed, he is the father of all who have faith, both Jews and Gentiles (see Gal 3:29 and Rom 4:16–17).

Among his immediate descendants, those who had faith in the gospel promises became heirs of those promises, but those who rejected them were cut off from the covenant community. That is played out most conspicuously in Esau's rejection of the promise (see Heb 12:16–17). Less drastic, but no less instructive, is the example of Lot. In the pursuit of individual success and happiness he chose to depart from the community and settle near Sodom. His choice was close to fatal as his individual wellbeing was impacted by the new community he chose to associate with. When Sodom is destroyed because of its wickedness, Lot was rescued but suffered great loss.

The experience of Hagar is also telling. She was appallingly mistreated in the covenant community both by Abraham (who illicitly takes her to be a surrogate wife for producing an heir), and by Sarai (who, in jealousy, deals with her harshly). She flees, leaving the community of which she is meant to be a part and where alone she will find blessing. Taking refuge in the wilderness, she is found by the angel of the Lord who sees her in her misery and takes care of her. His love and compassion for this individual is beautiful, yet he requires that she return to the community, to Abraham's house, because that is the house he will bless.

This complex interplay of the individual and the community is profoundly important for our own context. While the Genesis narratives show the dignity, independence and personal responsibility of each person, they also show that ultimate good can only be found outside of oneself. Keller rightly says,

> You cannot get significance through self-recognition; it must come in great measure from others. In the end, you can't name yourself or bless yourself ... We need someone from outside to say we are of great worth, and the greater worth

> of the person telling us so, the more powerful that recognition is to our identity formation. So, if we try to authenticate and validate ourselves, we place ourselves in an infinite loop of delusion that will lead to either narcissism or self-loathing.[65]

This is a truth our Facebook and Instagram addicted church members need to hear. We are easily caught in the endless pursuit of self-validation. But the 'unwinding', as Sayers calls it, of all communal ties, institutions and commitments leaves us free to go away, change our story, get married or divorced, hired or fired, go broke or start a business. We are left with a very fragile existence. Nothing is solid, fixed or stable.[66]

The gospel remedy is radical:

> To be shaped by grace in a culture of self, the most countercultural act one can commit ... is to break its only taboo: to commit self-disobedience. To acknowledge that authority does not lie with us, that we ultimately have no autonomy. To admit that we are broken, that we are rebellious against God and His rule. To admit that Christ is ruler. To abandon our rule and to collapse into His arms of grace.[67]

This, he argues, takes a resilience in our cultural context that can only be found in 'a life rooted in Jesus' sacrificial gift of grace'.[68]

As we preach the lives of the patriarchal family, or further back in the story, the lives of Adam, Eve, Cain or Lamech, we have ample opportunity to reveal the destructive consequences of pursuing individual freedom at the cost of others. We also have endless opportunities to challenge each individual to find their place in the world not by writing their own story but becoming part of God's story. We can affirm the dignity and worth of every individual, but we must also proclaim that true joy and lasting happiness is secured only when we abandon our own quest for self-affirmation and resolve to find blessing in Abraham's seed alone.

Conclusion

The Pentateuchal narratives in general, and the patriarchal narratives in particular, are not just great stories but foundational ones designed to be preached. Providing us with our deepest historical and spiritual roots, they enable us to assess the Australian cultural narrative in the light of God's age-long plans and purposes. Setting the trajectory for the entire biblical narrative, they are stories that we are invited not only to read but to participate in as we become a part of narrative through faith in Abraham's seed. In him alone there is ultimate blessing, and through him we find purpose and perspective on our journey in this country as we await the heavenly country our earliest forebears also awaited in faith.

Sample Sermon: Genesis 22:1–14

If you know the stories of Winnie the Pooh, you will know there is a character called Tigger. Tigger, a young tiger, is incredibly bouncy. He's always positive, outgoing, upbeat and confident, which tends to get on the nerves of some of his friends. Like Piglet, who is nervous and tentative, and Rabbit, who is practical, and Pooh, who really only thinks about eating honey.

> So, Rabbit comes up with a plan to 'unbounce' Tigger:
>
> 'Well, I've got an idea', said Rabbit, 'and here it is. We take Tigger for a long explore, somewhere where he's never been, and we lose him there, and next morning we find him again, and – mark my words – he'll be a different Tigger altogether.'
>
> 'Why?' said Pooh.
>
> 'Because he'll be a Humble Tigger. Because he'll be a Sad Tigger, a Melancholy Tigger, a Small and Sorry Tigger, an Oh-Rabbit-I-am-glad-to-see-you Tigger. That's why.'
>
> 'Will he be glad to see me and Piglet, too?'
>
> 'Of course.'
>
> 'That's good', said Pooh.
>
> 'I should hate him to go on being Sad', said Piglet doubtfully.
>
> 'Tiggers never go on being Sad', explained Rabbit.[69]

You know, I sometimes wonder if God doesn't at times take us on a long explore in order to 'unbounce' us. Not because he's in any way cruel or vindictive or annoyed with us, as Rabbit may have been. But because he knows that if we are to fully experience the riches of his love that he has won for us in Christ, we will need to look to him and nothing else. So, we'll need to be a more humble Tigger, a more dependent Tigger, a more 'Oh God, how much I want to see you' Tigger.

Certainly, that's what he did with the man who in the Bible is known as the father of the faith. Abraham is called by God at the ripe old age of 75 and then taken on a very long explore. His long journey of faith was designed to teach him what it means to really trust God. God had promised him great blessing – not merely personal blessing but blessing that through him would go to all nations, all peoples. In fact, the promises he made to Abraham, back in Genesis 12, were really the promises of the gospel.

Abraham believed those promises. He believed the gospel. But like us, he had to learn the hard way what faith in God really meant. As we take up Genesis 22, we are picking up after 25 years of training. That's a very long explore, isn't it?

We are used to things happening quickly. I hate a web page taking more than two seconds to load. We hate waiting in queue, or waiting for test results or waiting for someone who's a few minutes late. And we tend to carry our impatience over into spiritual life. We want rapid spiritual growth. We want speedy conversions and fast-track discipleship and quick church growth. But God is in no such rush. He knows that it takes time to learn deep faith. He will work with us over long periods of time. In fact, he'll work on us all our life, teaching us more and more about what it is to really live by faith in Christ and in the promises of the gospel.

So now, after 25 years, at age 100, God tests Abraham's faith.

We know how testing works, don't we? Students have tests at school to make sure they know what they've been taught. When a new medicine is developed, there is extensive drug testing to make sure that it is safe and effective. If you make some really great food you taste test it to make sure it is good, before serving it to guests. In each case the testing is not designed to make something fail, but to prove that it won't.

And God does the same with us. He tests us, not to make us fail but to prove the genuineness of our faith and to further refine it and strengthen it. That's what he now does with Abraham, and this test and the way Abraham handles it has much to teach us about the tests we will also face and what it means to live by faith.

There are three things here worth noting. First:

God may ask of us things that seem too hard

God actually had a track record of asking hard things of Abraham. Ever since God first called Abraham to leave his home country of Haran, he'd been teaching Abraham to rely on him no matter what. He'd been training him to obey even when it is hard (which it often was), not to take matters into his own hands (as he did on several occasions), and to believe that God can do the impossible (and he really did do the impossible in giving Abraham and Sarah a son).

But now God asks something that pushes his faith to its limits. Verse 2: 'Take your son, your only son, Isaac, the son you love ...' and sacrifice him to me!

It is an outrageous thing for God to ask. Everywhere else in the Old Testament, God hates human sacrifice. That is the practice of pagans, not followers of the Lord.

And more than that, this dearly loved son is the son the whole story has been waiting for. This is the son on whom all God's promises depended. God had promised elderly Abraham and barren Sarah descendants, and they had to wait and wait for this son to arrive. When Sarah finally conceived, aged 90, it was an astounding miracle. So how crazy to sacrifice this son! Surely Abraham is being asked to do something that seems far too hard. Something that doesn't make sense. Something unrealistic. Something impossible.

And that may be how it feels to us at times as well. Thankfully we will never be asked to do what Abraham was asked to do. But God may well put us in situations that seem too hard, unrealistic, impossible. I think we easily feel that, because for most of us life is pretty good. We're fairly comfortable. Life is pretty predictable. Most of our problems are first world problems. But sometimes God seriously rocks our boat.

He might place us in a situation of having to go somewhere we don't want to go. We have always lived near family and friends. We've always lived somewhere safe and comfortable. But we find God placing us in a situation where we don't know how we will cope. 'Lord, why are you asking this of us? It's too hard.'

He might place us in a situation of extreme financial need. We are used to financial security and money in the bank, but we find ourselves in circumstances where we are anxious and struggling financially and it seems far too hard. 'Lord, why aren't you providing for us?'

Maybe you've faced times when you have lost friends, or lost a loved one, or seen your church divided, or been betrayed by a close friend. The pain is enormous. We feel we can't cope, and we wonder why God has allowed it.

You may have seen the work of the gospel you have poured yourself into being undermined. The church plant crumbles. The new believer you've invested in so heavily walks away from faith. The faithful ministry you've built up over years is attacked by enemies of the gospel. We grieve, and we wonder where God is in it all.

I wonder if in the future we might not face persecution here in Australia. We are used to freedom of speech, and church on main street, and Christian values largely upheld by society. But all that is being undermined, and I wonder how we will cope if we have to suffer for our faith. We are so used to comfort we may well be crushed and think it is too hard.

But the fact is, as followers of Christ we are not exempt from trials and burden and suffering and hardship. In fact, we may face increased struggles for the sake of the gospel. And we may feel more keenly the agony of faith because we had expected God to look after us better. And we may find God putting us into particularly hard circumstances to refine us and change us. So, we find ourselves thinking God has asked of us something that is too hard, unrealistic, impossible. He did that to the father of our faith, and he may well do that to us as Abraham's sons and daughters in the faith.

So, what do we do? Well, let's go on in the chapter. We see next in this story that:

God calls us to trust him no matter what

That's what God had been teaching Abraham for a long time and so now he puts his faith into practice. The next morning, he gets up and prepares to go. He saddles the donkey, gathers his servants, gets Isaac, prepares the wood for the burnt offering and sets out.

What a long, hard walk it must have been. Seventy kilometres. Three days. I'd love to know what Abraham was feeling. If there'd been a tabloid reporter there, they'd have been asking, 'So how do you feel about what you have to do?' Abraham would tear up. and we'd have a powerful TV moment.

But there's none of that here. We're not told what he was thinking or what he was feeling. We're not told about the conversation en route for most of the three days. In fact, we're told almost nothing about the journey. We're just told he went. He obeyed.

And when they arrived, we see his faith strongly intact. He says to his servants, 'Stay here; we will worship, and *we* will return' (22:5). He believes, somehow, that he *and* Isaac will come back.

But then Isaac asks the most awful question: 'Dad, where's the sacrifice lamb?' How does Abraham reply? With great faith he says, 'God will provide' (22:8). Literally, he says God will 'see to it'.

My wife gets up to make cup of tea and I say, 'Sit down honey, I'll see to it.' A new employee is taken on and the boss says, 'Now don't worry, I'll see to it that you are paid well.' One of you kids upends the meal all over floor, but you quickly reassure them: 'It's all right, I'll see to it.'

To 'see to it' is to have it totally covered; to take care of it completely. And Abraham believes God has this sacrifice totally covered. Somehow, he'll see to it.

The book of Hebrews gives us an insight into the depth of Abraham's faith. Listen to this:

> By faith Abraham, when he was tested, offered up Isaac, and he who had received the promises was in the act of offering up his only son, of whom it was said, 'Through Isaac shall your offspring be named.' He considered that God was able even to raise him from the dead, from which, figuratively speaking, he did receive him back' (Heb 11:17-19).

That's remarkable, isn't it? Abraham believed in the possibility of resurrection from the dead, even though he'd never seen or heard of a resurrection. He believed that if he really had to kill the promised son, God could bring him back from the dead. God had given him from the dead womb of Sarah in the first place, and he could give him back from the grave if needed.

You see Abraham had walked with God long enough to know what he is like. To know that he can do the impossible. That he is powerful and loving and good. That he always keeps his promises. So, he believed that, somehow, God would see to it.

And that's what living by faith is all about. It is about obeying God and trusting that, somehow, God will see to it. When work, or finances, or relationships, or parenting, or ministry or life is too hard … we must trust that somehow, God will see to it. We don't know how. We can't understand why he has put us in this situation. But we know God is faithful, powerful, gracious.

Your finances fail. Your best friend betrays you. You are diagnosed with cancer. Your child becomes ill and dies. It's awful. But you know that somehow, God will be sufficient for you. Somehow, God will see to it.

I know a young pastor who's planting a church and who was recently diagnosed with cancer. When the diagnosis was made, he explained it to the church and then wrote:

> This news might be quite a surprise – it certainly was for me, but it isn't news that surprises God. He has known this about me since before I was born, and he has complete control. Although the negative possibilities might be the first that jump to mind, we have a good God who is the master of healing – please bring this to him in prayer.

That's the response of faith. But how can we have faith like that? Is that real faith or just naivety?

Well, in the third part of this story we are given the basis for this kind of faith; the ground for trusting God no matter what. We trust because:

God has provided for us in the ultimate way

We're not told the conversation that took place as Isaac was bound and tied on the altar. It's almost impossible to imagine. Somehow not only did Abraham do it, but Isaac submitted to it.

We're not told the conversation, but the narrative slows down, and we see Abraham build the altar, and lay out the wood on it, and bind Isaac and place him on the altar and then reach for the knife. The knife he used many a time to kill an animal and would now use to slaughter his son.

As he is about to plunge it into Isaac, the Lord calls out: 'Abraham, Abraham; don't do it; stop.' God stops him because he has passed the test. 'Now I know that you fear me because you have not withheld your son, your only son from me' (22:12).

At that moment, Abraham looks up and sees the Lord's provision. A ram is caught in a nearby bush. Abraham is able to catch it and bring it to the altar, slay it and burn it as an offering in place of Isaac. The Lord provided a substitute. So, Abraham names the place, 'The LORD provides.' The Lord sees to it.

It's wonderful. But even more wonderful is the substitute he has provided for us. You see, on that same mountain, Mt Moriah, the mountain of the Lord, another Father took his son, his only son, the son he loved, and laid him on the altar. Just before he went to his death, he asked his Father to spare him. 'If there is another way ... but not my will, but your will be done.'

But there was no other way. No other way for the promises to Abraham to be fulfilled. No other way for the gospel to go to all the nations and for God to fix a broken world. No other way for sinners to be saved.

And so, Jesus was bound to the cross. And there at Calvary, there was no last-minute rescue. There was no substitute, because he was the substitute. He was the sacrifice in our place – for all our sins, our failings, our disobedience, our rebellion. He was put to death in our place.

And then on the third day, God raised him from the dead. Abraham believed in the resurrection of the dead without ever having seen it. We believe in it because of the empty tomb. Jesus has risen and has conquered sin and death.

Through Christ, God has seen to it. He has seen to it that sin is defeated, the grave conquered, eternity secured. And 'he who did not spare his own son, but gave him up for us all, how will he not also, along with him, graciously give us all things?' (Rom 8:32).

On Christmas day the family came around for dinner. Everyone brought food and the provision was abundant. It was a feast. The table sagged and there weren't just seconds but thirds and then lunch and dinner the next day and beyond.

God's provision in the saving death and resurrection of Jesus is so ample, we are supplied for every circumstance of life. Yes, we can trust him to forgive all our sins. And we can also trust him trust him to bring good out of evil, as he did on the cross. And to provide for us and our families – maybe not what we want, but to provide strength, grace and perseverance. And we can trust that our children are in his hands, no matter what. And we can trust him to do what is right and just. And we can trust him to advance the gospel in the hardest places. And we can trust him when we face death. And we can trust him for the world to come.

The God who saw to our greatest need on the cross will see to every other need in life and in death.

Maybe God is taking you on a long explore. Maybe you sense he's making you a humbler Tigger, a more dependent Tigger, a more, 'O God, how much I need you' Tigger. If so, what he really wants is that as you look at the cross, maybe through tears, maybe with fear, maybe with no clue as to what God is up to, you will see that he has already seen to it. The God of Abraham gave us his son, his only son, the son he loves, to love us forever. The difficulties of life are not signs of his distance from us or his judgement on us. They are just his means of drawing us to himself, that we might trust him fully, always.

3

PREACHING OLD TESTAMENT LAW TO AUSTRALIANS

Martin Pakula

Introduction

I suspect that most Christians who set out to read the Bible cover-to-cover will face a challenge pretty early on. Genesis and the first half of Exodus are exciting; they contain lots of great stories and intriguing revelations about the character of God. But about half way through the book of Exodus, we get lots of chapters detailing the construction of, and the ministry pertaining to, the tabernacle. And it is given in long, painstaking detail. Leviticus comes next, with more and more laws about sacrifices and priests. And then more laws! And Numbers and Deuteronomy[1] don't get much better. Frankly, most Christians' eyes glaze over at this point. They find this part of the Bible boring. The narrative parts are good; the laws – not so much.

So, why preach on these Old Testament laws? I suppose the Reader's Digest version of the Pentateuch would keep just the exciting narrative parts. But if we cut out the laws, we would be omitting about half of the Pentateuch. And the Pentateuch is the foundation of the Old Testament, and the Old Testament is the foundation of the Bible. It's important to preach on the Old Testament laws because they are the word of God. But there's still more to it than that.

Exodus 19 through to Numbers 10 is all about the one year stay of God's people Israel at Sinai. The promises to Abraham (Genesis 12:1–3) are the key to understanding how the narrative unfolds in the Pentateuch and the rest of the Old Testament. By Exodus 1, Abraham's descendants have multiplied to become a great nation. God rescued them from slavery in Egypt primarily to bring them into the promised land, in fulfilment of the promises to Abraham. But first they stopped at Sinai. Why? Because God promised Abraham that he and his descendants would be blessed in the promised land. And a large part of that blessing is being in relationship with God.[2] That relationship was established at Sinai, and the laws expound what it meant to live in that relationship as the now saved people of God.

A large part of the Sinai laws consists of the building of the tabernacle (Exodus 25–31, 35–40) and the sacrifices and priestly ministry that are to take place there (Leviticus 1–9). These laws are perhaps seen as one of the most excruciatingly boring parts of the Bible. But they are critically important: they are the foundation of the meaning of a sacrifice for sin. Our whole understanding of Jesus' death on the cross as a sacrifice for sin has its basis in this part of the Old Testament. It is *crucially* important, and therefore we must preach on it.

There are other reasons we should preach on Old Testament laws. They convict us of sin by holding up God's standards.[3] And they show us what God desires for his people.[4] Clearly, we still think the Ten Commandments have great importance in this respect. But so too do the rest of the laws. Some Christians would divide the laws into moral, civil and ceremonial laws, and say that only the moral laws still apply.[5] However, I would urge us to examine and preach on *all* the laws and to see how they are fulfilled in the person and work of Jesus Christ.

A pastor friend of mine preached through the book of Leviticus. At first, most of his congregation groaned politely under their breath. But by the end of the book their reaction was far different. It opened their eyes to see how glorious and great the word of God is and how it all points to Jesus.

The Hermeneutical Task

Needless to say, it is not a simple task to preach on Old Testament laws. Maybe the Ten Commandments are easier pickings, but what about, say, Numbers 5:11–31 and the test for a wife suspected of adultery? How do we preach on such seemingly obscure Old Testament laws?

Within Christian history, there have been a number of approaches to the hermeneutical task at hand. In the past, the church preached allegorically on the Old Testament, but this approach does not take the passage literally in terms of its historical and literary context. We must exegete a passage in its original historical and literary context to understand what was said to the original hearers of the word of God. Most commentaries will be of great help here; however, I strongly recommend doing our own work first on the passage to understand its original message. Only after that should we consult the commentaries. I recommend using the grammatical-historical method of exegesis to gain an understanding of the what the text meant. This is a critical and important step in our process of preaching on any Old Testament text.

However, we must go further and not stop there if we are to understand what the text *means* for today. An allegorical approach offers few (if any) controls for how the text is to be applied to a Christian today. A typological approach has much more promise, because it takes seriously the original context in the Bible and how the Bible itself deals with such types.[6]

The typological approach to hermeneutics is based upon a sound process of exegesis.[7] It is based on the grammatical-historical method, but then proceeds to examine how the passage of Scripture fits into the context of the entire Bible, viewed as a unity. For example, the book of Hebrews speaks about the tabernacle, priests and sacrifices and how they are fulfilled in Jesus (especially chapters 7–10). These are types that find their fulfilment in the antitype (Jesus).

The prophets of the Old Testament themselves demonstrate a typological approach as they take up the promises to Abraham and David and speak of new saving acts in terms of the previous saving acts of God. They speak of a new exodus, a new David, a new covenant. Such a reinterpretation of past events does no violence to the original historical acts, because they are disposed to this reinterpretation from the start by their very nature.[8] There is 'an unmistakable "structural analogy" ... between the saving events in both Testaments'.[9] This 'structural analogy' is typological.

Gerhard von Rad notes, rightly, that the fulfilment of Old Testament types in their New Testament antitypes is not literal, but far surpasses what was expected.[10] He also notes that such typological interpretation will involve the entire Old Testament, and thus the 'number of Old Testament types is unlimited'.[11] Being based on sound exegesis, such a typological interpretation always emerges from the literal sense of the text.[12]

Sidney Greidanus discusses several different, but related, approaches to preaching Christ from the Old Testament: Redemptive-Historical progression, promise-fulfilment, typology, analogy, longitudinal themes, and contrast.[13] Greidanus defends the typological approach.[14] Some scholars view such approaches (typology, biblical theology and so on) as not being based on the grammatical-historical method.[15] The basic charge is that such an approach reads back into the Old Testament a meaning that was not originally there. This however is not the case (unless the method is used wrongly; Greidanus calls this 'typologising'). The original meaning of the Old Testament text is read in light of its fuller revelation in the context of the whole Bible. Greidanus notes that 'even though we *discover* this fuller meaning only retrospectively from a later stage of redemptive history, from God's perspective it was always there in his overall design of redemptive history'.[16]

There are three key hermeneutical approaches to the Old Testament that I would like to mention.[17] Firstly, the secular humanist approach arises from the Enlightenment and views the Bible only as a human document.[18] This approach is the basis of critical scholarship. The laws are seen as a late evolution in Jewish religion: part of the P source from post-exile Judah. The laws are viewed as providing a window into how the postexilic community operated, telling us little or nothing about the time of Moses. Clearly this view does not treat the Bible as the word of God. There is no application under this model, for it tells us what the Bible *meant* post exile, but not what it *means* today. Though this approach is clearly a dead-end for Christian preachers, it stands behind many of our modern commentaries. That is why there is usually no application in Old Testament commentaries and little or no discussion of fulfilment in Jesus.

Even if Evangelical commentaries disagree with this approach, their authors usually still move in the same world of critical scholarship. Sadly, such commentaries, while suitable for exegesis, usually give little help to the task of preaching on Old Testament law. The original meaning will be given, but little else. How such laws might be fulfilled in Jesus or apply to us today are passed over briefly if at all. Some commentary series are a welcome exception to this rule, such as the Bible Speaks Today series, the NIV Application Commentary series and the Australian Reading the Bible Today series.

A second hermeneutical approach, common today among many Christians, is to apply the Old Testament directly to us. This may seem an intuitively correct approach when it comes to the Psalms or the Ten Commandments. Moving straight from them to us in application often makes quite good sense. However, we might get into trouble with the book of Joshua. Should we declare jihad today and wipe out all unbelievers in the promised land? Is that not the direct application to us of the book of Joshua? And what about the tabernacle and sacrifices? There are many Christians today who want to rebuild a temple in Jerusalem, with literal priests and sacrifices. That would indeed be a direct application of this part of the Bible to us today. But I would suggest that this is not how the New Testament interprets the Old Testament.

The third hermeneutical approach is the biblical theological approach. A key Australian author, Graeme Goldsworthy, has written much to make this approach clear.[19] Biblical theology doesn't mean theology that is biblical. It means basically putting an Old Testament passage into the context of the whole Bible to see how it is fulfilled in the person and work of Jesus. While there are many human authors of the Bible, each book has a dual authorship of God and a human author. Psalm 110 is authored by David (Acts 2:34–35) and by God (Heb 1:13).[20] There is a profound unity to the Bible because ultimately there is one chief author: God. What's more, the storyline of the Bible moves forward from creation to redemption in Christ, then to new creation.

What this means is that we ought not to pluck out the laws and apply them directly to us today. When we preach on the New Testament, we can usually move straight from the passage to ourselves today in application. Hermeneutically, there is a critical extra step involved when preaching on the Old Testament: we need to put the laws in the context of the whole Bible as the story moves forward to its fulfilment in Jesus, and only then to apply the laws to ourselves. This is how the New Testament deals with the Old Testament. According to Jesus, the Old Testament, including its laws, is primarily about him.

> And beginning with Moses and all the Prophets, he interpreted to them in all the Scriptures the things concerning himself.[21]

> Then he said to them, 'These are my words that I spoke to you while I was still with you, that everything written about me in the Law of Moses and the Prophets and the Psalms must be fulfilled.'[22]

Likewise, the apostle Paul said that 'all the promises of God find their "Yes" in him'.[23] The Law of Moses is ultimately all about Jesus – about his person, death and resurrection. Reading the Law and applying it to us today by allegory or directly, by bypassing its fulfilment in Jesus, will lead to misreading and misapplying it. It goes against the way Jesus himself viewed the Scriptures. The Law of Moses must be read in the context of the whole Bible as it finds its fulfilment in Jesus.[24]

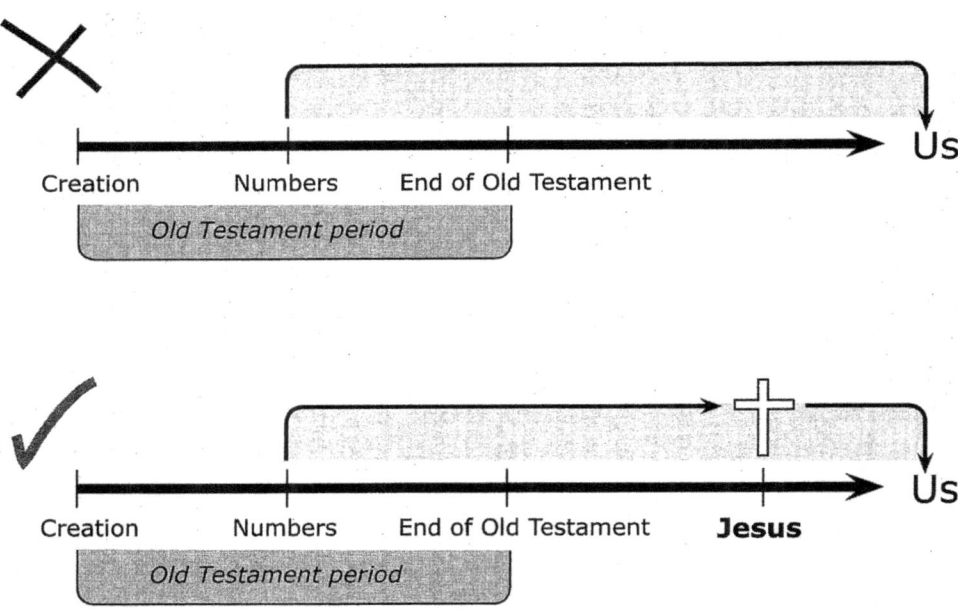

One of the criticisms of this approach is that every sermon on the Old Testament ends up tacking Jesus on at the end in a formulaic way. I think this is a possible pitfall for preachers, but only if the preacher is lazy. If detailed work is done on the Old Testament passage itself, many rich, multifaceted themes relating to fulfilment in Jesus will open themselves up for exploration.[25]

Let's think for a moment about preaching on the Ten Commandments. It's an excellent thing to do at church because it convicts us of our guilt before God as we hear of his right standards, and it causes us to turn in faith to Jesus alone for the forgiveness of our sins. We are urged to repent of sin and to live God's way. But jumping straight from the Ten Commandments into application for today is not a sound hermeneutic.

For example, the commandments 'Do not murder' and 'Do not commit adultery' are very literal in the Old Testament. They apply to a civil society and mean, literally, not to kill your neighbour and not to have sexual relations with your neighbour's wife. But that's not how they apply to Christians today. In the Sermon on the Mount, Jesus takes these two laws and *changes* the application. Actually, he raises the level of application. Under the old covenant, God's people were judged mostly on their external actions by human judges. In the new covenant, the law is written on our heart and God judges our hearts, not just our external actions. He judges our motives and thoughts as well. So, if you hate your brother in your heart, you are guilty before God of murder, Jesus says. If you look at a woman with lust, you are guilty before God of adultery.[26]

The tenth commandment, 'Do not covet', similarly examines motive, not just action. It applies to the previous commandments (not to covet the wife of another, or their possessions). This gives us the hermeneutical principle of applying the Ten Commandments as broadly as possible. God is not just interested in the physical act of murder, but also the thoughts of our hearts: whether we hate others.

And take the ninth commandment: 'You shall not give false testimony against your neighbour.' The third and ninth commandments go together: one is about honouring God's reputation, while the other is about honouring the reputations of others. False testimony means literally what we call perjury: lying about someone in court. Not only do we blaspheme God by lying, but we harm our neighbour. False accusations are devastating. If a school student falsely accuses a teacher, pastor or youth group leader of sexual abuse, then even if it comes out later that they are innocent, their reputation will be tarnished beyond repair and their career may be over. Breaking this commandment is therefore taken very seriously and can carry the death penalty: the penalty in the Old Testament for perjury is that you get the punishment that would have fallen on the falsely accused (Deut 19:16–21).

But the ninth commandment is not just about misrepresentation of a brother or sister in a court; the commandment extends to misrepresenting them in any situation. Thus lying, slander and gossip are forbidden in this commandment. We are not to misrepresent other people; instead, we are to value their reputation. We should not speak ill of others. And in the new covenant it will mean not only getting rid of words that harm others but even the thoughts that give rise to those words, for God examines our hearts. We are not even to think evil of others.[27] We are to so honour the reputations of others that we speak and think what is right concerning them. Rumours, gossip, slander, exaggeration about others, picking at their faults, seeing the worst in them – all such things break this commandment. We are to love each other in our speech and in our thoughts.

Let's move on now from our discussion about preaching on the Ten Commandments. When it comes to applying the Old Testament laws, we need to see what the New Testament does with Old Testament texts in general. For example, the food laws of Leviticus 11 are part of a section that concern all of life activities that would make an Israelite ceremonially unclean (chapters 11–15). But now that Jesus has come, his death on the cross makes us clean in God's sight. Furthermore, such food laws served to separate Jews and Gentiles, but now in Christ Jews and Gentiles are one new human (Eph 2:11–22). So, all foods are now clean (Mark 7:14–19; Acts 10:9–16; Col 2:20–23; 1 Tim 4:1–5). The fulfilment of these and many other laws in Christ is such that they no longer apply to us today. However other laws are fulfilled in Christ in such a way that they continue to have application to us today. Leviticus 18 and 20 set forth God's will concerning forbidden sexual relationships. These laws protect the family unit. It is clear in the New Testament that such teaching still applies (Rom 1:24–27; 1 Cor 6:9–20).[28]

At this stage, let me say a word about the length of a passage one might choose to preach on. With the Ten Commandments one could preach ten separate sermons, taking one commandment at a time. But in preaching through the book of Numbers, I might take a much larger passage, say two chapters or more. There's no 'right answer'. It will depend on one's congregation and preaching program. For example, I would preach on Numbers 5 and 6 in one go. There are a lot of different laws in that passage.

How would you preach on Numbers 5:11–31? Here we have an elaborate ceremony done at the tabernacle. This passage involves a wife who has committed adultery, but it has been done in secret and her sin has not been detected. So, she has broken the law, but it is a secret sin: there are no witnesses and so no one caught her in the act (v.12). But the husband has become suspicious (something tips him off) and this passage teaches what he is then to do. There is an elaborate ritual whereby God deals with the woman (if she is guilty). The ritual is highly symbolic and visual, but it's not about a 'magic potion'. God punishes the guilty, who sin in secret. In fact, the innocent are protected. If a husband is suspicious of his wife and *he* is wrong, she will be protected and found not guilty. The husband is not to take matters into his own hands, but is to give the situation over to God alone.

How then is this fulfilled in Jesus, and how should we apply it to us today? In the broader context, Numbers 5:1–4 says that the unclean are to be expelled from God's presence. God dwells among the army camp, and God is holy. Numbers 5:5–10 says that if someone realises that they have wronged another, they must make restitution. They can't continue among God's people in the camp as if nothing were wrong. And our passage (5:11–31) is saying that if someone in the camp has sinned in secret and become unclean, God will find them out.

We are reminded again of the seriousness of sin, that Jesus has dealt with our sin and that our secret sins are not secret. God dwells among his people now by his Holy Spirit, and he will judge us for our secret sins. No one will 'get away with it'. We must confess our sins, bringing them out into the open and repenting of them, turning to Jesus and seeking forgiveness in his name. And if we are suspicious of a wrong done to us, like a wife going astray, we are not to take it into our own hands. We are to give the situation over to God. Romans 12 reminds us never to take revenge, but to give vengeance over to God. In our modern Western context, we will also need to be sensitive about how we preach on this passage. We should apply it of course to both husbands and wives.

Finally, in undertaking biblical theology I have found a helpful model in the four-step process I learnt from Bryson Smith (now pastor of Bathurst Presbyterian Church). We answer the four questions: What's the story so far? (context); What's this episode about? (exegesis, detail of the passage); What does it show us about how God does things? (themes); What does it show us about how God does things through Jesus? (biblical theology).[29]

The Contextualisation Task

The 'Describing Australians' chapter outlines some of the features of Australian culture. No doubt some of this will come naturally to us. In our preaching style, we will probably shorten our words and use Aussie vernacular and slang. And I hope our style will tend towards the direct, frank communication of an individualistic mindset. Frankly, as one brought up Jewish, I think our Anglo culture is very softly spoken and careful. In sermons, this leads to a desire to be less direct, to not offend. It seems to me that Jesus and Paul may have been more Middle Eastern in culture, and therefore more direct. My church is in a lower socio-economic area, where our down-to-earth Aussies appreciate straight talk. But all of this is more about style than content.

In preaching, we expect that many of the features of Aussie culture will also come out in our illustrations. Sport will be common as well as popular culture (movies, TV series, YouTube, social media). But there's also no doubt about it – we need to think more about the features of Aussie culture, and Ian Hussey has helped us enormously with his careful analysis.

We saw that Aussies are, surprisingly, rule-based. Clearly, this will be the cultural point of most importance when preaching on law. What it means is that preaching on Old Testament law is not irrelevant for Aussies – in fact, far from it. We may be wrongly assuming that we can't preach from the books of Leviticus or Numbers.

We Aussies do indeed like laws and rules. We like the rule of law, justice and fairness. We want to have good systems of government and church organisation. These things matter to us. My Chinese friends have a different social orientation to rules. While rules are often very important to them, social interactions can be even more important. In preaching to them, I have to emphasise that God *does* care about such things. In their culture, it is more common to break copyright laws by downloading movies from the internet, which is stealing. It's not that Aussies are immune. At the Bible college where I studied, they had to put up notices on every photocopier telling students not to steal by breaking copyright laws. But my Aussie friends immediately understood that this would be wrong. Not so with my Chinese friends. (Given the multicultural society we live in, hopefully our churches will have many Asians among us, so we may need to give reasoned arguments for why downloading movies is stealing.)

But by the same token the Bible is not as tight and neat on laws as we would like. So as Aussie rule-based folk, we are chagrined by the lies of the midwives (Exod 1:15–21) or the lies of Rahab (Josh 2:1–7). Clearly telling lies is wrong (Lev 19:11). However, the Bible here is laxer on the subject than we might be. Perhaps our Chinese friends have some wisdom we can learn from. For them, offending someone is far worse than telling a lie. Relationships are more important than laws and rules.

The next of the 'big five' cultural dimensions that is pertinent to Old Testament law is the importance of distinguishing individualism from collectivism. This is something to which we may often be culturally blind, for we have very strong individualism in Australia. Take, for example, the fifth of the Ten Commandments: honouring one's parents. Our culture values individualism so highly that most children begin to be independent in their teens and are almost entirely independent of their parents by their late teens or early twenties. My Asian friends will be far more obedient to their parents, especially while still single. I suspect that their cultures are closer to the Bible than ours at this point, such that we should be preaching against our culture when it comes to obeying the fifth commandment.

But the Bible corrects Asian culture, too. Genesis 2:24 speaks of marriage, where a man will leave his parents and be united to his wife. A new family unit is formed. He *leaves* his parents. The husband or wife no longer answer primarily to their parents, and their parents should not interfere in the marriage. That is a helpful corrective to many non-Aussie cultures (who are with us in our multicultural churches).

Many Old Testament laws emphasise the *collective* nature of our society. What we do has effects upon our families and neighbours. Committing adultery isn't a 'private matter'; it hurts so many people around us. Our culture tends to view our own personal happiness as the highest good. God is a Trinity. The Father and the Son and the Holy Spirit are in triune relationship eternally. The Son seeks to honour and obey the Father. There is other-person centredness at the heart of God's very nature, and this is at the heart of our universe. We are therefore to be other-person centred, not just looking to our personal happiness. In fact, personal happiness comes from serving others. The path to happiness is given by God's laws. He is no mean-spirited killjoy. God gives the laws for our good, to show us the way to enjoy relationship with him. Committing adultery hurts me, my wife, my children, my extended family, my friends at church, my pastor, the woman with whom I have an affair, her husband, children, and so on. How on earth did we come to think that it's okay as long as it's not hurting anyone? The incidence of adultery has increased in the church, mirroring Western society. Our extreme individualism has taken us down a terrible path. The Bible's laws, in terms of both content and setting, often serve to correct our extreme individualism.

There is also, especially in Deuteronomy, the constant call in the law to look out in Israel for the Levite, the orphan and the widow. This again emphasises the collective nature of society and hopefully pushes us towards care for others and charity. Australians do seem to be a charitable lot, especially among Christians. We are more aware than ever of the plight of refugees in our global yet war-torn world. However, our materialism and individualism push us to look after ourselves and pay off the mortgage first. But the laws of Moses push us towards an other-person centredness that recognises the plight of the disadvantaged. What's more, these laws push us towards real action and giving, not just commenting on social media.

Yet, of course, there is an individualistic turn to the Old Testament laws as well. A life has value because a human is created in the image of God (Gen 9:6). What could be more individual than that? Certainly, we should be careful when preaching on Old Testament laws, or really any part of the Bible, to think through how our individualism may have distorted what we are preaching on. And we should think through how a collectivist attitude among many of our multicultural church folk may affect their thinking and actions.

Overlapping with this last point are several other features of Aussie culture. The first of the big five cultural dimensions was mastery over our environment. Although we are big on 'mateship', we are more concerned about personal success and achievement than personal relationships. No doubt this arises from our individualism but also from our materialism (we are wealthy and consumerist). I think this is a clear point at which we should preach against our culture. We should emphasise the importance of relationships. The laws are all given in the context of relationships: with God and with one another (our neighbour). God rescued his people Israel from slavery in Egypt to be in relationship with himself. The Ten Commandments begin this way (Exod 20:2; 19:4). Many of the laws describe how the Israelites are to relate to God (for example, laws of sacrifice, the tabernacle). And many of the laws describe how the Israelites are to relate to one another (for example, laws regarding stealing and property, injuries to one another, the disadvantaged, sexual relationships). Clearly, Christianity is intensely relational. We need to be careful when preaching on laws to apply them relationally, not as rules with no social context. We want to produce good neighbours, not Pharisees. We should also preach against materialism. The laws, especially in Deuteronomy, urge us to look out for the disadvantaged: the widow and orphan, the Levite, the slave. Our materialism needs to be challenged by clear biblical preaching that pushes us towards generosity. Preaching against coveting and stealing, for instance, should push us away from materialism towards generosity.

My last point may also have something to say about our being time poor and even anxious or depressed. Anxiety and depression may be physical of course (chemical), not just psychological. Though anxiety and depression can limit our ability to socialise, it still holds true that humans are fundamentally relational beings (we're created in the image of the triune God), and that therefore it's right to expect that being among other people should help us. Our extreme individualism may blind us to the reality that fellowship with others (and not just on Sundays or mid-week Bible study) should help those who are struggling with anxiety or depression.

The same is true of being time poor. Our rigorous focus on time and our general impatience dovetails into this topic (being monochromic in time-orientation). Again, the focus of Old Testament laws is very much relational. The laws are enacted within a society under God. We need to preach them that way and correct our extreme individualism. This may help us at a number of points where our culture is leading us astray. Perhaps we would read the Bible, pray and evangelise a lot more if we thought more relationally and less individualistically. Perhaps spending less time in church activities as rule-based tasks and more time with non-Christian friends, family and neighbours would help our evangelism. Evangelising together is much easier than doing so individually. Perhaps less time in individual prayer and more time at church prayer meetings would help our prayer lives. And we can read the Bible with others, too, not just alone.

Another of our big five cultural dimensions was our Aussie egalitarianism, which leads us to be suspicious of authority. Old Testament laws both promote authority and also speak out against the abuse of authority. Submission to authorities is a theme throughout the Bible, but the focus is sharp within the Law of Moses. Our lack of respect and honour of parents in Western society is corrected here when we see that cursing one's parents carried the death penalty (Exod 21:17). Speaking against leaders was often treated just as harshly (Numbers 16). Preaching on the law should lead to far more respect for authority and correct our culture on this point.

Furthermore, in our postmodern culture we are also anti-institutional. Abuse in the church is, I believe, still present at many levels. Perhaps more humility and self-criticism would go a long way to remedying this awful blight on the church. We need to apply the laws of the Old Testament not only to our congregations but also to ourselves. Moses was known for his humility (Num 12:3) and was also prepared to die for the sake of those he served (Exod 32:31). Preaching on the law should expose our own hearts to our utter sinfulness and our need to repent. Abuse of authority should be far from us as leaders and far from our churches.

Finally, I want to say in this section that while we must take our own culture into account, and while we are often blind to our own culture, we still have many commonalities that are very strong across all cultures. We are all sinful human beings. And we are all in need of redemption. Preaching on Old Testament law should major on exposing our sin and pointing us to Jesus.

Sample Sermon: Leviticus 16

Comments on the Sermon

Leviticus 16 is about the Day of Atonement and the ceremonies performed on that day. It seems obvious how to get from there to Jesus: Jesus' death on the cross atones for our sins. But that would be a very lazy application of the passage. The passage is far more detailed than that, and the detail will give a different angle and application. Here is my summary description of the passage.

Let's deal with the background first of all, the story so far. This passage occurs during the one year stay at Sinai. Israel had been rescued from Egypt and would move on to the promised land. Leviticus teaches about the sacrifices made at the tabernacle to bring forgiveness of their sins. In the early chapters of Leviticus, the main types of sacrifices are outlined. I agree with Gordon Wenham that the burnt offering is the main offering to atone for one's sin.[30] The 'sin-offering' was not about paying a ransom for sin but was about cleansing the inanimate objects of the temple from sin.

In Leviticus 10 two of Aaron's four sons approached God in the Most Holy Place. They were immediately struck down dead. Leviticus 16 comes back to this at the start of the passage. It teaches that no one could approach a holy God at the tabernacle. Even the high priest could not approach God, or he would die. Only once a year, on the Day of Atonement, he could approach God, and only then with a cloud of incense smoke so that he didn't see God and die (Lev 16:1–2, 12–13).

There are two sets of ceremonies in Leviticus 16, and both teach highly visual lessons. The first set of ceremonies were like a spring cleaning of the temple. The high priest entered the Most Holy Place and sprinkled blood everywhere, first for his own sins and then for the sins of the people. The blood cleansed the Most Holy Place from their sins so that a holy God could remain dwelling with them.

This was like an annual spring cleaning of the temple, but with blood, because blood/ death atones for sin. The penalty for sin is death. The daily burnt offering also took place as usual on that day. That is what atoned for individual sins (in terms of paying the ransom for their sins). Every day, morning and evening, sins were atoned for at the temple with the burnt offerings. But the Day of Atonement involved cleaning out the temple from all the sins the Israelites brought into it, so that a holy God could remain dwelling among them.

The second ceremony saw their sin placed on the scapegoat's head and the goat sent far away from the temple, far away from God's presence. The temple was cleansed of sin and the Israelites' sin was sent far away.

So, what do the Day of Atonement ceremonies show us? They show us that God is holy, that we are unholy, and that we can't approach God in our sin, or we will be struck down dead as we bear the penalty for our sins.

The fulfilment, of course, is in Jesus. Jesus' death on the cross paid the penalty for our sins. But what this means in Leviticus 16 is not just that our sins are atoned for – after all, the daily burnt offering did that. But it shows us that we can now approach God, because our sins have been atoned for once and for all. The curtain was torn in two when Jesus died on the cross. Access to God is now available to all who trust in Jesus. Hebrews 10:19–22 speaks of Jesus' death making a way for us, through the curtain, so that we can approach God with confidence.

Therefore, my application on this passage is about approaching God in prayer. Many non-Christians assume that if they are in trouble they can rock up to God and approach him in prayer. Leviticus shows that God is holy, we are unholy, and we cannot approach God. Even Aaron's sons were struck down dead for approaching God. God will not simply hear and answer our prayers. But now that Jesus has paid for our sins, we can approach God and enter his presence. He can and does hear our prayers. One of the most amazing things about prayer is the fact that we can now personally approach God because of the death of Jesus.

That is my briefest summary of the passage. Here are some excerpts from my sermon. In the introduction, depending on how much time I have, I speak about the Day of Atonement festival in modern Judaism.

Sermon Text [excerpts]

[Here I pick up at the end of the introduction]:

I think though that many Jewish people go to synagogue on this one day of the year because they do feel some sense of guilt before God. They know they are not perfect, and like most good Aussies, they think if they do a bit of good, put in an appearance, then 'She'll be right, mate!' It's not much different to your average non-Jewish Aussie really. I think that most Aussies reckon they're okay with God, and if they do a bit of good – 'She'll be right, mate!'

Do you remember Paul Hogan in the movie *Crocodile Dundee*? When Crocodile Dundee was asked about God he said: 'Me and God, we're mates!' We Aussies are just so laid-back we think that our God is, too, and we're just a couple of mates. It's like an ad that used to be on TV: 'When you get to heaven what d'ya think you'll say? I think I'll say: G'day!' We Aussies are okay with God and will rock up before him and say 'G'day', because God's me mate!

It's a comforting thought: God is laid-back like an Aussie and will welcome us all into heaven. The problem is, however, that when people meet God in the Bible it is very different: they fall down as if dead. That is very different to rocking on up before God and cheekily saying 'G'day'.

But *why*? Why do people fall down before God as if dead? The book of Leviticus says God is *holy*. God is perfect in holiness; he always does what is right one hundred percent of the time. He is perfectly holy. We, on the other hand, are not perfect; we do wrong things, we make mistakes. We are sinful and unholy. Here then is the problem: how can a holy God be in relationship with an unholy people? That's the problem the Day of Atonement is dealing with: how a holy God can live with an unholy people.

*

[Here's another excerpt as I explain the Day of Atonement ceremonies]:

The great thing about the temple was that God dwelt there. Israel was like no other nation; the God of the Universe was with her. She had God in her midst. But God could not dwell with unholiness. And all year as people came in and out of the temple, they brought their unholiness into it. It's a bit like kids with muddy feet coming in and out of the house. After a while the house gets dirty and needs to be cleaned.

Here is the spiritual equivalent: people have brought their unholiness in and out of God's house and it needs to be cleaned. You can't see muddy footprints in the temple – or 'unholiness' footprints – but it is a reminder: God will not dwell with unholiness.

So once a year there was a spring-cleaning ceremony, where the temple was cleaned out: all the uncleanness, all the unholiness, was cleaned out. And the reason? So that God could stay there with his people. That's what the Day of Atonement was for: it was for God to stay with his people and to be in relationship with them.

So, here's a dilemma: what do you clean unholiness with? It's obvious what you clean dirt with – with water. But what do you clean unholiness with? Most Aussies would say – with good deeds! Do a few good deeds and it will balance out the bad ones. That's modern Judaism's answer too. But it's not the Bible's answer.

What is the Bible's answer then? How do you clean unholiness? The Bible's answer is – with blood. Blood cleans unholiness as water cleans dirt.

*

[Finally, here's an excerpt from the final parts of the sermon]:

Our holy God wants to deal with our sin and unholiness so that he can be with us. Jesus' death means we have full access to God. Our sins are forgiven because Jesus has taken the penalty for our sins on himself: he dies in our place, instead of us. Now that we are forgiven, we have full access to God. We are no longer barred from God's presence: we can stand before a holy God as we are. Our unholiness has been dealt with once and for all.

When Jesus died, the curtain was torn in two: the curtain in the temple, barring the way to God, was removed. We now have access to God. We will not die when we stand before God. It is not now that only a high priest stands before God, and only once a year. Now all God's people can stand before God, anytime, because our unholiness has been dealt with once for all. Look at how Hebrews 10 puts it:

> [19] Therefore, brothers, since we have confidence to enter the Most Holy Place by the blood of Jesus, [20] by a new and living way opened for us through the curtain, that is, his body, [21] and since we have a great priest over the house of God, [22] let us draw near to God with a sincere heart in full assurance of faith ...

We have confidence now to approach God, to stand before him – without the curtain, without the veil, without the smoke screen, just as we are. We have *full access to God*. An unholy, but forgiven, cleansed, people: we have full access to God, because our sins are forgiven.

If we take this for granted, we have missed a huge point. The Old Testament shows that we can't just rock up before God whenever we want. Those who did that died in their sins. But now we are forgiven, and we have full access to God. We have relationship with God; we are friends with God. We're his mates! This is the most incredible thing ever – something the Old Testament prophets longed for and hoped for. We now have it. We have full, free relationship with God because of the death of Jesus.

Finally, I want to draw out one implication of this full, free access to God: *prayer*. Look at Hebrews 4:14:

> [14] Therefore, since we have a great high priest who has gone through the heavens, Jesus the Son of God, let us hold firmly to the faith we profess ... [16] Let us then approach the throne of grace with confidence, so that we may receive mercy and find grace to help us in our time of need.

We can now approach the throne of grace with confidence and ask God for what we need. Prayer is an immense privilege.

People who aren't Christian often just assume that God will hear their prayers (especially if they are in trouble). That's not true. God will not necessarily hear their prayers. How could he? How could a holy God listen to the prayers of an unholy people? If an unholy person was to approach God, they would die!

Does God forgiven the sins of Jewish people on the Day of Atonement when they pray to him for forgiveness? No! You can only be forgiven on the basis of a sacrifice for sin, namely Jesus' death on the cross. But for Jews and Gentiles who have put their trust in Jesus' death, our sins are now forgiven. And now with our sins forgiven we can approach the throne of grace with confidence. God can and does now hear and answer our prayers.

You see, what's the most spectacular thing about prayer? The fact that now we *can* pray to God because of Jesus' death for us. The curtain is gone, the way to God is open, we can come before him in prayer and he will hear our prayers. That is an *immense* privilege.

Are you taking this privilege for granted? I think I often do. How can we not pray? What a great privilege it is!

Comments on the Sermon

One of the key difficulties in preaching on any part of the Old Testament is that there is an extra step involved: the biblical theology step. It takes time to give the context of the passage and then do the biblical theology involved. For some of my sermons I give detailed application, but often there is only time for a broad sweep of application, as here.

The illustrations and language I used are clearly directed to an Aussie congregation. I think that is just natural in our preaching. There was no concerted effort to do that.

One comment I want to make about preaching on this text is to address our tendency to read ourselves into the text. This comes from our strong individualism. We misread Leviticus 16 as being about atonement for our sins, individually. However, it is more about atonement in the sense of cleansing the inanimate objects of the temple so that a holy God can remain dwelling with his people. I correct our individualistic tendency to read ourselves into the text and make it all about us, so to speak. It is more about God.

In terms of power distribution, the law of Moses and this passage are clearly very hierarchical. This goes against our Aussie cultural sensibilities. Only the priests can offer sacrifices at the temple, and only the high priest can perform the Day of Atonement ceremonies. The high priest, though, is a type of Christ (as are the sacrifices and the scapegoat). I think the gospel does tend to transform the hierarchical nature of the law into a more egalitarian fulfilment. Christ is our high priest and head. However, in Christ we are all equal and we believe in the priesthood of all believers (e.g., 1 Peter 2:5, 9). We do have leaders in the church, but they are not priests. In terms of our passage, biblical theology will actually push us towards an egalitarian outcome.

Of course, our passage, describing ceremonial law procedures in detail, looks very rule-based! However, biblical theology again transforms the fulfilment of the passage to be relationship-based. The application moved towards approaching God as we are, forgiven in Christ, and approaching him in prayer. Relationship with God is the key outcome of Christ's fulfilment of this very rule-based law passage. Perhaps our penchant for rules leaves us feeling vague about this application (I hope not!). We may prefer rules for how to approach God and how to pray. We may even approach our Bible reading and prayer times in a very rule-based manner. But this passage leads us to an open-ended relationship with God.

The application will also correct our monochronic tendencies. In Australia we tend to separate our work and personal life; we do one task at a time. The problem for us then is that we may tend to think little of God at work and spend little time in prayer there. Of course, we might rationalise that we should not waste our employer's time on such personal matters. Perhaps we could use our lunch hour for prayer and reflection. However, surely we can give the right amount of work time to our employers, while still spending moments in reflection upon God and in brief prayer throughout the day. This could be a specific application given at the end of the sermon when speaking about the privilege of prayer.

In the introduction, I spoke about the average Aussie thinking that they are okay with God. I wondered if this is still the case, but our statistics show that Aussies do indeed still think of themselves as Christian to a large degree. Many will still think this way. While connecting with our Aussie non-church going friends, then, the introduction does also challenge this belief by speaking of our sin and inability to approach God in our sin as we are (apart from Christ).

Finally, our Aussie contextualisation chapter spoke of our fear, anxiety and depression. The application at the end addresses this. God, in his love, has given his dear son Jesus to die in our place and atone for our sins. We now have access to God, just as we are. We can approach God with confidence. God is good. God is love. He wants our good, and he wants us. He brings us close to him, despite all our failures and sins. More could be said on this in the sermon to address our fears and anxieties and dispel them. Turning to God, trusting in Christ, is the antidote to our fears.

My hope for this sermon was to take what would be seen as a dry and perhaps dead boring passage (Leviticus 16) and make it clear and gospel-focused. People look almost fearful after the Bible reading of this passage! My aim is to use biblical theology to show how the passage is clear and can be understood, and why it is important to us. The focus on the gospel and the application about prayer is meant to inspire folk in a fresh way to see what a privilege it is to approach God in prayer. The hermeneutical approach is, I believe, critical.

My hope is that this chapter will inspire you to preach on Old Testament law passages using biblical theology to show how those laws are fulfilled in Jesus – and then how they apply to us today. With the application, the features of our Aussie culture can highlight new angles for us to bring God's word to bear more accurately on ourselves and our congregations.

4

PREACHING OLD TESTAMENT NARRATIVE TO AUSTRALIANS

Christine Redwood

Introduction

I love preaching the narratives found in the Bible. Yet I've come to discover that not everybody shares my love, particularly for Old Testament narrative. I was teaching an advanced preaching class recently, and I suggested we look at Judges 11 and think about how we would preach such a story. The students read the text, and then one of them closed the Bible and said to the student next to him, 'I wouldn't preach that.' I've heard similar comments from people in church. One scholar, Strawn, recently tried to measure how often the Old Testament was preached, and concluded it is on the decline.[1]

It shouldn't surprise me to realise that not everyone likes the Old Testament, yet it does. Now, granted, the Old Testament narratives are ancient stories formed in very different cultures to our own, and there are confusing and terrible things that happen in some of those stories. But when we cut ourselves off from the dark parts of the biblical story, it means we will have nothing to say to the many Australians who also struggle with these texts. I find Old Testament narratives fascinating, because we get to see people struggling to know and follow God in the messiness of life, and then, in turn, we get to wrestle with and often encounter God in a new way.

I'm going to take Judges 11 as our case study for this chapter to show how enriching this story can be. But before we dive into this particular narrative, let me say a few words more broadly about Old Testament narratives.

There has been fresh interest in narratives both in biblical scholarship and homiletics.[2] Many preachers have rediscovered the power of stories. One of the crucial insights that Long speaks about is letting the Bible speak into both the 'content and shape of the sermon'.[3] If this is true, then it means that expository preaching can be varied, for the Bible itself contains diversity. Narratives have a way of engaging the whole person, their minds and their emotions. They call for a response having the 'power to transform, to urge choice, and to command praise' as they point to God.[4] When looking at narratives, we need to pay attention to the plot, various scenes, structure and characters.[5] Furthermore, when approaching the Old Testament, I, like many evangelical preachers, operate 'within the framework of the evangel', the good news concerning Jesus Christ.[6] While reading an Old Testament narrative in its original context is essential, for Christians it cannot stop there. This means that when preaching from the Old Testament, I always have one eye towards the climax, which for me is Jesus Christ: his life, death, resurrection and coming kingdom.[7] Taking these general points into consideration, let's see how it works in practice.

The Hermeneutical Task

Parameters

The first step for a preacher is to set the parameters of the story. The great thing about narratives, although it might at first seem unusual or intimidating, is that we can cover huge chunks of Scripture in just one sermon. This is very different to preaching from one of Paul's letters, for example, where we might only cover a few verses because the arguments are so dense. Narratives are not meant to be preached one verse at a time. It also means the preacher does not have to feel bound to explain every detail in the text. A preacher can cover a huge story like the whole book of Esther or focus on a smaller story that appears in part of a broader book.

Make sure, when choosing the parameters, you read carefully to know where the limits of the story are. For instance, you could decide to focus on Judges 11 and make that choice simply based on the chapter divisions. But in fact, the story begins at Judges 10:6 with Yahweh frustrated because of Israel's continual sin. Knowing this will help a preacher make sense of the problematic parts later on in Judges 11, including God's response. Judges 10 raises the questions that drives the narrative forward into Judges 11: What is going to happen? Will God raise up another deliverer?

Plot

A preacher needs to understand the plot because Old Testament stories 'focus more on action' than particular characters.[8] We need to note what the major crisis is in the story. In Judges 11, it is the vow that Jephthah makes that results in his daughter's death. Old Testament plots often have many twists and turns and seem to thrive on 'ambiguity'.[9] Part of the challenge for a preacher is how to build that suspense into the sermon. The other challenge is to work out why characters make certain decisions. Before turning to the commentaries, spend time in the narrative yourself and try breaking the story down into scenes. This structure may or may not shape your sermon's structure.[10]

Judges 11 could be broken down like this:

Scene 1 (10:6–16): Dialogue between Yahweh and Israel.

Scene 2 (10:17–11:11): Dialogue between Jephthah and the Elders of Gilead.

Scene 3 (11:12–28): Dialogue between Jephthah and the King of the Ammonites (via messengers).

Scene 4 (11:29–33): Jephthah makes the vow to Yahweh.

Scene 5 (11:34–40): Dialogue between Jephthah and his daughter.

Scene 6 (12:1–7): Dialogue between Jephthah and the Ephraimites.

Point of View

It can be easy to forget, but biblical stories have a narrator. One of the things a preacher can pay attention to is how the narrator is telling the story.[11] In Judges 11, the point of view of the third person narrator is presented as reliable. The narrator aligns themselves with Israel and Jephthah's account of the history of the land. The narrator focuses on Jephthah's vow before God and the fulfilment of the vow. Scholars describe the tone of the narrator as being neutral throughout the narrative.[12] This does not mean disinterested; rather, the narrator gives space for the reader to respond to the story for themselves. Evans notes that in the book of Judges in general, the narrator rarely provides 'editorial comment'.[13] The narrator does, however, emphasise the grief of Jephthah when he realises the consequences of his vow; the narrator notes the way he tears his clothes and highlights the fact that he is losing his only child. There seems to be sympathy for him and admiration for the daughter. Yet also given that this narrative is situated in the book of Judges, it does seem that this story is meant to be viewed as tragic.

Characters

A familiar tension in Old Testament narrative is trying to work out a character's motivations. We don't get to hear their inner thoughts. The preacher will need to make significant decisions about characters' motives, which will shape the way they tell the story and what application comes out of the narrative. Subtle clues in the dialogue and narration can serve as a guide.

Jephthah

Jephthah is the main character in Judges 11, and the only character fleshed out in any detail. We learn that Jephthah's father was with a prostitute, resulting in Jephthah's birth. Eventually, his other brothers kick him out of his home in Gilead. This contributes to Jephthah's insecurity and mistrust.[14] Jephthah's other essential characteristic is his 'mighty power'.[15] Jephthah is the only judge not raised up by Yahweh directly.[16] Nonetheless, Jephthah does seem to recognise and depend on Yahweh – however flawed that might be.[17]

There is a lot of pressure riding on Jephthah. The elders of Gilead call him back home to help them defeat their enemy. They promise to make him their chief if he wins. He needs to have success.[18] Perhaps this explains the extra lengths he goes to. Firstly, he tries diplomacy with the Ammonites. We might be tempted to skip this section, as it goes into a lengthy dialogue about the differing claims to the land of Gilead, but we learn more about Jephthah's character. Jephthah wants to stress how careful Israel was in treating the other nations with respect. He argues it was only because of Amorite aggression that Israel was forced to fight and ended up winning the land that is now in dispute. Jephthah identifies Yahweh as the ultimate Judge, which is 'one of the most profound theological statements' in the whole of the book of Judges.[19] But at the same time, Jephthah also gets many details wrong in the negotiations. In verse 24, Jephthah says that the god of Chemosh is the god of the Ammonites. This is unusual, as Chemosh is commonly associated with Moab. Block suggests that this is an example of Jephthah's syncretism. He shows both contempt to the Ammonites by calling their god by the wrong name, and disdain to Yahweh by suggesting that Chemosh, not Yahweh, would give Ammon land.[20] The diplomacy fails, and so Jephthah prepares to fight the Ammonites.

This leads to the most intriguing part of the story, Jephthah's vow. Preachers will need to step outside the story and understand the role of vows in ancient Israelite culture. Vows appear to be commonplace, with instructions in the Torah to guide the making of such vows. Burnt offerings of animals are closely associated with vows.[21] Vows are to be treated seriously and to be fulfilled promptly.[22] Yet there is a clause that excuses people from their vows if they pay a fee.[23] Janzen also stresses that since the law actually forbids human sacrifice, Jephthah was under 'no obligation' to fulfil his vow.[24]

While scholars agree about the purpose of vows, they disagree about the particulars in this story. Firstly, it is unclear whether Jephthah was open to either animal or human sacrifice when he makes his vow in verse 31. It does seem that Jephthah is talking about making a burnt offering in his vow. Many scholars think that Jephthah was open to human sacrifice.[25] Webb points out when Jephthah uses the word 'to meet me', it is a word associated with people rather than animals.[26] Evans agrees and adds that if Jephthah were only thinking about animals, then a person walking out of the door, later on, would be irrelevant.[27] Many of the surrounding cultures did occasionally practice child sacrifices.[28] I have followed the consensus that Jephthah was open to human sacrifice.

The second question that is unclear is why Jephthah is making this vow. It seems like Jephthah is making a deal with God just like he made a deal with the elders.[29] Others, like Yoder, argue that Jephthah's commitment to the vow is praise-worthy; he is a leader who can be trusted in a time when leaders were not always trustworthy.[30] All this background information would not need to be included in a sermon, but it does show the responsibility the preacher has to choose how they'll understand the main character in an Old Testament narrative.

The Brothers/Elders

It is a standard feature in Old Testament narratives to cluster people into groups, individuals are 'not differentiated' but function together in one role.[31] Most other characters in Judges 11 tend to appear as groups. The brothers/elders function as one group who move the action along first as antagonists driving Jephthah out of the clan. Then they bring Jephthah back and establish him as chief. Biddle points out that the elders are not interested in restoring the relationship with Jephthah or admitting wrongdoing but seek to appease Jephthah by paying him off.[32] The Ammonites and their king appear as the next antagonistic group waging war against the Israelites and demanding the land back for themselves.

The Daughter

Jephthah's daughter appears as a brief sketch. But debate encircles her. Did she know about the vow? Most seem to say yes.[33] Jephthah's vow is public, and therefore some scholars note that Jephthah's daughter would have been aware of his words.[34] Her first words seem to affirm she knows what Jephthah had vowed and agrees with it. Her response can be read as representing 'the proper role of women', showing humility, giving complete obedience, and grieving the loss of marriage.[35] Ryan proposes she offered herself 'willingly' as a sacrifice.[36] Janzen describes her as complicit because she meekly surrenders.[37] This seems to be reading a lot into the daughter and probably reveals more about our views on what it means to be female than about Jephthah's daughter.

Yahweh

Lastly, there is God. Yahweh functions as a character primarily in the background though we hear Yahweh speak in Judges 10:16. Yahweh's response here is ambiguous. Firstly, Yahweh laments Israel's constant sin. Yahweh speaks in verses 11–14 declaring Yahweh will no longer save Israel, yet when Israel responds with repentance in verses 15–16, Yahweh seems to relent. Hamlin argues that this is because there is an action that accompanies their words, signalling the sincerity of their repentance.[38] Biddle likewise sees a change in Yahweh's response which is in keeping with the character of God.[39] Yahweh 'enters into authentic relationship' and so reacts to Israel's responses.[40] Fretheim agrees, emphasising the fundamental fact that Yahweh is deeply relational, a 'real' relationship between people and God is possible.[41] That means that God is affected by people's actions.[42]

Yet how God responds is still unclear. Either Yahweh is moved/grieved by Israel's suffering or Israel's continual sin exasperates Yahweh.[43] Younger describes the Israelites' cry as trying to manipulate Yahweh rather than a genuine cry.[44] In response, God is silent.[45] McCann states, 'God's quality of life is diminished ... suffers.'[46] This is a clue perhaps to how Yahweh must be feeling by the end of the story. In other parts of the Old Testament, like the psalms, the silence of God is linked with Israel's disobedience and God's lament.[47]

Yahweh's Spirit appears in the narrative, as Jephthah prepares for battle. This is the third time this has occurred in the Judges narrative. The Spirit also comes to rest on Othniel and Gideon.[48] Martin describes this as an act of grace to save the people from the Ammonites.[49] Along similar lines, Biddle states that Jephthah was the people's choice, not God's, but then God finally empowered Jephthah because the suffering of his people moved him.[50] A distinction is made between the Spirit enabling and the Spirit changing a person's character to pursue God's way of life.[51] The Spirit's role in the book of Judges seems to be to work through various individuals to help the Israelites supernaturally throw off their oppressors.[52]

God does not make Jephthah say his vow, but neither does God stop it.[53] In this story when humans choose destructive decisions, Yahweh does not intervene. The people of God are also silent; nobody objects.[54] McCann argues that Yahweh does not intervene because Yahweh does not tend to violate human freedom.[55] Even when God does intervene it does not seem to produce long-lasting change. People continue to choose things that lead to death and destruction. God's presence is best found with the women lamenting at the end of the story.[56] Judges 11 leaves us wondering where God can go from here. God still shows grace by saving the people, but the ending of the story suggests that sin is also prevalent and the relationship between Israel and Yahweh is still profoundly fractured.

The Contextualisation Task

The Underdog

I, like most Australians, love stories. I grew up playing and imagining stories with my sister and listening to stories before bed. As a teenager, I loved going to the cinema and walking out with my face damp with tears. Today the average Australian spends around ten hours per day connected to a screen.[57] Not all that time is spent engaged in linear stories, but a significant amount of that time is wrapped up in stories we either watch or craft in some way. We particularly love stories of the underdog. Our national stories celebrate the Anzacs and Ned Kelly. Our films champion the outsider, from *Muriel's Wedding* to more recent movies like *The Dressmaker* or *Jasper Jones*.

Preaching Old Testament narratives is a fantastic opportunity to tap into Australians' love of the underdog. Again and again, we see God work through the unexpected person. Think of Moses, a man who ran away from his people after he killed someone, who then encounters God through a burning bush. Then there is Ruth, the foreigner who chooses to stay with her mother-in-law after her husband's death, or David, the youngest son just looking after sheep who becomes king of Israel. In Judges 11 we met Jephthah, a man whose birthright was questioned, yet who becomes a deliverer. The Old Testament gives us characters who are real and flawed. Many of them are underdog figures.

Just as Jesus used parables, we too can tell a story that can work past people's natural reluctance to interact with the Bible. If you can tell a story in such a way that intrigues and draws Australians in, they might end up encountering God. Brown encourages preachers to engage their listeners, not only at the intellectual level but 'emotionally', telling the biblical story in a way that captures the drama and tension.[58] I suspect that a lot of Old Testament stories are not well known. This means preachers have an excellent chance to surprise people by introducing them to God.

Mastery

Old Testament narratives serve as a caution to Australians obsessed with achievement. Many of the Old Testament narratives focus on leaders, both their successes and failures. We see how our desire for mastery has ancient roots. Moses, in a moment of frustration, hits the rock to draw out water, and God rebukes him for failing to trust. Jezebel kills God's prophets and seeks to gain more power by taking a man's vineyard. Solomon marries hundreds of women to secure political alliances and make himself even more influential. Jephthah wants to be the leader of his clan, and he is prepared to do whatever is necessary to make it happen – even make a deal with God that involves human sacrifice. This desire for mastery often comes, I suspect, from a sense to prove ourselves, to escape our insecurities.

MacKay writes about how 'learning to live with insecurity' is one of the significant challenges facing Australians.[59] There are plenty of things we can worry about like climate change, job insecurity, changing technology, and a more fragmented society than in the past.[60] As the 'Describing Australians' chapter observes, we Australians, while appearing to have mastered so much, and living in a wealthy society as we do, also have incredible rates of depression and anxiety. This is a major issue in the church I work for; I live in one of the wealthiest suburbs around, part of the northern beaches in Sydney, and yet I meet person after person struggling with mental health issues. Stark writes about how Australians have grown up listening to stories that end with 'happily ever after'; we are pursuing our happiness as the ultimate goal, and there is a 'wellness' industry making billions of dollars as they help us.[61] We also have stories that tell us to rely on luck. We are the 'lucky country', after all. Perhaps it is not surprising that, shaped by such stories, Australians are 'world-leading per capita' when it comes to gambling losses.[62]

Yet the Old Testament narratives can provide a counter story. Firstly, they critique this drive to be masters by showing the results. Jezebel experiences a gruesome death. David, who is considered the greatest king Israel ever had, falters in his relationships once he experiences success. He uses his power to start and cover up adultery. He gains mastery over a nation, but his home life is a mess. By the end of his son's reign, the kingdom of Israel divides. The mighty and powerful often fall: think of Nebuchadnezzar in the book of Daniel, who orders a statue of himself to be made and worshipped, who ends up reduced to 'eating grass like an ox' and going through a time of insanity.[63] And Jephthah's story ends on a tragic note with the loss of his only child because of his vow.

The quest for mastery is shown again and again to be futile. Old Testament narratives, instead of believing in luck or a person's capabilities, stress the importance of trusting in God. The characters can draw Australians in, but these stories end up subverting our expectations by revealing that it's not the characters themselves who achieve anything, but God. One of the overarching themes in the historical narratives is the faithfulness of God.[64] Despite it all, despite people's obsession with mastery and control (which often leads to destruction) the Old Testament narratives speak about the persistence of God in bringing freedom and peace. This is a God of grace.

The Old Testament narratives can also serve as a caution when it comes to our mastery over the land. Australians have a complicated relationship with our land. Many of our stories are set in the bush or by the sea. We have a great love for the wild beauty of this land. Yet we also have mixed feelings about our history, particularly the colonisation of land and people. The land is a central theme in Old Testament narratives.[65] Many of the conflicts are centred on land. Lake traces how in the past these biblical stories were sometimes used to justify British expansion into Australia.[66] They shaped the colonial farmers' ideas about what farming the land should look like.[67] It was assumed that people needed to bring order into the wilderness, transforming the bush into productive land for the capitalist system. Yet the Bible was also used by a minority of Christians to speak out against some of the violent aspects of colonialism, arguing that the Indigenous peoples of Australia were also made in the image of God.[68]

More recently, Adam has argued that, though there a few instances of God reallocating land in the biblical narratives (particularly the book of Joshua), the overarching theme is that all land and peoples belong to God, and theft of land is wrong.[69] We see this concern in the debate Jephthah has with the Ammonites. He stresses how Israel did not go beyond the limits God had set. The nations, including Israel, are held accountable by God, to stay in the land they need to be committed to the covenant of God with its emphasis on justice and love for the alien and poor.[70] If Israel fails to keep the covenant, they too will be 'vomited' from the land.[71]

The Old Testament narratives show the realities of nations and land with all its complications and sin. Narratives give nuance to these discussions and could lead to some fresh thinking for Australians and our relationship to the land. It matters how we live in this place.

Individualism

Australians are highly individualistic. The temptation for preachers is to only concentrate on the flawed but interesting characters in the Old Testament narratives because that is what will connect with Australian listeners. The rise of postmodernism has just exacerbated our obsession with individualism.[72] Yet the Old Testament narratives are set in a much more collective society than Australia. Ancient Israel was primarily structured around the 'household and the kin group'.[73] This contributes to many of the Old Testament narratives feeling foreign to us. In the books of Joshua and Judges, the focus is on tribes. We see power struggles to be the chief of a clan. Deliverers regularly summon tribes to war, and when tribes fail to join, they are condemned. The importance of loyalty to the group is stressed. This is because many of the Old Testament narratives are about Israel developing its national/ethnic identity.[74]

A significant number of Old Testament narratives are concerned with telling the story of how Israel became a nation. Their national story celebrates how God saved a group of slaves out of Egypt and brought them to a land where they could live. People regularly invoke Yahweh's name. There is a recognition that ultimate power comes from God. Often the whole nation will suffer for one person's mistakes, like the story of Achan's sin in Joshua 7. Jephthah's daughter similarly seems willing to sacrifice herself for her father and the Israelite group. Old Testament narratives feature arranged marriages with expectations that family members will take care of other family members. This is because 'preserving the harmony of the community is everyone's primary goal' in a collective society.[75] In Australia, we conceive of ourselves as individuals before identifying with a particular group. The only group we might identify with is our nuclear family.

How does this focus on this ethnic nation, Israel, relate to Australia's multicultural context? Firstly, there is a note of caution. One of the primary themes in the historical narratives is the call for Israel to be faithful to the covenant it had made with God. The narratives show how dangerous it was for Israel to take on the surrounding culture and engage in the worship of other gods.[76] They regularly did. The trajectory of the Old Testament narratives is one of tragedy. This is reflected in the individual stories of 'initial hope' followed by 'distorted human ambition'.[77] When Israel becomes like the other nations, they have nothing to offer the nations. They were chosen by God to be a blessing to the nations, with the hope that the nations would come to know God and be part of God's people.

Christians are not part of this old covenant. We are not a nation. But what the Old Testament shows us is the tension we still face – to be in the world but distinct from the society around us. We too are called to be holy and live in light of God's kingdom. Live in such a way that the peoples and cultures around us might be intrigued and come to know Jesus for themselves. The Old Testament narratives are not there as a perfect model for us to replicate. Narratives show us what faith looks like in different cultures and times. In the Old Testament, the tribal society become a monarchy, the monarchy becomes conquered, and the people are scattered. It is okay to acknowledge that there are parts of the Old Testament stories that will seem foreign, maybe even oppressive, to Australians. Indeed, missionaries working in a collectivist society in Indonesia speak about how hard it is to 'present the values of a collectivist culture in a positive light' to Westerners.[78]

But what these stories do is remind us that this call to holy living is not done in isolation. Community is important. This is a message, I believe, that many Australians are yearning to hear and experience. A theme that runs right throughout the Bible is relationships. One of the downsides of individualism is loneliness. Loneliness is seen as such a serious issue in our country that there is an Australian Coalition to end loneliness.[79] The Old Testament narratives tell how God is forming a people for himself. Today there is the church, still called to be the people of God, still called to be committed to others – indeed, called to love one another.

Egalitarianism

Australians like to see themselves as an egalitarian society. We give everyone a 'fair go'. Since the publication of Germaine Greer's book, *The Female Eunuch*, which fought against the church's traditional teachings on women's roles, Australians have had to rethink gender and what it means for women to have a fair go.[80] This discussion has continued in the public sphere with new voices like Clementine Ford, Tara Moss and Tracey Spencer continuing to bring challenge. Moss, for example, has written about the low representation of women in politics and in the media (and I would add the church), and she challenges the labels women still get categorised with.[81] Such categories end up reducing women. This is probably not an issue many Australian preachers would consider, which shows how ingrained it is to see everything through a male gaze and think it is normal.

There are not that many female voices in Old Testament narratives. Most of the narratives are about men, with the few positive exceptions like Deborah, Ruth and Hannah. Many of the stories where women do appear, they appear as victims, like Jephthah's daughter, the Levite's concubine or Tamar. I think many Australians would be disturbed with these parts of the Old Testament. I can feel the temptation to want to smooth away the difficulties.

Take the story of Judges 11; what do we do with it? I want to reassure those listening that God does not endorse what happened to Jephthah's daughter, even though he works through the situation. I want to comfort and declare that God is good. I can feel the temptation to jump quickly to Jesus. Jesus is the good and only sacrifice we need. No more daughters need to die! I notice this temptation with beginner preachers when sharing this story to them. They wanted to celebrate the faithfulness of the daughter with the implication that we too should be ready to be faithful, even when it's for dubious reasons. Is that what God wants? Instead, I think we need to acknowledge that this is a difficult text. Australians appreciate honesty and people naming things as they really are.

This is needed more than ever in light of the Royal Commission into Institutional Responses to Child Sexual Abuse. After hearing stories of horrific abuse by Christians, Australians reports to having a more negative association with Christianity.[82] As Lake notes, just because Christians might know the Scriptures, it doesn't necessarily mean they will not inflict 'deep and lasting harm on vulnerable people'.[83] I'm working in a Sydney context where most of my congregation are University-educated, with many young adults taking a subject in gender studies through their degrees. I'm also writing this chapter in the wake of the #MeToo movement. The word 'feminist' is a very loaded word to say to some evangelicals, but I'm committed to learning from feminist scholars and their interaction with Old Testament narrative, because one of the jobs of the evangelical preacher is to communicate the Bible to a variety of people. Feminist hermeneutics has contributed to making people conscious of the fact that we read and preach as gendered beings. When a preacher speaks, they will naturally draw on their experiences to apply the biblical text. This is why it is essential to have a diversity of voices preaching.

A feminist perspective can help a preacher to be prepared that many people listening to the Bible will respond with outrage and sorrow to the biblical text. Trible focuses on the lament of the daughter and her friends in Judges 11, arguing that such action gives those listening to the story permission to lament for daughters today who have suffered due to 'faithless' men.[84] Old Testament narratives can be prophetic in speaking into our struggles. For instance, there is still a need for preachers to address such issues as gender violence and rape in Australia. A recent investigation by Baird reports how many women, when seeking help from their pastors about domestic violence in their household, were either not believed or told to 'submit to their husbands'.[85] This should be a cause to lament. Old Testament stories are spaces where we may relax, thinking they have no relation to us, when suddenly it hits those listening that the issues of religion and the abuse of power is still happening in Australia. Old Testament narratives give permission for people hearing their stories to acknowledge the hurtful and dark parts in our story. We need to be willing to listen. These stories call out to God for something more.

Secularism

Old Testament narratives are stories that encourage us to wrestle with faith. Cundall describes Judges 11 as a challenge to listeners about our loyalty to God.[86] The Old Testament tells stories of both God's presence and his absence. Many times, God is not actively involved; it seems like it is people driving the action. Jephthah and his daughter go through with the vow because of their faith. The question the sermon below tries to address is: what does faith look like when God seems absent or confusing?

This is particularly relevant to Australians. Secularisation has made everyone, even those with faith, feel a little less sure. Australians are moving away from Christianity, with more and more people choosing 'no religion' on censuses and surveys.[87] I have seen many young adults in my context walk away from the Christian faith.

Frame has done extensive work understanding unbelief in the Australian context. He says a significant portion of Australians think that belief in God is 'irrational and unreasonable' given the scientific and technological breakthroughs that have transformed our world.[88] There are other Australians who object to Christian theism because it causes damage to 'human beings and civilised society', especially when societal structures give religion prominence.[89] While there are philosophical beliefs and challenges, by far the most pervasive reason for not believing in God is people's experiences; people are 'repulsed by the attitudes and actions of those allegedly acting in God's name'.[90] This is no doubt why so many preachers can feel uncomfortable preaching from Old Testament narrative. In many of those stories, we see people do horrible things, invoking and justifying their actions by calling on God's name.

Even for those who remain Christian, they are aware that there are other options out there. We live in a pluralistic culture. Many Australians are pulled in different directions, feeling both the pressure to believe and not to believe.[91] Doubt is a strong part of the Australian Christian's experience. Smith argues that doubt is also the experience of those who don't believe; they too can be unsure, wondering whether there is more.[92] The fact that we are time poor and do not have the luxury to reflect on these matters can impact on our experience to connect to God. Preaching can be a gift, giving space to name out loud people's doubts and help people begin to navigate between faith and doubt.

Whenever you preach, you will have a range of listeners at different stages in their faith: some people are exploring the Christian faith, some like their faith to be neat and simple, and some can live with ambiguity and want a sermon 'that honours the complexities of a text and life'.[93] In the sample sermon, I am deliberately aiming both at Christian listeners who need to be shaken up because they tend to oversimplify faith and at those yearning for more. It is also a sermon that is aware of some of the postmodern influences in our culture. While there are many words in Judges 11, there is an equal amount of silence. Biddle describes 'a silence that hangs over the entire Jephthah story'.[94] This sermon focuses on perhaps the most mysterious person in Judges 11, God. It is God, or God's absence, that makes the story so problematic.

Sample Sermon: Judges 11

It's easy to get frustrated at God, isn't it? To see all the suffering and terrible things happening in Australia – the drought causing our farmers to worry, government and the revolving door of leaders, children stuck on Narau in indefinite detention – and to blame God. Why didn't you step in and stop it, God? Where are you? Many of the young adults I have mentored have asked this question. 'Where is God? I pray, and I can't hear anything. It doesn't feel like God is answering'. So, then I started praying, God, where are you? Make yourself known to these people; they want to know you. But a lot of the time, there doesn't seem to be an answer. And many of the young adults, people I have spent years catching up with for coffee, who have served in the church and once been so passionate about Jesus, slip away, leaving the church – and slowly, their faith – behind.

Silence. Have you experienced that? You're praying to God, perhaps pouring out your whole heart, and it feels like in the end there is nothing. You're just talking to yourself alone in your room. You ask for healing, but none comes. You ask for peace, but the fighting continues. You ask for direction, what should I do? You strain to hear anything, to see a sign, hear a word, feel something … love, joy. But there is nothing. It's easy to get frustrated with God, or maybe give up on God altogether. Many Australians have.

I've been reading and re-reading the story found in Judges 11. It is a story that troubles me, confuses me. I've been straining to understand, but for a long time, all I heard was silence. Have you ever had that experience when coming to the Bible? Well, eventually I went back a few pages and started reading Judges 10. It was more familiar territory.

> The people of Israel again did what was evil in the sight of Yahweh and served the Baals and the Ashataroth, the gods of Syria, the gods of Sidon, the gods of Moab, the gods of the Ammonites, and the gods of the Philistines. And they forsook Yahweh and did not serve him. So the anger of Yahweh was kindled against Israel ...

This happens a lot in the book of Judges. The people always have this choice before them: to choose to love Yahweh and be committed to the covenant or to choose to break away and serve other gods. Mostly, they choose to turn away. Like us. But this time, because I was thinking a lot about God, trying to understand his silence, what struck me was that it says: 'Yahweh sees.' And Yahweh reacts to the decisions the people make. This is a God that is not unmoved. But feels. You think it is only human beings who get frustrated?

No, God gets frustrated with us! It's mutual! When God sees suffering and terrible things happening because of the decisions we have made, when evil takes place, it disgusts God. When people repeatedly turn their backs on having a relationship with God, breaking their promises to listen and serve: God responds, God gets angry. That might make us uncomfortable. Maybe, after all, we'd prefer not God but some good force at work in the world; maybe we'd prefer the silence of a God who didn't feel things so strongly.

But the Bible shows a God who wants a relationship with us! God wants to speak. God wants good to flourish, for his kingdom to come. We, on the other hand, are a little bit more confused. We're not sure what we want: do we want to know God or do things our way? Do we want God to speak or would we rather not hear?

The Israelites tended to only come to God when they needed something. In Judges 10 they cry out to God. They want God's protection from their enemies now they are ready to confess their sin, but the rest of the time, well, they are happy to keep their options open, worship, serve ... anything that will help them get what they want.

This is a challenge for us. I've been guilty of getting frustrated at God for very petty reasons. A week or so ago I was driving to Scripture class, and I was running late, it was my fault I was running late, but I kept praying to God for help, just give me lots of green lights, but all I got was red lights, and then I started to get really angry at God. Can't you do it, God? Why won't you help me, right now? I needed to take responsibility for my choices. And admit when I have made the wrong choice, to myself, to others, and to God. When was the last time you stopped and ask God: have I hurt you? Are you angry at me?

In Judges 10 when the people cry out, God responds, saying:

> Did I not save you from the Egyptians and from the Amorites, from the Ammonites and from the Philistines?

(And many more, there is a long list!) Yahweh is good and has rescued his people time and time again, yet they always forget and go and serve other gods, so Yahweh says:

> Go and cry out to the gods whom you have chosen; let them save you in the time of the distress.

That's the last time we hear God speak for a while. I wonder if sometimes there is silence because God has had enough. God can't stand seeing all the evil that happens. It's like he wants to turn away. Maybe even for a time he does – he withdraws, almost.

> So they put away the foreign gods from among them and served Yahweh, and his soul was grieved/impatient/troubled over the misery of Israel.

There's a mixture of feelings going on for God here. Some have said that God's quality of life is diminishing under both the weight of evil he can see and the misery of his people suffering. God's soul aches. What happens to the people of Israel matters to him; he loves them, and to see them suffering is for God to also suffer in some way. Will he act, will he help them?

So, we come to Judges 11. In Judges 11 the people take action. They approach a man named Jephthah and ask him for help. They see in him the possibility of a leader. Jephthah is known to be a mighty warrior. He also is the son of a prostitute. His half-brothers kick him out of the house when he is old enough because of his parentage. But when the Ammonites make threats, and war seems to be coming to the land of Gilead, they turn to him for help. We don't just come to God when we need something. We go to anyone we think who can help us. This is especially true for us in Australia. Less and less people are turning to God. Instead, we look to the celebrities, gurus, ourselves, for help. The leaders of Gilead go to Jephthah, knowing he is probably hurt and angry with them, but they're desperate. They want protection from their enemies. Jephthah echoes God's words here:

> Why have you come to me now when you are in distress?

The elders side-step the question and instead make a deal with him; not only can he be their leader in this fight, but head of the clan. This appeals to Jephthah. Yes, to be master of it all – that would be nice. So he agrees, invoking Yahweh's name:

> If you bring me home again to fight against the Ammonites, and Yahweh gives them over to me, I will be your head.

Jephthah acknowledges here that he needs God's help if they are to win against their enemies. He's not certain that God will help. There's still silence. You know, sometimes there is silence because God wants us to make decisions. Right from the beginning, God shares his power. We are called to represent him in the world. God shows us the way to live that will bring life but also gives us freedom. So, we make decisions: some that are good, some not so good. We are called to make decisions knowing who God is, to make decisions that would please him even when we might not feel God.

The elders of Gilead agree to this bargain while also acknowledge Yahweh.

> Yahweh will be witness between us, if we do not do as you say.

Even though God does not speak, they are aware that God is present, a witness to these decisions that are being made. What would happen if Australians were more aware that God is with us even when we might not feel it – would it change the way we make our decisions?

Jephthah gets on with the job. He first tries to negotiate peace with the Ammonites. The Ammonites and the Israelites are both claiming to have a right to the land. So Jephthah puts forward the Israelite case for the land. In that history he again brings God into it:

> And Yahweh, the God of Israel, gave Sihon and all his people into the hand of Israel,
> and they defeated them. So, Israel took possession of all the land of the Amorites.

Jephthah remembers how God saved and brought the people of Israel to this land. He grew up on stories of Israel's journeys through the wilderness, how when those in power refused to let Israel walk through their land, they were defeated, and God gave the people more land. Land that the Ammonites never seemed to possess. When Jephthah looks back over the history of his people, he is reminded – and reminds the Ammonites – that God has actively been at work to look after Israel and help them find a home. And God acted justly through the whole process. This is worth doing. In times of silence, look back and see how God has worked. At the end of the speech, he says through his messengers:

> I therefore have not sinned against you, and you do me wrong by making war
> on me. Yahweh, the Judge, decide this day between the people of Israel and the
> people of Ammon.

The Israelites had discovered that God is not a detached being that just created the world and then let it run itself, nor is God an autocrat. There are limits. God cannot break a promise. God cannot do something against his character. God is just. And God is compassionate. Now Yahweh still has not spoken. And yet as Jephthah remembers the stories of his ancestors, he is confident that God will act and do what is just. We too can often find confidence by reading the Bible. We hear these stories to remind ourselves of the character and person of God. Immediately after the speech, we are told that God does indeed act:

> Then the Spirit of Yahweh was upon Jephthah.

When the Spirit comes in the book of Judges, it is powerful. The Spirit does not speak, but the Spirit is active, raising up people to be deliverers, rescuing the Israelites from oppressive foreign regimes and bringing relief. God has heard Jephthah's prayers and commitment. God has heard the cries of the people asking for deliverance and answers by giving Jephthah what he needs. God works with Jephthah. When we cry out to God, don't just listen, but look around and see what happens. But all Jephthah can hear is silence. He is not sure if God will give them victory; he needs more reassurance, so he goes one step further, he makes another decision, a vow:

> If you will give the Ammonites into my hand, then whatever comes from the doors of my house to meet me when I return in peace from the Ammonites shall be Yahweh's, and I will offer it up for a burnt offering.

Still silent. God does not comment on the vow (or deal, is probably a better word). Jephthah goes to war and Yahweh is present, giving Israel victory over the Ammonites. Praise God! Jephthah returns home to celebrate:

> And behold, his daughter came out to meet him with tambourines and with dances. She was his only child.

The first person to walk out of the house is his daughter. Jephthah tears his clothes as he remembers the vow he made to Yahweh. This is something that should never have happened. God never asked for this. In fact, he hates child sacrifice. We know because God has already spoken about this in the Torah. That is something the pagan nations surrounding Israel do. Jephthah should never have made such a vow where this could be a possible outcome. And yet God is silent. Silent when Jephthah first made the vow and silent here as the girl agrees:

> My father, you have opened your mouth to Yahweh; do to me according to what has gone out of your mouth now that Yahweh has avenged you on your enemies.

We speak, we pray, we talk to others, we invoke God's name, we make promises. I want to get angry at God for not stepping in and stopping this death. I want to see God's anger kindled at Jephthah. But maybe I need to get angry at Jephthah a little more for making such a poor decision, for his insecurity.

Like most relationships, our relationship with God is not simple. It's complicated. We make decisions all the time that are evil in God's eyes. And maybe all we hear is silence because there is so much that distresses God, that makes God want to leave, but time and time again God exercises restraint. God allows terrible things to happen, God respects people's freedom and yet also keeps moving towards mercy. Grace. The story ends with Jephthah's daughter and her friends lamenting. It ends with tears. And maybe this is where we can best find God, lamenting once more at sin, his soul grieved, this time weeping with the women.

The God of the Bible is a personal God, who feels, who is good, who loves, and yet he struggles because we break our promises, we turn away, we only want protection not a relationship, and we don't understand God. There is so much that we don't understand about this being who can intervene in such powerful ways but doesn't always do so. Who seems to value our freedom, who keeps accommodating us, coming down to our level and letting us wrestle between trust and doubt.

The story in Judges 11 shows a moment in history when God is almost at the point of not wanting to show grace. And no wonder why; Jephthah sacrifices his daughter, thinking God will be pleased. This is a man who both trusts God and gets God so horribly wrong. We might not like this story, but there something very real about it, right? We can be people struggling to both know God and get God horribly wrong, too. We want to hear more from God, but we don't even practice what he has already called us too. Yet God shows us grace.

And step by step God is working towards a new world, a world with no more tears and suffering, when Christ is established as king. When Jesus comes, he will raise girls like Jephthah's daughter from the dead. God calls us into a relationship, to trust him in the middle of a complex world. Sometimes we will hear God clearly, and sometimes all we will hear is silence. But even in the seasons of silence, don't give up. Keep making good decisions, confess if there is a need to confess, remember the ways God has worked, and look for where God is now. Because there is a God who cares deeply for Australia. Keep choosing to follow Jesus once more today, and keep wrestling with this God.

5
PREACHING WISDOM TO AUSTRALIANS
Marc Rader

Introduction

Is there any section of Scripture more apt for preaching in the Australian context than wisdom literature? To a society addicted to busyness and in mad pursuit of 'balance', the Teacher's message that 'there is a time for everything' (Eccl 3:1) rings with particular urgency.[1] Likewise, the Teacher's wise scepticism about the ultimate value of wealth and its pursuit could do with a hearing in a materialistic culture enjoying one of the highest standards of living in the world (though with little gratitude and even less generosity). Who more needs to hear the warning of the woman lost in the ecstasy of sexual enjoyment to 'not arouse or awaken love until it so desires' (Song 3:5)? Or in the face of ever-increasing suffering, what wisdom might the struggles of Job and his friends reveal about our own experiences?

The Hermeneutical Task

The wisdom literature of the Old Testament includes Job, Proverbs, Ecclesiastes, and less frequently, Song of Songs.[2] There are also wisdom psalms (e.g., Psalm 1) and scattered examples of the wise or proverbs in the narratives (e.g., 2 Samuel 14:2; 20;16–22; 1 Kings 20:11). Many of these are clustered in the stories of the monarchy, reminding us that the wisdom traditions that gave rise to the Old Testament wisdom texts most likely developed in relation to the establishment of this institution.

Characteristics of Proverbs

Though the wisdom demonstrated in Job, Ecclesiastes and Song of Songs are all worth exploring, the topics found in these texts are more easily preached than Proverbs.

They can be profitably explored in a preaching series. However, it is on the book of Proverbs that I'd like to focus. Not to be unduly reductionist, but the reason they are easier to preach is that they are thematically organised (e.g., suffering in Job, meaning in Ecclesiastes, sexuality and love in Song). Proverbs reflects the characteristics of wisdom literature to a greater degree than these others.

On top of that, if the preaching literature is to be believed, Proverbs is one of the least preached sections of Scripture. (Though to be fair, there would be a few candidates in the Old Testament. I'm looking at you, Obadiah.) The brevity of individual proverbs causes headaches for expository preachers as there simply isn't much text to exposit. Then there's the danger of moralising: reducing proverbs to nothing more than the power of positive thinking.[3] Long calls Proverbs 'nothing more than a deserted stretch of highway between Psalms and Ecclesiastes'.[4] McKenzie laments that 'most preachers, as well as most lectionaries, avoid biblical proverbs, preferring instead more familiar and accessible lessons from psalms and epistles or the Gospel narrative and parables'.[5] However, she goes on to point out the absurdity of this ignorance. 'While pastors are in their studies skipping right past proverbs on the way to somewhere else, their congregations are out in the world living by Proverbs.'[6] And she's absolutely right. The practicality of biblical proverbs parallels the practicality of contemporary proverbs, and they are everywhere – 'on billboards, T-shirts, coffee mugs, cartoons, magazine ads, bumper stickers, and posters'.[7] And that's not to mention memes and Instagram pics! For these reasons, I want to focus on preaching from Proverbs in this chapter.

There are some specific issues for preaching proverbs related to the genre. Proverbs are short, pithy statements of generalised truth. Usually (though not exclusively) two lines long, utilising the various features of Hebrew parallelism, the proverbs state what is universally true but in a generalised way. This means that there is an implied narrative in each proverb that can be exploited by the preacher. In other words, if the truth contained in a proverb is observed truth, what circumstances have been observed where the truth has been observed? Stories and anecdotes – biblical and otherwise – can be used to great effect. The generalised truth of proverbs and their very length mean that they do not state everything. They are rules of thumb, not manuals of operation. This means that there are times when the proverbs are not true. This is part of the genius of wisdom literature generally; the genre is designed to get us to think. This is true beyond Proverbs too. What else are we to do with Eliphaz's simplistic (and wrong) logic on why Job is suffering? We need to identify it as incorrect – if only because we have been told that Job is godly, but also because it is poor theology (and even poor observation of the world). What else do we do with the Teacher's refrain that 'everything is meaningless' or that the best we can do is 'eat, drink and be merry'. Surely, we don't believe that? This characteristic of wisdom literature is even more stark in

Proverbs. It invites us to play around with the proverbs and to consider when they are true and when they may not be true.

This, of course, points to the critical matter of timing in wisdom. It's not only knowing what to do or say that marks someone as a wise woman, but her ability to do or say the right thing at the right time. Saying the right thing at the wrong time can have as devastating a consequence as saying the wrong thing. And, of course, this reminds us that Proverbs, in a way that sets it apart from the rest of the wisdom literature, was meant to be used. From an application perspective, it is among the easiest parts of Scripture to apply because it is a genre of applied truth already.

Preaching Proverbs

While I am far from an expert on preaching from Proverbs, with only about a dozen sermons on individual proverbs,[8] I have been more deliberate in thinking about how to preach them to Australians than I have for many other genres. The challenges of preaching from a single verse (more on that in a moment) coupled with writing this chapter at the same time has proven a fruitful exercise. What follows are my observed and experienced nuggets of truth about preaching from Proverbs.

Thematic or verse-by-verse preaching

To begin with, it is necessary to ask whether we should preach Proverbs thematically or verse-by-verse. There are advocates for both sides, but I believe that verse-by-verse is the better option. It may be true that for a beginning preacher a single verse might be quite daunting, but proverbs are designed to be used as individual proverbs, not in sets of related wisdom. We use single proverbs in our day-to-day life and should, to be true to the genre, preach them that way too. A thematic approach strikes me as the soft option – one that provides some security by being able to find something to say from several proverbs, and also one that is more prone to offering up simplistic platitudes, since the sermon only skims over the various aspects of the theme rather than going deep into the wisdom of any particular proverb.

Having said that, there are some longer sections (e.g., the wife of noble character) that should be preached as a whole. Furthermore, in a series on Proverbs, one or two sermons that pick up significant themes, especially of some of the caricatures we encounter in the book (e.g., the fool or the sluggard) might be beneficial. These sorts of 'rules' for preaching Proverbs are meant to make us think before we break them.

Selection

As stated, proverbs are used individually, and therefore preaching on a single proverb is appropriate. However, if we are preaching a series on Proverbs, how do we select from the hundreds of proverbs which ones to preach on? I have used each of the following techniques.

Firstly, reverse-engineer them. What I mean is to select a contemporary news event and apply a proverb to it. This could be negative, where a proverb could have been useful but was not, or positive, where the wisdom of a proverb has been demonstrated in our world. This has the benefit of encouraging us to look for examples of the proverb's application in our day-to-day life.

A second selection technique I have used is to pick some of the well-known proverbs such as 'spare the rod, spoil the child', or 'iron sharpens iron'. What this does is remind our congregations that these are biblical proverbs. Our over-familiarity with the proverbs can sometimes breed contempt or, if not contempt, at least a disregard for them and their practicality.

Yet another technique is to select a particular theme (e.g., the power of words) and choose a single proverb to reflect on this theme. This allows us to make reference to other proverbs that speak about the same theme, but still focus on a single proverb.

The last technique is to select a proverb you find interesting. This should be done in moderation; our preaching is not just for us. However, nothing is quite so engaging as preaching on passages or texts that intrigue us. Our interest usually spills over into our preaching and brings people along with us.

Exegetical work

This is one of the most difficult aspects of preaching Proverbs, for the simple reason that there is so little material to work with. In general, two lines, reflecting some sort of parallelism and speaking of everyday situations and circumstances. There are, however, a few practices that are useful.

While I believe proverbs stand alone, paying attention to the context can provide a little bit of help. Searching for link words or themes that are at work in whole sections can provide some help. In a recent sermon on Proverbs 16:3 ('Commit your ways to the LORD ... ') the surrounding context (16:1–9) provided the insight that the focus in 16:3 was on our action in committing our ways to the Lord rather than the Lord's work of establishing them. This came from noting the emphasis in this section on God's sovereignty and our responsibility. The link between the proverbs wasn't as important as the light shed on the theme.

Familiarity with the characteristics of Hebrew parallelism or with the type of proverb (e.g., 'Better than' proverbs) can also provide a little bit of help for our consideration of the proverb. Some non-biblical frameworks can also prove useful, such as McKenzie's definition of proverbs 'for the harbour' and 'for the storm'.

> There is a kind of wisdom that helps us order our lives and factor out a degree of chaos, a wisdom meant to shelter us from trouble. We might call it wisdom for the 'lee places' of life ... Then there is wisdom for the storm. It consists of proverbs and life stories that acknowledge that tragedies strike the wise, injustices oppress the hardworking, and we can suffer from other people's stupidity (and vice versa!).[9]

I find it helpful to do a word study of key words in the proverb. I am no Hebrew scholar but have found the interlinear function on Bible Hub remarkably useful.[10] This process of identifying the meanings that lie behind a translation and finding the other places where similar words are used can open homiletical options. Preaching on Proverbs 16:3 and recognising that the word 'commit' has the sense of 'to roll' elsewhere was really helpful, homiletically speaking. Add to that Bruce Waltke's comment on this verse – 'The admonition *commit to* (*gol 'el*, lit. 'roll to/upon'; see Gen 29:3, 8, 10; Ps 22:8[9], 37:5) connotes a sense of finality; roll it unto the Lord and leave it there'[11] – led me down the path of using this metaphor in the sermon. While there may be a sense of finality to the admonition, too often, like Sisyphus, condemned to roll the same stone up the same hill every day, we find our lives sloped inward and as we roll our deeds to the Lord, we find that they roll back on us. Our plans are concave, and this proverb needs to be used every day rather than as a one-off. We are to continually commit our deeds to the Lord.

In another sermon on, 11:22, 'Like a gold ring in a pig's snout is a beautiful woman who shows no discretion', I was struck by the fact that the word for 'discretion' was also used to describe Abigail's actions in 1 Samuel 25:33. This led me to using that narrative of a beautiful woman who had discretion to illustrate the proverb (and to keep the focus on discretion, rather than on beauty!)

Commentaries

A word about commentaries on Proverbs. You will generally find that the exegetical information on any one single proverb to be a bit thin. Waltke's two-volume commentary (part of the NICOT series) is good, and he offers comment on each proverb. It is not unusual, however, to have next to nothing on a particular proverb. In general, I'll only need to spend ten minutes or so reading the three different commentaries I have on Proverbs. What I have found is that once the terminology is understood, the point is usually straightforward.

Consider the proverb I just cited, 11:22, and the following information gleaned from the commentaries. Murphy highlights the grotesque nature of the proverb and the sarcasm of a 'common ornament' (Gen 24:47; Isa 3:21) before noting that 'discretion' has a root reflecting 'taste' and giving the link with Abigail in 1 Samuel. 'Beauty without wisdom', he says, 'is the height of incongruity.'[12] Whybray notes that this 'rather crude' proverb would have been used to instruct young men on the choice of a wife –'Beauty is not a reliable guide'[13] – as is also reflected in Proverbs 11:16 and 31:10–31. He also notes that 'good sense' is literally 'taste'. And all in two brief paragraphs! Kidner suggests that the proverb is more forceful than we might think, and observes that we tend to place more emphasis on the external and therefore might be inclined to see the woman as 'a little disappointing'[14] rather than the monstrosity the Hebrew suggests. He also notes the parallel with Abigail.

The NIV Application Commentary is more useful due to its emphasis on preaching. In an attempt to connect the proverbs together, Koptak suggests that 11:22 may be addressing the wicked of 11:18 and pointing out that life cannot be measured only in terms of gold. 'Who would put a gold ring in a pig's snout? No one, yet we isolate beauty from discretion all the time, just as we want riches without wisdom. Neither is fitting.'[15] The proverb is directed to men, but, as he puts it, 'overheard by women'. He also observes that it is less of a putdown of beautiful women but of the men who might prefer them. While there are few useful exegetical nuggets here, the meaning of the proverb is no more obvious than it was when we first read it. This step should not be ignored, but the next is the most important for preaching Proverbs.

Play Around with the Proverb

This is the part that is longest and most important for the preacher who wishes to preach a proverb. McKenzie calls proverbs 'freeze-dried narratives', urging preachers to take them 'on the road' and consider the use of proverbs in everyday life.[16] We have to play with the proverbs, engage our sanctified imagination, open our eyes and really think about the proverbs. This is what they are meant to help us do.

There are a few questions that I ask myself, and of the proverb, as I am preparing to preach on one. There is a fair amount of overlap between them, but they can all be helpful to wrestle with the wisdom in the proverb.

When is it true? When is it not true? When would we use this proverb? If proverbs are short, pithy statements of generalised truth, we need to ask when the proverbs are proved true and identify the situation where it might not be true. Many commentators point out the general, though universally stated, truth of proverbs by contrasting Proverbs 26:4–5: 'Do not answer a fool according to his folly, or you yourself will be just like him. Answer a fool according to his folly, or he will be wise in his own eyes.' These seemingly contradictory statements demonstrate the value of these two questions. What are the conditions when you should *not* answer a fool according to his folly, and when might answering a fool be wise? Even proverbs that don't have a contrasting and contradictory parallel can be considered from this perspective. For the 'better than' proverbs, it can be useful to ask, for example: when is it *not* better to live on the corner of a roof than with a nagging wife? The idea is to seek to unpack the wisdom from its small container. Asking when I might use this proverb in my own life also engages my imagination.

Structures

I would not attempt to prescribe one particular structure over another when preaching from Proverbs. However, I have found that it can be valuable to integrate our thinking about the proverb in the sermon-as-preached. In other words, preach the dead-ends, insights, and wisdom you encounter as you prepared. If your first thought about a proverb proved unfruitful or led to a second, more fruitful observation, preach that. Model to your congregation how you engaged with the proverb; how it made you think and how you wrestled to really grasp the wisdom. As may appear obvious, this lends itself to inductive structures that are more conversational and invitational.

The Contextualisation Task

The wisdom literature is a section of Scripture that is white for harvest in the Australian context. For a secular, pragmatic society, the invitation to consider the ways that lead to success and, therefore, to consider God's ways may provide a suitable pathway to considering and discovering the claims of Christ, the true Wisdom of God.

In the spirit of full disclosure, I should state that I am a Canadian who has spent the last two decades ministering in Australia. I have spent more of my ministry life in Australia than in Canada, however, and have grown fascinated by the cultural distinctives of Australia.

Firstly, wisdom is intensely practical. The Hebrew term for wisdom (*hokmah*) means skill in life.[17] It is first used in the Old Testament to describe the craftsmen who were to be tasked with the construction of the tabernacle (Exod 28:3; 31:3, 6). Fee and Stuart define wisdom as 'the ability to make godly choices in life',[18] while Longman says that wisdom is 'a skill of living'.[19] Wisdom literature is in some regards, then, the ancient equivalent of success literature. Long argues that the rhetorical function of a proverb, for example, is 'to provide a general ethical guidance which the reader can then apply to various real-life circumstances'.[20] This practicality makes it ideal for Australian culture, which is pragmatic in its approach to life.

As we explored in the 'Describing Australians' chapter, Australians value performance-based achievement in pursuit of personal goals as a reflection of a deeper desire to control their environment. There is a pragmatism at work in this pursuit that tends to be willing to experiment with different ways to achieve those goals. This is in contrast with 'seniority-based' rewards that, due to their intrinsic nature, do not inspire innovation. Proverbial wisdom strongly links rewards with one's performance; wise actions lead to success (often in material terms). Proverbial wisdom also believes that sense can be made of the world; that mastery is achievable. Of course, there are differences between an Australian vision of success and a biblical one, but there is more than enough common ground to gain the attention of an Australian congregation.

A similar point of connection is between the proverbial wisdom as keys to success and the rule-based approach to life that Australians tend to have. I share Ian Hussey's perplexity at this one; the laid-back persona stands side-by-side with a dependence upon and desire for rules. This paradox is explored helpfully in Geoff Aigner and Liz Skelton's book on leadership in Australia, under the tagline, 'The tension between our desire and dependency for authority while simultaneously railing against it.'[21] Regardless of the reasons for it, the rule-based approach to life provides the preacher with an appeal to Australians. The proverbial wisdom represents universal laws and rules that are, in the words of Nardon and Steers, designed to be 'applied uniformly to everyone'.[22]

This application to everyone touches on the egalitarianism that is so critical to Australian society (and lies behind the so-called 'tall poppy syndrome'). The proverbial wisdom, as taught in the home by mothers and fathers, is for everyone. Even the proverbs that are directed, in context, to kings or those in their court can be applied to everyone.

Secondly, and related to its intense practicality, the wisdom literature is more 'secular' in character. We mustn't read too much into this designation, as wisdom was based on the sacred premise that wisdom's source is the fear of the Lord. However, the biblical wisdom literature makes few references to the sorts of things we would anticipate finding in the Bible. There are few or no references to redemptive history, the patriarchs, the covenant, the law or cultic practices. Its focus is success in life, and it therefore deals with everyday life. The 'secular' nature of wisdom literature is also evident in the inclusion of wisdom from other nations (Job isn't a Hebrew, and Proverbs includes the sayings King Lemuel's mother taught him, not to mention the clear parallels with the Egyptian Wisdom of Amenemope). The general nature of wisdom literature is equally helpful for the preacher who is looking for common ground with his or her congregation and with the wider Australian society that is increasingly secular.

While the biblical context was certainly more religious that contemporary Australian society, the secular nature of proverbial wisdom can be described, in the sermon, as 'differently' religious. Yes, the state and the population of ancient Jerusalem was religious in ways that ours is not, but the extrabiblical parallels demonstrate that the wisdom literature was, in a sense, one voice among many. This is not pluralism as we know it, but it diffuses the overt religiosity of the wisdom literature. This is, of course, a false diffusion, since the wisdom literature of the ancient Near East would have been birthed in a religious context too, but to contemporary modern ears the fact that there are extrabiblical witnesses to wisdom makes it more palatable for a society that is less and less religious.

Thirdly, proverbial wisdom is easily acclimated to the anti-institutional stance of Australians. Once again, in context the proverbs are more institutional and conservative than we might immediately think; however, they are not found in the mouths of priests or prophets, and that is not insignificant for an Australian context. Many would be more willing to listen to the Queen of England than to the Archbishop of Canterbury, and this same dynamic is at work in proverbs.

Fourthly, the wisdom literature is observational rather than revelatory. There are no angels, no prophets and no visions (apart from the theophany in Job 38). There is no need to ask people to ascribe to or believe in these things at all when preaching from wisdom. What we have in the wisdom literature is that which has been observed. Wright helpfully points out that the reliance of observation rather than revelation leads to a different tone from law.[23] Law, he points out, commands, while wisdom warns. This tone 'enables us to [discuss all kinds of social, political, and moral issues] without appearing to "lay down the law" or impose legalistic demands on people'.[24] Wisdom literature invites us to think about our common experiences. This more indirect and invitational approach provides a helpful tone for our preaching of wisdom literature. The invitation to think about the application of proverbs, or the permission to ask the tough questions in Job or Ecclesiastes,[25] are very helpful for preachers. This participatory tone is particularly helpful for an Australian context that is resistant to authority.

Fifthly, the underlying doctrine of wisdom is creation. There are certain rhythms and patterns that the Lord built into the created order, and these go beyond gravity, tides and astronomical movements. To say that the Lord created the whole world is to affirm that the Lord created the material universe and the moral universe. This connection is seen most clearly in Job. Many commentators point out that Job's opening speech (3:1–26) utilises language of un-creation. The implication seems to be that his suffering (as a righteous man), which called into question the moral universe, called into question the material one. Furthermore, the Lord's *tour de force* through the material universe in chapters 38–41 demonstrates to Job that if he cannot comprehend the material universe, he can hardly be expected to comprehend the moral. The foundation of wisdom literature is that by observing the material world, we learn how to live successfully in it: when to plant, when to harvest; and by observing the moral world, we learn how to live successfully in it: be honest, guard our tongues, choose our friends wisely. Why, for instance, is honesty the best policy (to cite a modern proverb) except that God made it that way? In this sense, there is a connection between the observed order of God's world and the revealed law of God; they are not distinct because they are both reflections of the one Lord's will. Access to them, however, is different. The wisdom literature can be grasped by any who are willing to see. There is, indeed, some truth to the saying, 'All wisdom is God's wisdom.' The doctrine of creation also provides a point of contact with all people, created by God. And, if God is morally consistent, then his standards should apply to all.[26] This resonates with the egalitarian Australian.

Finally, at a pragmatic level, for a time-poor society like Australia, proverbs can be appropriated more easily than some longer texts. With little or no narrative context to digest, the proverbs can be preached 'quickly'. In our recent series on Proverbs, we subtitled the series 'Pocket tips for better living from Proverbs' to emphasise the simplicity of the genre.

These characteristics make wisdom literature an important set of texts to preach to Australians. Wanting to be successful at life is a common desire of all people, and there is no end of advice to be had on how to achieve it.

Sample Sermon: Proverbs 14:12, 16:25

Last year, around this time, my family and I were planning to go overseas. We were going to spend some time in the United States to see my family and hopefully get up to Canada as well. And we were able to do both of those things. Around this time, I was spending a fair amount of time on the internet trying to figure out what we could see and do on the road trip from Los Angeles to Las Vegas on Route 66. We'd hired a car, we'd got our airplane tickets, we were all set to go; now, I wanted to know what we could *do*. And I was doing what most of us would do: we asked friends and family, 'Have you been to the place that I'm going? What would you recommend that I do, and what would you suggest that I don't do?' And we were trying to work out what we should and shouldn't do so that we got the most out of our trip. If you're going to take that much time and, ahem, spend that much money, you want it to be good, don't you? You don't want a holiday that's littered with horrible experiences so that when you get home people go, 'Oh, I could have told you, you shouldn't have done that.' You want to make the most of it.

And that's true, not only in terms of holidays and trips, but it's also just true in life, isn't it? If we're going to succeed in the journey of life, if we're going to have a good outcome, if we're going to have good experiences, we want, to the best of our ability, to get the best sort of advice. And the book of Proverbs is full of advice for success in the journey of life. In lots of ways, the book of Proverbs is much like the success literature that you might find in the bookstore at the airport. These titles might not still be there, but I'm thinking of titles like Dale Carnegie's *How to Win Friends and Influence People*, a whole bunch of principles that lead to success; or Stephen Covey's book *The 7 Habits of Highly Effective People*; or Malcolm Gladwell's *The Tipping Point*; or Jim Collins' *Good to Great* – all observations of the world and research of the world. The authors, they've kind of boiled it down and then written it up in a book so that we can be more successful, more effective, can win friends and influence people and all of those sorts of things.

But unlike books, which tend to be, shall we say, a little bit easily digested, proverbs are actually not that simple. They are in lots of ways a compacted truth, a dehydrated truth; all of the excess wording has been boiled away until you just have this wonderful two-lined piece of wisdom; which means, though, that if we're going to get as much as we can out of them, we kind of have to soak them a little bit. This is more like a degustation menu than it is one big meal; it's seven little meals all the way through. This is more test cricket than Twenty20.

We need to take some time to explore what these proverbs actually have to say and almost play around with them a little bit. And I've chosen, for this series, three proverbs that I would really like to hear on our lips as a community of faith. And the one that we're going to look at this morning is actually found in two places – once in chapter 14:12, but the second time in chapter 16. It's identical in both places, and it reads this way: 'There is a way that appears to be right, but in the end it leads to death.' *There is a way that appears to be right, but in the end it leads to death.* Now, at first glance, it seems that all this proverb is saying is: there are lots of ways out there, some look pretty good but end badly, so choose wisely. Right? We might talk about it in terms of our own modern proverbs as: 'Don't judge a book by its cover', or, 'All that glitters is not gold', or even, 'Beauty is only skin deep'. Right? This whole idea that you don't want to misjudge something just by its appearance. There's a way that appears to be right, but in the end it leads to death, so be careful about your choice.

But is this proverb only a warning against judging something by its appearance? I mean, if you've ever judged a book by its cover – you bought a book and you thought, this cover is brilliant, the contents must be equally good, and you've started to read it – the worse that will happen is you will be disappointed. You will kind of go oh, you know what? This book is still going to look great on my shelf, but I'm never going to open it again. I'm disappointed that I spent $12, $15, $40, whatever, on this book that looks great but doesn't have the content to back it up. I guess on the flip side you might also be pleasantly surprised, mightn't you? If you buy a book thinking it's not going to be very good, because obviously the publisher decided that this deserved no graphic work at all and it's just a horrible looking book, but its contents are brilliant, you might be pleasantly surprised. But this proverb seems to have a little more severe a consequence, doesn't it? 'There is a way that appears to be right, but in the end it leads to death.' This is more than disappointment.

In the book of Proverbs, of course, death is – and this is going to sound completely obvious – the opposite of life. But life is kind of a symbol for blessing and contentment and fulfilment and honour and all the good things of life, and death becomes the symbol for all of the opposites: for failure and shame and dishonour and impoverishment and all of the things that you want to avoid by reading the book of Proverbs so that you might make wise choices. This is a little bit more significant – 'There is a way that appears right, but in the end it leads to death.'

So, it got me thinking, what are the characteristics of a way that appears right? In other words, why might I look at a decision or an opportunity or a choice in front of me and say, 'This is right'? And I thought of four different things that might contribute to a sense of something feeling right. First one was that it was popular – if everyone's doing it, it probably doesn't lead to death because you'd figure if it led to death, it wouldn't be very popular. Sounds pretty logical, wouldn't you say? So if all of my friends are making the same sorts of decisions that I'm being led to make, if all of their friends are doing the same sorts of things, there's a sense in which because something is popular, because something is attractive to many people, it would appear right to us as well.

Along the same lines, it's sometimes true that there's a really nice kind of congruence between an opportunity and my own dreams and aspirations. Now I have to ask where my dreams and aspirations have come from and where they've been shaped. They're often shaped by our culture in fairly unhelpful ways. But there are times when I might look at an opportunity or look at a situation or a choice before me and think, you know what, to choose this way or that way really seems to fit with my dreams, my hopes for myself and for my future.

I think, thirdly, there might be a coinciding of my gifts and skills and passions and abilities and what-not. I might look at an opportunity and say to myself, you know what, I think I've got the skills to do that; I think I've got the passion to do that; I've got the time to do that; this is wonderful.

And then finally, sometimes, there are a number of little coincidences that lead up to a decision and we feel that maybe, just maybe, there's a higher power at work. Sound normal?

These are the sorts of ways that we often make decisions, and it's important to realise that these are fairly common ways. If you came to me and said, listen, Marc, I've got this situation in front of me, I've got an opportunity that I can take up, and it's popular with people around me, and it's seems to match my own dreams, and aspirations and I've got the skills and the passions and the time to do it, and there are a number of little things that have happened along the way that suggest that God might be in this – what do you think? I'd probably say it sounds like the right thing to do; it appears right.

So, is this proverb then only saying that there's no guarantee of success? You know: There's a way that appears right, choose as wisely as you can, but some of them end badly. Ha! Who knows? It's all kind of down to luck or fate. Is that what the proverb is saying? Is it just making an observation about life instead of giving us wisdom?

I don't think it is; there's something more going on here as well. Because if that were the case, that's not wisdom; we might as well all buy Magic 8 Balls and make our decisions that way. Should I do this? Yes, I should. Okay, done. And this is where we need to remember that when we're talking about Scripture – and any passage of Scripture, whether it be relatively easy to understand or more complex – is that Scripture informs itself. So the rest of Scripture, for instance, leaves no room for luck or fate. Without going into all the ins and outs of God's sovereignty, the Bible is very clear that God is the primary mover behind all the activity and action in the world. How that gets worked out is much more complicated, but the Bible is very clear that there's no concept of fate or of luck; that's not how the world works. The proverbs, instead, are built on the idea that God has actually invested into the world and built into the world, has created in the world, the patterns for our moral behaviour.

But the other thing to note, and this is really significant in the book of Proverbs, is that the book of Proverbs is very clear about the sorts of ways that lead to death. There are actually seven different ways that the book of Proverbs describes as leading to death.

The first of them, which is found primarily in the first nine chapters, the prologue of the book, is sexual immorality. Most of the time it's framed up as a father's words to his son to be aware of, and to beware, the adulterous or unfaithful woman; I think that we can expand that out to sexual immorality across the board. And what the father makes clear to his son is that that way is not the way of life, it is the way of death. If you go into her house, he says, you are entering into the grave. Ill-gotten gain leads to death. Gain and wealth that is got by dishonesty, that is got by cruelty or oppression – that will lead to death. Wickedness, just in general, will lead to death. Lack of discipline leads to death, whether it's just the pure lack of discipline in your life or the lack of discipline that is related to laziness. A lack of prudence will lead to death. An untamed tongue leads to death. The power of words is remarkable, and the book of Proverbs is full of sayings about the importance of what we say – an untamed tongue that says whatever it wants whenever it wants will lead to death. And folly itself will lead to death. In chapter 8, Wisdom, who is personified, says 'those who hate me love death'; folly leads to death.

So, there are seven ways that lead to death; the book of Proverbs is very clear on this, which means that when we come back to this proverb you have to ask, how in the world could you miss that? How could a way that leads to death that is marked by sexual immorality, wickedness, folly, lack of discipline, lack of prudence, an untamed tongue, all of those things, how could a way that's marked by those things ever appear to be right? You would have to be an absolute and utter fool to mistake a way that leads to death with a way that appears right. And that, actually, might be the clue we need; because in Proverbs 12:15, the proverb that we're looking at is slightly modified. It says this: 'The way of fools seems right to them, but the wise listen to advice.' Commentators, when they look at 16:25 and 14:12, the proverb that we're looking at this morning, suggest that what this proverb is about is about a decision made in isolation. There's a way that appears right to me, and if I am left to my own devices and the deceitfulness of my own heart, I can convince myself that a way that will lead to death is actually okay. This is what the proverb seems to be pointing at. And therefore, listening is critical. And this is true all the way through the book of Proverbs; you find that listening is critical to obtaining wisdom. It's found all the way through the book of Proverbs.

In Chapter 8, which I mentioned a little bit earlier, there are a number of places where this principle is spoken about. In verse 6, this is wisdom speaking, 'Listen, [she says] for I have trustworthy things to say; I open my lips to speak what is right. My mouth speaks what is true, for my lips detest wickedness.' So, listen to me. If you follow that down to verse 32, it says,

> Now then, my children, listen to me; blessed are those who keep my ways. Listen to my instruction and be wise; do not disregard it. Blessed are those who listen to me, watching daily at my doors, waiting at my doorway. For those who find me find life and receive favour from the LORD.

We are to listen if we are to succeed; we're to listen to others. But, of course, listening to others is not the end of it, is it? Because, as Proverbs 17:4 says, 'A wicked person listens to deceitful lips; [and] a liar pays attention to a destructive tongue.' There's listening, and then there's listening to wise Godly people, and nowhere is the devastating consequences of the wrong sort of advice found in Scripture than in 1 Kings 12.

1 Kings 12 narrates for us the story of the beginning of Rehoboam's reign. Rehoboam was the son of King Solomon; he was the fourth king of Israel. You might have heard of Solomon before – a lot of the proverbs have come from him. He had the wisdom of God, a wisdom that he had asked for and that God had granted to him. And Rehoboam, when he becomes king, gathers the people before him and the people ask him if he would become a little bit more lenient than Solomon, his father, was. For all of his wisdom, Solomon had been very oppressive in both his taxation and forced labour, and the people come and ask Rehoboam, would you kind of lighten the load? And Rehoboam, in wisdom, says, give me three days. Come back to me in three days and I'll give you my answer then. And in 1 Kings 12:6, we're told what he then does: 'Then King Rehoboam consulted the elders who had served his father Solomon during his lifetime. "How would you advise me to answer these people?" he asked.'

Now, just notice, he asked the men who had advised Solomon; even the wisest man who has ever lived had people to advise him; just keep that in mind. And these older men say to him this,

> 'If today you will be a servant to these people and serve them and give them a favourable answer, they will always be your servants.' But Rehoboam rejected the advice the elders gave him and consulted the young men who had grown up with him and were serving him. He asked them, 'What is your advice? How should we answer these people who say to me, 'Lighten the yoke your father put on us'?' The

young men who had grown up with him replied, 'These people have said to you. 'Your father put a heavy yoke on us, but make our yoke lighter.' Now tell them, 'My little finger is thicker than my father's waist. My father laid on you a heavy yoke; I will make it even heavier. My father scourged you with whips; I will scourge you with scorpions.

You can see the wisdom in both cases, can't you? The elders say, 'Listen, you need to give them a favourable answer, and if you will serve them, in this instance, they will serve you forever.' But you can also make some sense of the young men, can't you? 'Your father was a great man; you don't want your people thinking that you're weak. Give them a show of strength.' You think my dad was bad, wait 'til you get a load of me. I too am a strong king that you can put your trust in.

You can see the wisdom, can't you? And we can also see the great folly, can't we? Instead of listening to the elders who had served his father during the most prosperous time in Israel's history, he listens to the young men who had grown up with him. The result? The kingdom was torn apart by civil war and Rehoboam ended up with a rump state, two tribes instead of twelve, with devastating consequences on the kingdom, both north and south. He listened to advice; he just listened to the wrong advice. 'There is a way that appears to be right, but in the end it leads to death.'

And this proverb actually tells us something really important about the way God made the world, and that is, that God has made the world in such a way that if we are going to be successful, we must ask for counsel and advice. We must. Which points to this very important underlying principle, and that is that humanity was never meant to be, and will never be, self-sufficient; that's the dream, isn't it? That we would be selfsufficient; that I would be able to attain enough wisdom that I would be able to make a decision on my own. Theologically, biblically, that is rubbish. The only one who has ever been and who ever will be self-sufficient is God.

Do you remember in the garden, before the fall? The man, he was there in the garden – the garden that God had created, where he had been placed – and God looked at the man before the fall, before the effects of sin, and God's decision, his overall assessment, was, 'It's not good for the man to be alone.' He brings a companion alongside, the woman, and that is good. There is mutuality from the beginning. Even Adam in his created perfection was not self-sufficient. And while I don't know exactly what heaven's going to look like, we're not going to be selfsufficient in heaven either. We'll be made perfect, but we will not know everything. I will not be able to do everything, and neither will you, because we were never created to do everything. We will never ever be self-sufficient. And what this tells us about God's world is that we are not only better together – we were made to be together. That wisdom is never found on your own; it is always found in teams and groups and families and networks and communities. Success in the journey of life is always, always found in others. We will never be self-sufficient people, able to make decisions flawlessly.

When should we use this proverb? You should use Proverb 16:25, it should roll off your tongue every time you are absolutely certain that you know what needs to be done. Whenever you say to yourself, I know exactly what has to happen, you need to remember this parable. You need to remember that there's a way that appears to be right, but in the end it leads to death. You need to remember that we are not made as self-sufficient individuals. And can you see why this proverb is so hard for us to engage with in our individualistic age, the age that places so much emphasis on the self as the seat of wisdom and strength and of authority? We need to grapple with that and allow this proverb to sink deeply into our hearts. Because if we are going to avoid the deceitfulness of our own hearts, which can convince us that a way that leads to death is actually right, then we must set aside the myth of self-sufficiency and choose to press into wise counsel.

This is wisdom; this is how God made the world – that we should seek and obtain good advice from wise people, Godly people, in order that we might make good decisions that lead ultimately to life. There is a way that appears to be right, but in the end it leads to death. Let us live wisely.

6

PREACHING PSALMS TO AUSTRALIANS

David J. Cohen and Erin Martine Sessions

Introduction

In 1625, metaphysical poet – and Dean of St. Paul's Cathedral in London – John Donne commenced his sermon on Psalm 67:3 by stating that 'the Psalms are the manna of the church. As manna tasted to every man like that that he liked best, so do the Psalm's minister instruction and satisfaction to every man in every emergency and occasion.'[1] What was true millennia ago and true in 1625 is true today – the psalms minister to us all. But how do they minister specifically to Australians? 'The Psalms have been preached, are preached, and will continue to be preached, and when we preach them, we step into that tradition … humbly yet proudly joining that great chorus of witnesses in expounding the Psalter.'[2] How should we preach the psalms with the peculiarities of Australian culture in mind? This is, of course, not to say that we are uninterested in the psalms in their original context – far from it. These ancient Israelite views of God and humankind and faith and life, running the gamut of human emotion, will help us to see how the psalms can speak to us in our time and place. So, with these thoughts in mind, we now turn to examine some general features of the Psalter that need to be considered when one preaches the psalms.

The Hermeneutical Task

The Psalter is expansive, reflecting the prayers of individuals and communities. These prayers, composed and collated over a long period of time, originally express the concerns of Israelite people. In ecstasy they express praise to the God of all creation, while in humility they offer thanksgiving for deliverance. With provocative questions and complaints, they voice the despair of those who lament, and with assertiveness, the anger and frustration of the oppressed. The psalms take us from the 'mountaintop' to the 'valley', from the still water of a pond and its fertile surrounds to the raging seas of Leviathan and the parched deserts of an ancient land.

The images encountered within the Psalter and the emotions these evoke penetrate the heart of those who read and pray them like perhaps no other part of Scripture does. These psalms spoke to those who returned from exile and those who joined with them in worship, collectively becoming the prayer book of the Second Temple.[3] Beyond this period, Christians have followed their Jewish cousins' lead in continuing to use the Psalter as a prayer book for personal devotion. The church has employing the Psalms, albeit more selectively, as a font from which expressions of corporate worship can flow. Continued engagement with the Psalter throughout church history has aroused ebullient praise of the prayers it contains.

Athanasius hears the words of the Psalter as echoes of a person engaging with them, saying, '… the one who hears is deeply moved, as though he himself were speaking, and is affected by the words of the songs'.[4] He grasped the profound personal effect that the Psalter can have on those who pray these prayers. Perhaps inspired by Athanasius, John Calvin called the Psalter '"An Anatomy of all the Parts of the Soul"; for there is not an emotion of which anyone can be conscious that is not here represented as in a mirror'.[5] With her typical dynamism, Dorothy Day laconically declares, 'My strength returns to me with my cup of coffee and the reading of the psalms.'[6] While each of these observations is focused on the individual's response to engaging with psalms, they also, no doubt, reflect thoughts and emotions that pervade the communities of faith who collectively use psalms in sharing responses to, and reflections on, their lived experiences.

Recognising the depth and breadth within the Psalter presents particular challenges to the preacher. While focusing on a specific psalm or genre of psalms, it is also important to convey to listeners the richness of the tapestry found in this collection as a whole. In what follows, we will present some of the more significant features that ought to be considered when preaching psalms. These ought to influence both the way an individual psalm is understood, interpreted and reflected on by preachers and the way this is then conveyed to their audience. Given the depth and breadth of the Psalter, it may even be expedient to begin preaching psalms with an introductory sermon outlining the following features as a way of orienting the audience. By considering them, we begin to draw a kind of map to help us navigate our journey through preaching the Psalter, enabling us to lead those who accompany us as we preach the psalms.

So, what are the significant factors informing a preacher of the Psalms? We suggest five and offer some observations about why each is important and how they might affect the preacher's understanding of discrete psalms. They are:
- Shape of the Psalter
- Genre in the Psalter

- Poetry of the Psalter
- Lived experience in the Psalter
- Trajectory of the Psalter

Shape of the Psalter

In 1993 Clinton McCann edited an important collection of essays entitled *Shape and Shaping of the Psalter*, in which scholars explored how the Psalter in its present form came to fruition.[7] The title of the book implicitly suggests that the Psalter evolved into its current form over a long period of time. These studies remind the preacher that of the five books that make up the Psalter, books one to three (Psalms 3–89) was most likely the original corpus, with books four to five (Psalms 90–150) subsequently added. The growth of the Psalter in this way reminds us that when we preach a specific psalm we are always, and only, engaging with just a part of a collection.[8] Appreciating the growth of the Psalter also reminds us that these collections emerged from different people at different periods during history. So, while each psalm we encounter had a 'local' origin with a particular individual or community, it became more widely utilised. As a consequence, these 'local' writings acquired a more 'universal' relevance and application.[9]

While the details of how the Psalter was shaped are important, our focus here is on the relevance of this factor to preaching psalms. Appreciating the process by which the Psalter was formed reminds us that psalms are not esoteric, philosophical musings about the meaning of life, although they may approach this at times. Rather, they are responses to, and reflections on, the lived experiences of individuals and communities. The collection of these prayers reminds us that, whatever importance they held in their initial iterations for individuals and communities, their significance transcended this to become not only the hymnbook of the Second Temple but also, potentially, psalms for any person and any community.

Genre Within the Psalter

The second feature is that of genre. In the early twentieth century, Hermann Gunkel recognised distinct genres within the Psalter.[10] He identified the following five:
- Hymns
- Individual lament psalms
- Communal lament psalms
- Thanksgiving psalms
- Royal psalms

There are also several subgenres, such as wisdom psalms, Torah psalms, creation psalms, imprecatory psalms and others.[11]

Recognising this raises questions about each genre's unique features. As an example of this, it is interesting to note that just over a third of the psalms are either individual or communal laments.[12] The prominence of lament may cause the preacher (and audience) to wonder what the particular features of this genre might be as compared with others. If the genre of lament psalms is compared with the genre of thanksgiving psalms, it quickly becomes apparent that thanksgiving psalms tend to be primarily expressions of an individual. This realisation might provoke questions about why there are few communal thanksgiving psalms. Could one response be that thanksgiving psalms portray a different view of the individual? Perhaps an individual can embody the community when she speaks in thanksgiving psalms. A third major genre is that of hymns, or psalms of praise. Claus Westermann called these psalms of declarative praise because they simply declare what God is like.[13] This genre raises questions about what kind of God delights in, and in fact desires, human praise. What is the efficacy of praise offered to God for those who express it? Does God benefit in some way from our praise?

Transcending genre, we also encounter particular psalms that appear to have a special function within the Psalter as a whole. Psalms 1 and 2 are an example of this. It has long been noted that these two psalms taken together form a kind of introduction to the Psalter, in that they set the scene for readers or hearers.[14] We will say a little more about how these psalms achieve this below.

Psalm 89 is another psalm that seems to have a particular function transcending itself. Located at the end of book three, which we have suggested marked the end of the original corpus of psalms, it affirms that God is God of both creation and covenant. The particular covenant referred to in this psalm is the Davidic covenant.[15] However, it then proceeds to lament the demise of the Davidic kingship, implicitly questioning what might emerge in its place. If one can imagine the psalm as the conclusion to an earlier version of the Psalter, it may cause us to wonder what readers of this Psalter may have thought as they heard and prayed Psalm 89. For modern readers, a consequence may be wondering how we read Psalm 89 in light of what now follows in books two and three. Do books two and three of the Psalter, Psalms 90–150, respond to the dilemma with which Psalm 89 concludes?

Poetry of the Psalter

It has long been recognised that psalms are written in poetic style.[16] Preaching psalms needs to take this into account. While Hebrew poetry uses poetic devices, which we can find in poetry from other cultures and in other languages,[17] it has its own unique features that give it a distinctive quality.

The most important of these is 'parallelism', a descriptor coined by Robert Lowth in the late eighteenth century.[18] Lowth noted that most psalms consist of two-line phrases in which the second line reflects the first in various ways. Sometimes the second line simply repeats the first using different vocabulary, sometimes the second line states the opposite to the first and sometimes the second line extends the first by embellishing it. For the preacher, an awareness of the different types of parallelism can bring light to a particular psalm's emphasis and how it is achieved.

Lived Experience within the Psalter

When encountering psalms, it is not difficult to resonate with many of the experiences recounted in them. Psalms are reflective of the human experience in various ways. When the psalmist laments, we can feel their pain; when they rejoice, we can sense their joy. The titles found at the start of many psalms attributing them to David, Asaph, Korah and others indicate that these prayers emerged from lived experiences.[19] While the examples offered here are male, it is important to acknowledge that women may well have contributed psalms.[20] There is an ongoing discussion about Psalms' authorship, yet the titles remind us that these prayers originated with real people and emerged as authentic, prayerful reflections on real lived experiences.

This awareness is important for the preacher, as it means that psalms can be preached confidently as authentic expressions of individual human experience, be it that of King David, Hannah or someone else. In preaching, it is helpful to remember that the audience will not need much prompting to connect with these songs of life. As a result, they may even employ some as a vehicle for expressing their own experiences. This kind of approach avoids the pitfall where psalms are preached and appreciated for their theology, aesthetics and even for their profundity while holding them at arm's length for fear of engaging with them too deeply. In other words, preaching the psalms as lived experience invites an audience to find resonance, validation and language that they may lack.

The Movement of the Psalter

A question we might ask is, 'What do I notice when I read from the beginning to the end of the Psalter?' Westermann offers an important observation: 'The first half of the Psalter is comprised predominantly of Psalms of lament, the second predominantly of Psalms of praise.'[21] This varied concentration may present an aspiration for people of faith, encouraging a movement from lament to praise, while at the same time not excluding either from being expressed. Another way of approaching this is to characterise it as a movement from disorientation (lament) when one feels distant from God to orientation (praise) when one feels close to God.[22] The second view reminds us that the Psalter is deeply relational in its focus, being a dynamic book of prayer – a lived, and living, document.

The trajectory found in the Psalter reminds us that the life of faith is a kind of journey. At any point on the journey, one can be in a season of praise, lament, thanksgiving or something other. However, the situation will inevitably change. It also underlines the appropriateness and inevitability of all these seasons in life, offering validation. This is particularly pertinent with regard to lament, the expression of which seems difficult for many twenty-first-century Western Christians, perhaps even more so for contemporary Australians. It suggests that no matter how much praise and thanksgiving there may be in life, lament will always play a significant part in peoples' lives. Acknowledgement of lament in prayer and worship is critical in the journey of faith. The Psalter affirms such an acknowledgement.

Introduction to the Psalter: Psalm 1 and 2

Having considered these five factors and how they inform preaching of the Psalter, it remains for us to ponder the introductory role of Psalms 1 and 2 and appreciate the lens these psalms provide for viewing the whole book in a way that no other psalms in the collection seem to offer. Psalm 1 presents two contrasting ways of living; the way of the righteous and the way of the wicked. The description suggests that the outcomes of these two paths are clear and distinct. The righteous will flourish, and the way of the wicked will perish. Alongside the two paths of Psalm 1, Psalm 2 presents a clear picture of divine sovereignty.

Together, the images in these opening psalms sound both convincing and comforting. They may also cohere well with the theological frameworks of the preacher and congregation. However, from Psalm 3 onwards the propositions of both psalms are questioned and challenged. While we see glimpses of the Psalm 1 and 2 ideal in subsequent psalms, we are also exposed to situations where the principles are tested.

So, how do Psalms 1 and 2 function? They provide 'framing' of the divine ideal.[23] These ideals are then seen to be tested in the crucible of life experience, being refined through trials and endured through prayer. An awareness of the 'framing' provided by these psalms allows the divine ideal to be held in tension with the reality of lived experience. In addition, as a divine ideal they form the basis of an appeal to God when facing injustice, pain and frustration. The frame helps to remind us that God intends something better.

The Contextualisation Task

We've explored some considerations for preaching the psalms more generally, but what about when we preach them to Australians specifically? What aspects of our culture might we need to address? How do we contextualise our message without importing

Australian cultural values onto a centuries-old Hebrew collection of poems, which are the living word of God for all peoples and all times?

In what follows, we address such questions by discussing and providing mini-sermons on Psalms 22, 23 and 24. In examining Psalm 22, we take into account Australia's egalitarianism and high rates of anxiety and depression. Turning to Psalm 23, we consider the tendency of Australians to over-work and be task oriented. And finally, we explore Psalm 24 in light of the relationship Australia has with its land and environment.

Something we both have been asked is: 'Is there a female voice in the Psalms? What if a woman preaches the Psalms?' Enabling women congregants to hear the voice of women in Scripture and to experience biblical narrative and poetry from the perspective of female biblical characters, even in the psalms, must be a consideration when preaching – especially when preaching to Australians, since we perceive ourselves to be egalitarian. Now, what is meant by the term 'egalitarian' in the context of Australian cultural categories is not quite the same as when we use the term theologically or ecclesiologically. When we use the term 'egalitarian' in theological circles, we mean 'egalitarian as distinct from complementarian'. But identifying as egalitarian in wider Australian culture means that we believe in equality for all (if not quite achieving it); we are stridently anti-hierarchical (even though the vast majority of our businesses, organisations and churches are hierarchical), and this fierce egalitarianism is embedded in our culture of 'mateship' (but if you get too big for your boots we'll cut you down, even if you are our mate – this is called the 'tall poppy syndrome').

Churches will differ in their theology concerning women preaching, but that does not mean we cannot explore psalms that were written with women in mind – for example, Psalms 45, 68, 123, 131, 139 and others – and hear their voices and see their perspectives in our sermons. We may also consult the work of female translators and commentators to see not only the female voice they bring out in the psalms, but also the female voice they bring to their interpretation and application. We may consider an expository sermon on Hannah's Song and its similarities with Psalm 113. Or, in the harsh light of Australia failing to live up to its ideals of an egalitarian society, namely Australia's problem with gender-based violence, we may try – through the medium of a topical sermon on gender-based violence – to come to grips with how Tamar would have felt hearing Psalm 61 sung in the Temple, knowing that her father was not for her a refuge, nor did he hear her cries or seek justice. And, turning to our cycle of Psalms 22–24, we may explore what Psalm 22 has to do with Esther.

Psalm 22, a lament psalm of David and of the people of Israel during the exile, should be immediately recognisable to Christians. Especially the first line: 'My God, my God, why have you forsaken me?' We hear these words and are instantly transported to Jesus crying out from the cross in Matthew and Mark. In fact, although other psalms are referenced in the passion narratives, Psalm 22 was the one used most frequently.

But perhaps less well-known is the Jewish tradition of reading Psalm 22 with Esther's voice. As much as Christians associate Psalm 22 with Good Friday, Jews associate Psalm 22 with Purim, the Jewish holiday which commemorates the saving of the Jewish people from genocide at the hands of Haman, as recorded in the book of Esther.

While the tradition of associating Psalm 22 with Esther actually arose after the Christian tradition of seeing it as prophetic of Christ, there is some merit to this association. The *Midrash Tehillim* – exegesis of the psalms by ancient Judaic authorities, dating to the eleventh century – is at pains to explain how each verse of Psalm 22 applies to Esther. Rather than recounting this interpretation, what is interesting for our purposes is the more recent Christian practice of seeing types of Christ in Old Testament women. We are accustomed to this kind of typology – 'certain persons, events, and things (such as Moses, the crossing of the Red Sea, the Passover lamb) as prophetic indications of the Messiah'[24] – but seeing women in this role is relatively new. An argument could be made that Esther is a prophetic indicator of the coming Messiah, and her association with Psalm 22 would strengthen this. Though the psalm's original life setting may, or may not, have had Esther in mind, there is no reason we cannot carefully apply Psalm 22 to Esther's context, much as we may thoughtfully apply it to our own context and hear Esther's voice in the psalm.

Hearing the voice of women when we preach the psalms is just one way to engage with Australia's concept of an egalitarian society. Australian egalitarianism is also about 'a fair go for all'. So, how do we preach the psalms, in this case Psalm 22, to a congregation that expresses the desire for a 'fair go' regardless of status and wants to support the 'underdog', but which inevitably falls short of this ideal?

Allow us to frame this discussion with another distinctive identified in the 'Describing Australians' chapter: that Australian culture has a high incidence of anxiety and depression. The World Health Organisation's recent global health estimates showed that Australia comes in at equal second in worldwide rates of depression.[25] Depression and anxiety don't discriminate. These mental health disorders strike regardless of ability, age, ethnicity, gender, nationality, race or sexuality: any one of us could experience anxiety or depression at any time.[26] As we write this chapter, the recent devastating news that well-known and talented people like Avicii (Tim Bergling), Kate Spade and Anthony Bourdain – giants in their fields, perhaps even considered to be 'tall poppies' – have taken their own lives, highlights that none of us are immune. King David was a shepherd, a musician, a writer and a political leader and, arguably, he had bouts of depression – just as three million Australians are currently experiencing depression.

We must be extremely careful when preaching about mental health. It is dangerous to suggest that depression and anxiety in a person's life are caused by sin. It is even more dangerous to suggest that one will only overcome depression and anxiety by prayer or by turning to Scripture. This is not to say that God cannot heal a person of ailments and afflictions – and by all means let us pray and immerse ourselves in the Scriptures – but it must be stressed that anxiety, depression and other mental health disorders are exactly that: medical disorders. Going to the doctor for mental illness is the same as going for any other illness. It must also be said that 'worry' and 'anxiety' are not synonymous. And with that in mind, what can preaching on Psalm 22 teach us about depression and anxiety?

If you have been lucky enough to have not experienced depression, Psalm 22 gives us insight into how someone who is depressed might be feeling. For those of us who have battled the black dog or been afflicted with anxiety, this psalm gives us words to express ourselves when perhaps words fail us. A person who is depressed might require more sleep but find no rest (v.2). They may feel worthless (like a worm – v.6) or like they have been deserted and there is no one to help (v.11). Depression and anxiety can have physiological symptoms along with the neurological: chronic joint, limb and back pain (v.14),[27] numbness and fogginess, like the ability to feel has leaked away (v.14), and dry mouth (v.15).[28] The physical complaints of Psalm 22 reflect the physiological symptoms of anxiety and depression.

Most strikingly, Psalm 22 acknowledges there are times when we will feel as though God has forgotten us. It gives us permission to feel that way. To say it aloud. And to cry out in anger, anguish and abandonment to God – the very same God we feel has stricken us. Spurgeon puts it beautifully: Jesus 'keeps his hold upon his God with both hands and cries twice "My God, my God!" ... Oh that we could imitate this cleaving to an afflicting God ... For our prayers to appear to be unheard is no new trial ... No daylight is too glaring and no midnight too dark to pray in; and no delay or apparent denial, however grievous, should tempt us to forbear from importunate pleading'.[29] So, while Psalm 22 paints a picture of what it can look like when we are grappling with our mental health, it also strongly encourages us to trust in God (vv.4–5; 9); teaches us that we can cry out to God in the midst of our pain and confusion and when we don't feel like ourselves (v.1; 5); and reminds us that God has always been, is now, and forever will be our strength, one who hears us and the one who is worthy of our praise (vv.10; 24; 30–31).

Which leads us to Psalm 23, one of the most beloved – and arguably the best known – psalms. Henry Ward Beecher calls it the nightingale of the Psalms. 'It has poured balm and consolation into the heart of the sick, of captives in dungeons, of widows in their pinching griefs, of orphans in their loneliness. Dying soldiers have died easier as it was read to them.'[30] Psalm 23 has been associated with death and funerals in the US since the Civil War,[31] and while it has become something of an American icon, it has been an ever-present feature of Australian choirs and funerals, too. But what does the rural/pastoral language, imagery, and symbolism of Psalm 23 say to Australians, the majority – over two-thirds – of whom live in capital cities?[32] And, more to the point, what does a psalm of rest and trust say to Australians who are stressed, overworked and reticent to take holidays?[33] We think we are time poor, and we have a tendency to prioritise tasks over people; this is not consistent with the values of God's kingdom and at odds with the message of Psalm 23.

In the wise words of Maya Angelou: making a living is not the same as making a life. More than twenty percent of Australian workers spend fifty hours or more a week at work, and sixty percent do not take regular holidays.[34] Could the remedy to our unhealthy focus on time and task be to reprioritise? It should be obvious that working longer hours leads to dissatisfaction with one's 'work-life balance' (if there is such a thing), but you may not know that it also leads to higher absenteeism and lower productivity.[35] A culture shift towards valuing people and relationship over tasks, would benefit both the worker and the business. So, for what are we sacrificing our time: are we working for material gain, and have we forgotten how to rest? In the very first line of Psalm 23, David puts himself in the place of the sheep and knows that because he belongs to the Lord, he lacks nothing. It might be tempting to draw a connection between Australia's wealthy and consumerist culture and the idea that 'lacking nothing' means our material needs are met. But we need to be clear that this is not what Psalm 23 means; it is no prosperity gospel. David experienced poverty and hardship. It would be strange to suggest that all his needs were met, and he lacked nothing materially. David means he lacks nothing spiritually. Yahweh has given him – and us – a life, not a living; life is a gift from God, and what we do with ours should be a gift back to God.

Perhaps the key to understanding the first verse of Psalm 23 is the second verse. Perhaps the key to Australians understanding what it means to experience 'lacking nothing', in its true sense, is to rest. In this gift of life, Yahweh invites us to slow down, to rest. God refreshes us. The thing about sheep, though, is rarely do they lie down. If they've had enough to eat, and the flies aren't bothering them, and they don't sense any threats, only then might they lie down in green pastures. It should come as no surprise that Australians don't know how to rest either. For the sheep, their rest and refreshment depends on the protection and care of their shepherd – and so it is with us. God is the shepherd of our contentment, not material possessions; the shepherd of our rest, not working over fifty hours a week; the shepherd of our flourishing through loving God and loving neighbour rather than making idols out of trappings, tasks and time.

And the bigger picture here is that we are spending, sacrificing and making an idol out of time that is not our own. Our time belongs to God. Karl Barth, on New Year's Eve in 1960, preached from the Basel prison pulpit on Psalm 31:15. He began his sermon with a personal anecdote about a friend who had preached on the same passage. His friend said: 'My time is secure in your hands.' The sermon was stirring and alive, but soon after, his friend wasn't. That was the last sermon he ever preached. Barth then asked: 'How do I know that today's is not my last sermon, too?'[36] At the end of time, we will be asked what we did with our time. Will we be answering that we fixated on dividing our time up into increments and wondering where it all went? Or will we reflect on those times the Lord, our shepherd, refreshed, restored and renewed us? On God's time spent serving God's people and worshipping the one whose goodness and love follows us all the days of our lives? Our time is neither in our own hands nor in the hands of time-poor, task-oriented culture. Rather than our cups overflowing with busyness and belongings, our cups could overflow with green pastures and quiet waters. We can rest without the world falling apart; in fact, the world – and us – will be better off.

It is not only time that we try to control. Australians like to try to control their natural and social environment, too. Generally speaking, we want to have mastery over the land we inhabit rather than nurture it. Following the conservation movement, theologians have been pondering God's intended relationship between humanity and the environment. What do the Psalms have to say about humanity's relationship to the natural environment? What does it mean for Australians to be stewards of creation rather than trying to have mastery over it? What do Indigenous Australians have to say about this? To try to answer these questions, we've turned to Psalm 24.

It is generally agreed that Psalm 24 is an entrance liturgy, and while we may not be able to identify its original setting, we do know about its ongoing use in the cultic life of Israel. And its liturgical use continues today, with Christians still using Psalm 24 in their liturgy for Ascension Day. The psalm's composition has often been questioned because at first glance it can seem thematically disjointed, but the psalm has come to us as a whole and does have a theological unity.

So, what does Psalm 24 teach us about environmental issues and how Australians might relate to God's creation? Perhaps unsurprisingly, this succinct and masterfully written poem begins with poetic devices highlighting that Yahweh is both creator and owner of the earth and that his creation is carefully ordered. When Australian Christians think of the Earth's creation and its care, we tend to understand these concepts in conversation with the first chapters of Genesis. Our modern (mis)interpretation of terms like 'dominion' and 'stewardship' leads us to think we need control over creation and the vague idea that creation somehow needs us. Though the terms 'dominion' and 'stewardship' do not appear in Psalm 24, they require brief explanation. From the Hebrew 'radah', meaning to tread down, 'dominion' does not allow us to exploit the earth; rather, it means we are to care and take responsibility for God's creation. And Psalm 8 beautifully portrays 'stewardship' as the role humanity plays in God's domain, linking 'God's self-disclosure in creation with our vocation'.[37] Who are we that God cares for us? We are to care for everything God has placed under our feet.

The care and responsibility we are to have for God's creation is particularly relevant to those who are poor and marginalised, since they are the first to suffer the consequences of the abuse of the earth's resources. Australia's Indigenous peoples are some of the most marginalised peoples in our country, yet their care for country far exceeds that of non-Indigenous Australians. Predominantly city-dwelling Australians have a tendency to forget that we depend on the resources of creation. As we write this chapter, the whole of New South Wales is drought-declared, shaking many of us out of our complacency when it comes to our responsibility for and dependence on creation. The 'environment is to be understood as a delicate, fragile system of interrelated parts that is maintained and enhanced by the recognition of limits and givens and by the judicious exercise of choices'.[38] It seems to us that this sounds remarkably similar to the Indigenous Australian practice of 'treading lightly', which stems from an intimate knowledge of the land. In fact, we can say that our First Nations peoples 'created the world's first systematic approach to ecofarming'.[39] There is much the church can learn from our Indigenous brothers and sisters – good stewardship of creation is surely one of them.

While we are discussing what the church can learn from Australia's Indigenous peoples, Australia's non-Indigenous people, especially those of us who identify as Christian, need to partner with Indigenous peoples to end the injustices perpetuated against them. And we are reminded of one of the brilliant sermons of Martin Luther King Jr., who in 1966 took the familiar refrain of Psalm 24:1 and directed it right at southern discrimination: 'God has not decided to turn this world over to George Wallace. Somewhere I read, "The earth is the Lord's and the fullness thereof."'[40] The earth is the Lord's, and the Lord first entrusted Australia to over 500 different Aboriginal nations with diverse cultures, beliefs and languages. In the words of Aboriginal Christian leader, Brooke Prentis, aboriginal peoples are gracious hosts on ancient lands.[41]

When we preach from the Psalter, we are prompted to marvel at the country we call home. Psalm 104 shows us God's extravagant provision for all the creation we see around us, plants and animals that thrive in the Australian desert included – yes, even the ones that are trying to kill us! 'How many are your works, Lord!'[42] Psalm 8 teaches us our role in the stewardship of God's creation – we are given careful authority with the works of God's hands. And Psalm 24 reminds us why we partner with God in the care of this earth God has created – because the fullness thereof belongs to God.

As we have seen, the language of Psalms 22, 23 and 24 is bold and imaginative – and our sermons can be no less so.[43] Brueggemann argues that to preach truth in our world 'requires us to be poets that speak against a prose world'.[44] To be a preacher is to be a poet, and to be a poet is to be countercultural. As the co-authors of this chapter, one of our challenges is to model how we may interpret and preach the psalms, diversely and poetically, to Australians with the specifics of Australian culture in mind. While we approach texts from a similar perspective and hermeneutic, we preach very differently: David tending towards tradition and Erin preferring to poetically experiment. In the sample sermons that follow, we have combined our two styles into three mini-sermons, embedding poetry in each, since the psalms are poetry with a rich and lengthy tradition 'and we need not try to squeeze them into a narrative mould so they might qualify as preaching fodder'.[45]

The choice of psalms for these sermons is based on their close proximity to each other, the breadth of expression encompassed and the way in which each psalm informs the way we understand and interpret the others. The broad movement is from lament to trust, culminating in praise – or, to use Brueggemann's terminology: disorientation, orientation, new orientation.[46] The titles chosen for three sample sermons are:

- A Queen's Lament (Psalm 22)
- A Shepherd's Comfort (Psalm 23)
- A Worshipper's Ascent (Psalm 24)

Sample Sermons: Psalms 22, 23, 24

A Queen's Lament (Psalm 22)

Introduction

I wonder what it would be like to face the destruction of your family and yet feel like you are in a position of power to perhaps avert the catastrophe. That was Esther's position. Every year at the Purim festival, Jewish people continue to remember Esther's dilemma at her peoples' plight and her courageous response which led to their preservation. As Jews recall Esther's story, they also imagine that Psalm 22 expresses her lament. No doubt she experienced anxiety, maybe even depression, as she contemplated her peoples' possible demise, and she may have wondered if her people would ever get a 'fair go'. Perhaps Esther's story, viewed through the lens of Psalm 22, can help us better understand how to handle anxiety and how to respond when life seems unfair.

> The garden had linen hangings of white
> and blue, gathered with purple ribbon.
> Gold and silver couches rested on
> mother-of-pearl pavement. Oil and spices
>
> perfumed my robes and seasoned our feast.
> "Fit for a king" announced my attendants
> as they set the scene and I took my chance.
> But for three days of fasting you had forsaken me:

I was poured out from your wine
glass. My heart melted like a candle
at your table. My exposed bones were handled
like a burnt offering and my mouth was dry

as clay. Lots were cast to decide our fate
and we lay in sackcloth and ashes. But you
spun the tables: ashes to alms, sacks to
robes, and mourning to honour at the king's gate.

Now the man who raised me wears
blue and white royal garments
and fine purple linen. Each year hence
we mark the day our people remained heirs.

A lament for the anxious

For those of us familiar with Psalm 22, we readily associate its opening question with Jesus on the cross. But what do these words suggest? Crying out to God in distress is in some ways a struggle for some sense of control. This is a natural and normal desire. Distress, especially when extreme, wrenches control out of our hands. The sudden death of a loved one, loss of a job or being diagnosed with a terminal illness, to name a few.

Paradoxically, this opening cry of Psalm 22 expresses both doubt and faith at the same time: doubt about God's whereabouts, but faith that God hears prayer. Have you ever uttered a prayer like that? It is the cry of the anxious who feel desolate and despairing but still feel compelled to cry out to God. The psalmist also wonders why God doesn't help. It's a confronting but not uncommon experience.

With no immediate answer, the psalmist proceeds to use a series of graphic images to paint a picture of anxiety. Interwoven with these images, God's past goodness is recalled but the present circumstances are overwhelming. The psalmist feels worm-like, having enemies like raging bulls or ravenous dogs. The experience feels like being 'poured out like water', having 'bones out of joint' and possessing a 'heart of wax' that is melting (v.14). It's not a comforting picture. It describes a person who today would be considered anxious and perhaps even depressed, and it resonates with anyone who has these experiences.

However, beyond resonating, the words offer a pathway of prayer for expressing these emotions. It's an invitation from the psalmist to enter into their world – the world of an Esther or Jesus. In doing this we are encouraged to explore our own world and to lament the sadness within ourselves and around us. It's not only appropriate to do this, but Psalm 22 models to us both the necessity of such expression and a way to do it.

A cry for all ...

Psalm 22 and the characters associated with it reminds us that distress and the emotions it evokes transcend time. Not only is the experience common to us all but also often engenders feelings of injustice or unfairness. In a culture that values fairness, this psalm offers a voice to the voiceless. It models a way of expressing our feelings of unfairness to a God who does care for us and has our best interests at heart. Perhaps surprisingly, people who express their dismay at God's seeming absence, like the psalmist, actually find comfort in doing this. Conversely, those who are deeply distressed and yet discouraged from expressing their anxieties find that their feelings of grief, loss, anxiety and depression don't simply go away. They persist and can manifest in destructive ways. This psalm reminds us that expressing them through prayer is both appropriate and beneficial.

We can imagine that, in different ways, each voice we have mentioned above (the psalmist, Esther and Jesus) was crying out, at least in part, from a sense of unfairness. They seemed to believe that their voices would not go unnoticed by God. It is because of this belief that their cry could rise up from the abyss of distress. If we can grasp the same belief, then our cry of despair can be equally directed towards God as a healthy expression of faith. A remarkable thing happens when this is done.

We get a glimpse of it in the second half of Psalm 22, where a different tone emerges. The psalmist has somehow seen light in the darkness. Their world will never be the same, due to the distress they are experiencing, but their world can go on. It seems that when we learn to express our deepest anxieties to God, a renewed strength to trust in God's goodness and God's action emerges.

Reflections

Current research on Australian culture indicates clearly that anxiety and depression are significant problems across our society. People of faith are not immune to these issues, and in a culture of the 'fair go' some may see it as unfair that, while trusting in God, they still struggle with these challenges. As we look around it is not unusual to see deeply anxious and depressed fellow travellers in this life. Psalm 22 offers a response to this situation. It provides a voice that may be elusive to many of us. When people of faith encounter distress, the words of this psalm underline the value of expressing the generated feelings and thoughts. The contrast between the bleakness of the first part of Psalm 22 and the hopeful tone of the second part models a healthy and contained prayer. This psalm also responds to those who suggest that anxiety and depression are a result of faith that is lacking or sin that has been committed. It is not the case. As a result, we find ourselves drawn closer to God rather than repelled by God. The psalm offers hope amid anxious despair and an alternative to feelings of unfairness, affirming that God is for us, not against us, and that the healthy expression of our anxieties will only lead us into a deeper relationship with our God.

A Shepherd's Comfort (Psalm 23)

Introduction

Psalm 23 is so familiar to us that many could recite most, if not all, of it from memory. Psalm 23 encourages us to withdraw from the busyness of life and reflect on the one in whom we trust. How many times a day do you realise that you are rushed? Our busyness can distract us from quiet places in life, but this psalm reminds us that they are both discoverable and desirable. Slowing down and finding time to reflect may help us to discern between what we want and what we actually need as we navigate life. Psalm 23 offers some clues to us.

Trusting in the shepherd (in the pastures)

In the opening scene we find ourselves in green pastures; paddocks here in Australia of course. The still waters might remind us of peaceful billabongs offering respite from pounding summer heat and refreshing cool water to slake our thirst. It is idyllic, almost utopian. Seemingly impossible to imagine in the hustle and bustle of modern-day life, the psalm encourages us to stop long enough to experience something different. The backdrop to this is Psalm 22, which reminds us of the tumultuous potential of life. Psalm 23 offers a response, and perhaps an antidote, to these kinds of storms. Rather than the calm *before* the storm, Psalm 23 represents a calm *after* the storm.

We've all heard the idea that if you want something done, ask a busy person to do it! Busyness can be considered a badge of honour for some, and we may believe that our deepest needs are met in activity. But here we are reminded that our deepest needs are met in God. Astoundingly, the psalmist says that we will lack nothing as we trust in God. It is not a vision of material prosperity, even though some have interpreted it this way. Rather, these words offer an invitation to slow down and pause, reflecting on God's provision of *what we really need* and the refreshment of that provision. Our culture tends to feed desire. Advertising often capitalises on our desire to obtain something better than what we already have. But the capacity we develop to rest in God's presence, trusting in God's 'steady provision', is a key avenue to finding contentment; rest in the midst of activity.[47]

Fearing with the Shepherd (in the valley)

This psalm then gives us a jolt. Quite abruptly we find ourselves walking beyond green paddocks into the dark valley. Or, as Robert Alter puts it, 'the vale of death's shadow'.[48] There is no hiding from the inevitable dark places in life. The language of address shifts here from 'he' in verses 1–3 to 'you' in v.4b. It encourages us to re-focus from the dark shadow of the valley to the Shepherd, the Lord. It doesn't ignore the fearfully dark experiences of life but offers perspective: light and dark, comfort and discomfort, orientation and disorientation.

Psalm 23 urges trust within 'the vale of death's shadow'. It encourages us to look over our shoulder back to the images of green pastures as we contemplate our response. The Shepherd is trustworthy *in these times* and beyond these times. The reinforcing words 'you are with me' (v.4b) are the centre of the psalm and emphasise that acknowledging God's presence and resting in that presence is so important. While we might want control, the importance of placing ourselves in God's hands is reinforced.[49] It is because we belong to the Shepherd that God's presence is assured, and trust is justified.

So, to summarise, the psalmist acknowledges comfort in the midst of distress and trust that protection from God is tangible. This leads to the final image in the psalm of cups overflowing with goodness and mercy rather than busyness and belongings.

Feasting with the Shepherd (around the table)

How important are meal times to you? There was a time in Australia where families would sit together to eat and share the experiences of the day. The third and final scene invites us to such a gathering around a table. The shepherd (the 'you') in this scene, who has been with us in green pastures and dark valleys, prepares and shares a banquet. It is a meal provided by the one we love and trust. Yet we are reminded that our enemies are also somehow present. The realism of the psalm is both disturbing and authentic. It acknowledges that there is comfort in the one we trust, the Shepherd. But 'enemies' are not absent. The presence of God does not preclude distress, but it protects us from its causes.

Who are our 'enemies'? Perhaps people or events – but one also wonders whether our enemies in contemporary Australia might in fact be ourselves! Could it be that in seeking to control our lives and our environment through task-oriented, possession-acquiring activity we, in fact, lose our lives to these preoccupations? Psalm 23 reminds us that richest blessing – anointing and overflowing cups – happen when we turn to trust in the Shepherd. Apparently, blessing does not eventuate when we grasp for it. In Jesus' words, 'Those who find their life will lose it, and those who lose their life for my sake will find it.'[50] As if to reinforce the importance of relying on the Shepherd rather than ourselves, we are encouraged to see that the outcomes do not just 'follow' the one who trusts in God (v.6). The word typically translated here as 'follow' is better rendered 'pursue'.[51] This pursuit is by God, not for our harm but for our good.

> The nightingale of the psalms,
> its balm is poured out for six
> short verses. A little larger
> than a robin, the nightingale stands six
> inches tall. Her voice is strong
> and sweet, a liquid-slow melody
> winding like a stream through
> green pastures. Her song a remedy
>
> for shadowed souls, she trills
> from evening and into the night,
> urging us to listen and be still
> until we are refreshed for the light.

Reflections

Viewing Psalm 23 in its context is helpful. The images presented in this psalm contrast markedly with those found in the first half of Psalm 22 but also reinforce and affirm the hymn of praise that ends Psalm 22. Psalm 23 also reminds us of the importance of pausing to reflect on the lived experiences of trust in God in times of darkness and light. The images of Psalm 23 reflect glimpses of God's favour. They affirm the importance of meaningful relationships and of feeling safe. The psalm depicts an intimacy between God and humans around a meal table that gathers whether life is difficult or easy. The meal table may also prompt us to think of those around us who lack safety and security, those that we might reach out to and invite to join with us in the meal of blessing.

For a culture that struggles with a sense of being time poor, Psalm 23 also implicitly reminds us to slow down, to dwell beside the still waters and enjoy the green paddocks, at least for a while. Rest is important and recreation critical to our wellbeing. Perhaps as we acknowledge that we lack enough time we might find the time that we actually have. When feeling distressed, perhaps even oppressed in some way, this psalm urges us to pause to give thanks for a trustworthy God – to show gratitude. Psalm 23 also reminds us that while some material goods are necessary, true provision is found in relationship with God and God's presence. Trusting in God, we 'shall not want'.

A Worshipper's Ascent (Psalm 24)

Introduction

The steep ascent from the old city of David up to where the temple was located in Jerusalem is somewhat arduous but also rewarding. It's not difficult to imagine ancient Israelites making this ascent regularly to worship their God. There's something about going up to a high place. It offers a different perspective on life and the world around us. Psalm 24 describes such an ascent through its majestic and brief portrait. While we might picture ourselves clambering up the temple mount, this psalm reminds us of what is more important: that the God we encounter there is Yahweh, the owner of all creation.

But this is not the whole story. While the psalm is a canvas on which a portrait of Yahweh's relationship to creation is offered in broad brushstrokes, it also alerts us to humankind's responsibility for creation. In doing this, it urges an ethical approach to the environment for us as worshippers of Yahweh. As Yahweh is presented as the God of *creation*, it reminds us that we must listen to all the voices who have an interest in our environment, Indigenous and non-Indigenous alike.

Let's consider this psalm through three lenses that challenge us to be more aware of our environment and the land in Australia and how we might act responsibly towards it.

> Many Heads, carved from Cambrian earth
> and moated by russet dirt, throws an atlas
> of shadow over mountain trails. The wind circles
>
> like a yidaki and sentinel stones
> chart the symphony of the land. I stride
> towards Kata Tjuta, tasting metal since
>
> time has scored the iron ridges to drifts.
> Each red-streaked rock, desert gorge
> and weathered dome is eloquent of epochs.
>
> Rust colours strike through the outcrops
> like strokes of sinopia in an oil painting
> and a singular eucalyptus tree juts
>
> from a sandstone easel. The Artisan chiselled
> the land to make sacred sites of roseate
> stones and to leave a lithic legacy.

Yahweh as the creator and owner

The opening to Psalm 24 urges us to focus on God's relationship to creation before we explore our responses to creation. This is an important beginning point, because we can sometimes imagine that we 'own' creation. Those of you who have purchased a house might recall being given the keys and feeling like you possessed that house and the land where it was located. Australia's colonial history, our post-war aspirations for the 'great Australian dream' of home ownership and the complex relationship between Indigenous and non-Indigenous peoples all feed into our perception that we somehow possess the place where we live. Affirming Yahweh as creator *and* owner of all, Psalm 24 challenges our egocentrism. It offers us a visionary space to consider our place and role as tenants within the community of creation. Imagining peoples' role in creation in this way will also be enriched through the voices of Indigenous Australians and hearing how they traditionally view themselves as custodians of the land.

By stating that the earth is 'to/for the LORD', Psalm 24 also stretches our thinking beyond God possessing creation.[52] It reinforces that creation exists for the benefit of Yahweh and not the other way around.[53] That doesn't mean God is only interested in what can be gained from creation. In fact, God doesn't *need* creation. However, God does derive enjoyment from creation functioning well.[54] Beyond God's presence and enjoyment in creation we hear of a God who is also acting. In other words, this is not the watchmaker God, winding up creation and then exiting, leaving it to its own devices. Verses 1–2 speak of a 'carefully ordered creation'.[55] So owning creation means that God has an ongoing concern for creation's wellbeing in the same way as a homeowner cares for their garden. But does this dual notion of God owning creation and caring for creation offer us a model that can inform how we might act towards creation?

Humans as co-creators

As we read Psalm 24, it does help us to begin to contemplate our place and role in the community of creation. In considering our damaged environment, we may begin to see we have a responsibility. Perhaps this responsibility could be called 'co-creation'. For the psalmist, any personal response to creation begins with an encounter with the God of creation and an awareness of the need for human transformation. The transformational encounter is encapsulated in two questions: 'Who shall ascend the hill of the LORD? And who shall stand in his holy place?' (v.3). These questions show an awareness that authentic encounter with God in worship transforms people. Clean hands and a pure heart are the beginning point (v.4). This might seem overly individualistic, but when individuals worship God and are transformed, these same people shape transformed communities. One writer underscores this, saying that images of clean hands and pure hearts indicate 'only a well-oriented community'.[56] Well-oriented communities are deeply concerned for the environment and motivated to act ethically towards it. This is about our identity as people of faith. Our worship (of Yahweh in Psalm 24) reflects our identity. Our identity affects what we do, and these should not be separated easily.[57] Personal piety in the world is critical, but not enough. The psalm goes on to emphasise intentional action towards our creation through an ethic that cares.

In a remarkable vision of hope, verse 5 portrays worshippers as those who 'will carry blessing from the LORD and rightness from the God who saves them'.[58] What a privilege to carry divine blessing into creation and to take up the responsibility of putting things right! In doing this, we fulfil the mandate of Genesis positively.[59] We partner with God, co-creating the world as God intended. Of course, we need to know what that 'intended world' looks like, and Genesis 1 and 2 provides a response.[60] Worshipping the Lord ought to inspire us to seek God as the psalmist did, then take the blessing received into creation (vv.3–6).[61]

Yahweh, the God who completes creation

It might seem onerous for humankind to bear the responsibility of caring for the community of creation and to repair damage done to it. But we are not alone in this task. Verses 7 to 10 summon us to lift up our heads and see something that transcends our immediate situation. There is a final act to be played out. The King of Glory wants to enter into creation. But how can it be that the owner of creation seems to require something from us to enter? It's like needing to ask someone for the key to your own house! Yet not once but twice the psalmist instructs listeners to 'lift up your heads … *that the king of glory may come in*'. 'God stands outside the gate, not as a threat but as a welcome arrival. He is seeking access to the centre of his own world – the sanctuary from which blessings are disseminated to all parts of the world.'[62] Creation culminates with the entry of the Creator.

Yahweh wants to enter the community of creation, and humankind has a key role in making this happen. This psalm acknowledges Yahweh's desire to participate in creation with us. This precedent was set back at the beginning. God walked in the garden. Then in Jesus, who 'moved into the neighbourhood' with us.[63] God is willing to work with humankind in re-creating a well ordered world that will be completed with God's final arrival.[64] In this description we see the significance of human involvement in the stewardship role of re-creation with Yahweh, while at the same time recognising that it is only God who can bring creation to its divinely intended completion.

Reflections

As already mentioned, the co-creator role is an echo of the original creation story where humankind is commissioned to work *with God* in creation but not *as God* in creation.

Psalm 24 reinforces this idea. In a radio interview in 2010, David Suzuki stated, 'We are trying to be gods, but we don't know how to be gods.'[65] The Genesis creation narratives remind us of our responsibilities and what happens when people attempt to be gods. Psalm 24 offers an ethical vision which ought to encourage us to use natural resources wisely, reduce waste and recycle more. As tenants, we must not abdicate our responsibilities in this regard. In our Australian context, Indigenous people, who view themselves as custodians of the land, have much to contribute to our understanding. So listening well to each other will lead to acting well together in restoring and preserving our environment.

Nick Spencer reminds us of the magnitude of our responsibility in saying:

> Christians should care for creation because it has an eternal destiny in Christ: it will be transformed along with our bodies in the new creation, and *the work we do now to shape and to care for the world is of eternal significance.*[66]

Conclusion

Our exploration of the Psalter for preaching has provided us with much food for thought – 'manna', if you will. As we contemplate communicating the message of the psalms through preaching, it is critical to consider the general features explored at the beginning of this chapter. Alongside this, examining significant markers of Australian culture enables us to ponder the connections between the psalms and the lived experiences of Australian people of faith. The psalms speak equally profoundly to individuals and congregations.

With these resources in our preaching toolkit, the mini-sermons on three specific psalms offer examples of the way in which each could be communicated in light of these factors. In doing this we have aimed to provide a solid platform for preaching more *from* the psalms and more *of* the psalms. The sermon examples may also offer a catalyst for imaginatively engaging with the psalms in creative ways that fit a particular local context. It is our hope that such a pursuit might encourage people who hear the psalms afresh and utilise them more in their own study and devotion.

> The Psalms foretell what I, what any,
> shall do and suffer and say. – John Donne

7
PREACHING THE PROPHETS TO AUSTRALIANS
Kirk R. Patston

> ... to them you are nothing more than one who sings love songs with a beautiful voice and plays an instrument well, for they hear your words but do not put them into practice.
>
> Ezekiel 33:32

> They say to the seers,
> 'See no more visions!'
> and to the prophets,
> 'Give us no more visions of what is right!
> Tell us pleasant things,
> prophesy illusions.
> Leave this way,
> get off this path,
> and stop confronting us
> with the Holy One of Israel!'
>
> Isaiah 30:10–11

Introduction

It has never been easy to be a prophet. As the verses from Ezekiel 33 and Isaiah 30 suggest, the prophets were not received well by their contemporaries. Ezekiel was reduced to a source of entertainment. Isaiah reported an outspoken resistance to the prophets' words. Jeremiah was contained in stocks and thrown into a pit.

As I've been thinking about how to preach the prophets to Australians, a sense of unease keeps confronting me.[1] The prophets might be tolerated as quirky or entertaining, but the substance of their message seems irrelevant and even offensive in our current context. They preach about the seriousness and culpability of sin and connect it to terrifying images of God's rightful judgement. Neither sin nor judgement makes much sense in secular, postmodern, individualistic Australia, where moral choices are viewed as matters of personal and private preference. A stance of tolerance appears more reasonable and kinder than the judgemental threats and derision uttered by the prophets. I find in many of the sermons I have preached on the prophets, I am offering an apologetic defence of both the validity of sin and the surprisingly positive value of a God prepared to judge.

To be fair, the prophets speak of sin and judgement as elements in a process of transformation. Judgement is not really an end in itself. It can be an action that makes manifest the glory of God, especially in Ezekiel. Importantly for secular Australian ears, it is a process that can do *good* to people and for people. Clearly in Isaiah, but also in other prophets, judgement creates a remnant community of people who have been purified. The prophetic vision of the future is actually full of hope, in a way that Australians may find inspiring. The frustrations that Australians feel in trying to master a difficult environment, for example, can find an answer in the renewal of creation that the prophets describe. The gnarly discouragement of depression and anxiety can find relief in a vision of the future in which a good God generously and gently makes things right.

The preacher's task in bringing the prophets to Australians is to bring together the prickly strangeness and the comforting hope contained in their words. The preacher needs to explicitly recognise how strange Isaiah, Jeremiah, Ezekiel and the Twelve can be. But once the strangeness is sensed, there can be great satisfaction in showing Australians how precious and attractive these books of Scripture are. As preachers, we will need to help people interpret these books with reference to the faith and history of Israel and the ancient Near East. We will also have to guide people to make sense of the prophets' strange communication techniques.

It will be possible to contextualise the prophets by pointing out that God does not change, sin is still sin and judgement still matters. The prophets speak of a transformation that, from time to time, is offered beyond the borders of Israel, even to distant islands (see, for example, Isa 42:4). So, in a way, the prophets are about us.

The Hermeneutical Task

Task 1: We Need to Read the Prophets Within the Faith and History of Israel and the Ancient Near East

The prophets understood the people of Israel and Judah to be a people in covenant with the Lord. The covenants with Noah and Abraham create an important backdrop of God's relentless commitment to life and blessing. The prophets seek to hold the nation of Israel accountable to the terms of the Sinai covenant. The privilege of living in the promised land could be removed if the nation turned from the Lord's ways. Similarly, the Davidic king lived within a covenant arrangement and could choose a path that would lead to blessing or discipline.

This means it is illegitimate to preach as though the moral and social issues raised by the prophets are *immediately* relevant to Australians. The eighth-century prophets are famous for speaking against social injustice. Isaiah confronts those who ally themselves with thieves, practise business using gifts and bribes and who fail to defend the cause of the fatherless and the widow (see Isa 1:23). There is some value in taking up their words to critique practices of politicians and business leaders and Australian actions towards the homeless and those without family support. But in the texts of the prophets, these social and ethical sins sit within the covenant that Moses made with the nation of Israel. No such covenant arrangement sits around Australian political and social life. If we are to urge Australians to be kind to the homeless because an Old Testament prophet says so, we need to consider why we are not preaching the full Sinai covenant, including the need for Sabbath observance or circumcision. If we are to make application to Australians, it will need to be grounded in the unchanging character of God, for example, not simply the terms of the covenant.

The prophets' thinking about God and his people is deeply embedded in the ancient covenants. They articulate their future visions using the vocabulary of the past. Isaiah's way of describing God's future is to imagine a day when the nations will stream to a temple on Mount Zion to receive teaching of God's law (Isa 2:2–3). Jeremiah, while clearly critical of the Davidic kingship, hopes for a better Davidic king and a renewed Levitical priesthood (Jer 33:14–26). He dreams of a new covenant but also finds assurance in the fact that God's faithfulness to ancient covenants cannot be annulled. Ezekiel is thoroughly disgusted with the idolatry that persisted in Israel despite the jealous claims of the Sinai covenant. Still, his vision of a new world is one dominated by a temple (Ezekiel 40–48). These hopes cannot be literally directed to the future of Australian society. Good preaching will take time to make the unique theological history of Israel clear. Overviews of covenantal and salvation history can provide good orientation here for preachers and keen listeners.² The Bible Project videos can be an efficient way of communicating some of this theological context succinctly.³

The way that the prophets understand history is worth noticing, because it assumes a distinctive – and not naturally Australian – view of time. The prophets of Israel speak of a coming Day. Over sixty times, we will meet the expression 'In that day' in the prophets (especially Isaiah), and a similar expression, 'days are coming', appears frequently in Jeremiah as well as Amos. The prophets do not count hours and minutes as modern Australians do. They inhabit epochs. They see how God is moving to bring an end to unfaithfulness and to renew his people in a world of peace and flourishing. Implicitly, they expose a pettiness in Australian impatience and punctuality. Our lives are better understood by counting centuries and millennia. It will be worth exploring how this different vision may be valuable to Australian lives.

Australians will benefit from a more expansive view of time as they situate the prophets in ancient history. Australians will also read the prophets more accurately by realising that the prophets' messages generally relate to the historical realities of their day. In simple terms, Amos, Hosea, Micah and Isaiah 1–39 are warning God's people in the 700s BCE that their covenant unfaithfulness will result in Assyrian invasion. Habakkuk and Zephaniah can see that ongoing apostasy and immorality will lead to a Babylonian exile. Jeremiah urges the people of the late 600s BCE to submit to Babylonian attack, while Ezekiel attempts to elicit a sense of shame and responsibility in the exilic community in Babylon. Isaiah 40–66 show that a new exodus is coming and that Cyrus will open a way for God's people to go home to Palestine. Joel's images of judgement are not historically referenced and might fit with Assyrian or Babylonian contexts. Haggai, Zechariah and Malachi confront complacency as the people of God try to build life again in the 500s BCE, after the Babylonian exile.

Wider horizons are offered by Obadiah, Nahum and Jonah and the oracles concerning the nations in the prophetic books. Obadiah condemns Edom for rejoicing in an attack on Jerusalem, perhaps the Babylonian attack. Nahum announces judgement on Nineveh, the Assyrian capital. Jonah tells a story of how hard it is for a prophet from Israel to tolerate God's mercy towards the Assyrians.

Rhetorical criticism of the Old Testament has highlighted the importance of noticing layers of historical contexts. The texts describe a prophet pronouncing oracles to a particular audience and the preacher needs to represent the dynamics of this. At the same time, the text itself reflects and effects a communicative engagement with readers from later generations. When we read and preach from the prophets, there is a dynamic of over-hearing messages meant for someone else that needs to be appreciated. There can also be a deepening awareness of a text's significance across political and theological history.

I have tried to demonstrate the layering of meaning in applying the prophets in my study of the book of Isaiah.

For example, Isaiah 42:18—44:23 discusses the deafness and blindness of Israel in the task of being a messenger. It also discusses the folly of idolatry. There are accents of meaning depending if one reads in the time of the Assyrians, Babylonians, Jesus or today:

> Following his own miraculous healing, Hezekiah had an encounter with Babylonian envoys in which he seemed to say nothing about God. And it seems he did not want the meddling Isaiah to come and criticise him for his actions (Isa 39:1–8). The Babylonians would have gone home without being challenged to give up their idols. Hezekiah acted like a servant who had grown deaf and blind.
>
> For C6th readers, this text would have been a deep challenge to reject the idols that Israel had served at home or had been tempted to serve in Babylon. Idolatry was less of a problem in postexilic Judaism than it had been before the exile. In this, Isaiah 40–48 may have made a difference.
>
> The deep generosity of God expressed in this section of Isaiah finds its fullest expression in God's own coming to earth in the person of Jesus and in sharing his Spirit with those who trusted Jesus. The language of ransom in this passage (Isa 43:4), which seems to be pointing back to the exodus, also points forward to Jesus' generous act in paying the price for the freedom of others (Mark 10:45).
>
> So many of the hopes of this passage have come true for Christians who have experienced the Holy Spirit breaking through their deafness and blindness to God and drawing them to Jesus. It would make no sense for such privileged people to live lives in the service of created things instead of their Creator and Redeemer.[4]

In some sermons, I may draw explicit attention to the way I interpret the prophets with a layered view of history:

> Zephaniah sometimes spoke of judgement on Judah and sometimes spoke of judgement on the world. It's a common feature of the OT prophets. Sometimes they see into history just a few decades ahead. Sometimes they see into history centuries ahead.
>
> Imagine placing four cartons of milk perfectly in a line on a shelf in your fridge. From some angles, it looks like one carton but, from another, it looks like four.

In a way, the judgement on the world that the prophets speak about will happen once, and we are waiting for it to come. But from another angle the judgement on the world happens over and over again.

In the 500s BCE, the Babylonian invasions would devastate Judah and other countries nearby, and it was as though the whole world came to an end. In 70 CE the rebuilt Jerusalem fell again, this time to Rome. It was the end of the world. One day you will die and that, for you, will be the end of the world. And one day, 2000 years ago, Jesus died, strangely summing up into himself the end of Judah and the end of Jerusalem, strangely taking into himself your end, your death, absorbing the judgement of God on the whole world.

Listen to Zephaniah's words and think about the terror, loneliness, earthquakes and the unfathomable darkness of Easter Thursday and Friday:

The cry on the day of the LORD is bitter;
the Mighty Warrior shouts his battle cry.
That day will be a day of wrath –
a day of distress and anguish,
a day of trouble and ruin,

a day of darkness and gloom,
a day of clouds and blackness –

Did you notice that in Zephaniah 1:7 the day of judgement is presented as a day of sacrifice, as though the leaders of Judah are going to die for the sake of their people? Zephaniah was anticipating something hundreds of years later, when the true king of Jerusalem would become a sacrifice at the hand of foreign soldiers.

However distant all this might seem, the preacher needs to make sure Australian listeners have a grasp of this history, or the prophetic voices will not make sense.

Task 2: We Need to Acknowledge the Prophets' Strange Communication Techniques

Isaiah, Jeremiah, Ezekiel and the Twelve are not just historically distant; their communication techniques and literary conventions are unfamiliar and will need explanation.

As well as preaching sermons (Jer 7:2) and delivering verbal oracles, the prophets performed *sign acts*. Isaiah walked around with his buttocks bare to picture the humiliation that was to come on Egypt and Cush (Isa 20:1–6). Jeremiah buried a linen belt and used its ruined state to picture the judgement coming to Judah (Jer 13:1–11). He wore a yoke to symbolise Babylonian oppression (Jer 27:1–15), bought a field as a picture of hope in a day when normal social and economic life would be restored (Jer 32:1–44) and threw a scroll into the Euphrates as a picture of Babylon's defeat (Jer 51:59–64). Ezekiel lay on his side, shaved his head and built models of the city of Jerusalem (Ezekiel 4–5). Even the death of his wife functioned as a kind of parable (Ezek 24:15–27). Hosea married a woman who had been (or would become) unfaithful (Hos 1:2). The prophets gave striking, symbolic names to their children (Isa 7:3, 8:1; Hos 1:4–9). Perhaps Australians can make sense of these by comparing them to political rallies where people wear symbolic colours, wave flags and even burn effigies. There may be value in making connections to performance artists. More and more Australians would be aware of performance artists like Mike Parr, who recently spent three days buried under a major road in Hobart. The trouble is, Australians tend to be a bit sceptical about artists and poets. I have dealt with this in a sermon on Ezekiel, which appears at the end of this chapter. In the sermon, I take on this sceptical voice as I role-play a monologue offered (fictitiously) by Ezekiel's brother-in-law.

Another major dimension of the prophets' communication techniques that will need explaining is the prophets' use of *imagery*. I can remember preaching on Jeremiah and becoming overwhelmed with how many metaphors he used within a small slice of text. In discussing exile and return, Jeremiah uses language of an unruly calf, a weeping woman, wearing a yoke, a persistent wound, a king like David, streams of water, a level path and so on. I self-consciously drew attention to the way we use metaphors, in the hope of helping my congregation feel confident with the poetry. I had pictures of an old rusted car and a slick red sports car to help people feel familiar with attaching emotions and significance to images. I used examples of metaphors gone wrong, which I had found online, to give my listeners a sense of mastery. Here's a portion of the script: Someone with an ear for clumsy phrases has heard people say the following. Can you notice what's wrong?

> We could stand here and talk until the cows turn blue. I wouldn't eat that with a ten-foot pole. I can read him like the back of my book …

I transitioned to the metaphor-rich text of Jeremiah by suggesting that Jeremiah was not a clumsy metaphor mixer but a prophet whose emotions were overwhelmed with the importance of what he had to say.

Another important device for preachers and listeners to be aware of is *parallelism*. This works at the level of individual verses, as well as for whole books. In Isaiah 42:6, for example, the Lord speaks to the servant and says, 'I will keep you and will make you to be a covenant for the people and a light for the Gentiles … ' Unpacking the meaning of this will mean deciding if the word 'people' has the same meaning as 'Gentiles' (synonymous parallelism) or whether there is an expansion from the 'people of Israel' to the 'Gentiles' (climactic parallelism). At the level of whole books, sometimes obscure passages take on a clearer meaning when one realises that there is a parallel text within the book that addresses a similar theme. It is possible, for example, that the unexpected story of Rechabites who do not drink wine (Jeremiah 35) offers an example of not drinking a literal cup *and* the symbolic cup of God's wrath (Jer 25:15–18).[5] David Dorsey suggests that most of the Old Testament books use parallelism to organise their structure, and often he discusses this in a way that clarifies the large movements of thought across the text. Australian listeners are often reasonably rehearsed in finding parallelism in literature, as it is a feature of television drama.[6] There is, of course, a danger in taking this too far. I suspect that overdoing literary analysis may alienate rather than illuminate congregations of Australians.

As we prepare sermons full of imaginative language, it is worth praying that the poetry touches something beyond the rational mind and engages hearts and wills.

The Contextualisation Task

God Does Not Change

Some of the most profound portraits we have of God are from the prophets. If we assume that God has not changed from the time of the prophets to today, there will be truth to preach that is immediately relevant to Australians. But, in the age of the New Atheism, speaking of God is not straightforward. The impressive complexity of the God we meet in the prophets is vital for Australians to grasp. Our culture seems to have adopted a thin vision of God – and then dismissed him as an undesirable constrictor of freedom or an unnecessary imaginary parent. In secular Australia, the New Atheist voices have been granted a high level of credibility. When one examines the God they don't believe in, however, the descriptions of God fall short of what is presented in Scripture. The prophets are well suited to be conversation partners with Australians on the matter of God. The prophets do not surrender to unbelief just because God eludes human comprehension. They urge loyalty to him while being honest about the strangeness – the otherness – of his ways.

The prophets are shocking in what they say, and their message can be one of judgement that can do nothing other than offend the listener. The God they present has been deemed 'the most unpleasant character in all fiction'.[7] Jeremiah laments that God is not always easy to live with (Jer 20:7–18). Habakkuk faces hard questions about God's inactivity in the face of human injustice (Hab 1:2–4). There are difficult tensions created by juxtaposing mercy for Nineveh in Jonah and judgement in Nahum. Ezekiel can speak shocking words that are almost pornographic.[8] The Lord's failed relationship to Israel is pictured in terms of seduction and violence in Ezekiel 16 and 23. God can seem thoroughly self-absorbed in Ezekiel, driven only by concern for his own glory (Ezek 36:22). The prophet Hosea is called to live out a dysfunctional family life that mirrors the deep dysfunction going on between God and his people. The people's appalling carelessness with the covenant elicits a bewildering swing of responses from the Lord. He will be a judging, menacing presence to them, like maggots and rottenness (Hos 5:12), a devouring lion (Hos 5:14), a fowler capturing his people in a net (Hos 7:12), an arsonist (Hos 8:14) and a baby-killer (Hos 9:12). In the same book, God's love is compared to that of a doting parent (Hos 11:1–4), a protecting lion (Hos 11:10) and a nest (Hos 11:11). Provocatively, Walter Brueggemann suggests that there is a similarity between the Lord and an abusive intimate partner.[9] God is far more complex than the god many Australians no longer believe in.

Alongside the disturbing claims, the prophets furnish us with some of the most moving and encouraging portraits of God. The book of Isaiah is famous for its grand poetry about God as creator and redeemer. The Lord is presented as a tender shepherd, as one who can help people to soar on eagles' wings and as a nursing mother who can never forget her baby (Isa 40:11, 31; 49:15). Jeremiah testifies to God's relentless faithfulness (Jer 31:35–37) and Ezekiel longs for the climactic privilege and blessing of the presence of God (Ezek 48:35). Often the Lord is pictured in imagery of growth, life and fertility. His compassion on even the animals in Nineveh is astounding. As the book of Zephaniah ends, the God who is mighty to save is also a God who sings over his people (Zeph 3:17). Isaiah is glad that God is strange, because he is not what we expect. His mercy exceeds what we imagine is possible (Isa 55:9).

In the Old Testament prophets, the message lunges from wrath to mercy with no explanation, leaving the reader confused and dismayed. The prophets have the challenge of testifying to the wrath and the mercy of God without the story of the cross of Christ to offer resolution. When the apostle Paul spoke of the foolishness of the cross, he was aware that it would not satisfy Jewish demands for power or a Greek preference for wisdom. Similarly, the jarring of judgement and mercy will not find an instant connection point with Australian values and stories. It is, necessarily, strange. While we have work to do as preachers in making our communication as skilled as possible, the prophets will not make the profound connection that they need to with Australians unless there is a deep work of the Spirit of God.

Sin Is Still Sin

Many of the dimensions of sin that trouble the prophets are captured in a sermon delivered by the prophet Jeremiah. It is worth quoting several verses.

> Do not trust in deceptive words and say, 'This is the temple of the LORD, the temple of the LORD, the temple of the LORD!'
>
> If you really change your ways and your actions and deal with each other justly, if you do not oppress the foreigner, the fatherless or the widow and do not shed innocent blood in this place, and if you do not follow other gods to your own harm, then I will let you live in this place, in the land I gave your ancestors for ever and ever. But look, you are trusting in deceptive words that are worthless.
>
> Will you steal and murder, commit adultery and perjury, burn incense to Baal and follow other gods you have not known, and then come and stand before me in this house, which bears my Name, and say, 'We are safe' – safe to do all these detestable things? (Jer 7:4–10).

Jeremiah perceptively links theological impulses, such as loss of trust in the Lord and idolatry, with social ills, such as theft, murder and idolatry. Australians, in contrast, tend to explain social problems as arising from a lack of education or poor mental health. Jeremiah expects faithful people to treat vulnerable people well. Australians struggle with how to balance this vision with sensible self-interest. The prophets take issue with people who are affluent and self-indulgent. Australians may feel insulted. When the prophets are outraged by idolatry, Australians may feel that this is irrelevant until the dynamics of idolatry are explored: ancient idolatry grew out of human fear and anxiety, a desire for mastery and accommodation to the worldview of others.

The preacher addressing an Australian congregation can connect the portraits of sin to Australian Christians by asking what the new covenant expectations are for Christian behaviour. It will often be possible to find that the specific sin named by the ancient prophet is reiterated in the preaching of Jesus or the instructions of the apostles.

The preacher addressing an Australian congregation may be able to draw connections to Australian society on the grounds that human beings have not really changed, while being careful not to ignore the unique covenant demands that inform the prophets. The book of Amos, in a stirring rhetorical move, adds another strand to the contextualisation task by addressing the world beyond Israel and Judah. Amos claims that Gaza will be judged for capturing people and selling them (Amos 1:6); Tyre, too, for selling communities of people, disregarding 'a treaty of brotherhood' (Amos 1:9); Edom, Ammon and Moab come under censure for dehumanising and cruel actions. Admittedly, this serves to persuade Israel and Judah of the importance of his message. The persuasion, though, depends on there being a reality to the prophet's claims. God the creator of all human beings expresses his intent to make all humanity accountable. This is important for applying the prophetic vision to social and political life today. Brueggemann has proposed:

> This rhetoric permits Israel to enunciate the claim that under the aegis of Yahweh's sovereignty, there is a kind of international law or code of human standards that seems to anticipate the Helsinki Accords of 1975 in a rough way, a code that requires every nation to act in civility and humaneness toward others. Any affront of this standard is taken to be an act of autonomy, arrogance and self-sufficiency, which flies in the face of Yahweh's governance. Thus, Yahweh is the guarantor, not only of Israel, but of the nations in their treatment of each other.[10]

Taking Amos as our guide, there is some scope to apply the prophets' denouncements of sin to Australians in general. Australian history – including the history of the Australian church – has not always expressed the values of the prophets when dealing with the vulnerable and the outsider. There can be a harshness and fear that leads to inhumane treatment of First Nations Australians, migrants and refugees. Beyond Amos, the prophets' preaching against the nations focuses on the human sin of pride. The Australian veneration of individual freedom and choice, even at the expense of the other, may well fall under their critique.

Intriguingly, discussions of sin in the prophets assume a collectivist point of view. The 'characters' in their books are, by and large, groups: Israel, Judah, Jerusalem, Assyria, Egypt, Cush, Babylon and other nations. Collectivism may have been a tacit assumption of the prophets and their audiences but, still, the prophets were able to contend with some of the faulty assumptions and inferences that collectivist thinking can bring. People in Israel and Judah could see themselves as privileged and protected, especially in comparison to the nations who were not descendants of Abraham and children of the exodus. Amos, Jonah, Isaiah, Jeremiah and Malachi all insist that this is a distortion. On the other hand, collectivist thinking could lead to a sense of helpless determinism. As invading armies marched in, it would be easy to think that personal choices were immaterial. In this context, it is vital to note that Jeremiah and Ezekiel saw a connection between hope and individual responsibility. The prophets saw that repentant individuals would form remnant communities even in the midst of large-scale acts of divine judgement.

Unlike the prophets, the Australian preacher will need to start with a sense of individualism and expose the weaknesses of it. The preacher will need congregations to see how thoroughly individualism has taken hold of the Australian imagination. Recent discussions of both the political right and left suggest that border protection, economic rationalism, sexual liberation and the right to define one's identity are among our most pressing concerns. These can be construed as a valuing of individual rights and choice. The effect of our choices on our families, suburbs, towns and natural environments falls out of political view.[11] The theme of being fellow human beings is too rarely explored. Importantly, we Australians now want to investigate the absence of the common good in our practices in banking and aged care.

Christian preachers could try to connect Australian individualism to the gospel. There is a popular tradition of thinking of the Old Testament as collectivist and the Christian gospel as individualistic. In this paradigm, Jeremiah and Ezekiel speak of a new, individualist covenant. This arises, however, from too simple a reading of the new covenant texts in the prophets and also from insufficiently noticing God's engagement with households and churches in salvation (Acts 16:30–34) and judgement (Rev 1:9–3:22) in the New Testament era. Both Old and New Testaments cannot be reduced just to collectivism or just to individualism. But the assumption of collectivism in the prophets and the assumption of individualism in Australians will mean that preachers must work carefully to bring horizons together.

Judgement Still Matters

For the prophets, to talk of sin was to talk also of judgement. This need not be beyond the grasp of the Australian imagination. The covenants of God bear witness to a good ordering of Israel as a microcosm of the creation. Australian society's rule-based nature (see the 'Describing Australians' chapter) can be used as a way into seeing that the prophets' exposure of sin and insistence on judgement serves good order. When preaching on Zephaniah 1, I was struck by how relentless the portrayals of judgement were and thought that Australian listeners would not connect with the text. I tried to reach for the sense of good order that Australians currently find in clear rules about food hygiene and gun control. I asked my congregation to look at Zephaniah 1 by looking inside their refrigerators:

> What do you do when you're cleaning up after dinner and you notice a good two centimetres of cheese sauce at the bottom of the saucepan? Well, you find a small container and self-righteously put it in the fridge, ready for the next time you cook corned beef. What about when strawberries are only a dollar or two for a punnet? Well, you stack them up in your trolley with dreams of strawberry smoothies for breakfast and strawberries and cream for dessert.
>
> What do you do three weeks later? When there are bluey-grey dots all over your cheese sauce and your strawberries have grown furry white beards? You can push these things to the back and shut the fridge door or you can face up, clean up and throw out. Facing up, cleaning up and throwing out are what the Old Testament prophets are all about.
>
> Zephaniah is a book with some of the most tender and beautiful language about God's love for his people but that's not how it starts … or at least not in an obvious

way. So, today's sermon is thoroughly about the fact that God is a judge. I hope you can read Zephaniah, though, and say, God is a judge: thank God for that.

Zephaniah moves between pictures of judgement on the whole world and judgement on Judah. We're going to think about two reasons why he does that. And we're going to look at the place of the judgement of God in our lives as Christians today.

But first: let's get our bearings.

The reign of Josiah was very late in the history of Judah just a little before Jerusalem would fall to Babylon. He was a godly king, associated with important reforms: getting rid of other gods, getting people focused on the temple again, taking the words of Moses seriously.

Despite all this, Zephaniah presents a pretty sickening picture of Judah, maybe because some of Zephaniah's preaching was before the reforms really kicked in. Then again, maybe Zephaniah preaches during or after the reforms but still presents a rotting picture of Judah because he could see more deeply than a political program.

You know, you can clean up your fridge and get all your little jars lined up neatly in the doors of the fridge, but the jars of jam and the jars of olives might not be in a good state. The kings of Judah could get all the jars in order, but the prophets took the lids off and looked for the furry white mould, the things that were going rotten in people's hearts and minds and wills.

In the reign of a reforming king, Zephaniah brings us shocking poetry about God's plans to judge the whole world. Look at verses 2 and 3:

> I will sweep away everything
> from the face of the earth,
> > declares the LORD.
>
> I will sweep away both man and beast;
> > I will sweep away the birds in the sky
> > > and the fish in the sea –
> > > and the idols that cause the wicked to stumble.

It's like Noah's flood, but this time no animal will survive, not even the fish. It's like God is pressing 'rewind' on his whole creation. Chapter 1 ends with the same idea. Consider verse 17:

> I will bring such distress on all people
>> that they will grope about like those who are blind,
>> because they have sinned against the LORD.
>
> Their blood will be poured out like dust
>> and their entrails like dung.
>
> Neither their silver nor their gold
>> will be able to save them
>> on the day of the LORD'S wrath.

When your strawberries have their furry beards and your white sauce is white and blue and grey, why do you drop them in the bin? Well, you know that mould, and the bacteria that may well be growing with it, can have a dreadful impact on your breathing, your immune system. The cheap but mouldy strawberries could leave you with vomiting and diarrhoea. You don't want that for you or for anyone in your household, and so you do good by sweeping them away.

We live in a time when we easily fall into simplistic ways of understanding the judgement of God. The God who judges in the OT prophets has been described as jealous and petty, impulsive and violent because of passages like Zephaniah 1, but surely that's too quick a reaction. You can do good by facing up, cleaning up and throwing out. You can do good by sweeping away.

You know, sometimes refrigeration serves solemn purposes beyond preserving our punnets of strawberries. In April 1996, the morgue refrigerators in Port Arthur Tasmania suddenly had to deal with thirty-five dead bodies because of a young man and a gun. In the months that followed, around 700,000 fire arms were surrendered by the Australian public and our politicians crafted stricter gun laws. The gunman was charged and imprisoned. The authorities acted to judge, not because they were petty, impulsive and violent but because something seriously wrong had happened. To judge was to defend and value life. You can show love and care as you face up, clean up and sweep away.

God is a judge. Thank God for that.

Australians spend a lot of time judging bachelors, home renovators and aspiring chefs on reality TV shows. Judgement can express a commitment to truth, beauty and goodness and perhaps the Australian love of rules and order shows an unexpected commitment to holding humanity to account.

Another Australian angle on judgement may be our identification with the underdog. While being regulated is the Australian way, we still hang on to the notion that we are a nation of larrikins. We have a sense of connection with the Bradbury way of winning gold medals. We sing of a thief who throws himself into a billabong rather than surrendering freedom. In a way, the prophets are anti-establishment underdogs, whose lives are experienced through the judgemental gaze of others. Australians may find this a valuable way into grasping the gospel that is foreshadowed in the prophets' words and lives.

The prophets position themselves not just as preachers of judgement but also as people who . There is a profound thought at work when one reads across the prophetic books. The prophets feel the weight and sadness of judgement (Isa 24:16b) and question whether justice is working out fairly (Hab 1:2; Jer 12:1). They themselves become the victims of human judgement (Jer 20:2). Their life stories mirror the pain that sin causes to God (Hosea and Ezekiel). Their bodies come to symbolise the pain of judgement (Isa 50:6). And an anonymous servant-prophet seems to suffer as a substitute for others (Isa 53:5). It may be possible to frame the prophets as underdog heroes and so create a connection point for Australian listeners. Postmoderns, who are suspicious of raw power, may also identify with this dimension of the prophets.

Most strangely, and especially in Isaiah, the underdog has a kingly and exalted quality (Isa 52:13, 53:12). We are caused to wonder if the formidable God identifies with the suffering of the humiliated prophet.[12] The prophets' presentations of judgement prepare the way for the Christian good news about Jesus.

Transformation Can Include Us

The prophets knew that the God of Israel was really the God of all the nations. Australian preachers can interpret the days we are living in – days when even Cush, Tyre, Egypt and Assyria participate in true worship of God (see Isa 18:7, 19:24–25, 23:17–18). Isaiah knew that the islands would put their hope in the servant and the justice he would achieve (Isa 42:4). Given this eschatological program, Australians can find themselves in the prophets.

That is not to say that Australian understandings of how things are transformed match the vision of the prophets. The Australian worldview positions human beings as agents who exercise control over the physical environment. This is not always a rational belief. People die in Australian floods and fires. The evening news, however, always assures us that some brave volunteers will sort everything out. Even when some Australians propose that environmental degradation is *human* in origin, the story we tell ourselves is that human science and technology will fix things. We work with similar assumptions about human resourcefulness in our health and education programs.

The prophets see reality differently. They point to God as the only dependable source of hope. Human wisdom and strength, military exercises and political manoeuvres all come under prophetic critique when they are pursued in place of God. At times, the prophets move into an apocalyptic mode of thinking that accents the hopelessness of human enterprise. They hope for a day when the world will end, and a new creation will begin. Australian preachers will need to point out how countercultural this is.

Despair about human efficacy is an important message in contexts where human resources have come to replace any need to trust in God. To be responsible to the Bible's broad teaching, however, preachers will need to offer a nuanced account of the valid place of wisdom and technology when these things are accepted as the gift of a kind creator, not as products of human autonomy. In a sermon on the radical trust that Isaiah asked of the people of Jerusalem, I tried to synthesise the Old Testament perspectives of wisdom (human skill is important) and apocalyptic prophecy (human effort is futile):

> Your brakes are squeaking. You pray: Lord, help me to include you in this experience.
>
> You ring a mechanic and book the car in. You pray: Lord, thank you for all the stability and peace in our society that the phone lines work and the mechanic has skill and that I have money to pay for this. You pick up your repaired car. You pray: Thank you for your involvement in this in ways that I can't even see. And who knows the countless ways you might sense God's presence and care in this experience?
>
> When I imagine that scene playing out, I get a picture of a person who is calm and kind of good to be around. Because they have a thankfulness about them that gives hope and contentment.

A picture of a calm and hopeful person would be attractive to Australians, many of whom will have stories to tell of anxiety and depression robbing themselves and their families of calmness and hope. I know that the images of intimate relationship and magnificent redemption in the book of Isaiah have been favourite resting places in my own times of troubled emotional life. Perhaps Australians can come to develop a love for the transformed creation in the context of mental health challenges. If negative emotions are fuelled by fear, it is important to realise that the prophets contrast military invasions and cosmic destruction with many pictures of safety and flourishing.

Isaiah knows that the Lord can be a refuge, offering water in the desert and making trees clap their hands. Jeremiah sees an end to tears and knows that it is worth buying land because of a safe future. Ezekiel pictures a triumphant defeat of the enemies of God and a future held safe by the glory and presence of God; the new creation will be impregnable since God's presence at its very centre (Ezekiel 38–48). Hosea imagines experiencing God as life-giving dew (Hos 14:5) and Joel, too, offers images of pouring rain and even the pouring out of God's Spirit (Joel 2:23, 28). Amos speaks of an agricultural abundance and homecoming (Amos 9:13–15). Obadiah pictures a kingdom of the saved

(Obadiah 21). Jonah testifies to scandalous mercy (Jon 4:11). Micah pictures a future of farming, not war, and of settled life with no reason for fear (Mic 4:2–5). Nahum knows that the war-makers cannot endure (Nah 3:19). Habakkuk finds reason to rejoice in God, even in troubled times (Hab 3:17–18). Zephaniah pictures homecoming song and celebration (Zeph 3:14–20). Haggai, Zechariah and Malachi are certain that God has his kingly, priestly and prophetic agents who will guarantee the Lord's good purposes (Hag 2:23; Zech 3:8; Mal 4:4). This is the kind of news Australians need to hear.

The preacher of the prophets has a challenge to connect another period of salvation history, ancient geography and politics and unusual literary techniques to Australian listeners. But the prophets will be a way of offering some of the Bible's deepest portrayals of God and most profound critiques of individualism. Their teachings about judgement and transformation match some of our deepest longings. To borrow again from the song, *The Word*, we need to trust that the prophets' madness can make us wise. We need to pray that the prophets' foolish, radical faith will capture and then recapture us again.

Sample Sermon: Ezekiel

Comment on the Sermon

My understanding of the rhetoric of the book of Ezekiel is that the reader is meant to grow into a sense of shame and responsibility for the exile. The sign acts are meant to achieve this effect. Ezekiel's brother-in-law experiences this, and by presenting him as a first-person voice speaking in a colloquial tone, I am hoping to give the congregation this same sense of discovery.

Sermon Text

My sister is dead. We weren't expecting it. She was only thirty-one. You can go and see her body if you like. It's still there in Ezekiel's house, cold and grey. And that husband of hers says we're not having a funeral. He's dressed in his usual clothes. He has done his hair. He doesn't want our wailing songs, our prayers. Nothing. Now, I know that we're in exile. I know that some people have given up on all our Judean songs and ceremonies. You can't sing the Lord's song in a strange land, they say. But not even for a funeral?

Oh, it gets worse. We're exiles over here in Babylon. And we've just got news that Nebuchadnezzar's army has done the impossible. They've got into Jerusalem. They've got into the temple. It wasn't that long ago that Yahweh killed as Assyrian army who tried to take Jerusalem. Those were the days … when we had real prophets like Isaiah. We've just had that crazy Jeremiah telling us to give in to Nebuchadnezzar … and all the carrying on of my weird brother-in-law, Ezekiel. I don't know what's worse: Jerusalem, our dear Jerusalem – I don't want to picture those pagan soldiers and what they're doing to our holy city! My sister, my dear, dear sister – I don't want to picture her lying dead with no funeral!

If I'm going to be honest, the last five or six years have been really strange for all of us. The Babylonians have worked out a clever way of crippling a culture. They packed up a lot of us from Jerusalem and brought us way over here. Families have been split up. Our plans for our futures are in tatters. And then ... and then ... things started to go funny with Ezekiel.

It was around the time of his thirtieth birthday, when he should have been becoming a priest. He reckoned that he had seen God one day. He tried to describe it to us: wheels and eyes and thrones. But he didn't tend to use words to communicate with us. It's like he's turned into Marcel Marceau or something. He really got into this whole mime thing. I don't know if you've been to those art galleries where people vomit up paint and hang themselves with hooks. Well, it was like Ezekiel had turned into one of those weird performance artists. But this wasn't a biennale here! We were in a camp for exiles. This is not Venice. Although, we are living near a big canal.

One day Ezekiel found a lump of flat clay – a brick that hadn't been sun baked yet – and in the soft surface he started drawing a map. A few of us were there trying to console my sister about her husband going strange. He drew a map of Jerusalem and, before we could get too nostalgic, He made little clay models of siege ramps, battering rams and camps of soldiers. We got the idea: one day Jerusalem would be under siege.

Then he went and got a big flat griddle from the kitchen. I guessed he was going to flatten the models he'd made of those invading soldiers. Yahweh likes to do that sort of thing for us 'cause we're his chosen people. But he did something else instead. He put the pan like a wall and then he positioned himself behind the wall like he was out of reach of the city.

He didn't explain what he was doing, and I found myself thinking about it for days. If Ezekiel had seen God, as the rumours were saying, did he position himself in God's place in the model? Was he trying to tell us that one day God would remove himself from Jerusalem, that he would abandon his city and let the invading soldiers in?

And then he got some rope and pulled it around himself and lay on his left side without a word. We stood and watched and waited and watched and waited, till after about half an hour we were sort of annoyed and bored at the same time and we just went home. What a ridiculous thing to do! Tie yourself up with ropes and then lie on your side next to a model of a city. I could see the strain in my sister's face. What was Ezekiel thinking?

Next day, after work, Ezekiel didn't eat the meal my sister had made him. And she's not a bad cook. I mean, things aren't flash for us in Babylon, but Ezekiel acted like things are worse than they really are. He meticulously measured out some wheat and barley. He got some scales and portioned out some millet and spelt. Then he did it all again with some beans and lentils, and he measured out some water, about enough to fill an old milk bottle. Ezekiel's not into fad diets or anything. There's never been any suspicion of anorexia or bulimia. But here he was, limiting himself to war rations.

He made a little damper mix and – like you do – started to get a fire ready. And here came the surprise. We'd normally get leaves and twigs and some logs, but he got a handful of cow manure. Now I admit that we hadn't been quite as kosher with our Jewish food laws in Babylon but Ezekiel – Ezekiel! A man from a family of priests! – I mean, really, what was he doing, cooking his food on manure?

This was strange enough. But he did it the next day. And the next. Some of my mates started to keep a calendar. Twenty days, thirty days, a hundred days … In the end we counted 390 days when Ezekiel would silently lie on his left side, 390 days of eating war rations cooked to become unclean – and then there were forty days when Ezekiel lay down on his right side.

My poor sister! Watching her husband act so miserably for so long, more than a year of this … We didn't want to eat at their house any more in case the food tasted like – well, you know – and we were getting sick of Mr Misery-Guts Ezekiel.

Still, some of my friends were talking: 390 days – he definitely did 390 days. It must mean something. Well, I'd been thinking about it too, and 390 days was a pretty good match to the number of years from the glorious King Solomon to now. It was like Ezekiel was paying a fine. For every year of the life of our nation, there was a corresponding time of pain and imprisonment. And when he did the forty days on the other side, we couldn't help but think of the forty-day flood in the days of Noah. And the time when our people roamed in the desert for forty years as God's punishment until a generation had died.

Maybe he was saying that there would be a generation who would be punished … you know, I think a lot about that as I long for my life back home and as I spend day after day surrounded by Babylonians who speak a different language and who don't understand us. Are we that generation? Is this the judgement of God?

Well, if we were in any doubt, Mr Show-Off Ezekiel had something else for us to see! He'd somehow gotten himself a big sword – don't ask me how he did it – and he wasn't looking his best. He'd lost weight, his hair and beard were all straggly, and with just a few people watching, he flashed this ridiculous sword around and started to hack off his own hair.

The people called out to passers-by, who sent their kids to get other neighbours, and before long there was a crowd watching Ezekiel humiliate himself as he hacked and cut clumsily with his sword, shaving off all his hair and his beard. He looked a mess: little bleeding nicks here and there and his shiny scalp. But what made us feel repulsed was watching a priest do this ... Why must Ezekiel keep making holy things unholy?

And still he wasn't finished. He had some scales, and in his obsessional way, he began to measure the weight of his hair and whiskers. He took a third of it and with a startling fizzle dropped it into his cooking fire. You can picture the sudden burst of light and get a whiff of that offensive smell of singeing hair. He took a third and tossed it in the air and swiped at it furiously with his sword. The last third he threw high so that the wind could sweep it away.

We watched, feeling hopeless, as his hair scattered and was lost, because we could see that his hair represented us – God's people now under God's judgement.

But you know what hair and whiskers are like. There were still a few around and Ezekiel gathered them up. It reminded me of how Isaiah would always talk about a remnant, how when God judges, he always saves a few ... like Noah. But then, in an act that made me mad and frightened all at once, Ezekiel took the few stray hairs he was holding and dismissed them to the fire, too.

We stood completely silent. Three hundred and ninety years of history and then siege and fire, sword and scattering. Is this what being in Babylon means? The end of 390 years of history? This dreadful sense that God was punishing and scattering ...

Ezekiel would later speak God's words to us:

I will make you a ruin and a reproach among the nations

You will be a reproach and a taunt

a warning and an object of horror

to the nations around you

when I inflict punishment on you in anger and in wrath and with stinging rebuke.

There was Ezekiel ... my own brother-in-law, skinny and starved, a defiled humiliated priest, a shameful figure. At the time, I wondered if he'd just sit in the ashes and die.

But the years have gone by, and now it's my sister's turn to be the performance piece in this absurd theatre that Yahweh is producing. It's my sister now: cold and grey, lifeless and hard, and Ezekiel shaming us again. By refusing a funeral, by not singing the laments, by getting dressed and tidied up like nothing has happened.

And news today is that the Babylonians have got into Jerusalem. I can just imagine them grabbing gold from the temple. Soldiers with swords and flames, screaming people and buildings eaten up by flames. I can see the charred city, cold and black, lifeless and empty.

Don't talk to me about shame. It's all around me.

This is what it means to be God's chosen people? Weren't we meant to be a priestly nation?

Weren't we meant to be the glorious point of meeting between God and all the families of the earth? But look at us. Look at Jerusalem. It's like we've been starved and attacked. Our head has been shaved and we're sitting with bloody sores, looking stupid. Our life has been taken away. My sister is not the only one who's dead.

I think I know why Ezekiel doesn't want a funeral. He wants us to own up to something ...

We've been killing Jerusalem for 390 years. We've put up with worshipping Yahweh – and Molech and Baal and the Queen of Heaven. We've argued with each other about Moses' laws, but we've done too little for the people those laws love: the alien, the widow, the orphan.

You know what we've done? We've broken God's heart. I can see it now; I can feel it now. In all of Ezekiel's pain and sadness we're meant to be seeing Yahweh's pain and sadness. But, why me? Why Ezekiel, why my sister?

Yahweh, the one who lives forever, what do you know about what we're going through here? Sure, sin may break your heart ... but you're not going to feel what it's like to go into exile. You're not ever going to feel like a stranger. You're never going to know what it's like to be surrounded by soldiers who tease you and poke at you with their spears. Yahweh, the one who lives forever, you're not ever going to know what it feels like to die.

I left the questions hanging in this sermon. The prophets poignantly train us to expect that one day the Lord will personally know the experiences of exile, torture and death. Perhaps this is the strangest message of them all.

8
PREACHING NEW TESTAMENT NARRATIVE TO AUSTRALIANS
Tim Patrick

Introduction

Passages of New Testament narrative are often preached as though the narrative does not really matter. There are two primary expressions of this error. The first is when individual passages are preached in abstraction, removed from the overarching narrative. The second is when individual passages of narrative are preached without sympathy for – or perhaps even consciousness of – the fact that the narrative form is significant to the text achieving its intended purpose.

In this chapter we will consider both of these concerns, and we will especially consider how the narrative form found in the Gospels and Acts supplies important cues for how those texts should be preached to modern Australians.

The Hermeneutical Task

It is all too common for preachers to disregard the overarching narrative from which a given short passage of text has been extracted. This is clearly displayed when churches deliver sermon series with titles such as 'The Parables of Jesus', or 'Different Responses to the Gospel', or 'The Apostles' Speeches in the Book of Acts', and which are made up of sermons on individual texts that have no natural macro-narratival connection to each other. In these cases, the preacher has invented (or copied) a synthetic category for their sermon series, then populated it with texts freely lifted from their places within larger narratives. In doing this, the individual texts are severed from their critical contexts, the overarching story disrespected and cast aside in favour of a preferred new arrangement for biblical revelation – almost as though the preacher has better ideas about how God's word should be packaged than God himself! This disrespect is perhaps even more stark in that occasional piece: the one-off sermon drawn from a short passage of biblical narrative.

The practice is problematic, because narrative is not only a style of writing (contra, say, poetry or apocalyptic) but also supplies *book-level structure*. This means that the New Testament's narrative books, the four Gospels and Acts, can only be fully understood when each is approached as a coherent whole. Conversely, each subsection or short passage in these books can only be properly understood when taken in its intended place in the full narrative. Every narratival work has a start, a middle and an end, through which it progresses linearly (even when the storyline is not chronological) and meaningfully. And every individual part is important to the whole, as the whole is important to every part.[1] To take short passages of biblical narrative out of their book-level context is akin to reading a selection of chapters from a novel but never reading the whole work from cover to cover, or like watching a number of scenes clipped from a film without ever sitting through the work in its entirety. In these cases, while it may be possible to get some sense of the author's or producer's intentions and a taste for their values, the integrity of the original work is damaged, and there is considerable risk that the major purpose of the whole work may be missed.

Given this, the first lesson for preaching New Testament narrative is a simple one: preach through each book from start to finish, chapter and verse, in order. Begin a preaching series on Luke's Gospel at Luke 1:1 and finish it at Luke 24:53. Start Acts at Acts 1:1 and conclude at Acts 28:31. Of course, this will mean having to plan for long preaching series (or even series of series), but if we want to be true to these texts, which were inscripturated as meaningfully coherent wholes, this is work worth embracing. To do anything less would be to abandon the full narrative and preach something other than what was given. The Gospels and Acts make best and proper sense as complete works and should be treated as such by those entrusted with expounding them.[2]

Moving beyond this macro-level consideration, the second way that we preachers commonly mishandle New Testament narrative is by failing to preach each individual passage of narrative *as narrative*. This may be because we have adopted the too-common practice of preaching every text as though it were a Pauline epistle. The standard preacher training model seems to presume that all texts are essentially repositories of facts and arguments, and that the preacher's job is to distil those facts before arguing for them again, clearly and faithfully – ideally with an anecdotal introduction, a few fresh illustrations from pop culture or personal experience and an imperative application. While this model may suit some texts (and it may not, in fact, actually suit many of the Pauline epistles), it will not serve for all. In particular, it will not serve for narrative. To treat narrative as though it were simply a source for propositions misunderstands the genre and will also prevent the text from doing much of what it was intended to do.

Before turning to examine what *are* the purposes of New Testament narrative, however, it is helpful to briefly consider approaches to genre within Scripture more generally.

Genre in General

Some preachers address genre as though it were a kind of literary code that needs to be cracked, or a distraction to be dealt with, before a text will give up the otherwise partially obscured underlying meanings that are the reader's primary interest. Others treat genre as an artistic flourish, whimsically chosen by the author for the sake of style – or perhaps to inject some variety into the Scriptures in order to prove to subsequent generations that its human authors were real individuals with their own personalities and situations. In both of these cases, genre is acknowledged but considered to be of no final consequence to the text's meaning.[3] Of course, this is an old-fashioned misunderstanding of what genre is and does; to preach narrative (or indeed, any text) well, we need a better view.

Genre is now widely recognised as being essential to the purpose of a text.[4] The medium may not ultimately be the message, but messages are completely inseparable from their media, and genre is the top-level category for media.[5] It is genre that constrains subject matter, suggests vocabulary and determines the broad form of a text; through setting these kinds of parameters, a text's genre uniquely enables that text to accomplish its author's purpose.[6] Moreover, each genre achieves things that other genres cannot (and cannot achieve things that others can).[7] A graphic novel can grow young readers in their capacity to endure long texts, but it cannot effectively communicate the result of yesterday's sporting fixtures. A scientific paper can report the percentage of aluminium in a certain type of synthetic mineral, but it cannot tell someone how much we love them. A legal contract can establish the terms of a business relationship, but it will not be useful as a record of our reflections from our recent holiday.[8] In each of these cases, we know intuitively that form, or genre, is closely tied to purpose, and the same is true for the different forms or genres of the different books of Bible. Therefore, the need to preach narrative *as narrative* is again clear: if we do not, we risk losing the ability to communicate the full meaning, and to achieve the intended purposes, of the passage.

Narrative Genre

Like all other genres, narrative has its own defining characteristics, through which it achieves distinct purposes.[9] To 'narrate' is to tell a story, and stories are recognised by their language, settings, characters, themes and unfolding plotlines. It is when we recognise and follow these features that the narrative begins to have its effect upon us.

The first purpose of narrative is to 'create worlds' for us to mentally enter into (as listeners and readers).[10] Narratives paint particular scenes and populate them with particular people, ideas and tensions that we are meant to engage with or even 'live through' as we read.[11] Thus, when we only try to 'crack the narrative code' in order to extract general facts or doctrines, we risk losing this primary purpose, even if we have a measure of success in determining some of the author's underlying convictions. But the author is not just delivering facts; they are showing us how certain facts, doctrines, ideas and convictions manifest in the lives of particular people, in particular circumstances, as they inhabit a particular world.[12] And through doing this, the narrative works to create and shape whole worldviews that transcend whatever points of abstract information may be possible to discern from the text. Doctrines do not just hide behind the narrative waiting to be discovered, but rather are there in order that they might be witnessed as they are played out in a given set of circumstances.

So, for example, the story of Jesus raising the widow's son in Luke 7:11–17 is not just a convenient literary vehicle for establishing the general truths that Christ is compassionate and powerful. It is a story that shows how Christ's compassion and power were expressed in one instance of great sorrow. It is an example of the truth in live human action, not truth in abstract proposition buried in an incidental story. Here is a chance to see doctrines uniquely expressed within the particular plot circumstances of a deliberately presented narrative, and as we witness this, our understanding of the doctrines is filled out and thickened up. New Testament narrative therefore helps us see that even black-and-white absolute truths – which it does not deny – are found in a world of colours (and even greys). In that world, the light of truth is reflected and refracted differently in different situations.

Beyond creating these colourful worlds and inviting readers into them, the second purpose of narrative is to call its audience to take a moral or convictional position. That is, the reader is not only imaginatively drawn into the world of the text but is also encouraged to adopt and own a certain point of view on its people and events, and indeed to look at the whole of the narrative's world from a certain perspective.[13]

This end is largely achieved by the narrator, who controls the reader's perspective, 'taking sides' in the world by casting certain characters as virtuous and others as evil, or presenting situations, events and outcomes as either positive or negative.[14] And the narrator has great power to do this. Unlike the forensic chronicler, they can throw selective light and shade on different aspects of the world and disclose the hidden thoughts, intentions and motives of the people in the story.[15] Because of this, we readers gain a privileged understanding of the narrative world and can even have a greater sense of pathos for the story's characters than is possible for other characters in the text to have. To be sure, our special insight comes at the cost of submitting to narratival bias, but this is not a shortcoming of the narrative genre so much as its clear purpose: to establish readers in a certain stance within the world of the text.[16]

New Testament Narratives

The New Testament narratives are also *historical* narratives. This means that they do not just tell us *any* kind of stories but rather present stories about the truth of the past. Historical narratives are therefore able to advance the two purposes of narratives in two other ways.

Firstly, rather than merely 'creating' worlds for us to imagine, they present the *real world* that we already live in, albeit often at a different time, in a different place and with different experiences.[17] Given this, it can be far easier for us to 'enter' the world of the historical narrative as we read. We do not need to suspend reality; instead, we can draw on our existing knowledge and experience of reality to help us. Unlike a work of fantasy or science fiction, we do not need to learn a whole new set of rules in order to imagine ourselves into the text's world. While the context may be very different to our own, the laws of physics are the same, the laws of human nature are the same, the human condition is the same and the global metanarrative is the same.

Secondly, because the 'world' of the historical narrative is the real world, these texts go beyond merely encouraging us to adopt a certain perspective *within* the story to calling us to view the real world with that same lens. In a sense, we are meant to continue inhabiting something of the New Testament world when we have left the New Testament narrative. The authors do not have the limited goal of only absorbing us into the world of the text for its own sake. They have the more comprehensive aim of thoroughly soaking us in a worldview, in order that we might then continue living at all times in the real world by that worldview.[18]

At this point, it is worth asking if readers ought to be forewarned about these agendas of historical narratives. After all, it could be possible that some authors have a devious desire to imbue us with an enduring *immoral* worldview – and that they have used the persuasive power of historical narratives to do so. Two simple responses can be given with regard to the New Testament narratives. The first is simply that they have no covert agenda, no secret to keep. At various points they unashamedly make their own persuasive intentions explicit (e.g., Matt 28:19–20; John 20:30–31; Acts 26:27–29); the writers' motives are not hidden but highlighted.[19] The second is that, through a well-worked doctrine of inspiration, we know that these texts have God as their primary co-author, working in, through, above and behind the human authors.[20] Given that God and his purposes are fundamentally good, it follows that it is good to adopt the view of the world that he desires us to adopt and that it is good for us to engage with the world in the way that he wants us to engage. Christians – or people who are spiritually open to the faith – do not enter into reading the New Testament with suspicion but with excitement, keen for the chance to grow in their ability to see through God's eyes and to participate in his story.

This leads directly to our final point on understanding New Testament narrative. Just as historical narrative takes us further than other narrative by giving us the point of contact between the world of the text and the real world, biblical narrative takes us further again. The God whom we encounter in the narrative is the same God we relate to in our personal devotions and disciplines. This means that biblical narrative does not just inform a worldview that is to be lived in the world, it gives a theology that is meant to be carried into our personal relationships with God, other people and the whole creation. And in the New Testament narrative, it is not a generic god the reader meets in the text, nor even merely the God of Old Testament Israel, but the three persons of the Trinity. The Gospels usher the reader into the world of Jesus and let them 'get to know him personally' by following him around, hearing his words and witnessing his works. And the book of Acts does the same with the Spirit, working in and through the Apostles. (Of course, the Father and the Spirit are also met in the Gospel narratives, just as the name of Christ is writ large across Acts.) Thus, through the New Testament narratives, and of course the inner illuminating work of the Holy Spirit, each reader meets Jesus Christ, and through the Son they can come to know the Father. Growing this personal, relational knowledge of God is the ultimate purpose of these parts of the Scripture.

The Contextualisation Task

Preaching New Testament Narrative

Our understanding of the nature and purpose of New Testament narrative has significant implications for how we preach those texts. Perhaps the most important is that we, as preachers, need to work hard to draw listeners into the text and its world. This notion is in stark contrast to much of the common practice of preaching the Gospels and Acts, which sees the readers *taken away from* the text and its world. As noted already, this can happen if we effectively disregard the narrative as narrative, focusing instead on extracting and arguing points of doctrine. While it would be going too far to say that sermons on the Gospels and Acts should never mention doctrines or universal truths that are clearly of importance to the narrative, this approach alone will never achieve all that the authors intended from their texts. To preach biblical narrative well, the congregation should be taken *into* and *through* the text itself as part of the sermon. Highlighting major doctrinal paradigms at play in the story ought to happen as part of bringing the story to life, not by changing the sermon into a kind of scholastic theology lecture.[21]

Another way that preachers take their listeners away from the narrative instead of into it is by recasting the story using contemporary parallels and illustrations. An example of this would be if a preacher made a comparison between Jesus entering the temple to teach during the Festival of Booths (John 7:14) and a street preacher stepping up onto their soap-box during market day in the congregation's local town. The intention in this type of illustration is to bring the listeners closer to the event or tone of the text by using something known in their own experience (preaching at the market) to give a sense for something foreign in the passage (teaching in the temple during festival). The preacher may feel that there are enough helpful parallels to merit the comparison, but they must recognise that there will also be many significant differences too: the temple did not have soft drinks, nor pop music, nor men and women co-mingling throughout, nor a stall advertising the local mosque. While any one of these differences between the text and the illustration may only be superficial, the real problem is that when the preacher talks about the local marketplace, the scene imagined by the congregation is not the scene narrated in the text. In the sermon illustrated this way, the congregation does not enter as much into the world of first-century Jerusalem where they can 'meet' Jesus and have their worldview shaped and readied for their return to daily living. Instead of being taken to that different time and place, they are taken somewhere that is already part of their daily lives, and it is a place where the Son of God is not encountered in the flesh, and where the prevailing worldviews, concerns and tensions often have little in common with those of the text. Although the preacher has worked to 'bring the text to life', what they have actually done is left the congregation in their own world, which they have used as a substitute for the narrative's world. Because of this, the intrinsic purposes of the narrative cannot be fully achieved.

Again, this critique does not mean that sermons on New Testament narrative should never carry any illustrations. But it does mean that we must seek to illustrate from *within* the story and aim to cast more light on *its* world, not to provide pathways straight out of it.

Preaching New Testament Narrative to Aussies

Some might worry that this insistence on attempting to draw congregations deep into the world of the text is an approach that would simply be too foreign to modern Australians, but this is not at all the case. From childhood onwards, Westerners are soaked in imaginative play and entertainment that regularly delivers them into very different worlds. Negatively, we call this 'escapism', as viewers disappear into television dramas and soap-operas or readers plough through trashy airport novels and glossy magazines as a means of disengaging from their daily grind. But more positively, it is simply a natural way that human beings explore different points of view and develop pathos. It taps into our imaginative skills and helps us broaden the way we look at the real world, its people and circumstances. For young children, there are endless games where they imagine themselves as superheroes, princesses, space warriors and the like, and while playing at these they explore different moralities (goodies versus baddies), different power dynamics and responsibilities (mummies, daddies and babies), and different life experiences (monsters, rock stars). This crafting of play-narratives allows the development of alternative, sometimes more nuanced, perspectives on life. Furthermore, it continues right through to adulthood: the growing obsession with virtual reality, online console gaming and cosplay only underscores how much older people are willing and able to fully absorb themselves in alternative worlds. This is also the reason for the great popularity of the immersive experiences offered by modern widescreen, surround-sound cinema. Much the same thing is going on in high culture too. Opera, drama ('plays'), classic novels and even fine art all aim at drawing people into different worlds, ideas and points of view, and then generating from them a fresh personal response. To be sure, there are differences between many of these media forms and New Testament narrative, but nonetheless it would seem very hard to argue that today's Australians have limited capacity to mentally enter into imaginative worlds. There is therefore no reason for preachers to shy away from crafting narrative-based sermons that tap into this innate human capacity for exploring realities outside of our normal experiences.

To do this well, one thing we will require is a good working knowledge of Palestine and the Mediterranean in the first century. Each preacher needs to be something of a local expert on this 'world' in order to serve as a kind of tour guide for their audiences. Most theological colleges provide their students with a substantial background in this setting and all of its relevant facets: Roman occupation, Hebrew and Greek language and culture, Second Temple Judaism, ancient agricultural societies, geographical and climatological features and so on. And nowadays a great deal can also be found in an ever-growing number of readily available reference books and online resources. As preachers, we need to invest the time and effort necessary to accrue a decent working knowledge of all of these topics, which fill out the standing backdrop to the New Testament narratives we are preaching.

As another important part of what we might call our 'meta-preparation', and returning to the opening of this chapter, we need to have a good understanding of each of the Gospels and the book of Acts as literary wholes. Once again, resources are relatively easy to come by, with countless commentaries, monographs and web pages now dedicated to each book of New Testament narrative. While it would be unreasonable to expect each one of us to become a global authority on these books, or even to keep abreast of the endless stream of scholarship, we are nonetheless obliged to be reasonably well-acquainted with the complete primary texts. We should at minimum have some clear sense of the distinct structure, flow and emphases of each of the Gospels so as to avoid treating them as a grab-bag of interchangeable short stories. Having this knowledge will not only enable us to preach each text with a conscious awareness of its literary framing, but also to share some of that fuller narratival context with our congregations.

Preaching New Testament narrative also requires good systematic theology, not just in order to insert it into our sermons at appropriate points, but so that we let the narrative do its work of progressively refining and colouring our congregation's doctrine without distorting it by blunt or imbalanced interpretations of individual passages. For example, a preacher with an under-formed theology of the Holy Spirit might preach a sermon on Acts 2:1–13 and assert that the coming of the Spirit is always accompanied by the capacity to speak in other languages, thus taking a particular event and universalising it. But a preacher with a more balanced theology would draw people into the moment of this text so they might witness a particular manifestation of the Spirit at a particular juncture in salvation history, and in doing so would further develop their still bigger view of the Spirit's ways.

Finally, we will need to be good storytellers or 'world-crafters'. This is not because our task is to just retell the passage of Scripture for our congregation (although it is remarkable how powerful it is to hear New Testament narrative read out loud really well), but because we need to preach in a style that is sympathetic to the narrative genre. Just as epistles should be preached personally, prophecy preached pleadingly, poetry preached emotionally and apocalyptic preached intensely, narrative must be preached *immersively*, with the preacher not merely explaining the text but leading the listeners in and through it. This requires skills in capturing the mood, personalities, tensions and movement of each passage, and then in preserving and communicating these to the congregation. Unfortunately (or perhaps not), there are no formulae or standardised techniques for any of this. Rather, it requires us to read closely and soak deeply in each text as we prepare to preach it to others. In short, we must first enter and dwell in the story ourselves before we seek to lead others there.

New Testament Narrative and Australian Culture

The 'Describing Australians' chapter of this volume presents some of the general features of Australian culture. Armed with this data, preachers might at first be tempted to assess whether the New Testament narratives as a whole either affirm or challenge our various cultural propensities, asking whether these narratives endorse or rebuke our environmental mastery, monochromic relationship to time, postmodernism and so on. If we attempted this, however, we would find it impossible to make many firm binary determinations. This is because narratives, as we have seen, do not always yield such absolutes and are often more likely to provide a range of complementary perspectives on our cultural dispositions. That is, as different passages of New Testament narrative present different people, situations, tensions, moments and so forth, they may cast different light on our cultural propensities and show us how, from God's perspective, each might manifest as good or bad depending on the particular circumstances.[22] Some examples may help to illustrate.

We have recognised that Australians are individualistic. But rather than giving us an unequivocal assessment of whether this is pleasing or displeasing to God, the New Testament narratives in some cases – such as Luke 12:4–7, where Jesus teaches that even the hairs of our heads are counted – show that God does have an intimate knowledge of and concern for every individual in their uniqueness. However, other passages – like Acts 4:32–37, which details the early Christians' sharing of possessions – present Christ's church as profoundly communally-oriented. Of course, these passages are not teaching different things about individualism and do not stand in any kind of formal contradiction; neither one is, in fact, primarily about individualism at all. Each only intersects this cultural attribute while narrating stories about other matters. Indeed, the worldview behind both of them relativises the very category of 'individualism' and submits it to the text's own perspectives and priorities. Therefore, the preacher who takes the congregation into and through these passages actually leads them away from a self-understanding that is either 'individualistic' or 'collectivist' and towards a mindset that instead is primarily and fundamentally Christ-like. It is only from within this Christian worldview that they will then find which expressions of individualism are to be celebrated and which rejected, and their journeys through the New Testament narratives will progressively hone their understanding of what is appropriate at different points.

Australians are also more egalitarian than hierarchical, yet again we cannot preach through the New Testament narratives and conclude that this preference of our culture is uniformly good or bad. Instead, we find that in some cases – such as Jesus' radical interactions with the Samaritan woman in John 4:1–42 – God disapproves of the stratification of society, whereas in others – such as Jesus' great admiration of the centurion's views on authority in Matthew 8:5–13 – he calls for it to be respected. This shows us that egalitarianism per se is a position neither rejected outright nor embraced without qualification in the Gospels. Instead, these texts present instances where the expression of egalitarianism is consistent with Christ's priorities, and others where it is not. If these narrative priorities are respected in preaching, we will resist any urge to quickly extract a universal truth about an attendant matter from any one passage without first having considered all of the rest to confirm whether the idea is truly pervasive, or instead a belief given a particular nuance that is appropriate to a certain set of circumstances when those are engaged by the worldview of Jesus.

As a final example, Australians have been recognised as time poor, and this is yet another trait that the narratives of the Gospels and Acts will neither praise nor decry in toto. Luke 10:38–42 famously records Jesus rebuking Martha for not finding the time to sit at his feet with Mary, but in Mark 7:24–30 we find Jesus seeking a time of solitude, yet willingly accepting that this will not be available to him if he is to give himself to responding to the need of the Syrophoenician woman. Again, these different sections of narrative give us different windows into Jesus' views on time-poverty, which are situationally determined and controlled by the narrative's higher perspective.

These brief examples show us that the New Testament narratives prevent us from making blanket assessments about our various cultural traits and characteristics, be they individualism, egalitarianism, time poverty, or any and all of the others. Instead they help us filter our dispositions through the larger and primary lens of the Christian worldview, with the promotion of this worldview being a principal purpose of these narratives. By involving us in the truth-of-Christ-in-action, or the truth-of-Christ-in-particular-circumstances, the Gospels and Acts allow us to understand each aspect of our culture even-handedly; they are neither fully sanctified nor fully condemned, requiring celebration in some circumstances and restraint in others. And faithfully preaching through the great diversity of the New Testament narratives with all of their God-ordained particularities trains believers to recognise which and when. These books of the Bible are not vehicles designed merely to deliver quanta of truth but real-life stories that bring us to Jesus, in and around whom we see the gospel truths expressed in many and various ways as necessitated by the complex world in which he lived. The preacher of New Testament narrative is tasked with leading today's Australians into that world of Jesus and his first followers, and then bringing them back to be his followers in this time and place.

Sample Sermon: Matthew 22:23–33

As we continue travelling alongside Jesus in our reading through of Matthew's Gospel, today we come to a part of his ministry that many of us may have heard about before, although I wonder if it is an incident in Jesus' life where the meaning of his words are very often misunderstood. It's not uncommon to hear people jump over to these verses in the Gospel to interrogate them for what they may or may not teach us about marriage – or even sex! – in the afterlife. But while this passage may have something to contribute on those questions, they are not really what is primarily on view. No, there is something else that we learn from Jesus today, something else about our way of thinking that is being challenged or reframed. To see clearly what that is, we really need to start by coming at our passage from its broader context, both glancing back at where we've been in the past months and also remembering how this part of our story fits into what Jesus is doing in this part of Matthew's Gospel.

After having concentrated on Jesus' ministry in Israel's northern region of Galilee from chapter 4 through to chapter 15, Matthew has now had us down south with Jesus in Jerusalem from chapter 21, and we will stay there through to almost the very end of his Gospel – just his final few verses will take us back to Galilee. So now, we are with Jesus as his teaching and ministry have left behind the more rural towns and countryside and have arrived in the capital city, where power and authority and control have long been centred for the Jewish people. While Jesus is in Jerusalem, much of the power is held by the occupying Roman forces, who are garrisoned here along with their soon-to-be-infamous regional governor, Pontius Pilate. Many of the different Jewish leaders are also based here. There is the ruling council, or Sanhedrin, that oversees the religious life of the people and formally interfaces with the Romans. King Herod has a place here too. He has significant authority but does not rule like the kings of old. His conflict with John the Baptist reminded us of his high-handed refusal to be humble and faithful before the God who he is meant to be representing. And then there are the Scribes and Pharisees; those experts in the Jewish laws who nit-pick at rules with the common people and also make it clear that they consider themselves to be part of a spiritual elite. It is amidst all of these groups with their different positions of spiritual, political and social power that Jesus is now ministering. And he is challenging them and recasting both the understanding of God, and of how people stand before him, that they are promoting.

Now, not only is Jesus ministering in this relatively intense context, but from 21:12 through to the end of chapter 23, we are with him as he does so in the Jewish temple complex. The temple is, of course, by far the largest building in Jerusalem and it represents the very presence of God among his people. Indeed, we remember that in Old Testament times, God's presence had been physically and dramatically manifested in the temple. He is not always so clearly tangibly present there these days, but the temple is still imposing and still the bustling heart and hub of the city and of Jewish spiritual life. This is the place where people came to do their business with God, and where they still expect God can be, and needs to be, approached in a special way. And so, it is a very charged place for Jesus – the Messiah of God – to be challenging the religious norms and religious leaders.

And challenging the leaders he is. In fact, for most of this time he is spending in the temple, Jesus is in confrontation with the Pharisees, who are very much out to get him. So, see 22:15, 'Then the Pharisees went and plotted to entrap him in what he said.' And 22:41, 'Now while the Pharisees were gathered together, Jesus asked them a [challenging] question ...' And then 23:13, 'Woe to you, scribes and Pharisees, hypocrites!'

– a cry that Jesus repeats over and over in 23:23, 25, 27, 29. It's all going to culminate in 23:37 when Jesus will lament over this city of Jerusalem before walking out of the temple and predicting its destruction in 24:1–2.

So, we find ourselves now with Jesus as he brings his message and ministry right up to the establishment – and particularly to the Scribes and the Pharisees – and challenges their interpretation of the faith as well as their hypocritical behaviour. Last week we saw that Jesus had just silenced the Pharisees after they had tried to entrap him on the question of whether or not to pay taxes to the Roman oppressors. They thought that if he said yes, he would prove that he was not on the side of God's people, but if he said no, he would be advocating a dangerous political rebellion. But Jesus showed them that the biggest question was not about what tribute was given to the emperor, whose image is found on the coinage, it was actually about what tribute was given to God by those who bore his image and likeness. Jesus exposed their inconsistency, and the Pharisees withdrew from him for a moment, before they returned to engage again.

And it's in this brief interlude between his interactions with the Pharisees that Jesus is now approached by another group: the Sadducees. These are also Jews who are represented in the power structures of Jerusalem; there are Sadducees who sit on the Sanhedrin. But they are an anomalous group, with some quite different beliefs to the Pharisees. Acts 23:8 tells us that these include different beliefs about the angel (presumably the angel of the Lord, who we meet several times in the Old Testament), the Spirit, and the resurrection, and they have come to Jesus now in an attempt to expose him as foolish for maintaining the common Jewish belief about the resurrection from the dead; the idea that there is God-given new and ongoing life after death.

Their plan is to unfold to Jesus a hypothetical scenario, which they are thinking can only lead to a completely unacceptable predicament if there really is to be a resurrection from the dead. Not only this, but they are premising the whole thing on a provision made in the Old Testament. In the book of Deuteronomy, commonly attributed to Moses, chapter 25 verses 5 and 6 say,

> When brothers reside together, and one of them dies and has no son, the wife of the deceased shall not be married outside the family to a stranger. Her husband's brother shall go in to her, taking her in marriage, and performing the duty of a husband's brother to her, and the firstborn whom she bears shall succeed to the name of the deceased brother, so that his name may not be blotted out of Israel. (Deut 25:5–6 NRSV-A)

This, then, is a provision to enable a family name to be perpetuated throughout the generations of Israel. If a man dies without a male heir to carry forward his name, his brother will marry his widow, thereby maintaining the family connection, and will ensure that their firstborn son carries forward the first husband's name. While many other cultures might find this practice strange, perhaps even disturbing or inappropriate, it reminds us how important family and heritage and ongoing identification with God are for the Jewish peoples around Jesus. No one wants to be eternally forgotten by God. Certainly, the Sadducees are not now objecting to this arrangement, but only to its implications if there is to be a future resurrection of the dead. So, they ask Jesus to tell them who the woman's husband will be in that eventuality. Which brother would she be married to in the resurrection life? Indeed, in the extended example that our Sadducees are putting before Jesus, the woman had married each of seven brothers, and so the question is which of those seven would she be married to in the resurrection? The first? The last? All of them? They feel that the absurdity of this problem clearly demonstrates the foolishness of belief in life after death.

Well, Jesus responds in a way that perhaps we really should be expecting by now. He doesn't actually answer their question at all; instead, he shows the Sadducees that they have bigger questions they need to answer and that their own questioning is based on a poor understanding of both the Scriptures and the power of God. Jesus explains in verse 30 that 'in the resurrection they neither marry nor are given in marriage, but are like angels in heaven' (NRSV-A). Now we must not hear Jesus saying anything like 'new marriages cannot be solemnised in heaven', or 'angels don't have sexual relations, so neither we will in the afterlife'. Whether or not those statements are true, they are really not the point. Remember that the challenge Jesus is engaging is about the truth of the resurrection. And the purpose of the family marriage provisions made in Deuteronomy is to raise up descendants who can carry the family name forward for generations, to prevent the name from dying out. Actually, it is to prevent that family from being forgotten and so cut off from God.

With that in mind, we see what radical a thing Jesus is now saying. He reminds us that God is the God of the living, not the God of the dead. He *is* the God of Abraham, Isaac and Jacob, those ancient founding fathers of the Jewish nation. Note that: he *is* their God. Not, he *was* their God. He *is* their God, still. And the reason that he is still their God is because they are still alive – even though they died long ago! That is, they live with him now and will one day be resurrected to live with him eternally, and this means that *their names will be carried forward forever because they themselves will carry them*! Jesus is helping us see that there is actually no need for widows to raise up sons to perpetuate their dead husbands' names if their husbands were faithful believers. If they were faithful believers, then they will *maintain their own names* forever before the Lord as they live eternally with him as part of the new creation.[23] And we will too, if we are counted among his faithful believing people like Abraham, Isaac and Jacob. People do not assure their place in eternity through their descendants any more than they do by their achievements or institutions or other legacies. Neither do people inherit a place in the presence of God from their parents or ancestors or culture. Each faithful person themselves stand eternally in the presence of God, simply because it is God's great plan and purpose to maintain each faithful individual in eternal life.

So, the Sadducees aren't getting the answer to their disingenuous little puzzle, but they are hearing that their failure to embrace the reality of resurrection is a failure to embrace their own eternal life.

Of course, all of this is significant for the Pharisees, too. In verse 34, we'll come to them hearing about Jesus silencing the Sadducees, and we'll see their reaction to that news. Sadly, it will be to bring another test to Jesus. I have to say that this seems profoundly foolish to me, and a mark of the Pharisees' incredible stubbornness. You see, in his interaction with the Sadducees, Jesus is actually siding with the Pharisees. He's confirming that the Pharisees' thinking about the resurrection, a belief of the greatest importance, is correct, and that the Sadducees – with whom the Pharisees are in disagreement, but who they find themselves needing to share power with – are wrong! Now, when you have already been confounded and clearly shown up as hypocritical by someone, you wonder if you might stop your offensive against them and find the humility to open up your ears to them a little more. And if that person then goes on to show another group from your own that you are correct and they are not with regard to a most significant and controversial matter of belief, you wonder if you might realise that in significant ways this person is offering you an opening for acceptance. You might wonder if perhaps now is the time to come together on that common ground and see if there is an even greater union on offer.

But what on earth would motivate you to go back in and attack again the one who you have already found to be impenetrable? What would motivate you to reaffirm your opposition to the one who has just undone your enemies? Some kind of stupid, stubborn pride. Some kind of need for power and control. Some kind of blindness that you seem unable to see. It's not going to end well for you if you continue in opposition to the man who has shown you that he knows both the human heart and true faith far better than we ever could. But such are the decisions that some people make.

Jesus will continue to engage and teach and offer his gift of eternal life to those who continue to draw near. And we will return to journey further with him again next week. Until then, we will walk his walk as we live in his world to his glory. Amen.

Comments on the Sermon

In the attempt to preach this passage as narrative, a few things can be noted. Firstly, in seeking to bring the congregation *into* the story, it has been mostly delivered in the present continuous, or historical present, with regular temporal markers (e.g., 'now') and repeated proximal markers (e.g., 'here'). There are also no illustrations that would take the congregation out of the story, and even an attempt to avoid language that might jar, such as the term 'levirate marriage' which would be anachronistic if used in this context. And even the acknowledgement of how distasteful levirate marriage will be for many is made from an embedded position, rather than from the outside. Secondly, I have tried to explain the narrative – both in its broader context and in the finer details of the passage – without breaking the flow of storytelling. In this, I hope to have given the meaning of the story as originally intended, rather than extracting dot points of doctrine from it, although there is clearly plenty of doctrinal content communicated. Thirdly, I have not stepped out of the story to prescribe a certain response, or application, but have preferred to let the sermon's main work be in shaping the worldview of the listeners. There are some obvious implications of the passage, but precisely because they are so obvious, it would seem clumsy to labour them. And of course, to do so would also be to break out of narrative mode.

When considering the ways that this Gospel sermon might engage with Aussie culture, we see that it does a number of things, albeit tacitly. For example, it affirms our individualism, saying that each person can have an enduring place in the presence of God, who not only cares about family or community groupings, but also about unique people. It challenges our rule-based thinking by rejecting a use of the Mosaic Law to create relational problems. (Interestingly, the text does not even attempt solve the Sadducees' problem, but simply refocuses them to a more important truth.) The sermon also affirms something of our anti-institutionalism by highlighting the extent of Jesus' confrontations with the Pharisees. In a way it is multicultural, or at least non-tribal, as neither the Pharisees nor Sadducees are favoured. To some extent it speaks against wealth and consumerism, as its great focus on the resurrection shows that there is more to human experience than just the physical and temporal. And that same focus on the resurrection may be of some help in relieving anxiety and depression as eternal hope is laid before the faithful. Of course, a preacher could easily develop any of these engagements with our culture further if that were deemed to be appropriate to the needs of their congregation.

9
PREACHING PAUL'S EPISTLES TO AUSTRALIANS
Tim MacBride

Introduction

The fundamental challenge when preaching Paul's epistles is their occasional nature: in the first instance, they were addressed to a particular audience at a particular time in history. Although they are rich in theological reflection, they are not abstract theological treatises sent, as an afterthought, in the form of a letter. Rather, they seek to apply theology to address the particular needs and concerns of their original audience. They are letters with a particular purpose, not reference books.[1]

However, the epistles also belong to the collection of texts we call the New Testament. Very early on, the church recognised these particular texts – whether they were directly written by an apostle or not – to be written instances of the apostolic teaching about Jesus; or, as Witherington more poetically puts it, 'the literary residue of the orally proclaimed word of God'.[2] As such, they have a function that goes beyond their original setting. Like the Hebrew Scriptures to which Paul refers, they are 'useful for teaching, rebuking, correcting and training in righteousness, so that the servant of God may be thoroughly equipped for every good work' (2 Tim 3:16–17). That is, these very particular letters also have something to say to all communities of believers in all subsequent times.

A key task of the preacher, then, is to show how such particular texts are relevant not just to the original audience, but to his or her own congregation. This involves two main challenges, which will be the focus of this chapter.

The first challenge, **the hermeneutical task**, involves determining the function of the text. We do not seek simply to understand what the text is saying, but also what the text is seeking to do in its original setting. It is not enough to discern and communicate what Paul is saying about, for example, the nature and use spiritual gifts in 1 Corinthians; we must also determine to what end Paul is saying it if we are going to use the content of the text the way Paul did. Since Paul is writing applied theology, faithful exposition seeks to apply it along the same lines.

The second challenge, **the contextualisation task**, involves recognising and overcoming the differences between the setting of the letter and the setting of the sermon, often involving a modification of the text's rhetorical strategies, so that the text can have a similar function. This flows from a conviction that the sermon should say and do what the biblical text says and does.[3] While the first challenge is essentially the same for all interpreters, the second challenge will be significantly different depending on the cultural and situational particularities of the contemporary audience, hence the necessity for this volume to be focused specifically on Australian audiences.

In this chapter, I approach these tasks in a manner that is a little different from most of the other chapters in the book. I will be describing a *process* by which Paul's epistles can be applied to Australians rather than providing suggestions for what the end result of that process might look like. This is for two significant reasons. The first is essentially practical, in that the breadth of the Pauline corpus – and the wide variety of topics Paul addresses in his letters – makes it impossible to cover everything adequately in the space available. I am using 1 Corinthians as our working example throughout the chapter, before concluding with an example sermon from Galatians to demonstrate the process that can then be applied to Paul's other letters.

The second reason comes more from a methodological conviction that Scripture consists of individual texts, each with specific intended function. It does not come in the form of an abstracted theological treatise. Nor is it a series of 'puzzle pieces' required to be put together to form an abstracted systematisation (a 'Pauline theology', for example), which exists independently from the texts from which it was derived,[4] and which then becomes the subject of our preaching. This does not mean, of course, that Paul did not have a consistent theological framework, but that this framework is not what is canonical for us. Rather, the specific applications of that theology are what have been recorded for us in Scripture, and these should not be loosened or detached from their situational moorings. As I argue below, this is because we preach not only the *content* of a biblical text (which, to some extent, *could* be so detached) but also its *function*. Therefore, I will not be offering a thoroughgoing sampling of how various topics in Pauline theology might be applied to Australians; rather, I will be suggesting a method of applying Pauline texts to Australians.

This also provides a rationale for the different direction taken in this chapter regarding application. Instead of looking first to the Australian setting and asking what the Pauline corpus might have to say to it (which will often necessitate detaching texts from their original function), we will look at the first-century settings Paul does address and then find similarities within the Australian setting into which Paul's message might function similarly. That is, we will be using Scripture to exegete Australian culture, rather than using culture to enquire of Scripture.

A Process for Preaching Paul's Epistles to Australian Congregations

A Hermeneutical Model

I need firstly to be clear about the hermeneutical model I will be using. Often, hermeneutical models have, in practice, focused on a narrow aspect of meaning, namely, content. We ask first, 'What is the text *saying* in its biblical setting?' and secondly, 'What might it *say* to us today in our own setting, given the historical and cultural distance?' This is not wrong, of course, but it can be a bit narrow, so that our preaching ends up being a bit simplistic. For example, in 1 Corinthians 1–4, Paul describes a church divided around its leaders and tells them that this situation is bad; so, we ask whether we are similarly divided around our leaders, because that is bad, too. Or we notice Paul calling them to account over the sexual immorality described in 1 Corinthians 5; so, *we* point out that this sort of thing can happen among us, too, so we should also be vigilant. This can shift further into topical preaching under the guise of exposition, in which we riff on the general topic Paul addresses in our assigned text.[5] In the case of 1 Corinthians 14, we could end up preaching a message along the lines of: *Everything you always wanted to know about spiritual gifts but were afraid to put up your hand in church and ask (in case someone thought you were Pentecostal)*.[6] Again, these may not be entirely wrong, but they often do not allow the biblical texts to 'bite' as much as they could.[7] Sometimes they land a glancing blow where the text was aiming, rather than hit the audience with the full force of the text.

If, however, we expand our idea of meaning to include content plus function, the text takes on a slightly different life. This is because language does not simply *say*; it also *does*. For example, when I go into one of my boys' rooms and announce, 'There are dirty clothes all over the floor', it is not merely a statement in the indicative; there is an implied command. The intended response is not, 'Yes, Dad, that's an accurate observation of the state of my room, your powers of observation are sharp, as always'. They are supposed to pick the clothes up; they are meant to do something in response. 'Language doesn't just say. It also does.'[8]

For the past four decades, this has been a theme in the study of homiletics. Biblical texts do not simply communicate content; they were also designed to do something in the lives of their first hearers. The biblical writers were intending to persuade, exhort and effect change. Our sermons, therefore, ought to do likewise. As David Buttrick notes, 'The question, "What is the passage trying to do?" may well mark the beginning of homiletical obedience.'[9] Fred Craddock put it more simply: 'Does the sermon say and do what the text says and does?'[10] My suggested model, then, is not just to work out what the text was saying in its first-century context, but also what it was doing – in order that our sermons cannot just say but also do something similar in our own contexts.[11]

When we satisfy ourselves with merely communicating the content of the text apart from its function – or only loosely connected to its function – we can miss some of what is going on in the text. As a result, we can misapply the text or simply miss out on some of its application – things that may not be quite as obvious until we ask the question of what the text is doing. (I will provide some examples of this below.)

Now, of course, we all do this instinctively to various degrees, so it is doubtful that as a result of this model we are going to have an epiphany and discover a whole new way of preaching texts. Here, I am simply offering an explicit methodology to help us to do it as accurately and consistently as we can, rather than relying on instinct. At the heart of this methodology is something called the 'rhetorical situation'.

The rhetorical situation (sometimes called the 'rhetorical setting') is similar to what commentaries often call the 'occasion' or 'setting' of the epistle, but it is more acutely focused on the factors that are open to change by persuasion. In a landmark essay in 1968, Lloyd Bitzer defined a rhetorical situation as containing an 'exigence ... an imperfection marked by urgency ... a thing which is other than it should be ... ', which can be 'positively modified ... by discourse', which seeks to influence an 'audience ... capable of being influenced by discourse and of being mediators for change' within 'a set of constraints made up of persons, events, objects, and relations which are parts of the situation because they have the power to constrain decision and action needed to modify the exigence'.[12]

To put it more simply, a rhetorical situation contains something that is not right, but a good speech – such as an epistle read aloud to a congregation – might persuade the audience to do what they can to fix it.

Once we have described the rhetorical situation of a given text in those terms – exigence, audience and constraints – there are at least three probing questions we can use to interrogate it to gain a fuller understanding:
1. Why is the situation like it is?
2. What needs to happen to change it?
3. How does the text try to produce this change?

If we apply this to the earlier situation of my boys' messy rooms, we can see that the exigence (or 'urgent imperfection') is that the room is messy; the audience consists of the rooms' inhabitants; and the key constraints are that the audience is under the authority of me, the speaker, but they are unlikely to act upon this. To this point, it is quite straightforward. However, we now introduce our three probing questions:

1. *Why is the situation like it is?* Being teenagers, they are in the 'individuation' phase of life, where they are frequently in rebellion against parental authority.
2. *What needs to happen to change it?* The audience needs to be persuaded to acknowledge that authority and act upon it.
3. *How does the speaker attempt to produce this change?* This is the question of rhetorical function. The persuasive task is to talk about the room in such a way as the audience will be motivated to act upon it and clean the room. One strategy might have been a direct order to clean up the room; however, from experience, this would probably create immediate resistance and spark teenage aggravation. So the chosen strategy is to make a pointed observation so the audience could then respond with at least the illusion of freedom, just like Paul does with Philemon.[13] (Granted, this is also unlikely to work, but the advantage is that no-one yells at me in response, so we can count that as a win.)

Although this example is intentionally trite, it illustrates the pattern we can use with more significant and serious rhetorical situations, such as the one going on in Corinth as addressed by Paul in 1 Corinthians, to which we will now turn.

1. Why Is the Situation Like it Is?

We begin by describing the rhetorical situation being addressed by Paul in 1 Corinthians. This is achieved through the hard work of carefully applying the historical critical method, making use of three significant resources: firstly, a prayerful and attentive reading of the text itself, noting down all of the clues we find in regard to rhetorical setting;[14] secondly, the use of introductions to Bible commentaries; and thirdly, the implications of the rhetorical genre and structure of the epistle as they relate to the function of the text.[15] There is no shortcut to this approach, and the examples that follow are, of necessity, a case of 'here's one I prepared earlier'.

However, we will go beyond simply describing *what* is happening in Corinth and ask *why* it is happening – the first of our three probing questions about rhetorical situation. We will look at the dynamics and behavioural patterns in play that could bring to light more and broader application. That is, a focus of our hermeneutical task will be to look at the reasons for the situation, not just the situation itself.

We will then link it to our own situation, exegeting our own culture and then comparing. The aim of our contextual task is to craft a similar description of our own setting and how Paul's epistle might speak into it in an analogous way. If we can show our congregation how their situation is similar (despite the obvious surface differences) to the situation of the original audience, half of our 'application work' is done. *How are the Thessalonians like me? How are we sometimes 'foolish and bewitched' like the Galatian readers? How is the Corinthian church like ours?* Once our own audience has grasped that, when it comes down to it, we are not so different from Paul's original audience, they will have been primed to listen to what Paul wants them to do in response.

Corinth and Australia

There are some broad similarities between Corinth and *urban* Australia in particular: most Australian cities are port cities which are important transport hubs; there is a constant influx of tourists and migrants; and our cities are a multicultural melting pot of different languages and ethnicities.[16] This makes both Corinth and urban Australia conducive to tribalism, where people are inclined to stick to the people with whom they have things in common.

A significant issue in Corinth was one of social status. In an honour-shame society, status was always important, but in Corinth this was particularly acute because it was a new city, only about one hundred years old. It had mostly been settled by military veterans who had been granted land, as well as by freed slaves, which meant that there was very little in the way of 'old money'.[17] Wealth and status had to be *earned* rather than simply inherited, and it needed to be displayed rather than simply assumed.[18]

That, by and large, is Australia – especially its largest cities. In global terms, Australian cities are young, and the rest of the world tends to view us as brash and flashy. There is plenty of 'new money', made all the more significant by our egalitarianism and rejection of inherited class distinctions. If everyone is indeed given an Aussie 'fair go', there is the opportunity for everyone to improve their wealth and status. As a result, we have an upwardly mobile culture, with an army of aspirational immigrants who have arrived wanting to make a better life for themselves and their families. Status and success are proved – to ourselves and to those around us – with the size and location of our house, the currency of our interior design, the model of car we drive, the job title we hold, and the schools to which we send our children. Australians, too, seek to create and display status.

Status through association

One of the specific ways a person could seek to gain and display status in the ancient world was through public oratory. This was true throughout the empire, but again, particularly acute in Corinth, being one of the key forms of public engagement and entertainment.[19] It thus provided a whole world in which to compete for status. The orators themselves gained status through their ability to persuade and, increasingly, to entertain. Those who owned homes big enough to host these speakers also gained status by association.[20] Everyone else sought status by becoming fans of their public-speaking heroes. They would pick a team, so to speak, barrack for their chosen speakers, and trash-talk the opposition, hoping to bask in the reflected glory if their hero 'won'. This is how one observer described the scene – and he was clearly not impressed at the dynamic, either:

> That was the time, too, when one could hear crowds of wretched Sophists [eloquent speakers] around Poseidon's temple shouting and reviling one another, their disciples, as they were called, fighting with one another, many writers reading aloud their stupid works, many poets reciting while others applauded them ... [21]

This is not all that different from the way Australians try to display status by association, seen most obviously in how we divide into tribes based on sporting teams and act out the same scenario described by Dio Chrysostom. However, sport is by no means the only area in which this pattern is displayed. There is the great divide between (typically) males over a certain age: are you Team Ford or Team Holden? We try to display status through choices in music styles or coffee. We pick favourites on reality TV and then barrack for them each week against their rivals. Often, we choose a political 'team' at a young age, and barrack for them no matter what they do. The specifics might differ, but the pattern is the same: we divide into teams and barrack – often blindly – for our own, because our choice of team displays our 'brand', and a win for our team is a win for our status.

Style over substance

However, our barracking is not always blind; often there are serious issues behind why we chose that team in the first place. This was the case in Corinth, too, with the population divided between two styles of public speaking. Some preferred their oratory to be serious and functional, reflecting its origins in the law courts and the political forums. Others liked to be entertained with grand displays of verbal eloquence; to hear someone showing off, rather than speaking for any real purpose.[22] The latter – called *sophistry* – appears to have been more popular, reflecting a society that consistently chose style over substance.[23]

This is seen in Australian society, too: in the shallow judgements we make about contestants we hardly know on reality TV shows; in the politicians we are attracted to; and in the kind of entertainment we consume. Even our news these days needs to entertain us, not just inform us.[24] This is the dynamic of our society – not of every individual, but collectively. We chase and display our status through division and barracking, and we mostly choose style over substance. If this is the dynamic of our world, how might that affect the dynamic of our *churches*?

A Tale of Two Churches

Before we answer that question for *us*, we need to take a look at how it affected the church in Corinth. It seems that they, too, had continued this tribalism and status-seeking around speakers, as Paul details in his narrative:[25]

> My brothers and sisters, some from Chloe's household have informed me that there are quarrels among you. What I mean is this: One of you says, 'I follow Paul'; another, 'I follow Apollos'; another, 'I follow Cephas'; still another, 'I follow Christ.' Is Christ divided? ... (1 Cor 1:11–13)

Now these are unlikely to be significant *theological* divisions,[26] since Paul condemns the existence of his own faction, and throughout the epistle the issues have strong undertones of socio-economic division – most obviously in chapter 11, where the poor are being excluded from participating in the Lord's Supper.[27] More likely, the reasons for the division around leaders are the same as for the rest of the world: namely, as a means of projecting status. This would have been particularly the case for the wealthier members of the Corinthian church, whose houses were of necessity used to host gatherings where the likes of Paul, Apollos and Peter would have spoken. The likely assumption was that the usual rules of society should apply: the host gains status.[28]

Paul goes on to imply that one of the divisive issues is his refusal to engage in the sophistic style of rhetoric that was in vogue – which, for some, made for an unfortunate comparison with Apollos' style.[29]

> For Christ did not send me to baptise, but to preach the gospel – not with wisdom and eloquence [literally, 'the wisdom of speech'], lest the cross of Christ be emptied of its power. (1 Cor 1:17)

In other words, the Corinthians' judgements about the worth of the various speakers were made with regard to *style* rather than *substance*.

An interesting side note is to ask which socio-economic grouping Apollos' more 'learned-sounding' rhetoric appealed. The majority view is that Apollos appealed more to the status-chasing wealthy elite, while a minority sees him as appealing to the *lower* classes who were latching on to what they thought was sophistication.[30] Either way, Paul's point is that they were judging speakers the way the world did, which is no longer appropriate for the new community. Indeed, Paul reminds his largely *non*-elite audience that worldly judgements had left them well down the food chain – so why would they want to bring *that* into the church community?

> Brothers and sisters, think of what you were when you were called. Not many of you were wise by human standards; not many were influential; not many were of noble birth. (1 Cor 1:26)

Later, in chapter 2, Paul goes on to contrast the wisdom of the world with the wisdom that comes from the Spirit:

> The person with the Spirit makes judgments about all things, but such a person is not subject to merely human judgments ... we have the mind of Christ. (1 Cor 2:15–16)

In essence, the Corinthian church was not simply divided around their leaders. It was divided because they had brought the world's way of judging things and the world's preferences uncritically into the church.[31] This is the dynamic in play, and understanding this opens up a far broader connection with our own experience than just being divided around the leaders. We are now dealing with the cause, not just one of the symptoms.

It is not hard to see how we, too, have uncritically brought the world's way of judging things into the Australian church. The way we respond to different preachers can sometimes be like we are in the audience for an episode of *So You Think You Can Preach?* Just like the ancient Greeks, we turn up ready to judge the quality of the oratory. Furthermore, our egalitarian culture biases us towards sitting in judgement over our preachers rather than accepting their authority. This is even more significant in the individualistic podcast generation, where, if we judge our local pastor unfavourably, we can just download someone more famous and entertaining – shopping around to find something that satisfies *my* spiritual wants, *right* now, in the style that *I* like.

Likewise, we can bring our status in the secular environment with us into the church and then treat others accordingly. We value the opinions of some and devalue the opinions of others, based on their secular occupation. (We are only egalitarian to a point, after all.) We accept some people and ignore others because of their style rather than their substance. We reflexively cut down perceived 'tall poppies' the way we would elsewhere in society. Or we display attitudes towards the ethnic 'other' that are derived more from our own tribal origins than the gospel ethic. When we are not careful, the values and standards of our culture become our default settings in the church as well, despite the fact that the gospel explicitly calls us to check our status at the door – along with our money, our degrees, and our ability to play the world's power games and win. The church was formed to be a haven of servanthood and mutual submission rather than yet another place to act out the same old social scripts.

If space allowed, we could apply this same detailed approach to Paul's other letters (as we will do at the end of the chapter, with Galatians). For example, in Philippians Paul draws on the language of citizenship, as Philippi was a colony that had quite recently been granted Roman citizenship, and its inhabitants were enthusiastic in their embracing of citizenship ideals.[32] He does this to call the Philippian Christians to a citizenship that is of a higher order, based not at the heart of human civilisation in Rome, but in heaven (1:27; 3:20). In preaching Philippians, we might similarly explore the ways in which we value and live out Australian citizenship – mostly in a far more laid-back manner than either the Philippians or, for example, our US counterparts – as the first part of a 'how much more' argument to value and live out our heavenly citizenship.[33] The oft-cited Aussie value of 'mateship' can be explored as pointing towards the kind of citizenship that puts the needs of others ahead of their own, modelled in Philippians by Timothy, Epaphroditus and Christ himself.

Likewise, Paul writes to a Colossian church in danger of following an alternative 'philosophy' (2:8) which, despite seeming on the surface to be attractive and compatible with faith in Christ,[34] was just a pale shadow (2:17) of the fullness and freedom believers now have in Christ (1:15–20; 2:9–10), and resulted only in enslavement.[35] We might also explore the attractiveness of the alternative 'philosophies' found in Australian culture – particularly those that attempt to cohabit with faith in Jesus, such as teachings about material prosperity – to prepare our audience to hear Paul's passionate presentation of the superiority of Christ.

Thus far, we have outlined the process for describing and comparing in detail the rhetorical situation – in both the first-century text and twenty-first-century Australia. This, I would argue, is the most significant step in the contextual task, because the content of the biblical message (to the original audience of the text and to our own) is, in essence, the same. The foundational contextual task is to show a twenty-first-century Australian audience how their situation, despite the surface differences, is similar to the situation addressed in the text, readying them to hear Paul's message as a word on target also for today.

2. What Needs to Happen to Effect Change?

We now move to the question of *what* needs to happen to change it and *how* that change will be effected, both in the world of the text and in the world of our hearers. This is called the rhetorical function: it asks the question, what is Paul trying to do in 1 Corinthians (the hermeneutical task), and therefore what should our sermon also do (the contextual task)?

At this point, I advocate the judicious use of insights gained from the field of rhetorical criticism, which considers texts as acts of persuasion and is therefore interested not just in their content but also their *function*. In relation to the Pauline corpus, this is based on the observation that his epistles employ, to varying degrees, the genres, structural arrangement and techniques of Graeco-Roman rhetoric as outlined in the surviving handbooks by orators such as Aristotle, Cicero and Quintilian.[36] Since the majority of the population was illiterate (and access to photocopiers limited), Paul's epistles were intended to be performed aloud.[37] They thus naturally tended to follow, broadly speaking, the conventions of speechmaking. Understanding Paul's written-down speeches against this backdrop helps us to discern the intended function of each part of the text, and the text as a whole, with greater confidence. Space precludes a fuller treatment here.[38] For now, let's focus on what is perhaps the most practical insight for our purposes: the part of the speech the handbooks called the *propositio*, or thesis statement.

The Proposition

The standard[39] ancient speech consisted of: an introduction that raised the topic and established rapport; a narrative outlining the situation the speech would address; the central proposition of the speech; a series of proofs, or arguments, in favour of the proposition, along with a refutation of any real or hypothetical objections; and an emotive, persuasive appeal at the end.[40] All of these parts of the speech work together to persuade the audience to accept the proposition, meaning that the proposition is central to understanding what the speech – or epistle – is attempting to do at each point. That is, it tells us the rhetorical *function of the whole epistle* and acts as a *hermeneutical control* over each section.

Returning to our example of 1 Corinthians, the proposition is the first imperative found in the epistle, introduced by a solemn formula:

> I appeal to you, brothers and sisters, in the name of our Lord Jesus Christ, that all of you agree with one another in what you say and that there be no divisions among you, but that you be perfectly united in mind and thought. (1 Cor 1:10)

It tells us that the epistle, in all its complexity, is essentially an appeal to concord in light of the division described in the subsequent verses – and different snapshots of what that concord might look like when lived out in the community of believers in Corinth. The purpose of 1 Corinthians as a whole is to persuade the people of God to be united rather than divided.

The proposition also acts as a hermeneutical control over all of the other parts of the epistle. This tells us that the rhetorical function of a given textual unit in 1 Corinthians is to support, in some way, the proposition, narrowing down our options of what each unit might be doing. This similarly narrows down what our sermon ought to do, if indeed the function of the text is to determine the function of the sermon.[41]

For example, the function of 1 Corinthians 13 is, in isolation, to hold up the virtue of selfless love so that the audience might be persuaded to pursue this virtue all the more.[42] However, in relation to the overall epistle, it encourages selfless love as the path towards unity in the church. In the same way, a sermon on 1 Corinthians 14 ought not to be an abstract discussion of the role of tongues and prophecy but should encourage the use of all spiritual gifts in a way that builds unity, rather than building up the individual. That is, 'every sermon in 1 Corinthians should at least be framed by an overarching appeal to church unity in *light of the particular content of the passage*'.[43] (Likewise, each sermon in Philippians should relate to the calling for believers to live as good citizens of heaven, 1:27f; each sermon in Colossians should in some way point believers to the superiority of Christ over rival worldviews, 2:8f.)

This gives us the answer to our second probing question: what is needed to change the situation? The simple answer to the hermeneutical task in this case is: Paul, an authority over the audience, needs to speak a word of unity into the Corinthian church. As in the case of my boys' messy rooms, there might be some resistance to that authority – largely due to some comparing Paul unfavourably with Apollos – which necessitates the supporting argumentation that follows.

The contextual task, when viewed at this fundamental level, is then quite straightforward and not culturally contingent. That is, our own Australian audiences will need to hear an authority – namely God, through Paul's words, through our sermon – speak a similar word of unity. light of the particular content of the passage' on 1 Corinthians *will be* the function of the biblical text.

Where it becomes a bit more complicated is when we get to our third and final question: *how* does the text of 1 Corinthians seek to achieve this aim of producing unity? And therefore, how might our sermons do likewise?

3. How Does Persuasion Happen?

This step again involves our two tasks: the identification of the rhetorical strategies used by Paul to persuade his audience of his proposition (the hermeneutical task: what are the texts doing?), and the appropriation of those strategies in our sermon to persuade our hearers similarly, taking into account the differences in the respective rhetorical situations (the contextual task: what should our sermons also do?). Here, we will again demonstrate this principle in action with a brief selection of rhetorical arguments from 1 Corinthians.

Be united: reject the world's judgements about status

In chapter one, Paul's first argument addresses the divisions around leaders outlined earlier, in which the Corinthians had brought the surrounding culture's way of judging things into the church – in particular, the preference for style over substance when it came to public speaking – with the result that Paul was judged unfavourably. Paul's strategy is to demonstrate that his refusal to pander to human pretensions is in line with how God works;[44] the 'foolish' message of the cross certainly did not pander to Jewish or Greek expectations (1:22–23). Furthermore, God is in the habit of bypassing those of worldly status and working through those who are ordinary and unlikely (1:27–29), just like the majority of the Corinthian believers he addresses, who were *not* judged favourably by the standards of their culture (1:26).[45] In essence, he used their own status as 'underdogs' to make his point.

Now in the Graeco-Roman world, this appeal to the underdog was a *counter-cultural* argument, and Paul has to provide the theological rationale – Yahweh as God of the underdog – for it to work. In Australia, however, this argument already has the wider culture onside from the beginning. Our strong egalitarian leanings mean that Australians are primed to barrack for the underdog, and we celebrate the achievements of the ordinary 'Aussie battler'. Our war heroes tend to be the unsung digger and the Anzac spirit collectively, or ordinary individuals (like Simpson and his unlikely asinine accomplice) doing extraordinary things, rather than the generals (with our egalitarian dislike of authority leading us to view them as elite and out of touch, treating their soldiers as expendable pawns and sending them to the wrong beach).[46] One way of translating Paul's argument would be to show how a unified church that refuses to judge one another the way the world does can be seen as embodying egalitarianism and the Aussie love of the underdog.

In chapter three, Paul then argues that it is foolish to be divided over leaders (like Apollos and himself) because they are united in purpose, just with different roles. To illustrate this, he draws on some of the stock imagery from the first century to illustrate: farming (sowing and watering) and construction (foundation-laying and building). Making a similar argument in chapter twelve, he employs a common image of different parts of the body having different functions for the benefit of the common good.[47] At first glance, this does not need much in the way of contextualisation, since most analogies of this kind are immediately *intelligible* to twenty-first-century Australians, although some may need brief explanations. However, intelligibility is not what makes analogies resonate with an audience, as that largely relates to the *content* being communicated. Where Paul has chosen examples from his audience's lived experience, we will need to do likewise if they are to have the same function.[48] While some of Paul's imagery may connect with the lived experience of different congregations – farming in the bush, building in the cities – we will need to use the stock images of our *own* culture if the images are to have the same effect on our hearers.[49] In the case of 1 Corinthians 3, Australians' love of sport makes it obvious and appropriate to speak of the different roles and skills needed on a sporting team to achieve the common goal of winning.

Be united: do not compromise with the world's sexual ethics

In chapters five to seven,[50] Paul addresses the disunity within the church that has arisen as a result of the differences between the values of the gospel and those of the world in the areas of sexual behaviour and marriage. In regard to the former, some in the church were perpetuating the patterns found in the wider community of allowing immoral behaviour by male heads of households to go unchecked,[51] without regard to how their behaviour dishonoured the rest of the body collectively (the 'one batch of dough' in 5:6) as well as dishonouring the individuals they thus mistreated. In regard to the latter, some were buying into a secular debate on the value of marriage, essentially between the Stoics (who saw procreation through marriage as fundamental to the good order of society) and the Cynics (who saw it as a waste of time).[52] In both cases, a desire to accommodate the ethics and 'water cooler discussion' of the surrounding society is at the heart. Paul's response is to remind them of how their new identity in Christ makes continuing their previous sexual behaviour untenable (6:11, 19–20), affirms a mutuality to the marriage relationship in which both partners are honoured (7:3–4) and forms a completely different basis upon which believers are to evaluate the wisdom of marriage (7:32–35).

Paul's message to twenty-first-century Australian believers, then, is far more profound than simply a contextualisation of the specifics – 'don't sleep with your stepmother, visit prostitutes or dishonour your spouse' – although the message to honour one another with our sexual and marital behaviour is clearly important. We live in a culture that has rapidly changed its position on the ethics of sex, gender and marriage, to the point where holding to a biblical viewpoint is no longer seen as merely quaint and mostly harmless, but a subversion of the social order. Furthermore, our secular, postmodern culture is actively pressuring Christians to conform to these new ethics, not only through sustained attacks from some sections of the media, academia and politics (essentially an epideictic shaming of deviant behaviour), but also through more practical means such as threatening access to public money and taxation concessions. As with any minority group, this external pressure to conform can incite internal division as individuals respond in different ways.[53]

In appropriating Paul's message, then, we firstly need to insulate our audience from this pressure to compromise in the same way Paul did: by refusing to accept the world's assumptions, resisting the temptation to always appear 'reasonable' to a society that has a fundamentally different worldview and instead grounding our appeal in our new identity, which by its very essence will cause us to behave differently from the world. Secondly, Paul also speaks briefly to the opposite response, reminding his audience that it is not their business 'to judge those outside the church' (5:12). This may be more significant for us than the Corinthians, due to the long history of Christian morality being the dominant ethic of the majority, with some sections of the Australian church seeking to use whatever power or privilege they have left to hold back the cultural shift. Compromise and judgementalism are both out of step with how we are called to relate to the wider culture, and both can cause division within the church community.

Be united: act for the good of others, not your own

In chapters eight to ten, the presenting issue is that the eating of idol food by some is leading others to defile their consciences (8:7) – again, a cause of disunity within the body of Christ (8:11–13). Although the specifics do not tend to arise in twenty-first-century Western culture, our increasing Asian population has put this topic again, as it were, on the table. Discussion of whether a Christian can, in good conscience, participate in the cultic practices of ancestor worship is very much a live issue within Asian congregations,[54] and any twenty-first-century Australian contextualisation of this text must resist a Western bias to gloss over the most direct application before looking further afield.

It is difficult, although not impossible, to find direct parallels in a secular culture, since there is rarely a cultic aspect. One instance may be the experience related by a ministry colleague who had been a self-confessed gym junkie and idolater of his own body; upon becoming a follower of Jesus he decided to remove himself from that world entirely for a time as he learnt to realign his priorities with the kingdom. His resolve, however, was not helped by some well-meaning members of his church, who could not understand why he was resisting their efforts to get him to join the gym and indoor sports centre that was a flagship ministry of the church. Idolatrous associations take on many different forms, and Australia's idolatry of sport and health may need more attention from the pulpit than is frequently given.

However, the most significant application is the dynamic behind Paul's seemingly conflicting instructions (8:13; 10:21, 25–27, 28) about eating idol food. That is, on morally neutral matters, do what is helpful for others rather than exercising one's own rights, seeking the common good rather than that of oneself as an individual (10:24, 32–33). In first-century Corinth, this message aligned to some extent with the more collectivist culture of Graeco-Roman society and its goal, in aspiration if not always in practice, of the common good.[55] In twenty-first-century Australia, however, this cuts against the grain of our entrenched individualism, while perhaps finding an ally among the more collectivist aspirations of Australian millennials.[56] Furthermore, Paul frames the issue as being between the relationship between the 'strong' and the 'weak' (here, and in Rom 15:1–2), and hints at the division having an ethnic connection (1 Cor 10:32). Australian churches are also ethnically mixed, and maintaining unity requires a commitment by all groups to put others' needs first – especially the majority that holds the power ('the strong' in this case) giving up its rights so that minorities are built up rather than further marginalised.

Be united: do not compromise on your worldview

Moving to chapter fifteen, Paul deals with a potential source of division in which 'some' (15:12) deny the idea of bodily resurrection. It is likely that the 'some' are of an educated Greek background, for whom the idea of bodily resurrection is absurd, given that one of the foundational concepts of Greek philosophy is Platonic dualism, in which the spiritual is superior to and seeks escape from the material, and the body carries with it connotations of mortality.[57] In rhetorical form, this chapter is an example of *refutatio*, in which both known and anticipated objections are dealt with by the speaker; the former can be seen in 15:12 and the latter in 15:35 ('but someone will ask … '). The function of the chapter, then, is to answer real and potential objections to the Christian teaching on resurrection, countering those who are influenced by the worldview of the intelligentsia in the surrounding culture.

In preaching this chapter, we will need to pursue a similar function, firstly showing how the same kinds of objections exist in Australian society today. Most obviously, the objection to any form of resurrection, bodily or otherwise, is found in secular atheism.[58] Additionally, although Australians with religious backgrounds may embrace some idea of a continued existence after death, for many the goal is similar to that of the ancient Greeks: to escape our material existence. This is true for many Eastern religions, as well as for those who may culturally identify as Christian but have been more informed by the Platonic assumptions underlying much Western thought, along with the persistent imagery of clouds, harps and angel wings. Secondly, being true to the principle of *refutatio*, we will go further, anticipating objections that may not have been part of Paul's culture. These include atheistic presuppositions, a suspicion of history itself, and a postmodern mistrust of anything that claims to be a metanarrative.

In answering these objections, we will employ Paul's arguments, recognising that not all of them may be equally appropriate for our setting. Most obviously, the logical conclusions Paul draws from the historical evidence for Jesus' own resurrection are still just as valid today (although the greater historical distance will require more detailed supporting evidence than the brief list of eyewitnesses mentioned in the creedal material Paul cites). His reference to the practice of being baptised for the dead is less directly relevant (15:29), although the idea behind it is quite broad: showing how particular human behaviours (which Berger has termed 'signals of transcendence'[59]) give evidence of an underlying hope that this is not all there is. One such example can be found in one of Australia's civic religions, the celebration of Anzac Day and the 'Anzac spirit' which lives on in us all, exemplified in Dame Mary Gilmore's poem performed at many dawn services:

> They are not dead; not even broken.
> Only their dust has gone back home to the earth;
> For they, the essential they, shall have rebirth
> Whenever a word of them is spoken.⁶⁰

Finally, we will need to be clear that, just as in the original setting, our apologetic is addressed first to those within the church, before also to those outside. As with the discussion on sexual ethics, the danger is that the increasingly secular, anti-supernaturalist worldview of the surrounding culture will make it increasingly difficult for Australian Christians to articulate doctrines like the resurrection without facing ridicule from the largely secular humanist institutions of academia and the media. The temptation for believers will be to conform to these anti-supernaturalist presuppositions or at least to 'soft-pedal' key biblical teachings. This, too, has significant potential for division, as those in the church who prioritise respect and acceptance in the secular marketplace of ideas may end up endangering the faith of others (15:2, 17, 33–34).

Although much more could be said, the preceding discussion of some of the key rhetorical arguments in 1 Corinthians has provided suggestive examples of how every Pauline text can be applied to Australian audiences: exegete the strategies Paul employs, focusing on identifying their function, then use these strategies where appropriate (and adapt them when they are not) so that they function in our sermon in a way analogous to their function in the biblical text.

Sample Sermon: Galatians 2:15–21

Comments on the Sermon

Thus far, we have worked through a hermeneutical method for preaching Paul's epistles, focusing on an analysis of the original rhetorical situation, which helps to identify ways the epistle might function within the rhetorical situation of a sermon to twenty-first-century Australians. Having used 1 Corinthians as an example, let us now turn our attention to a different epistle, Galatians, which will serve both as a recapitulation of the process and an example of what a finished sermon might look like.

My chosen text is Galatians 2:15–21, which by any reckoning is at the heart of the Galatians argument. In rhetorical theory, it functions as the proposition of the epistle, taking the form of a division: an outline of the key points which will be argued in the remainder of the speech.

I first describe the rhetorical situation, in which the recipients are in danger of being persuaded by some 'agitators' (Gal 5:12) to add the Mosaic law – and circumcision as its sign – to the gospel of justification by faith in Jesus, making it 'a different gospel'

(1:6). Now, I could simply stop at this point and make the application of the sermon relate to anything and everything we might be tempted add to the gospel. This would not be wrong, although not much of it would be all that similar to the Mosaic law; and for the most part, we do not explicitly add them as requirements for justification, merely as cultural boundary markers to be accepted in a given church fellowship.

However, I probe a little more deeply and ask the first question: why? What made the Mosaic law attractive to Gentile converts? The answers to this, as will be seen in the sermon, show that while the surface details are indeed quite different from our own situation, the underlying motivation of behavioural change is strikingly similar. We are no less susceptible than the Galatians to attempt behavioural change through the power of self rather than the indwelling Spirit. (Given the ongoing debate over the specifics of the Galatian situation, not everyone will agree on all the details of the analysis I present in the sermon; however, the point here is to illustrate how an exegesis of the rhetorical situation can guide a sermon, rather than defend a particular reading of Galatians. Supporting references are given in the endnotes.)

The answer to the second question about what needs to happen to bring about change is straightforward: both Paul's audience and ours need to be shown that this is not how the gospel works – that behavioural change is also the work of Christ.

The third question regarding rhetorical strategies is, as always, a little more complicated. Paul speaks authoritatively and harshly (1:6; 3:1) – appropriate, given the tone of Asiatic rhetoric generally, his role as the founder of their church and the imminent nature of the crisis. We Australian preachers might need to be a little more circumspect, particularly in the absence of marauding bands of Judaizers in most Australian churches. For the most part, he employs logical, rational argument, especially in the chosen passage; so I do likewise.[61] Importantly, the text forms the division of the speech, foreshadowing the other arguments given in the remainder of the speech; it is appropriate, therefore, to draw in those arguments and examples, such as justification being given to Abraham before the law was given (3:17), keeping in step with the Spirit (3:16) and carrying one another's burdens (6:2).

Readers will also note the generally Australian tone of the sermon, which contains plenty of colloquial expressions and Aussie irreverence.

Sermon text

Transformation. Growth. Improvement. It's part of what makes us human – to want to change things for the better.

Just look at the publishing industry. Out of all the non-fiction books sold, the two top selling categories are about building your wealth and transforming yourself. Classics like Stephen Covey, *The 7 Habits of Highly Effective People: Powerful Lessons in Personal*

Change; Tony Robbins, *Unleash the Power Within: Personal Coaching that will Transform Your Life*; and Paul McKenna, *Change Your life in 7 Days*. And we could go on. Listing books that tell you how to change, how to grow as a person. How to be transformed.

As Christians, we believe in change, too, right? We might dress it up in more important sounding words like 'spiritual transformation' or 'spiritual growth'. But essentially, we want to be better people. We want to become what God intended us to be. It's clearly a biblical idea.

But as true as that may be, it makes me stop and think – are we clear on what spiritual transformation is? On why we want to change? Because whenever the church and the world are sending similar messages, spouting similar phrases – when there's this synching of slogans, there's always a danger of losing our Christian distinctiveness, isn't there? Of equating the kind of transformation the world wants with the kind *God* wants to see in us.

If we're not clear about what we're on about, there's always the risk we'll start to buy into our culture's values. Seduced by the similarities, we become blinded to the differences. So that our message ceases to be distinct. Radical. Unique. We're just another voice saying the same thing, with a few out-of-context Scripture quotations thrown in to make it sound biblical.

Let me read some other book titles, this time by a wide cross-section of Christian authors, to see if you can spot the danger: Joel Osteen, *Become a Better You*; Joyce Meyer, *Change Your Words, Change Your Life*; John Ortberg, *The Life You've Always Wanted*; Tim Keller, *You Can Change*; John Piper, *Don't Waste Your Life*.

Now, hear me correctly: I'm not actually having a go at these books or these authors. Most of them aren't bad. Some of them are radically counter-cultural in what they say. And at least two of them would be in my top ten spiritual formation books. But my point is this: they look a lot like the other ones, don't they? The titles. The marketing pitch. The promise of improvement and change – that things will get better for you, if only you do what my book says.

It makes us question: are we in danger of becoming just another self-help, self-empowerment option in an increasingly crowded marketplace? Are we truly distinctive, truly Christian in our pursuit of spiritual transformation – both when it comes to the goal of this change we're chasing, as well as the means by which we're seeking to achieve it?

They're the two questions I want to ask today as we begin to deal with our topic of transformation. What's distinctive about Christian transformation – both its goal and its means?

The Galatian situation

So, I thought that the obvious place to start was with the debate over circumcision in Paul's letter to the Galatians.

What was happening in Galatia? Let me give you a quick run-down. Basically, it was a church Paul had planted, mostly made up of Gentiles – people who weren't Jewish. But then a bunch of Jewish believers had turned up, trying to get these Gentile converts circumcised and obeying the law of Moses. 'Cause the two go together: circumcision is the sign of being part of God's people, and obeying the law the way of life for God's people. Even the apostle Peter has been drawn into this back in Antioch, to the point where Paul calls him out on it:

> I said to Cephas in front of them all, 'You are a Jew, yet you live like a Gentile and not like a Jew. How is it, then, that you force Gentiles to follow Jewish customs?' (Gal 2:14)

Why would these hard-line Jewish Christians, why would these Judaizers (as we call them) want to do this? What's it to them if a bunch of uncircumcised Gentiles become Christians?

Later in the letter, Paul is quite explicit about their motives. He says the Judaizers don't want the embarrassment of being associated with lawless Gentiles: 'All the other Jews'll make fun of us. Persecute us. And after all, we were God's people first. So if they want to join our club, they have to become like us.'[62] I struggle to think of a modern analogy [as a picture of One Nation Senator, Pauline Hanson, briefly appears on screen]. So far, it makes sense as far as the Judaizers go.

But did you ever think for a moment: what's in it for the Gentiles? Why didn't they just send them packing? I can't see it being an easy sell. Kosher food and circumcision. I mean, imagine yourself, as a Gentile, hearing the Judaizers' pitch for the very first time: 'Okay, so to sum up, you want me to give up ham completely and just cut back a little on the salami? Right, um, no thanks.'

So why were they 'bewitched' by this, to the point that Paul had to write a letter to convince them otherwise? What's the attraction?

I suppose it's possible that the Judaizers had convinced the Galatians circumcision and the law were the way to *becoming* right with God. That Christ's sacrifice wasn't enough. And yet, at the beginning of today's reading, Paul seems to imply that this wasn't really in dispute; that all the players agreed justification was by faith, not works. Have a listen:

> We who are Jews by birth and not sinful Gentiles know that a person is not justified by the works of the law, but by faith in Jesus Christ. (Gal 2:15–16a)

Even Jews didn't really think that doing the law *made* you right with God. It was more the sign that you belonged to God's covenant people.

And that's probably more what's at issue here in Galatia. Making the Judaizers' message a little more subtle, more along the lines of: Christ has made you Gentiles a part of us, God's people. So now, get circumcised and obey the law. That's how you fit in – both with us, and with God's expectations.[63] The law is the process by which you unrighteous Gentiles learn to behave righteously, like us. The law is what helps you change. What makes you grow. What enables you to be *spiritually transformed*. (Told you I'd get there.)

Now we're on exegetically safe ground so far, but if we step a little closer to the edges, I think we can see the possibility of an even closer correlation with our own situation. Where there's evidence from first-century writers like Philo of Alexandria – evidence that for at least some pagan Gentiles, the Jewish law was attractive.

Why was it attractive? Because it was portrayed – it was sold – as a means of achieving self-mastery. To the Greek philosophers' ideal of being able to restrain your passions, the law and some of its practices were held out as a means of achieving them.[64] As a kind of self-improvement strategy to achieve your best life now.

Maybe if Philo had gotten himself a contract with a North American Christian publisher, it would have looked like this: Philo of Alexandria, *The 7 Habits of Highly Observant Jews: Powerful Lessons in Self-Mastery*. [Book cover appears on screen with the tag-line: 'Take a tip from me, and let them take the tip from you.']

It's not all that different from how the moral code of Islam can be attractive for people wanting to change. A number of years ago, troubled rugby league star Blake Ferguson converted to Islam through the witness of Anthony Mundine. Interviewed by *The Sunday Telegraph*, Mundine spoke about Ferguson's motivation in embracing Islam:

> He's just looking forward to changing his direction in life. At the moment he's in good space – no drinking, no drugs, no parties ... He wants to be a better person ...[65]

And given the background of rugby league's culture of immorality – portrayed by Islam as part of Western, 'Christian' society – you can see the attraction it held. For someone in trouble, wanting to change his life. More broadly, converts to Islam in the UK are citing the social laws and disciplined lifestyle as the major attraction. It gives people boundaries to live by, helps ex-prisoners stay out of gaol, and provides good values for the next generation.

Or what about the way in which many people who *aren't* Christians send their kids to Christian schools. And when you ask them why they do this, what's their number one answer? Survey says: *to give them good values*. It seems that even today, the Christian faith is seen by some in society as a good way of training morality – just as long as you go easy on the whole Jesus bit.

So, if we're not careful, the gospel message, this promise of spiritual transformation, becomes just another competing philosophy in the marketplace of ideas. Another product that promises to give results: the life you've always wanted. It becomes an attractive moral code, like Islam to wayward footballers or Judaism to frustrated Greek philosophers. A path to virtue and fulfilment.

So, what does Paul say to all of this? Is this gospel we believe any different from everything else on offer?

The gospel is not a self-help strategy

Let's take a look at our text for today, from Galatians 2. We're starting from verse 15, where Paul starts with the basics: the law doesn't make us right with God. Paul starts on common ground with Peter, in Antioch, and by extension the Jewish believers attempting to bewitch the Galatians. He says this:

> We who are Jews by birth and not sinful Gentiles know that a person is not justified by the works of the law, but by faith in Jesus Christ. So we, too, have put our faith in [have trusted] Christ Jesus that we may be justified by faith in Christ and not by the works of the law, because by the works of the law no one will be justified. (Gal 2:15–16)

How is a person right with God? How do we become part of his people? Not by obeying the law, but through faith. And in chapter 3 of Galatians, Paul supports this point at length – showing how Abraham was justified by faith four centuries before the law ever turned up saying breathlessly, 'What did I miss?'

Then Paul turns to what *is* in dispute: does the absence of the law promote sin? It's a fair question. Now that I'm part of God's people through faith, how am I spiritually transformed? If I don't have the law as my self-help strategy, what is there to stop me being like the immoral Gentiles? This is how Paul puts it:

> But if, in seeking to be justified in Christ, we Jews find ourselves also among the sinners, doesn't that mean that Christ promotes sin? Absolutely not! If I rebuild what I destroyed, then I really would be a lawbreaker. (Gal 2:17–18)

What does it mean that we 'find ourselves also among the sinners'? There are a few options:[66]

Once we're stripped of the law's restraint, do we discover just how sinful we are? Like when I got married, I discovered how much chocolate I could happily consume in one go, once freed from my parents' regimen of doling out two tiny squares with a cup of tea after dinner?

Or does it mean that we become *labelled* 'sinners', no better than the lawless Gentiles in the eyes of law-observing Jews?

Or does it simply mean that we no longer have the law to restrain our behaviour, which leads lawlessness, to abusing our freedom, like Paul's opponents would argue? And like he defends against later in the letter?

Probably those ideas aren't mutually exclusive. And Paul's point is to raise the question: if I pursue right standing with God through Christ, rather than through the law ... and if the result is that others see me as being 'lawless', with no restraint on my sinful nature, no external rulebook to act as a check on my freedom to do what I like ... does that make Jesus a promoter of sin?

Or more simply: if we chuck out the law, does that mean we end up back where we started – enslaved to our passions? If we rule out the self-help book, are we left with no help at all?

Paul answers with an emphatic 'No way!' In fact, turning up the irony, he says that if we build the law back up after it's been done away with, *that* would make us lawbreakers! And then in chapter 4 he cranks the irony dial all the way up to eleven.

Paul says that if we go back to the law, we'd have more in common with the child of Abraham who *didn't* have the law. The slave child, Ishmael, rather than the free child, Isaac. Not how any Jew would want to end up!

Paul says that if we go back to the law, we're just as enslaved as when we were captive to our passions and desires. Not where any good Greek philosopher would like to be, either.

Paul says that if we go back and submit to the law, it's like going back as an adult to live under your parents' roof and rules – something that was good and helpful for an adolescent, but not where a free, mature adult should want to remain, no matter how big a deposit you're trying to save.

In light of what Christ has now done, the law is a step backwards.

But why can he say this? What is it that Christ has done that's such a game changer? That makes the Old Testament law just another self-help book? What's changed?

The gospel is not about 'self' at all

Here's the answer; let's read it slowly:

> For through the law I died to the law so that I might live for God. I have been crucified with Christ and I no longer live, but Christ lives in me. The life I now live in the body, I live by faith in the Son of God, who loved me and gave himself for me. (Gal 2:19–20)

Do you get it? The gospel is far superior to any self-help strategy, because it's not about 'self' at all.

Where the goal of 'self-mastery' ceases to exist, because in one sense, 'self' ceases to exist. 'I' no longer live. The self that was enslaved by passions and desires is crucified with Christ; it died with him. It's gone.

And far more than that. It's not just a death of self, but a resurrection. No longer do 'I' live – it's Christ who lives in me. His life. His goodness. His faithfulness. That's what replaces self.

Where the law or Islam or Greek philosophy or Tony Robbins or even a Christian school teaching Christian values – where they can only stand on the *outside* and tell me what to do, the power of Christ-in-me transforms me from the *inside*.

Who needs Ten Commandments, when we have Christ? Who needs the four pillars of Islam, when we have Christ? Who needs seven habits or steps or tips from any highly effective human being, when we have the supremely effective power of the resurrected Christ in us?

Does the absence of the law or any other external guide promote sin? No way! Because we have Christ in us.

And that is the essence of spiritual transformation, for a believer in Jesus. It's not a relentless pursuit of self-mastery, so that we can live up to what we always wanted to be, or to what God always intended us to be. If righteousness could be gained that way, then Christ died for nothing (says Paul in v.21).

For us, spiritual transformation is the death of self, and in its place living by the power of Christ-in-me; living by the Spirit. And that's what makes the gospel radically different from all of those self-help regimens on offer. Different in means – how it's done. Different in goal – in what it's aiming for. So, in the time we have left, let's unpack these two aspects to see what it might mean in more concrete and practical terms.

The means of transformation: Christ-in-me

Firstly, let's look at the means of transformation. The way in which change comes about. 'Cause the world's idea of personal growth is that it comes through direct effort. Through self-help. Do these seven things and you'll get there. Work at this all week, and you'll see improvement by Friday.

Christians can fall into this trap easily. We want to grow. We want to please God. And so, we spend our lives looking for stuff to do better. Sometimes succeeding. Sometimes failing.

And much preaching doesn't help. As Henry Cloud says – wander into any given church on any given Sunday, and the sermon probably boils down to the same three points: God's good, you're not, try harder.[67] And we wonder why people fall into the trap of self-improvement!

Yet what's the alternative? Sit back and wait for God to do his thing? Continue in sin? Not put effort into doing what's right? That's the opposite error Paul wants to avoid. What he had to defend his gospel against.

> You, my brothers and sisters, were called to be free. But do not use your freedom to indulge the flesh; rather, serve one another humbly in love. (Gal 5:13)

Paul makes it clear that there's something active we need to do. A 'getting on board' with the Spirit's program, rather than sitting around waiting for something.

> So I say, walk by the Spirit, and you will not gratify the desires of the flesh. (Gal 5:16)

> Those who belong to Christ Jesus have crucified the flesh with its passions and desires. Since we live by the Spirit, let us keep in step with the Spirit. (Gal 5:24–25)

Walk by the spirit. Crucify the flesh. Since we have the Spirit in us, keep in step with it. Don't keep trying self-help but co-operate with Christ-in-me.

What this precisely means, how this works out in daily life, is I confess something of a mystery. And if I could fully explain this tension and how to live it, you'd be reading about this in my own seven-step book on the shelves at a Christian bookstore near you.

But here's one helpful idea I picked up from one of the books I mentioned earlier; John Ortberg's *The Life You've Always Wanted*. It's a book on spiritual disciplines. And he talks about the idea of doing stuff that puts you in a place where God does *his* stuff. Well, that's my paraphrase, anyway. Actively putting yourself in a space where God is most likely to transform you.[68]

He uses the analogy of training for a sport. 'Cause you don't normally improve much in a sport just by going out and trying hard to play it. No, you also do a bunch of activities – often unrelated to the game – to build skills and fitness, that then come in handy in the game. You don't score points on the field for how much you can bench-press, but it contributes.

It's the same with spiritual growth. It's not about going out there with gritted teeth and *trying* to be more Christ-like. To be more humble or more loving or more patient. Or to stop this sin or that sin. That's generally pretty ineffective – the typical self-help approach.

But there are things you can do that build spiritual habits. Build spiritual muscle. Give spiritual opportunities. You don't score points for them with God. But they put you in the kind of place where God tends to do his mysterious work of transformation.

You want specifics? Well, Ortberg starts with the obvious ones. Regular immersion in God's word, so that what's feeding your thoughts is from God rather than from the temptations of the culture around us. Disciplined rhythms of prayer that get us in the habit of talking to God and taking time to listen.

But some of the other suggestions – they're about setting up little practice sessions. If you play tennis and you want to work on your returns, you'll get someone to practise serving at you a whole lot of times in a row, right? So, think of the areas you need to grow in, and set up little practices that give the opportunity for God to grow you.

Struggling with pride? Volunteer for a really humble act of service each week. Struggling with patience and irritability? Practice 'slow days', where you deliberately choose the longer queue; let others in ahead of you. Struggling with trusting God rather than self? Do something in ministry totally out of your comfort zone. Deliberately put yourself in situations you'd normally struggle in, and ask God to teach you through them.

And don't do this on your own. Do it in community, where those who for the moment are stronger can use their structure and discipline to help those who are struggling. 'Carry one another's burdens', as Paul says in chapter 6.

Now does this sound like just another self-help strategy. Yes. It can be, if you treat it like one. If I bench-press two Bible readings, crunch out ten prayers every morning, I'll have a new set of spiritual abs in six weeks. If we do all these training exercises thinking they'll guarantee spiritual growth, then we'll probably be in for disappointment and be asking for our money back, less postage and handling.

But if we realise all we're doing is acknowledging our inability to self-improve – that every time we throw ourselves into God's word, every time we drag our weary minds into his presence in prayer, every time we force ourselves into a situation where our natural instinct would to be un-godly – what we're doing is placing our faith not in our own ability or activity or strategy. We're placing our faith in Jesus' faithfulness. Trusting in the fact that it's Christ who lives in me. Saying, 'I can't do this! ... but I want to be in the place where if I *am* to do it, it's going to be Christ-in-me who does it.'

For us, Christ-in-me is the means of spiritual transformation.

The goal of transformation: Christ-in-me

And Christ-in-me is also the *goal* of spiritual transformation.

This may seem obvious, since the definition of spiritual transformation is to become Christ-like. 'Be imitators of me, as I am of Christ', says Paul. But often our success-oriented culture can get us side-tracked in our goal of spiritual growth, too.

I mean, who are the successful Christians in the world? The famous ones, right! Why are they famous? Because they write books with steps to success, or have big churches, or big hair and teeth, or big PowerPoint presentations involving golf balls and laminin,[69] or whatever it is they've done that's different, that makes people notice them.

They may well be godly people – we don't really know – but the fact is they're famous because they've been successful in something measurable or outwardly noticeable. You can count it, or you can see it.

Now I trust that's not the way we *consciously* measure growth. But does that feed in to how we subtly start to evaluate ourselves? Numbers and metrics and outcomes. Because they're more visible. More tangible.

How have I grown this past year? Well, I've led two people to Christ. The kids in my youth group are treating me more as their spiritual mentor. I think I've prayed more times. I've read through the entire Old Testament in a year … Or, conversely, we look at the numbers and are disappointed in them.

But what's growth actually supposed look like, if we're serious about the goal being to see Christ formed in me? Not a series of accomplishments or a set of skills or a metric of outcomes. It's character, formed over time, that works out in our behaviour. Or as Paul puts it to the Galatians:

> But the fruit of the Spirit [the fruit of Christ-in-me] is love, joy, peace, forbearance, kindness, goodness, faithfulness, gentleness and self-control. Against such things there is no law. (Gal 5:22–23)

It's character, not skill set. It's behavioural traits, not specific accomplishments. Skills are important. But not as fundamental to who we are as Christ-like character. Set some character goals for yourself. Some specific ways in which you know you need to become more like Christ-in-me.

Pray diligently for God to change you. And then work out some things you can do to put yourself in the best possible place for that to happen.

And although how that works and when that works and what the finished product looks like is something of a divine, untameable mystery, you will look back at what God has done and be able to say: it is no longer I who live, but Christ who lives in me.

10

PREACHING THE PETRINE EPISTLES TO AUSTRALIANS

Mike Raiter

Introduction

I train preachers. I divide my time between conducting preaching workshops and coaching preachers. In my coaching sessions, which are normally with groups of three or four, the members either preach to the group a sermon they've recently delivered, and then receive critical feedback, or bring the first draft of a sermon they are working on. From my experience, preachers turn to the New Testament letters more frequently than any other biblical genre. And 1 Peter is a particular favourite.

The Hermeneutical Task

The Appeal of the Letters

What is the appeal of the New Testament letters for preaching?

Firstly, in the flow or progression of biblical revelation, the letters are the last stage. The letters are the outworking of the implications of the gospel in the lives of God's people. Almost all our key Christian doctrines find their fullest exposition in the letters. What's more, the letters address many key dimensions of Christian living.

Secondly, while much of the Bible is culturally distant from us, particularly we who live in the West, this cultural distance seems much smaller with the letters. In part, this is because they are largely written to urban communities. Much of the Old Testament is addressed to a theocratic nation, bound together by a common language and culture, occupying a common piece of land. The New Testament letters address God's people scattered across the Roman Empire. Further, the theological depth and complexity of many of the themes addressed in these letters suggests that at least some of the recipients were literate and well educated.

Connected to this is the fact that the letters were written to Christian churches and we are preaching to Christian churches. I recently heard a preacher expounding Judges 19–21, one of the morally darkest parts of Scripture. Repeatedly, the preacher claimed, 'and we are just like this'. I have been a member of a number of Christian churches, and none of them has resembled the idol-worshipping, brutal tribes of Israel in the days 'when everyone did what was right in their own eyes' (Judg 21:25). We don't feel the same moral and spiritual distance when we read many of the letters of Paul, Peter and John. The issues they address are the very issues we face today. That's why preachers find applying the letters of the New Testament to our contemporary context far easier than applying the Old Testament.

Thirdly, the length of many of the letters makes them appealing to preachers. How does one set out to preach a Gospel? For example, an expository series on the entire Gospel of Matthew, which attempts to treat every passage in some depth, would be a very long series. For that reason, many preachers choose to preach Matthew in sections (e.g., chapters 1–4, 5–7 etc). While this allows for passages to be dealt with in depth, the compromise is in losing the flow of the Gospel's narrative.

While Romans and the Corinthian correspondence present the same challenges, in most cases one can preach a New Testament letter right through without sacrificing a sense of its thematic coherence.

The Structure of the Letters and the Structure of the Sermon Series

When it comes to launching a sermon series (and my assumption throughout this chapter is that we'll be preaching a sermon series on 1 Peter or 2 Peter), one of the first decisions we have to make is determining the length of the series. There are a number of issues to bear in mind here that are informed by our understanding of the nature of the genre of the letter.

Letters normally have a discernible structure. We will want the structure of the series to reflect the structure of the letter. Many of the New Testament letters were dictated, and while we can sometimes detect the writer digressing from his subject (e.g., 1 Pet 3:19–22), or when writing 'finally', actually having far more to say (e.g., 1 Pet 3:8), nevertheless we can normally detect the flow of the author's argument.

Further, a letter normally has a particular purpose. There is a reason (or reasons) why the writer is addressing his audience. Unlike, say, the Old Testament historical books, the purpose of the author of the letters is usually transparent. So, for example, in his second letter Peter writes, 'Dear friends, this is now my second letter to you. I have written both of them as reminders to stimulate you to wholesome thinking' (2 Peter 3:1).

It's important to keep the purpose of the letter before the people. The danger in a very long sermon series is that the people lose the forest for the trees. For this reason, near the beginning of each sermon I briefly recap what the writer has already written so that the people understand both his big idea and the flow of his argument.

The Homiletical Issues

All of this, and more, impinges on our decision about both the content of each sermon (how many verses we will expound) and the length of the sermon series. We want to expose our people to as much of God's word given to us through Peter as we can, but there are some qualifiers. Firstly, we have a very big Bible, and we may find it hard to justify dedicating six months or more to the exposition of 1 Peter (although there is certainly enough in 1 Peter for twenty-six sermons, or more). But every week exposing people to Peter is a week when the other sixty-five inspired books are not proclaimed. Secondly, the New Testament letters are very dense. Just think of the opening two verses of 1 Peter. Here are the topics that could be profitably explored:

- Authorship
- Recipients
    - elect
    - exiles
    - geographical location
    - chosen
    - divine foreknowledge
    - Fatherhood of God
    - sanctifying work of the Spirit
- Purpose
    - obedience
    - sprinkling with Jesus' blood
- Greeting
    - grace
    - peace

There we have a twelve-point sermon – and that's only two verses. If we try to cover everything, we run the twin risks of information overload or dealing with each point so superficially that one wonders as to the value.

In summary, one of the appeals of the Petrine letters is that they are comparatively short, and so amenable to a preaching series. At the same time, the depth and richness of their content raises questions about the length and number of sermons.

Allow me to add one more comment. It is important to remember that, when it comes to the length of the sermon (how much to cover) and the number of sermons, the preacher is the master of the sermon series; the sermon series is not the master to which I owe slavish obedience. My responsibility is to be faithful to the passage and, to the best of my ability, the author's purpose. However, for the sake of clarity, coherence and impact, I am free to decide not to cover every verse, or I am free to lengthen or shorten the sermon series.

The Contextualisation Task

Understanding Our Context: Preaching to Aussies

What makes this book on expository preaching if not unique then certainly special is its focus. The book examines preaching the Bible to *Aussies*. However, the challenge of preaching to Aussies is complex, because 'Aussies' are complex. The 'Describing Australians' chapter has already very helpfully diagnosed some important distinctives of being Australian, but I want to add a couple of observations about the Aussies we preach to week by week in our churches.

The Aussies we are preaching to are diverse, not just in terms of age, gender, profession and so on, but also geographically, ethnically and theologically. We have to ask ourselves, to which kind of Aussies are we preaching? Space only permits a few brief comments.

One of the features of the modern church, particularly in our cities, is the 'Asianisation' of the church. While most of my evidence is anecdotal, it appears that the majority of converts to Christianity in Australia today are from a non-Anglo-Saxon background, and many from a non-English-speaking background. I live in inner-city Melbourne. Just a walk down Swanston Street demonstrates the extent to which the city's demographic has changed in the last thirty years. Thanks to the many overseas students and young workers, inner-city Melbourne has morphed into an Asian city. Urban geographer Seamus O'Hanlon suggests that by 2030 the 'typical Australian' will as likely be a young female professional of an Asian background living in a new high-rise apartment in inner-city Sydney.[1] Already, as O'Hanlon notes, Sydney and Melbourne are no longer 'Australian' in the older racially and culturally accepted forms of the term.[2] These changes are reflected in the makeup of our churches. While the number of people who tick the box 'no religion' continues to rise in our surveys, Asian immigration is saving the Australian church from even more serious numerical decline.

This has significant implications for our preaching. Since an increasing number of those attending our urban churches don't have English as their first language, then this must impact both our content and our delivery. We will need to speak more slowly and in words and sentences that aren't too complex. I preach from a full text, and so I often print out my manuscript and give it to those whose English might be poor or who may find my accent hard to understand.

Of course, a wide range of cultural issues arise when preaching to Asians. Some years ago, I was invited to speak at the wedding of a young Chinese couple. I began the sermon with an illustration of a funeral. I remember at the time the congregation appeared unimpressed. I was informed later that in the Chinese culture you don't talk publicly about funerals – let alone at a wedding! There are very important issues of honour and shame, obligations to one's parents and expectations of ancestor worship, to name just a few, which impact 'Aussie Asian' culture. From time to time, the application of our sermon must address these kinds of issues. In other words, there may be applications of a given passage that would not occur to preachers whose heritage is white Anglo-Saxon but in fact speak powerfully to people of another culture.

There are also a variety of theological 'tribes' across the Australian church. These tribes often cross denominational boundaries. For example, I spent many years living and ministering in Sydney. To a significant degree, the Anglican Diocese of Sydney, and Moore College in particular, and even more specifically a number of important leaders (tribal chiefs, if you like) have shaped the theological culture of many Christians – and not just Anglicans. One finds members of the same 'tribe' in Presbyterian, Congregational, Baptist and Independent churches. The tribe has many distinctive theological emphases (and one could add, rituals and songs). Let me give just one example. This Sydney Anglican tribe gives a prominent place to the mind. The preferred approach to preaching is grammatical-historical exegesis. Preachers normally spend hours of preparation in reading and researching. The body of the sermon mainly comprises explanation of the text, often with little attention to application. Recently, at a national conference held in Sydney, a visiting preacher from the United States chided the audience for giving too much attention to matters of the heart, and too little attention to serious intellectual engagement with the text. The target audience was 'Aussie Christians', but for the majority in the audience that part of the sermon missed the mark. The preacher, understandably, didn't comprehend the particular Christian subculture or tribe being addressed.

One could say so much more. Different tribes have different views of expository preaching. Some esteem it as the only faithful way of preaching, while others despise it. Some tribes demand 45–50-minute sermons, while others are committed to 20–25 minutes. All this is to say, our term 'Aussie' is more diverse than perhaps we imagine.

Preaching Peter to Aussies: Worlds in Common

While separated by 2000 years and about 15,000 kilometres, the church worlds of twenty-first-century Australia and first-century Asia Minor are remarkably similar. Consequently, part of the appeal of preaching the letters of Peter is the relevance of their issues for today.

The scattered believers who received these apostolic letters were living in an environment largely hostile to the gospel. Most commentators agree that at the time of writing (probably the early 60s CE), these churches were not suffering from violent persecution. Rather, much like Australia today, the opposition was occasional, localised and expressed in abuse, slander and discrimination. However, for them as for us, intensification of the persecution didn't seem too far away.

The letter is addressed to the scattered exiles (1:1). The term 'exile' is surely meant to bring to mind Israel's calamitous exile into Babylon in 587 BCE. There, for a time, many lived among a strange people, whose customs and beliefs were not just foreign but, in some cases, abhorrent to God-fearing Jews.

It would be fair to say that until recently in much of the Western world, Christians did not feel particularly alienated from the surrounding culture. Certainly, they were distinctive in some of their behaviours and attitudes, but ideologically they shared much in common. I spent my early childhood in England in the 1950s and 60s. My mother was a cultural Christian. She practised occasional church-going, and she had her children baptised into the Church of England and sent them to Sunday School. She did this, not just to give herself a deserved break from the demands of parenting, but because she believed a Sunday School education was good for them. She believed in God, and to the extent that she understood the teachings of the church, she believed them. While her spiritual rebirth would take place many years later, her thinking and behaving was significantly influenced by Christianity. In the government primary school I attended, we held regular chapel services (and I can still sing word-for-word the hymns we sang). Scripture was a subject taught and examined by our classroom teacher, along with all the other disciplines.

Increasingly, that is not the world I have brought my children into. Just one example will suffice. In 2015 on the ABC's popular television program Q&A, panellist Paul Ehrlich, the renowned ecologist, made an off-the-cuff remark that Scripture teaching in schools is child abuse. When the surprised host, Tony Jones, asked him to explain his provocative remark, Ehrlich elaborated that 'teaching children about non-existent terrifying monsters like God' could only be described as child abuse. But here's the important thing: the audience broke out in applause. Of course, not all the audience, but a significant number. In the early twenty-first century, Australian Christians feel like exiles in a foreign and increasingly hostile land. To such a church in such a context, 1 Peter speaks with particular resonance.

Homiletical Issues in Preaching 1 Peter to Aussies

Space does not allow me to deal with all the exegetical and homiletical issues that 1 Peter throws up for Aussie Christians, so I will focus on just four.

Our urban context

Like most of the Western world, Australia is urbanised. Two thirds of our population live in our capital cities. Similarly, many of Peter's first readers were urban dwellers who lived in cities like Smyrna.

The Graeco-Roman world in which Peter and the other Christians first proclaimed the gospel was every bit as pluralistic as our urban Western context today. The New Testament documents addressed multiracial and multicultural communities. The world of the first century was a veritable smorgasbord of religious commodities. Citizens were required to worship the emperor. There was the pantheon of gods like Neptune, Apollo and Artemis. Throughout the empire there were various expressions of the worship of the gods of the Egyptians, Isis and Serapis. Mystery cults abounded in the Mediterranean world, and then there were sacred rocks and mountains. Apart from all this, virtually every city and people had their own patron deities.

The abandonment of the White Australia Policy in 1973, and the subsequent removal of many of the racial and cultural prohibitions on immigration, has catapulted Australia into being a multifaith society. Apart from the numerous recognised religions, Australia is now host to diverse spiritualities. Just a walk around Australia's annual Mind, Body and Spirit festival will demonstrate the extent of Australia's spiritual diversity. So, when apostles like Peter announced to their multifaith world that 'Jesus is Lord', they were well aware of how provocative such a message was. While Aussies trumpet 'tolerance' as one of our nation's most important virtues (see the 'Describing Australians' chapter), in reality many are just as intolerant of any claims to exclusivity as those of the Graeco-Roman world.

How did Peter encourage his churches to respond in a context that was pluralistic, suspicious and often openly hostile to Christians? It is remarkable that Peter, like Paul, makes no reference to evangelism. Given that evangelism is one of the identifying marks of evangelicalism (as the name implies), it is puzzling that the apostles speak so little of it. Of course, there is an inherent logic in the gospel that demands that it be proclaimed, but to our modern evangelical ears it is surprising that the apostles, at least in their letters, rarely lay this obligation, at least explicitly, on their congregations. The closest Peter comes is, 'Always be prepared to give the reason for the hope that you have' (3:15). In other words, when challenged about their beliefs or practices, whether in the setting of a formal trial or more informally with family and neighbours, Christians should be ready with a timely and appropriate answer. Presumably, this would include both a rebuttal of mistaken ideas about Christian faith and practice as well as a clear explanation of the good news about Jesus. However, giving an *apologia* is the most assertive that Peter appears to expect his people to be.

So, in such a hostile environment, how ought Christians respond? Peter's answer is by living good lives. Even when giving an answer, the believer is to do so 'with gentleness and respect'. Repeatedly, Peter's word to his churches is be holy in all you do (1:15) and 'live such good lives … [that] they may see your good deeds and glorify God on the day he visits us' (2:12). The evidence is overwhelming that in the first three centuries after the church was born, it was the lives of Christians that made the biggest impact on the unbelieving world. Church historian Alan Kreider writes,

> The sources rarely indicate that the early Christians grew in number because they won arguments; instead they grew because their habitual behaviour (rooted in patience) was distinctive and intriguing. And the sources indicate that it was their habitus more than their ideas that appealed to the majority of the non-Christians who came to join them.[3]

The implications for the Aussie church are obvious and important. Peter's repeated plea is for his hearers never to suffer because they have deserved it. Sadly, the Australian church in the early twenty-first century is, to a significant degree, suffering deservedly. Too many Christian leaders have brought shame to Christ and his church by godless, predatorial conduct. Perhaps surprisingly, according to Business Insider Australia, ministers of religion are still ranked #13 in most respected occupations, behind accountants, public servants and lawyers![4] Sadly, too many Christians do not live lives that adorn the gospel. The message of 1 Peter speaks powerfully into this context. You often hear the refrain, 'Christians aren't perfect, just forgiven'. In the light of 1 Peter, that cop-out just doesn't work. Christians are, and must be, much more than 'just forgiven'. Peter's exhortation is to 'continue to do good' (4:19). Therefore, any proclamation and application of 1 Peter to contemporary Aussies must reverberate with the same exhortation.

Peter and the authorities – 2:13–17

In chapter 2, Peter addresses the question of how Christians should conduct themselves in hostile circumstances. He looks at the relationships between the governing authorities and subjects, slaves and masters, and wives and husbands.

Australians are notoriously disrespectful to authority figures. We see this, for example, in our preference for addressing people by their first name, not their title.

I am writing this chapter shortly after Scott Morrison replaced Malcolm Turnbull as Prime Minister of Australia. The media have raised the question of whether we should continue to address our head of state as 'ScoMo'.

This cynicism towards governing authorities may go back to our historical roots. The contrast with the United States of America is noteworthy. America was settled by religious refugees who, while fleeing corrupt governments, nevertheless held a strongly Christian view of respect for the God-appointed authorities. Australia was settled by convicts with little respect for authority.

In his book *Evangelical Christianity in Australia*, historian Stuart Piggin colourfully draws the contrast between the early religious scene in Australia and America:

> America started with convictions; Australia with convicts. America was established by dissenters; Australia by disreputables. American free settlers valued religious liberty; Australian convicts valued personal liberty to practise a more hedonistic religion. The first settlers of America believed America to be the promised land; they did not have to work to make it so. It was already heaven on earth. The first convicts thought of Australia as a God-forsaken hell on earth.[5]

Australia's first church building (on the corner of Hunter and Bligh Streets, Sydney) was built by the first chaplain, Richard Johnson, in 1793. On 1 October 1798, it was burnt down by disgruntled convicts.

Piggin goes on to make the point that this heritage has to a large degree influenced the character of our modern, secular way of life. The convicts were so numerous that their influence continued through the years. Indeed, it wasn't until 1827 that free settlers outnumbered convicts. In fact, the peak year for the sending of convicts was 1833.

How do we apply this command to respect the governing authorities when addressing Aussies? Let me say three things.

Firstly, we need to acknowledge that we live in a very different world from the first-century Roman Empire. We are not ruled by an all-powerful emperor or dictator. We live in a parliamentary democracy. Our rulers govern by the will of the people; we elect them into office, and we can remove them from office. Along with that, as citizens of Australia we all equally have rights. We have a separation of church and state enshrined in our constitution, which affirms, 'The Commonwealth shall not make any law for establishing any religion, or for imposing any religious observance, or for prohibiting the free exercise of any religion ...'

Unlike Peter's readers, we can freely practise our Christian faith, and freedom of speech and worship is protected by the law. As I write this chapter, the question of freedom of speech, and the degree to which this can be exercised, is hotly debated. However, the key point here is that, in this respect, our world is very different from

Peter's world, and Christians (along with everyone else) have the right to speak out, advocate, protest and work to protect their constitutional rights.

Secondly, Peter tells us that the governing authorities are 'sent by him' (2:14). Whether this refers to the emperor (the most natural reading) or God, nevertheless there is little doubt that Peter would have believed that God had ordained all these authorities (see Rom 13:1–7; Dan 2:37–38). Peter's point is that these authorities exist to promote justice (v.14). Their policies may not reflect God's will; indeed, they may actively oppose God's will, but Peter's call nonetheless is for Christians to respect these leaders. As we've already implied, this doesn't mean silent acquiescence, but it does mean we must exercise restraint in our words and actions.

Of course, what Peter says here (and it is very similar to Paul's teaching in Romans 13:1–7) is not the entire biblical picture when it comes to the governing authorities. The book of Revelation portrays rulers as beasts who serve the Satanic dragon (13:1–10). So, we must never be surprised when the men and women sent by God to govern us and promote justice (1 Pet 2:14) actually subvert the very principles they've been appointed to protect. Most likely, the Roman emperor at the time of Peter's writing was Nero, who was notorious for his cruelty and, later in his reign, the persecution of Christians. Yet Peter still called on his people to be blameless in how they spoke of him and responded to him.

Recently, I heard the ex-Premier of NSW, Mike Baird, speaking. Mike, who is a Christian, spoke of the pain and difficulty of facing daily criticism and abuse. Both he and his family suffered considerably. This is the lot of a politician. But politicians are human beings and need both encouragement and criticism. I wonder at the difference Christians could make if, rather than just delivering words of criticism, we also gave words of encouragement (and assurances of our prayers) – and not just to the Christians like Mike Baird, but even those whose agendas we strongly disagree with. I'm sure this comes under the rubric, 'Honour the Emperor' (v.15).

Thirdly, given what I said earlier about the diversity of Aussie culture, a preacher with a mixed Anglo-Saxon and Asian congregation may need to bring two different applications. Respect for authority figures is deeply rooted in the Asian culture. In China, for example, this attitude may owe more to Confucius than Jesus. Sometimes, though, respect for authority means that Asians are silent and acquiescent when authority figures are doing wrong or teaching error. In short, the practical application of submission to governing authorities may be different in different cultural contexts.

Peter and slaves – 2:18–25

In 2:18–25, Peter turns to the issue of slaves and masters. However, unlike the apostle Paul, who has commands for both groups (Eph 6:5–9; Col 3:22–4:1), Peter's focus is entirely on slaves. Peter's words are addressed, in particular, to those slaves whose masters are unfair or brutal. In short, Peter's exhortation to slaves is to submit to their masters, no matter how harshly they abuse them. He bases this on the example of the Lord Jesus, who left us an example to follow in his steps (2:21).

Of course, there are a number of significant homiletical issues in this section. One is the fact that Peter appears to accept slavery as a societal norm and doesn't challenge it. The preacher will need to decide whether or not to devote space to a discussion of the nature of slavery in the Roman Empire, and whether to engage in an apologetic for Peter's silence on a practice we consider inherently evil.

Particularly, though, how do we apply these words to our Australian context? We cannot draw a direct line from masters and slaves in the first century to employers and employees in the twenty-first century. Thankfully, most workers today have rights that protect them from unjust or bullying superiors. Do we always stand on these rights? When is it appropriate for an employee to seek litigation for unfair dismissal? What are our obligations to a boss who asks of us something contrary our conscience? What do we do when there is a conflict between loyalty (submission?) to the boss and our other competing loyalties, like family and church?

There are no easy answers to any of these questions. Indeed, we need to be wary of any 'one size fits all' answer to any situation. Each situation is different and calls for wisdom and discernment. Let me just make a couple of comments.

Firstly, we live in an increasingly litigious society, in which people quickly move to stand on their rights. What does it mean for a Christian to 'bear up under the pain of unjust suffering' (2:19)? Sometimes, it may mean not going to the court for unfair dismissal, but rather leaving the matter to God, who one day will bring justice. It may be better to look to God's word of commendation (v.20) rather than your day in court. It is particularly disturbing when one hears, with increasing regularity, of Christians taking each other to court. Again, there may be a time when it's right and appropriate to do that, especially for the sake of others. But there may also be a time – and this is too quickly forgotten – to bear injustice, trusting in the vindication of God.

Secondly, sometimes the demands of our bosses in the workplace may call for a radical rethinking of our priorities. Some years ago, I received this email:

> God spoke to me that my priorities have not been totally aligned with his, and indeed, my spiritual life had stagnated since I was an enthusiastic new convert in 2003. I remember at that time, I had naively told my bosses in my first few months at work that all that I wanted to do with my life was to serve God, and that career was not a big priority. That enthusiasm soon got lost and choked by the weeds of ambition and worldliness as I pursued a bigger salary and a job with better prospects. To that end, I wound up working in the finance industry in the last two years, through which I grew in materialism, greed and also in ungodliness.

God has been merciful to give me a wake-up call. The first practical step that I have taken is to resign my finance job, for personally, I know it has been a hindrance to my spiritual growth. I am currently serving notice and will leave my current company on 4 September. I am looking for another job in public service with more altruistic objectives. I am also in the process of signing up to volunteer for the Salvation Army in tutoring disadvantaged children. I have signed up for a mission conference in September and hope to be able to embark on my first mission trip soon. Another step I plan to take is to take up a theological diploma and grow in the word.

Sometimes the demands of the boss and workplace may so conflict with other, greater, commitments that we have to say 'no'.

Peter and wives – 3:1–7

Perhaps even more contentious in our present environment is Peter's words to Christian wives. The issue Peter is addressing here is the unbelieving husband and the command, again, is to submit. If there are harsh, unbelieving masters, there are also harsh, unbelieving husbands. Many women know the pain of living with such men. As I write this chapter, much of the Western world is in the grip of the #MeToo movement. Rightly, women are rising up and speaking out against the sexual abuse and harassment they have been forced, for so long, to endure. Recently, a number of Christian women have come out and exposed the abuse they've received at the hands of their Christian husbands, some of whom are pastors and church leaders. Some are laying the blame for this spousal abuse squarely at the feet of the biblical command for wives to submit to their husbands. In a recent ABC report, Julia Baird wrote, 'And in very many cases the local pastors did not believe the women when they told them of their stories. Or they told them to submit to their husbands, endure and stay.'[6]

On top of all this, there are the deep differences of opinion among Christians on the roles of men and women. I don't think there are many issues more divisive in our church today than the divide between complementarians and egalitarians. It is into this climate that a preacher is called to expound 1 Peter 3:1–7. In your congregation there will be women (and let's not forget, some men, too) who are victims of spousal abuse. There will be people on both sides of the 'women in ministry' divide. And there will likely also be the 'stranger' in our midst. What will the unbelieving visitor make of words that strike many as archaic, patriarchal and, indeed, inciting of abuse?

So, an exposition of such a passage requires care, clarity and sensitivity. And I should add, courage. We don't want to sound like we're embarrassed about, or apologetic for, Peter's divinely inspired words. We need to maintain fidelity to Scripture. An appropriate application will recognise that the role and authority of women Australia today is very different from women in first-century Roman Empire. We may need to address questions like: What does it mean today that women should not have elaborate hairstyles or wear gold jewellery and fine clothes (v.3)? What about the call to submission? Today, many Christians remove from their wedding promises any reference to the obligation of a wife to submit or obey her husband (and I've never heard any bride address her new husband as 'Lord'!). Rather than erase this command from Scripture, we need to display the goodness, virtue and indeed the appeal of wise and godly submission. What does Peter mean when he describes the wife as 'the weaker vessel'? Of course, given the high profile that domestic violence is given today, both within and without the church, there is no shortage of evidence that too many husbands abuse their power and physical strength.[7]

So, what kind of answers might we give to these questions?

To start, I would not be too prescriptive about how women (and men for that matter) adorn themselves. Clothing, makeup and things like hair dyeing and plastic surgery are matters of Christian freedom, not legislation. Nevertheless, God, through his servant Peter, makes it clear that 'a gentle and quiet spirit' is of greatest worth in his sight (3:5). It is therefore entirely appropriate for a preacher to challenge the congregation about whether the time and money spent on outward adornment is matched by, or better surpassed by, the time and money spent on developing the beauty of the inner spirit.

What about the contentious issue of submission? Of course, husband and wife relationships have changed, not just since Peter's day, but in the last fifty years. My mother was typical of women of her generation. She didn't work outside the home and was given little encouragement or opportunity to develop her various skills. Dad was the sole bread winner, and in that respect no negotiation was entered into. In Australia today, it would be fair to say that most marriages are partnerships, with husband and wife sharing equally in the decision-making and often in the financing of the household.

In such a changed domestic environment, what does headship and submission look like? The first thing to say is that submission by a wife, however that might express itself, is something gladly and wilfully given, not something to be demanded by a husband. The apostle Paul makes clear the husband's obligation: to lay down his life for his wife. The husband does not 'lord it over' his wife but serves her and the household so she can flourish in every way possible.

As I said, practically most Christian marriages are partnerships, marked by mutual love and decision-making. However, at the end of the day the husband is ultimately responsible for the wellbeing of the family. In particular, I need to ensure that my children are taught the gospel and that I have done all in my power, as husband and father, to ensure that they continue as Christ's faithful servants until their life's end.

Homiletical Issues in Preaching 2 Peter to Aussies

Distant worlds

Generally speaking, 2 Peter is one of the more neglected parts of the New Testament. Two of the three chapters deal with the Day of the Lord, judgement and the coming destruction. These are not topics frequently addressed in many Australian churches. If we are undertaking an expository series on 2 Peter, do we want repeated sermons on the theme of judgement? The letter also addresses false teachers in the most scathing terms. While there is an important place for warning and rebuke in our sermons, many are cautious about 'calling out', in the kind of terms Peter uses, those who preach the contemporary 'destructive heresies' (2:1).

However, it is for this very reason that we should be incorporating into our preaching program a series on 2 Peter. If the church has jettisoned the 'fire and brimstone' preaching that appeared to be a regular diet of some sermons a hundred years ago, the pendulum has clearly swung too far in the other direction. We tend to speak too little of topics that the Bible makes much of, like the fear of God and the coming judgement.

Peter and authorship

At this point I want to address the important homiletical question of how much time a preacher should give to background issues like date, audience and authorship. These are particularly important for 2 Peter, whose authorship is questioned by many scholars. Ernst Käsemann described it as, 'perhaps the most dubious writing' in the New Testament.[8] Outside the world of conservative biblical scholarship, most would argue that 2 Peter is pseudepigraphical. Such background issues are intensified in 2 Peter, because, on a few occasions, the author is almost certainly drawing upon Jewish traditions that can be located in intertestamental writings like 1 Enoch. To what extent should these kinds of questions occupy the time and space of the sermon?

In short, my answer is none at all. Our work is to explain the passage, apply it to the lives of our congregation and proclaim its timeless truths. Let's not confuse the academy with the church. In the lecture hall, it is appropriate to discuss issues such as date and authorship, but they are generally unnecessary and unedifying in the pulpit. Speaking of 1 Peter, John Piper writes,

> Is the setting of those Roman provinces in Asia Minor important? Let 1 Peter tell you whether or not they're important. Frankly, I think it would make a colossally boring first session to put up a map and work that over. You've probably done that; I've done it. I get done doing it and realize they're going home with a little geography in their head, but their marriage stays the same, their kids stay the same,

pride stays the same, everything stays the same. You can teach a very faithful and powerful series on 1 Peter without being an expert on first-century geography or Roman culture or exactly what the persecution was. Commentaries write whole introductions on what the persecution was. I say, just read it and see what Peter wants to tell you about the persecution. I think that's the most faithful and safe way, because if you start bringing stuff in from outside, you might bring stuff in that he doesn't want brought in.[9]

Grace and warning

Expository preaching takes seriously the meaning and purpose of a passage. The goal of an expository sermon, as the word implies, is to expose people to the Bible. The preacher's work is to explain the meaning of the passage, as intended by the original author, and then demonstrate what this means for the people at this place and time.

As we have been implying, our people need to hear all of 1 Peter and 2 Peter, not just verses here and there. This is particularly important with 2 Peter. Much of the letter consists of words of warning and exhortation. The danger in simply preaching a passage in 2 Peter in isolation from the rest of the letter is that we end up with a sermon heavy on demand and light on grace. For that reason, it's important to begin where Peter begins. The foundation Peter lays for all he will go on to write is the gospel of grace. The addressees are those 'who through the righteousness of our God and Saviour Jesus Christ have received a faith as precious as ours' (1:1). The salvation we enjoy is a gift we have received. Peter continues in that vein when he reminds them, 'His divine power has given us everything we need for a godly life …' (1:3). So, the exhortation to them, and to us, 'to make every effort' (1:10) is built upon the fact that God in his grace has given through 'his very great and precious promises' all we need to participate in the divine nature and escape the corruption of the world (1:4).

Peter and judgement

Another challenge facing Aussie preachers in expounding 2 Peter is that the central part of the letter is a high voltage attack on false teachers, who are deceptive in their teaching and immoral in their lifestyles. Peter holds nothing back in his condemnation of them: they are depraved, greedy, ungodly – bold and arrogant blots and blemishes, like dogs returning to their vomit.

This is not the kind of language one hears in most churches. We want our churches to be welcoming to people. We want preaching that is positive, not negative. We want to display the benefits, both for the present and for eternity, of knowing Jesus.

The two things that we might baulk at here are the talk of a coming judgement, and the attack on false teachers. However, the very topics that might cause us to hesitate to preach on 2 Peter are the very reason why it is such a timely word for our church. I am hard pressed to think of a greater lack in the preaching of the contemporary Aussie church than preaching on judgement and the concomitant fear of God. One of the great high points of evangelical history was the tremendous social achievements of people like William Wilberforce and the Clapham sect in Britain in the nineteenth century. The abolition of the slave trade was only the most famous of their many godly endeavours. But what motivated them? Wilberforce famously said, 'Great indeed are our opportunities. Great also is our responsibility … The time of reckoning will at length arrive. And when finally summoned to the bar of God to give an account of our stewardship, what plea can we have to urge in our defence?'[10] For him and his contemporaries, the reality of the final judgement and an afterlife of rewards and punishments was the most significant motivator in their tireless labour for God and the good. Such thinking seems foreign to much of the Australian church.

The Australian church's happy compromise with materialism and society's changing attitudes on sex, marriage and gender are, in part, due to the absence of any robust preaching on the coming judgement, specifically the certainty and nature of the judgement of Christians. It is important for preachers to speak of this judgement as persuasively and faithfully as possible. Indeed, this is one of the many reasons expository preaching should be the regular diet in our churches. If the bulk of our preaching is topical, the temptation will be to preach on those topics we feel comfortable with, and that the people will enjoy and commend us for. We will preach what they want to hear more than what they need to hear. However, if we preach letters like 2 Peter, then we will expose our people to truths and exhortations that, in the end, are good and necessary for their spiritual wellbeing.

Another significant feature of contemporary Western society is the unwillingness of many to say anything that might cause hurt or offense. And Christians don't want to seem judgemental. How, then, we do apply Peter's blistering attack on the false teachers?

There are two difficulties. The first – and homiletically less serious – difficulty is ascertaining the precise nature of the false teaching Peter is condemning. It seems that these teachers were denying the return of the Lord Jesus. Anything more specific than this isn't given to us. Since these teachers were also encouraging people to join them in lives of immorality, it would make sense that they are mocking the idea of a day of reckoning.

However, the harder task is applying Peter's warnings to our own context. What are the contemporary false teachings that are actually threatening the eternal security of our people? For make no mistake, Peter's warning is that both the false teachers and those seduced by their teaching are bound to destruction (2:12). Most of us are preaching to churches that are theologically orthodox. Perhaps the false gospel that is most prevalent at the moment, right across the world, is the 'prosperity gospel' in its different shapes and forms. Christian television programs are awash with prosperity gospellers promising people untold wealth and almost perfect health if they'll simply have faith. It is a gospel with no call to suffer or deny oneself. Many who proclaim such a gospel live lavish lifestyles, a far cry from the poverty and humility of Jesus and the apostles. It is not the path to godliness, Christian maturity and a life that pleases God. Indeed, it appeals to our baser desires of greed and self-satisfaction. Personally, I prefer to leave the question of the salvation of those who proclaim this gospel to the Judge of all the earth, rather than announce, 'like animals they too will perish' (2:12).

Perhaps the most dangerous false teaching that our Australian churches are exposed to is from the lips of those who redefine homosexual practice. The Australian church is still coming to terms with an appropriate response to the legalising of same-sex marriages. All of the statements I hear from evangelical preachers express, appropriately, attitudes of love and understanding to those who are same-sex attracted. A number of excellent books have been written by godly Christians who are same-sex attracted and have remained faithful to the Bible's teaching on sexuality and marriage.[11] However, there are others who have reinterpreted the Bible, especially Paul's statements on homosexuality. Typically, they argue that the practice Paul is condemning is promiscuous homosexuality, not loving, committed gay relationships. Or, Paul is simply ignorant. If he knew then what we know now about the nature of homosexuality, then he would have expressed himself differently. The consequences of this false teaching are every bit as serious as the false teaching Peter was addressing. If Paul is right that those who engage in homosexual acts (and any who are sexually immoral) will not inherit the kingdom of God (1 Cor 6:9–10), then those Christian teachers and scholars who call 'good' and 'natural' what the Bible calls 'sin' and 'unnatural' are encouraging a lifestyle that leads to destruction. And Jesus offered a solemn warning to anyone who causes one of his little ones to stumble (Matt 18:6).

Sample Sermon: 1 Peter 3:18–22

Comments on the Sermon

This sermon was preached at St James' Old Cathedral in West Melbourne. It is the oldest church in the city. It is an evangelical Anglican church, and its style of worship is traditional and liturgical. The sermon was delivered at the baptism of the daughter of the pastor of the church. The preaching is normally expository, and this sermon was part of a series of expositions on 1 Peter. Being a baptism, I knew that family members and friends would be there, and I could not assume all would be confessing Christians. So, I had three audiences that morning (apart, of course, from the Audience of One). There were the parents and Godparents of the little girl, Pippa. There were the regular members of our church. Finally, there were the guests who had come just for this service.

In our church we normally preach for twenty minutes. I have tried to maintain the flavour of this sermon as a preached message, while slightly formalising it for the sake of reading and publication.

One of the distinctive features of this collection of essays is the denominational variety of the contributors. While the volume is published by Morling Press, the publishing arm of a Baptist College, there are contributors from Anglican, Reformed and Presbyterian churches.

One Anglican distinctive is its view of baptism. Anglicans are paedobaptist; we baptise babies. Anglican pastors differ in their practice of baptism. Some ministers have an open practice of baptism; they will baptise any child who is presented for baptism, as long as the family have some connection – and it may be tangential – to the church. Other ministers insist that the parents of the child are confessing Christians, and active in the life of the church.

I thought, for the sake of this volume, that there might be value in seeing how a convinced paedobaptist would preach on the only reference to baptism in 1 and 2 Peter. And I was asked to preach on this passage at the baptism of an infant.

It's fair to say that 1 Peter 3:18–22 is one of the most perplexing passages not only in 1 and 2 Peter but in the entire New Testament. Interpretations vary widely. I have preached on this passage three times, and each time I have changed my mind as to its meaning.[12] Therefore, I present my current view with a degree of tentativeness. I freely admit that most commentators hold a different interpretation from the one I am presenting. Having said that, the main point of the passage is clear. So, whatever view one holds about the interpretation of the more contentious verses, or the meaning and mode of baptism, Peter's comments here are important and relevant.

How does a preacher approach a passage over which there is significant difference of opinion? First, of course, he or she must decide which of the various views is the one they find the most persuasive. In this case, I confess that I spent hours in my study, comparing the different opinions. Then, the preacher needs to decide whether or not to expose the congregation to this exegetical debate. Of course, this may depend on the nature of your audience. For example, you may preach differently to a chapel of theological students than you would to a typical Sunday morning congregation. There may be some passages which, because of their importance for Christian doctrine or ministry practice, demand that the preacher fairly outlines the different points of view. Generally, though, such discussions are a distraction from the sermon.

What I wrote about background issues, such as date and authorship, equally apply to exegetical debates. While they may fascinate the preacher, they are usually of little interest to our audience. Put simply, our people want to know what the passage means and its application to their lives, and not the range of scholarly opinions. My job is to work out, prayerfully, thoughtfully, and with careful and diligent research, what I think the passage means. Then all the research is left behind in the study, and I stand and proclaim the fruit of my research. Sometimes I will admit that the view I am presenting is only one of a range of views. I may admit that I hold this interpretation tentatively. And, on occasion, I may even admit that I simply don't know what the divinely-inspired author meant by these words. But, normally, I need a compelling reason to use valuable pulpit time to engage in such questions of exegetical debate.

Well-known Australian preacher David Cook likens preaching to flying a plane: you need maximum power for take-off and maximum power for landing. In other words, the sermon introduction and conclusion are very important. I will normally give plenty of time to both, but that was particularly the case on this occasion. I was aware that there would be guests at the service that morning, and so the introduction was designed both to acknowledge it was a baptism, and to show the relevance of this ostensibly obscure passage for today.

There were two points of application. The first was a story of how God changes lives. My target audience here was the unbelieving guest. The target audience of my second point of application was the believer. In applications, there can be great value in bringing different words to different groups in the congregation.

One final word of exhortation: preach the letters of Peter! Our churches need them.

Sermon Text

The day God baptised Noah

I want to add my welcome to the families and friends of Matt, Jenny and Pippa, and say how delighted I am to speak at Pippa's baptism.

Giving birth to a child, and baptising the child, is a wonderfully happy experience. There is the unspeakable joy of welcoming a beautiful new life into the world. And the recognition that this child is a wonderful blend of her mum and dad. For years to come, Matt and Jenny will be the centre of Pippa's little world, and for always, she'll be more precious to them than even their own lives.

This morning at this baptism we are affirming that Pippa is part of God's family. She is a member of the church of Jesus Christ, the community of the redeemed. So, it is a wonderful time for family and friends to give thanks to God and celebrate this special gift.

But sometimes, parents – in the midst of the joy and excitement – do pause. Sometimes, perhaps when it's late at night and the baby has finally dropped off to sleep, they may watch the depressing late-night news and start thinking. Perhaps they start wondering, what kind of world are we bringing this child, our child, into?

And I think Christians might feel that even more acutely. It is sobering to consider our society's rapidly changing attitudes towards Christianity. The world that I was baptised into was so different from the world today. When I was baptised as a baby, there was an underlying respect for God and the church. The Christian religion was seen to be good for society. It was beneficial for children to 'have a good dose of religion' in Sunday School or Scripture in the classroom.

I wouldn't say those days are gone entirely, but they are disappearing fast. It would be true to say that general respect for God, and particularly the church, has widely been replaced by indifference. Even that is morphing into something like contempt and disdain.

Of course, to a degree, we have only ourselves to blame. What other word could you use but 'contempt' for those sexual predators in the church who have abused the very ones they were entrusted to spiritually care for? Or, those pastors who preach sacrifice and self-denial and live opulent lifestyles? While such leaders are the notorious minority, nevertheless they have helped change peoples' attitudes.

Bishop Lesslie Newbigin, after decades working in India, retired to England and began church planting in the working-class areas of Birmingham. He called Britain – and he could be speaking of Melbourne – 'the most difficult missionary frontier in the contemporary world'. He went on to say that there is 'a cold contempt for the Gospel which is harder to face than opposition'. 'A cold contempt.' As I watch Q&A on a Monday night on the ABC or read *The Age*, I hear and see an increasing cold contempt for the gospel.

This is the Australia Pippa has been born into. In the decades to come, as she grows and matures as a disciple of the Lord Jesus, she may need a degree of courage and confidence in the gospel that perhaps we haven't needed so much in the past.

Peter's world

Now I mention that, not to be a wet rag on a happy Sunday morning, or to throw – if you'll excuse the pun – cold water on her baptism, but because our passage this morning on baptism is from 1 Peter.

Virtually everything Peter writes in this letter is to encourage a church who are doing it very, very tough. They are facing much more than a 'cold contempt for the gospel'. They're facing open hostility and persecution. And when people abuse you and ridicule you and unfairly accuse you of things you haven't done, it's hard just to sit there and take it on the chin.

To Christians facing this kind of abuse, Peter encourages them not to pay back evil for evil: 'For you were called to this, because Christ also suffered for you, leaving you an example that you should follow in his steps' (2:21). Rather, they are to repay evil with good.

If our critics in the media are sarcastic, cynical and sneering, then our response must be respectful, gentle and kind. Peter then reminds them, 'Who is going to harm you if you are deeply committed to what's good? But even if you should suffer for righteousness' sake you are blessed' (3:13–14). In the end, if we are going to suffer, then it's better to suffer for doing good than doing evil.

This leads us to our rather perplexing little passage in 1 Peter 3. I'm not sure what was going through your mind while 1 Peter 3 was being read out. Jesus speaking to spirits in prison? Baptism is something like Noah on the ark? Let's be frank, it's one of the more unusual passages in the New Testament. But its basic meaning and intent is clear: Christian, when things are tough, and when you're abused and people buy into the lies of the atheists that Christianity is one of the most malevolent, pernicious movements in the world, then know full well the great good that many of your brothers and sisters are doing quietly and unassumingly.

Emboldened by their example, we are to keep our resolve. Don't hit back. Don't say, 'Oh, what's the point', and just retreat into a cave somewhere. No – keep on believing, keep on trusting, keep on doing good. As Jesus did: 'Therefore, since Christ suffered in his body, arm yourselves also with the same attitude' (4:1).

True baptism

Peter begins this section with a wonderful summary of the good news: 'For Christ died for sins once for all, the righteous for the unrighteous' (v.18). He then reminds us that after Jesus was put to death he rose again, 'in' or 'by' the Spirit. So, here is Jesus, our great example, the perfectly righteous man, the truly good man who was mocked, ridiculed, and put to death, but then vindicated by God who raised him from the dead.

Then we have a digression as Peter tells us that this risen Christ made a proclamation to the spirits in prison (v.19). With these verses, I take Peter to mean – and this is by no means the only interpretation of these verses – that when Noah was preaching the way of righteousness to the unbelievers of his day, it was actually the Spirit of Jesus preaching through him. Earlier in this letter Peter wrote that when the Old Testament prophets like Isaiah, David and Zechariah predicted the sufferings of Jesus, in fact it was the Spirit of Christ speaking through them (1:10–11). So, just as the Spirit of Jesus spoke through David, Isaiah and Zechariah, so he was preaching through his servant, Noah. And the people to whom Noah preached, and who mocked and rejected his message, are now in 'prison'. Just like an accused criminal today is held in a prison cell, waiting for his day in court, so all who've mocked and rejected God's message are in the celestial prison, waiting for the coming judgement (v.20).

But why does Peter particularly mention Noah? Because here was a righteous man who was living a godly life in a hostile world. This faithful man believed God's word that judgement was coming and expressed his faith by building an ark. So, while the world mocked and ridiculed him, Noah stood firm. He equipped himself with 'the same resolve', just like Jesus. And like the Christians of Peter's day. And like us today.

But then Peter goes on to talk about Noah being saved through the water (v.21). The flood, if you like, was Noah's baptism. There they were, Noah and his family, and they all went into the waters of judgement, or the waters of death. Yet, they came through them, safe in the ark. This was like Jesus, who on the cross went through the waters of death and came through them by his resurrection.

And that, says, Peter is like our baptism. We go down into the waters, symbolising our death, but emerge to a new life, saved by his resurrection. And how many were saved in Noah's day? Just eight. A handful. A negligible, insignificant minority. Just like the believers Peter is writing to, scattered across the Roman Empire. And just like this tiny group of Christians on the edge of Melbourne. All around us are thousands of people enjoying the delights of the Vic Markets on the east side or the aisles of plentiful goodies in Costco on the west, and we are sitting here in our little ark called St James'.

But if some aspects of this passage are a little hard to get our minds around, Peter's definition here of baptism is, I think, the best in the Bible. So, if you want to know what's going on when someone gets baptised, you couldn't go to a better place than 1 Peter 3:21. Peter makes it so clear by telling us very plainly what baptism *is not*. And then what baptism *is*.

Firstly, it is not the removal of dirt from the body. Now of course he doesn't mean that people actually think that Pippa, or anyone who's baptised, is having a bath or a shower when they get baptised. The dirt Peter speaks of here – and the word is actually 'filth' – is moral dirt. So, he makes it clear that nothing magical is happening this morning. The Pippa who is to be baptised will be the same person after her baptism that she is now. She's not going to be morally cleaner or spiritually cleaner or closer to God. She's not going to become a Christian in a sense that she isn't already. In that sense, nothing will change. Any kind of religious ritual or rite doesn't remove moral dirt.

A while ago there was a very moving article in *The Age* written by a young university student named Anna Neylan. Anna was brought up a Catholic and went to a Catholic school. But later she fell pregnant to her boyfriend. She was now faced with the most painful and difficult choice of her life: whether or not to keep the baby.

Her conscience, informed no doubt by her Catholic upbringing, told her to keep the child. Indeed, she wanted to be a mother. But her boyfriend, and numerous counsellors, advised her to abort. And in this very honest article she described her moral struggle, and what she did after the abortion. She describes how she dealt with the enormous weight of guilt that she felt. She said that she'd already stopped going to Mass or confession. Yet, she felt so unclean. The article describes what she calls the long process to 'self-forgiveness'. Some months after the abortion, she told her father what she had done. He took her into the back garden, where they lit a fire. He told her to stand in the midst of the smoke, because he had read that in many cultures smoke is used as a cleansing substance. Then he drove her to a nearby nursery, where they selected a strong young eucalypt tree. Together, in a simple ceremony, they planted it in the garden. 'Life to acknowledge life', her father said.

I think that's a tragic story. Here's a woman who rightly knows she's committed a dreadful sin, and in her desperation and folly stands in some dirty smoke to cleanse herself. Indeed, in the light of what Peter is saying, even being re-baptised wouldn't have helped her. Baptism can't do that. It's not the removal of dirt from the body. What Anna needed was the cleansing of the Lord Jesus, who died for sins, once for all, the righteous for the unrighteous.

So, secondly, if baptism doesn't change us, what's it about? Peter tells us: it's the pledge of a good conscience towards God. You see, Peter is reminding his readers that when they were baptised, they were asked about their faith in Christ. At that time, they confessed, 'Yes, we trust Christ.' Then they were baptised. In other words, they made a promise or a pledge that they would keep on living for Jesus. They pledged to live good lives and to do so with a clear conscience before God.

So, in that sense baptism is like a wedding. On my wedding day I was asked, 'Do you Michael, forsaking all others, take Sarah as your wife for the rest of your life?' And I confessed, gleefully, 'I do.' Then there was a sign. I gave her a ring, and she gave me a ring. The old words were, 'I pledge you my troth', or I pledge my life to you. We were promising to always do good for each other and to live before each other with a clear conscience. In effect, we were promising that, whether we're together or apart, this person, and this person only, will be the love of my life.

And that's what you said to God when you were baptised. It's not uncommon nowadays for people to renew their marriage vows. Sarah and I don't think we need to do that, but I do regularly remind myself of the solemn promise I made to her. And it's good to remind ourselves from to time, particularly when it's tough being a Christian, of the solemn promise we made at our baptism.

So, this morning, on her behalf, Pippa's parents are making a promise that she will serve the Lord Jesus, and him only and him always. Of course, in the years ahead they're going to teach her about the Lord Jesus and all he's done for her, and one day, by God's grace and power, she'll own this pledge for herself.

Conclusion

Let me just say a couple of things to conclude.

Firstly, baptism is a great reminder of the glorious news of what God has done for us in the Lord Jesus.

I have just spent two weeks in Kuala Lumpur teaching in St Mary's Anglican Cathedral. I met a very impressive guy called Raj. He's on the ministry staff of the church. But for twenty years he was a heroin addict and one of the city's leading gangsters. He spent time in prison and realised that he needed to turn his life around. Four years ago, he was given a job as the night security guard at the church, and the minister gave him Christian books to read to pass the time. Raj devoured them and began to study theology. He's now one of the pastors in the church. He is a wonderfully mature, passionate disciple of Christ. He's come from death to life. God has removed the dirt from his heart and made him new. And baptism reminds us of the gospel that changes lives. That Jesus died, once for all, the righteous for the unrighteous.

Secondly, whenever I attend a wedding and hear the couple make these great promises, I am reminded of what I said to Sarah at our wedding. At that moment, I quietly, to myself, pledge myself to Sarah again. In a few minutes Matt will say to Pippa: 'Live as a disciple of Christ, fight the good fight, finish the race, keep the faith.' As I hear those words, I'm going to be thinking of Pippa, but I'm also going to be thinking of me, and I'm going to again, with resolve, pledge myself to the Lord. I'm going to promise to keep on living a life that pleases him. I'll make a pledge to never repay anyone evil for evil, be they family member, neighbour or work colleague. And should I in some way suffer, then I promise never to suffer deservedly for any wrong I have done, but only for joyfully bearing the name of Christ. Will you join me?

11

PREACHING THE JOHANNINE LETTERS TO AUSTRALIANS

Bill Salier

Introduction

All you need is love? Love wins? Are these the thoughts that spring to mind when thinking about the Johannine letters? There is a story from the early church concerning the Apostle John and his preaching towards the end of his life. The aging apostle would be carried in on his chair, would exhort the congregation, 'Little children love one another', and then be carried out.[1] This was no doubt mercifully short and to the point – and is a model perhaps many contemporary preachers would do well to emulate. But is it an accurate representation of the breadth of thought of the inspired apostle? Certainly, the love of God and his sent Son, Jesus, dominates the Gospel and letters of John, but to think that this is all the apostle has to say would be to sell short the theological and pastoral riches to be found in the letters normally attributed to John Zebedee.

As we turn to think about preaching the Johannine letters, we need to acknowledge that these short letters contain many challenges for the preacher who aspires to encourage others with their content. But there are also many rewards for patient perseverance with the text. As John exhorts his readers, he presents a rich perspective on the person and work of the Lord Jesus Christ. All three letters show us a pastor at work with his congregation, applying the gospel clearly to encourage right belief, right practice and right affections for the triune God, who has made himself known in the person of his Son.

The Hermeneutical Task

When it comes to interpreting these letters, 1 John is the 'problem child', with long discussions concerning genre, purpose, structure and argument appearing in the scholarly literature. These issues are more clear-cut when it comes to 2 and 3 John. Arguably, the 'issue' with these latter letters is neglect in preaching programs due to their brevity and relative obscurity. I will deal primarily with 1 John in the discussion that follows, and then make some separate comments on 2 and 3 John.

Of the many issues that are normally addressed in the introduction to a commentary, the most important for the preacher to interact with when it comes to 1 John are the questions of purpose and structure and argument.

Purpose

While there is often discussion about the precise genre of 1 John, it is at least clear that it is an exhortation in a loose, extended letter format addressed to a specified community and context.[2] The overall purpose is discerned between explicit statements in the letter (1 John 1:3, 5:13) and also a more general regard for its contents. The question of purpose is closely connected to attempted reconstructions of the background circumstances that lie behind the letter. The key passage here is 1 John 2:18–19, which appears to point to an incident, usually described as a schism, in the community to which the letter is written.[3] At some point in the past, a number of members of the community to whom the letter is addressed have left. Precisely why they have left is to be worked out from the letter's contents, but there appear to be significant differences at play in the schism: doctrinal, moral and social.[4]

Commentators differ as to the influence of this background on the purpose of the letter. For those who see the schism as the major impetus for the letter, the primary thrust is polemical, either directly against the secessionists, or to the Johannine audience with their 'heresy' very much in mind. Consequently, much ink has been spent on the difficult task of identifying the secessionists.[5] According to some older commentators, the letter was thought to supply three tests or laws for orthodoxy with respect to the secessionists: the so-called doctrinal test, moral test and social test.[6] Whether or not there is merit in the reconstruction that prompts these three observations, they do provide a neat summary of three of the letter's concerns: right belief about the person and work of the Lord Jesus; right response to that belief expressed in love; and the expression of that love in fellowship with the Christian community.

Against this interpretation, a series of newer commentators question the significance of this schism.[7] This non-polemical or pastoral approach sees the letter as one of more general assurance to a congregation written by their pastor to encourage ongoing faith in Christ and the appropriate response.

And a more recent monograph takes a mediating position between these two broad positions, suggesting that it is a letter written to reassure a congregation, noting the trauma of a schism and the ongoing need to 'talk things out'.[8]

There are numerous statements scattered through the letter where the author explicitly states why they are writing (1:4; 2:1, 7, 8, 12, 13[x2], 14[x3], 21, 26; 5:13). Three of these are followed by purpose clauses indicating the reason for writing (1:4; 2:1; 5:13); seven are followed by causal clauses, again indicating a reason for writing (2:12–14, 21) and three describe the content of what is being written (2:7–8, 26). The combined effect of these explicit statements, especially 1:4 and 5:13, lend themselves to a reading of the letter as a letter of pastoral encouragement and exhortation, with the 'schism' very much in mind as part of the experience of the audience. The following structural comments will nuance this analysis further.

Structure and Argument

It is important for the preacher to think about the structure and argument of a text. Decisions need to be made concerning how to break down a text for preaching, and it will also be helpful to have a grasp of the movement of a text as a whole so that the individual parts can be related to one another over the course of a teaching series. Unfortunately, there is little consensus on either the structure or the argument of 1 John, with as almost as many outlines of structure and argument as there are commentators.[9] Jensen notes five general approaches to outlining the argument of 1 John: 'There is no developed argument, there is an association of ideas, there is a cyclical and spiral form argument, it is parallel to John's Gospel, and it is chiastic.'[10] This is either very confusing or an opportunity to chart a new course.

It is a complex discussion, with no simple way forward. The following reading is indebted to Jensen's proposal concerning the structure and argument, which combines text-linguistic analysis with thematic and vocabulary analysis.[11]

Commentators tend to agree that 1:1–4 and 5:12–21 form a prologue and epilogue. There are clearly some sections that form units based on repetition ('if we say' 1:6–2:2; 'the one who says' 2:4–11; 'and you' 2:18–28; 'and we know' 5:18–20). 1 John 2:12–18 is also delineated by the *inclusio* 'children' and eschatological themes. The highly structured nature of 2:12–14 marks it out as a unit as well. John also tends to use vocatives to mark sections (2:1; 2:7; 2:12–14; 2:18; 2:28; 3:2; 3:7; 3:13; 3:18; 3:21; 4:1; 4:4; 4:7; 4:11; 5:21; see also 3 John 2, 5, 11).

If the 'I write' clauses with a purpose following are significant for thinking about the overall purpose of the letter, then, as Jensen notes, the combination of the verb 'I write' with vocatives (e.g., 'my little children', 'dear friends') are also significant (see 2.1, 7, 12, 13, 14) for establishing the overall structure and argument.[12]

John 2:12–14 is a major section that breaks the letter into two sections. This division is further emphasised when we observe that the first explicit imperative occurs in 2:15. This has the effect of making 1:1—2:11 an extended introduction, leading to a concentrated and poetic form of address to the recipients of the letter (2:12–14), followed by the first explicit command – to not love the world. The rest of the letter is, therefore, to be read in the light of this command.

Jensen also notes that the two early occurrences of 'I write', combined with a vocative, highlight the ideas of 'sin' and love' (2:1; 2:7).[13] When we look at the way that John discusses sin and love in the letter ,we see that the vocabulary of sin and love clusters in blocks (love: 2:15–17; 3:1–2; sin: 3:4–9; love 3:10–23; love 4:7—5:3; sin 5:16–18). In the blocks of text where neither sin nor love is mentioned, the language of 'truth' and 'lies' is prominent (2:18–28; 4:2–6; 5:41–5). This suggests that one of the gateways to sin and its wide-ranging consequences is through a denial of the truth and embrace of error (or lies), especially with respect to the person and work of Christ.

The letter, therefore, establishes through its long introductory section the importance of Christology (1:1–4) for thinking through issues of sin and love (1:5—2:11). The readers are explicitly addressed as those who benefited from the work of Christ (2:12–14) and then exhorted regarding their participation in the world (2:15–17). This is a world marked by sin, as evidenced by the existence of those who have left their community and the presence of antichrists (2:18–28). These antichrists believe and encourage false beliefs concerning the person and work of Christ. However, the readers have been born again as children of God and are to live faithful lives uncharacterised by sin (3:4–9; 5:16–18) and instead marked by love (3: 10–23; 4:7—5:3). The letter comes to a close with a ringing assurance of their victory over the world and the eternal life that is theirs (5:1–5; 18–20) and finally finishes with a stark warning about living in the world, summed up in the exhortation to flee idolatry (5:21).

The overall purpose of the letter is to encourage the readers concerning their status in Christ and to exhort them to live out the implications of what has been done for them in Christ by resisting sin and seeking to love.

Preaching 1 John

The discussion above gives some food for thought when formulating a teaching series on the letter. The way that John has structured his letter, and the way that themes repeat and are developed through the letter, can lend itself to a more thematic series. A series of sermons on emergent themes – things like God is light; God is love; the person and work of Jesus Christ; the world; sin; love; Christian assurance; truth – would enable a teacher to bring disparate parts of the letter in thematic treatments. This can stop a series feeling repetitive when a topic is revisited. On the other hand, such a thematic series avoids the need to read the letter as it has been written. Perhaps the teacher needs to grapple with the repetition and development of themes, show how they unfold and relate to one another as John has written them and explore the benefits and challenges of his particular style.

2 and 3 John

In terms of genre, 2 and 3 John are more clearly recognisable as New Testament letters, with the characteristic features of addresser, addressee, blessing, prayer report and final greetings all present. That said, they are also clearly exhortatory in their intent.

The structure of both letters is straightforward, with an address (2 John 1–3; 3 John 1–4), a body (2 John 4–10; 3 John 5–12) and a conclusion (2 John 12–13; 3 John 13–14). They give us insight into the minutiae of pastoral life in the first century.

In 2 John, the text more overtly reflects some of the themes we have identified above with respect to behaviour in the world, with the mention of antichrists (2 John 7) and the warning not to sin by following them into christological error (2 John 8–9). This is accompanied by a strong exhortation to walk in love (2 John 6).

However, 3 John reflects the situation of the first two letters less directly. The focus is very personal (3 John 1), with primary focus on offering hospitality to itinerant missionaries (3 John 5–8). The same general issues of right behaviour flowing from right belief are in evidence. Recognition of authority is specifically addressed (3 John 9).

Together, these letters raise questions concerning hospitality and its importance and limits, as well as the exercise of pastoral leadership in the congregation.

The Contextualisation Task

The overall exhortation that emerges from the Johannine letters is to live faithfully as a child of God in the midst of the world. This means faithfulness to Christ expressed in a life spent resisting sin and embracing love, within the context of knowing what has been achieved and gifted to the believer by the risen Christ. At various points, this teaching will come into tension with the various worldviews that surround the believer in our contemporary secular and postmodern culture, where religion is one voice among many.

John's letters represent the outworking of a worldview profoundly shaped by the knowledge of God as revealed in the person of Christ. John works with theology (God is light; God is love) mediated through Christology (Jesus reveals God in his person and work). The two are so intertwined that at a number of points it is difficult to see whether John is referring to the Father or the Son with his pronouns.[14] In a real sense, it does not matter, as John works outward from his doctrine of God, as revealed in the person of his Son, to every area of exhortation he makes in the letter. The single-mindedness and rigour of this thought stand as an encouragement and challenge to the contemporary Christian, where immersion in a pluralistic culture will weaken thoughts of the uniqueness of Christ and his revelation of God and perhaps even undermine the value of such 'hard' thinking.

From this profound theological and christological base, John's letters encourage us to think about our relationship to our world, its attractions and perils – and how to live out the identity as a child of God, which is gifted to the believer and lived out in the midst of a community.

Relating to the World

I have suggested that the exhortation in 1 John 2:15–17 is key for understanding the structure and argument of the letter. This first explicit imperative to not love the world or the things of the world highlights the challenge of how the believer is to live faithfully in the world. In 1 John 2:15–17, the choice is presented in stark terms. The initial exhortation to not love the world is followed up by a statement contrasting this with the love of the Father. The world is then defined and finally declared to be passing away.

This is a challenging statement for contemporary Australian Christians, who may at times feel a little too much at home in this world. The statement taps into a wider narrative in the Bible more generally and the Johannine literature specifically, in which the people of God have always been depicted as living in the midst of a world of unbelief that poses the twin threat of opposition and allure.

Resisting the allure of the world

John begins focusing on the allure side of the equation. He describes the world as consisting of the things we desire, see and rely upon to shore up life and make it worthwhile. In doing this, he moves the focus from the things 'out there' to the inner world of desires, and pride and moves very close to a Pauline concept of the flesh. The problem he describes is one of disordered loves and desires that fix upon externals, misplacing them on created things and not their creator.[15] The meaning of 'the world' in this sense is not the physical creation. This is created good, as is humanity, with all sorts of potential for creativity and production of good things. It is almost *too* good a world, and therefore a potential rival to God for the affection of the people of the world.[16] In John's sense, then, the world is a construct that arises when sin-tainted humanity engages with the physical world both individually and en masse.

The obvious application here is consumerism, and the reality that Australians live in a world full of stuff. We need clothes, houses, foods and other kinds of goods to live, but the temptation is to fix our eyes on these things and make them the main thing rather than the good gift of a good Father, to be received with thanks. The Johannine concept of the world expressed here is clearly seen in the phenomenon of consumerism.[17] As the

'Describing Australians' chapter suggests, one of the defining features of contemporary Australian culture is wealth and consumerism. The negative effects of consumerism are clear and all around us. They include a sense of entitlement, a lack of thankfulness, a focus on the self at the expense of others and a sense of dissatisfaction. Consumers are self-centred, thankless and discontent. This description is far from the values of the kingdom of God.

It is not helpful, though, to simply rant at consumerism and call for repentance; the theology of consumerism also needs to be considered. In a very real sense, we are created to be consumers by a loving and generous God, who delights in giving his creation good things. The question is not whether to consume or not, but rather how to live as a consumer without being overly attached, without fixating, without being seduced into giving too much power to things we consume by necessity and capitulating to the negative effects of the ideology of consumerism.[18]

We need instead to encourage one another to consume as children of God; to consume with thankfulness to the Lord who is an abundant and generous provider; to consume therefore without a sense of entitlement; and to consume with love, expressed in a sense of generosity and equity towards those around us.[19]

Responding to the danger of the world

John also reminds us that this is a world filled with danger: antichrists who will present teachings that can cause believers to drift from the truth. It is the world into which the antichrists departed, despite having travelled with the Christian community for a while; it is a world full of spirits to be tested (1 John 2:22, 4:1; 2 John 7–8).[20] John depicts a world that is full of dangers for the believer and does so in vigorous language.

John is clear as a writer that there is an 'us and them' (1 John 2:19). He advises his congregation not to invite false teachers into their houses (2 John 1–11) and threatens to publicly rebuke Diotrephes for not acknowledging his authority (3 John 9–10). This sounds exclusive to a culture that values inclusivity and is loath to judge others. John's language is binary: darkness and light (1 John 1:6); truth and lies (1 John 1:8–9); love and hate (1 John 2:10–11); believers and the world (1 John 2:15); sin and righteousness (1 John 3:7–8). He uses the emotive term 'antichrist' (1 John 2:18, 22; 2 John 7). This all sounds very harsh to postmodern ears and appears to provide an unhelpful model of division and hatred of others for the sake of the truth, especially in an age when truth is relative and personal. It will be difficult for the contemporary believer to live out this teaching in a world where 'pluralism' and 'tolerance' have greatest currency, as the 'Describing Australians' chapter reminds us. One of the first challenges is to be convinced ourselves that there is truth in the gospel and that people can be correct and incorrect about matters of God and faith. It is difficult to disagree in a world that preaches tolerance.

One point to emphasise is that for John, and the Bible writers generally, the truth matters, not the least because it is a revealed truth from God. This will jar in a secular Australia that is sceptical of truth claims and is also now well acquainted with the concept of 'fake news'. Yet John is insistent. There is such a thing as truth, and it matters because of the consequences that follow from knowing this truth: eternal life (1 John 5:11–12). John writes as a pastor keen to see his audience grasp the truth and live by it, because he knows that this truth means life. He states that knowing his audience enjoy that life makes his joy complete (1 John 1:4; 2 John 4; 3 John 3).

Yet this language needs to be heard within the wider context of statements concerning God's love for the world (John 3:16). Thompson makes the point that while John's dualism is absolute, the reality in life is that it is not so easy to discern, and this is perhaps indicated in John's exhortation to 'test the Spirits' (1 John 4:1).[21] The language is descriptive and directed at believers, with the purpose of encouraging allegiance as well as the life of love and righteousness that God, who is light and love, requires.[22] How we live will be an important testimony to the truth of what we say.

Reflecting on this further, I suggest that we can too easily pit truth against love and compromise on the truth that people might need to hear, thinking that it is out of love that we are not speaking the truth as fully or as clearly as we might. This is not love; it may in fact be closer to the more anaemic 'tolerance', which can also be vaguely patronising. Love of others will mean speaking the truth, especially if it is a truth we believe leads to life. We do not need to be rude or overbearing, but we can be clear, direct when appropriate and willing to bear responsibility for the consequences of our speech.

The pluralism of our age is akin to the pluralism of John's time, a world full of philosophers and gods, jostling for space. It might be worth considering that one of the benefits of our pluralist and even postmodern age is that the Christian voice, while simply one among many, can claim space to be heard, simply because it is one among many. We can, with clarity and humility, offer the truth of God for consideration to our contemporary audience.

Christian Identity in an Age of Fluidity

Despite its allures and dangers, John also speaks of a world in which the believer can live with a robust sense of identity. John brackets his exhortation concerning the world with statements of Christian identity. In 1 John, he begins with an extended statement of Christian identity. It is an identity founded in the resurrection of the incarnate Christ (1 John 1:1–2)[23] and based on knowing God as Father, light and love. In chapter 3, John summarises his thinking on Christian identity when he declares that his readers recognise the love that has been shown them: that they might be called children of God

(1 John 3:1). This identity is a gift, neither earned nor constructed, and one in which John encourages his readers to walk faithfully.

One of the features of a postmodern world, as noted in the 'Describing Australians' chapter, is a fluid concept of identity: self-constructed, shifting and changing as everyone is invited to write their own story, because the grand stories of the past no longer apply.[24] John speaks directly to this uncertainty by proclaiming the possibility of both knowing God as Father and knowing you are loved beyond belief. This identity is grounded in the grand story of Christ and his love and sacrifice. Perhaps one of the antidotes to the rising levels of anxiety in contemporary Australia is the recovery of the robustness of this sense of identity.

John is insistent on the nexus between life in the Son, right belief and obedient practice. Identity has consequences for practice. John emphasises this by constantly entwining statements of belief and behaviour around one another. This is challenging in a world where it is tempting and easy to split thought and action, belief and its consequences. This call for consistency or congruency has resonance among Australians, who appear to dislike hypocrisy, especially in others, and especially in those who espouse high moral standards.

Moreover, as Yarbrough points out this relationship is further informed by a 'deep-rooted devotion of the heart for God. This is love'.[25] This love for God is to be expressed in love for others. The love that Christians are to demonstrate is a love that is operative in word and deed and is to be ultimately inspired by and modeled on the love shown to the believer by the sending of the Son to be the propitiation for our sins.

John's extensive discussion of love and its meaning should give food for thought among believers, where the obligation to love is so well known that we risk our familiarity descending into contempt for the command, especially its practice.

It is also provocative in a culture where slogans such as 'love wins' and 'all you need is love' are popular. John's exploration of love stands in contrast to contemporary concepts that are characterised by sentimentality, erotic desire and individual rights. John's speaks of a love that is indiscriminate, active towards others, sacrificial and creative. It is a love that takes its lead from the cross of Jesus Christ and not modern romantic theories, which idolise and idealise love, or modern naturalistic theories, which reduce love to biological states, chemical processes and urges that must be obeyed and indulged. It is difficult in the contemporary world to hold onto the Christian teaching, as the believer is constantly assailed by images on screens and loud voices in the media reinforcing anything but a Christian notion of love as faithful, sacrificial, self-controlled and expressed within limits – particularly when it comes to notions of sexuality.

This chapter is being written in the aftermath of a vigorous debate in Australia over legalising same-sex marriage, where the Christian position was seen as discriminatory, unkind to others, selfish and conservative in the extreme. Discussing the Johannine (biblical) concept of love apart from its moorings in the grand story of God's creation, his plan for humanity and the sacrificial work of Christ will inevitably mean that it is misunderstood.

Christian Assurance in an Age of Doubt

One of the key notes of John's letters is his desire that his readers be assured that they know God and all that this means. This is an interesting teaching in an age where doubt, especially in spiritual matters, appears to be considered a virtue and almost essential.[26]

John is adamant; he writes so that his readers may know that they have eternal life (5:13). This assurance is based on the objective truths they have been taught, the inner work of the Spirit (1 John 4:13–14) and the anointing they have received (1 John 2:27). John's first letter concludes with three bold statements of what his readers may know and then a warning against what might chip away at that assurance (1 John 5:18–20).

This sense of assurance could, of course, tip over into arrogance, but this is forestalled by John's acknowledgment all along that any assurance is based on God's grace towards the reader (1 John 3:1): his grace in revealing himself (1 John 4:19); his grace in acting in mercy by providing forgiveness for sins (1 John 2:1–2); and his grace in providing the witness of the Spirit to assure his people (1 John 4:13–14).

In light of this, doubt may well be a reality, but it is not a virtue. Doubt may come in the face of apparent fellow believers leaving and no longer walking in the truth (1 John 2:19); doubt may come in the face of the false teaching of antichrists (2 John 7–8); doubt may come even as a response to the apparent unfaithful actions of other community members (3 John 9–10). But these doubts need not be fatal or final.

Christian Community and Authority in an Age of Individualism

The 'Describing Australians' chapter observes that one feature of Australian culture is its individualism. The New Testament generally, and the Johannine letters particularly, challenge this orientation with their commitment to community. In the Johannine letters, this is expressed in the exhortations to love the brothers (1 John 2:9; 3:16; 4:20), the use of family language generally to describe the Christian community (1 John 2:1, 18; 3:15; 2 John 1), and exhortations to provide hospitality to wandering 'strangers' (3 John 5–8). One issue that might prove especially provocative in these letters is the exercise of authority among the community.

Australians have an ambivalent relationship with authority. On the one hand, there is a pride in egalitarianism, which cuts against any ready acquiescence to authority. On the other hand, we are, generally speaking, rulemaking (if not always abiding) people.[27]

We also see a desire for strong leaders, recognising that good leadership is essential to the proper functioning of any organisation and country. Yet this is tainted with a general disillusion and cynicism with political and corporate leadership in Australia as this essay is being written.

I suspect that the implied spiritual authority expressed through all these letters will rankle many. The concept of spiritual authority is tricky anyway, in the light of the apparent abuse of such authority as unveiled by the Royal Commission into Institutional Responses to Child Sexual Abuse. But the apparently heavy-handed approach by John in his third letter when dealing with Diotrephes (3 John: 9–10) as well as the implied understanding that his words will be heeded and followed sits at odds with a sense of independence and equality that struggles with the notion of authority.

How do the Johannine letters speak into this? We see a model of leadership in action that is parental without being paternalistic, firm without being overbearing, clear and direct without being overly assertive and irrational. Yarbrough describes 3 John as 'almost painfully intimate'.[28] As John instructs, it is clear that he does it with love for his spiritual children (1 John 2:1, 7; 2 John 1; 3 John 1) and models an affectionate, caring and yet authoritative exercise of leadership (2 John 12; 3 John 2–4).

John's theological method also invites responsible engagement and not blind obedience. At times there has been puzzlement concerning the apparent contradictions in John's letters, most famously his statements concerning sin. On the one hand, he speaks of provision made by God for sinful transgressions (1 John 1:8–9); on the other hand, he speaks of the impossibility of believers sinning (1 John 3:6, 9). His letter circles around and back to a handful of issues, approaching them from different but complementary perspectives. All of this works to give the reader a number of fixed points within which to think about the issues John is writing about. There is room for responsible agency in working through these tensions. While John writes with affection to his 'children', he treats them like responsible adults. In doing so, he helps us to also think about how to do theology and apply the knowledge of God in a pastoral context. Space is made for a conversation that hears alternative but complementary perspectives, invites dialogue and conversation, but is also insistent on practical outcomes and not just talk (1 John 3:18).

Sample Sermon: 1 John 2:15–17

'What in the world has gotten into you?' Have you ever had those words said to you? What in the world has gotten into you? I first heard this as a kid when I stole a kitchen knife and for some reason slashed the bench seat in my parents' new Ford. I actually learnt a few other new words that night, but that's another story.

What in the world has gotten into you? When we say this, we mean that something else has apparently taken over, something from outside of us that is not part of the family or what we do around here.

This question is sometimes asked about the church … what in the world has gotten into the church? I found a string of quotes down the centuries, lamenting along these lines. This one from Spurgeon gives us the flavour: 'I believe that one reason why the church has so little influence over the world is that the world has so much influence over the church.'

Is he right?

The topic of how Christians ought to relate to the world around them is a big one, and our passage, 1 John 2:15–17, gives us a reason to think about this. The word 'world' is used in at least three different ways in the Bible. It can mean the physical world, the creation. It can mean the world of people, generally. But the special sense of the world we are thinking about here is the sense of a world of people in rebellion against God. It is one of John's favourite words in his Gospel and letters, and it has an important use in this passage. Let's look at it now.

Our passage, 2:15–17, occurs at an important point in John's letter. John has just spent a fair bit of time establishing what it means to be a child of God in chapter 1, and he sums it all up in verses 12–14 of chapter 2. To be a child of God means to know God, to know Jesus, to have sins forgiven, to have overcome the evil one, to be strong and to have the word of God live in them.

This is a great picture.

John tells them who they are, and now he tells them what this means. What does he want them to do? They are not to love the world. This little passage then sets up the rest of the letter. The children of God live in the world but are not to love it. John writes to encourage his readers to live as the faithful children of God in our world.

This is clearly something we need to hear, don't we?

However, a really interesting thing happens as John talks about the world. Did you see it? As he defines 'the world', John moves from 'out there' to 'in here', to the realm of desires and pride. There is a relationship to the physical, created world, but John's attention is moving between this external world and the more internal response of people to it.

John is comprehensive. His children are not to love the world or the things in the world. What are these things? He mentions three things.

The first thing is the desires of the flesh. Now we need to remember that this is John talking and not Paul. We are used to understanding the desires of the flesh as perhaps sexual desires. John's term is more general; the desires here are for the things the flesh needs. One writer suggests the translation, 'what the body hankers for', which I kind of like. The point is that there's a whole bunch of things we need and want, simply as people. We are people made of flesh: flesh that is weak and needs to be fed, clothed and so on.

These fleshly needs are legitimate; that's the way God has made us. But the problem is that we obsess about these things. We turn wants into needs. Legitimate needs go wrong, get overdone and turn into obsessions and industries … food, sex, pleasure, entertainment. We need food but end up with *MasterChef*, endless magazine pages about the next exotic ingredient and all sorts of food porn on our TVs. We need clothes and we get the fashion industry; we need housing and we get *The Block* or *Grand Designs*. We can't help ourselves.

The next phrase, 'lust of the eyes' is more specific and speaks again to desires. Sins such as greed, envy and covetousness in all areas of life seem to be hinted at here. We want what we see around us.

It is easy to see the applicability of this, especially in our highly visual culture, with its emphasis on images in so many areas of life. There is a constant stream of titillation for the lust of the eyes, to make us covet what we see. We see this through advertising and the constant bombardment of images encouraging all manner of desires, covetousness and envy. We are so used to sex selling anything and everything, even Tim Tams used sexual images at one stage! Who would have thought they needed the help to sell?

The third feature mentioned is the pride of life, or 'pride in life'. The word used for life is quite broad and covers things like life, livelihood, everyday goods and possessions. Through the use of the word pride, we move beyond the necessities of life to the thought that we find security in what we own. The pride of self-sufficiency. More than this, we can also desire the pride of status and acquire stuff with a view to impressing others – to keep up with the Joneses.

So, we have a trinity of what the body hankers for, what the eyes see and what people toil to acquire. If we put the three together, we get a picture of excess, too much – selfish human desire that is stimulated by what it sees, then acquires to satisfy its desires as we whisper 'I want that, I need that'; this creates a sense of security so that we can reassure ourselves with the thought that 'the more things I've got, the safer and more comfortable I am'. We can even show off a little, asking our neighbours to 'look at all my toys'.

What do you think? Do you recognise this as the material world of today?

John says that this boils down to a question of loves. Who do you love? If you love the world, he says, you cannot love the Father. The love of the world expels the love of the Father. John is saying that the world is a rival to God for our affection. There is no multitasking on this one. It might be okay to multitask at home or at work or school, but to attempt to love God in multitasking fashion – dedicating a portion of your love towards the world and then the rest to God – is fruitless, because it fails to acknowledge God as he truly is.

This passage feels a little like my daughter grabbing my face, holding it close to mine and saying, 'Listen to me. Pay attention!'

But there is a dilemma here in applying this. We need stuff to live, don't we? We need food, clothes, drink, relationships. There are lots of good things there. We need some stuff, don't we? It seems that the problem is not that the world around is so *bad*; the problem is that, from one perspective, it is so *good*. It is almost like God has made the world 'too good'. Too distracting.

This is easy to see in Australia. We live in a good world with good things: vaccinations against disease, mass transport systems, communication technologies, plasma screens, five-bladed razors, football, meat pies, kangaroos and Holden cars. So many good things to see, want, desire.

I think the picture is that we are like the dogs in that kids' movie, *Up*. This movie was on high rotation in our house when my girls were younger. Maybe you have seen it. There's a pack of dogs running at various points through the movie; they are running along all right, when either deliberately or accidentally, someone will yell, 'Squirrel!' And all the dogs stop where they are going and what they are doing and stare in the direction they're pointed. Their attention is diverted. They are distracted.

That is us walking the Christian walk. We are going along all right, when suddenly we hear the word 'squirrel'. It might be a career; it might be an attractive romantic option; it might be an ambition; it might be a desire for recognition. It might be something that promises safety and security; it might be a talent. All of these are good things, but we get distracted; we make a good thing the main thing, and we forget the real thing.

We attach ourselves to parts of our world way too hard: too intensely, excessively, obsessively and destructively. This works both individually and collectively.

The young man loves sex and freedom – squirrel! – so much that he won't commit to a single partner, and 'the world' develops a sex industry to give him what he wants.

The scientist desires cures and recognition so much – squirrel! – that she overlooks the personhood of the embryo and keeps on experimenting, and a bioethics industry develops to justify.

The Australian person loves having a good time – squirrel! – and a thousand industries, travel, entertainment and so on spring up to supply this, along with a philosophy that says you deserve everything you have and ought to enjoy it.

There is nothing wrong with sex and freedom, nothing wrong with cures and recognition, nothing wrong with enjoying life. But they so fill the horizon, desire grips us so intensely, that any room for love for God is eventually displaced and driven from us.

The world is given to us as a gift, but we think we have made it. In the city, of course – perhaps any built environment – this is easy to believe. We talk about remaking ourselves, creating wealth, building a life, shaping ourselves and our identities. We can even resurrect a career. We don't need the word of God because we can do it ourselves. Man does not need to live by bread alone, because we have foams, mousses and ragouts.

And so, we have created a world in conjunction with our desires, where even though many of us claim to be believers, we find it is easy to live as if God does not exist! This is where love of the world leads.

One of the main ways I think this is expressed in our world today is in what we call consumerism. This is the dominant faith in the world around us. It goes back to all that stuff we were mentioning. In the immortal words of those great theologians, Depeche Mode: we just can't get enough.

The fact of life is that we are always consuming, but it is more than what we do or buy; it is a mindset, how we think. It is there in our language: we 'buy into' ideas, 'shop around' for churches, 'invest' in relationships; put ourselves 'in the market'; need to 'sell ourselves' better, look for people who are 'good value' ... we start to unconsciously value people as resources rather than valuing and loving them as beings created in God's image.

Consumerism is a world of choice. We choose our location, lifestyle, recreation and religion, occupation, partners. We choose our identities through our consumer choices.

What is the problem here? Consumerism puts us firmly at the centre of everything. That is what is so attractive! The customer is always right. The most important person in the world is you.

Consumerism is predicated on unlimited needs and wants. The market is based on the idea that you will always want more; it is founded on endless dissatisfaction. And so, consumerism engenders endless discontent.

Consumerism breeds ingratitude and entitlement. Consumers don't give thanks because they have paid and are entitled. Do you need to thank someone who has served you in a restaurant or shop?

A consumer society is a self-centred, thankless and discontented place to be. This is a long way from the values of the kingdom, the values of the family of God. The Christian life is more like a service industry than it is a consumer culture.

Here's the thing ... from a Christian perspective, there is no way out of being a consumer; we are created to consume. It is what kind of consumer we are that is the important thing. God is an abundant provider, but he asks us to consume with thanks, without a sense of entitlement and with a sense of generosity and equity towards those around us.

We are created to consume – but not to be consumed by it all. We are to use the world wisely, but not be used by it. 'Do not love the world', John says.

We are not to pray 'My kingdom come, my will be done' and erase God from his universe. But we live in a culture, a world, that reinforces this at every step of the way.

What am I saying? We need to hear John, heed his warning and work out how to live faithfully in the midst of our desires and a world that feeds them. It is not always a 'no', of course. There's so much that is good and to be received with thankfulness, but I want us to hear John at full blast: Do not love the world or the things of the world.

Why does all this matter? Why would we heed this warning?

There is a reason that taps into the broader storyline of the Bible, and it's hinted at in the last clause of our passage: 'The world is passing away.' The world – in the sense of humanity – has a problem. It is helpless and hopeless; it has rebelled against God and faces his certain judgement. This rebellion is expressed in the indulgence of desires that disobey God's good word, in the creation of a world within God's good world that is a rival to him. In short, it is a world that needs saving. A world that needs rescue.

Humanity takes the world to heart, worships the created thing and not the creator and is condemned to a Godless eternity.

The world's solution is the love of God. You know the famous words: 'For God so loved the world that he gave his one and only Son, that whoever believes in him should not perish but have eternal life' (John 3:16).

Our world needs to hear people speaking the message of the gospel. Our world needs to hear there is a way out.

And our world needs to see people living to show a better way – not just going along with the herd, but living in such a way that demonstrates that God's way is viable and better, that his word is good, that God is good and that to live with Jesus, not the consumer, as king is actually the best way.

To love the world is to be taken up by all or part of that which constitutes the world instead of seeking to do the will of God. At the heart of John's concept of the world is humanity with the world at its heart.

Jesus loved the world but did not take it to heart. His followers are to do the same. We need to be like the Lord Jesus, who loved the world but did not take it to heart. Brothers and sisters, we live in the world; let's not love the world, and let's do this for the sake of the world.

12

PREACHING HEBREWS, JAMES AND JUDE TO AUSTRALIANS

Brian Harris

Introduction

In this chapter we explore some of the joys and challenges of preaching from Hebrews, James and Jude, with a special focus on preaching from these Scriptures in a way that is likely to connect with Australian congregations.

Given that a common author does not unite these letters, readers might well question the rationale behind grouping these three New Testament books together, perhaps suspecting it to be a pragmatic decision, as though we're sweeping together a few miscellaneous letters that don't comfortably fit elsewhere, none of which are substantial enough to require a chapter on their own. Their placement at the tail end of the canon certainly gives the impression that these letters are probably not the most important part of Scripture, and indeed, the right of each to be part of the canon has been contested at various times.

Should we therefore consider this chapter to be in the 'also-ran' category, included for the sake of completeness but otherwise saying very little?

I hope not – and if this is the final conclusion you reach, the fault will be mine as the author rather than the messages of Hebrews, James and Jude. Consider quickly the underlying themes of each, for there is nothing also-ran about any of them.

Hebrews helps us to dig deeply into the 'Who is Jesus?' question, boldly asserting that whatever view we have of Jesus, he is actually greater. At a time when we are deeply distrustful of superheroes, Hebrews reminds us that we should place some limits on our scepticism and listen calmly to the cumulative evidence pointing to Jesus as not only the one who 'is the radiance of God's glory and the exact representation of his being' (as if that were not enough) but also as the one who has 'provided purification for sins' and is now 'seated at the right hand of the Majesty in heaven' and ... well, the list goes on and on as we work our way through Hebrews.[1]

Though Luther famously dismissed the letter of James as a 'right strawy epistle', his claim simply reminds us that Luther, while brilliant, had some serious lapses of judgement.[2] Speaking to a community whose faith was being tested by a range of conflicts, both within and without, James is one of the most helpful of the New Testament letters. Be it on the relationship between faith and works, the importance of endurance, the risk of prejudice within the Christian community, the danger of idle gossip, the folly of self-confidence, the risks inherent in being wealthy, the power of prayer – enough said. Any preacher knows the treasure trove that this list opens and has probably drawn from the wisdom of James over and over again.

The letter to Jude – all one chapter of it – packs a punch that its twenty-five verses might not initially reveal. It is not the letter Jude wanted to write, but the letter he felt compelled to write. While his preference would have been to expand on the wonder of salvation found in Jesus, Jude quickly dives into his worrying context, one in which he has to 'urge' his listeners to 'contend for the faith that was once for all entrusted to the saints'. You sense his concern. His language is strong and unrestrained. The stakes are high – indeed, the truth of the gospel is at stake. What a fascinating letter to preach from, for in our perhaps overly tolerant times, Jude is uncompromising. True, he does instruct us to 'be merciful to those who doubt' – but Jude himself has little doubt as to what the truth is or of how to interpret the events of his day.[3]

While this thematic overview asserts the importance of each of these letters, it still does not address the question of why we should group them together, unless we consider pragmatic considerations to be reason enough – and after all, pragmatism goes a long way in the Australian context.

Witherington suggests that one reason to study Hebrews, James and Jude together is that each seems to have been 'written by and primarily for Jewish Christians'.[4] Witherington views each of these letters as essentially a sermon or homily, going so far as to title part one of his commentary, 'The Sermon to the Hebrews', part two, 'James the Homily' and part three, 'Jude – Another Brother's Sermon'.[5] If Witherington is correct, when we preach from these epistles we are preaching about another preacher's sermon or constructing a sermon about a sermon.[6] Given that Aussie audiences tend to be a little wary about preaching, this double dose of sermons about sermons could seem a little rich, especially as the worldview of the original congregation is both chronologically and culturally far from our own, though the barrier is not insurmountable. The fear dissipates a little when we view the task as getting into the 'zone' that the original preachers were preaching in, understanding that space well and, with similar heart, preaching to the concerns expressed – albeit the concerns as they now express themselves in a twenty-first-century context.

In short then, in this chapter we explore three sermons preached or written by and to Jewish Christians. In a book about preaching, this has to be a challenge worth rising to – to preach about a sermon and to do so with all the passion, integrity and insight of the original preachers.

But I am running ahead of myself. Are Witherington's assertions likely to be correct? And what are some of the background considerations we should keep in mind before preaching from Hebrews, James and Jude?

In many ways, it is a benefit not to be certain as to who wrote these epistles (or perhaps better, who preached these sermons), as too lengthy a focus on date and authorship can obscure the message conveyed. We rather need to sit with those first congregations, aware of the vulnerability of that time and the particular struggles they faced, and hear each of these messages being preached. Once we have listened carefully to and thought deeply about the impact of the preaching on its first hearers, we can think about our own congregations and how the messages of Hebrews, James and Jude can speak to an Aussie congregation as powerfully as each originally spoke to their first listeners, the vast majority of whom were converts from Judaism – at times wavering converts, but converts to be sure. But then, aren't our congregations also filled with wavering converts, conscious of being Christ followers in a post-Christian era, bombarded with accusations that faith is intellectually vacuous, morally suspect and experientially empty?[7] It might not be as difficult to be a follower of Jesus in twenty-first-century Australia, but it has its challenges, and there are more than a few who have abandoned the faith they once firmly held to.[8]

With this background, let's dig a little into the background of each of Hebrews, James and Jude.

The Hermeneutical Task

Hebrews

Before embarking on a quest to determine the authorship, audience and setting for Hebrews, it is as well to note Kenneth Schenck's cautioning: 'The only legitimate place to start interpreting Hebrews is with what the text of Hebrews itself tells us. Studies that begin by deciding on a highly specific author, audience, or situation are bound to lead us astray. Such starting hypotheses make it hard for us to hear Hebrews with open ears.'[9]

While the authorship of Hebrews has speculatively been assigned to several possible candidates, most notably Paul, Barnabas, Clement, Luke or Apollos, Origen's conclusion that 'God only knows' is the one we must live with.[10] It is the only New Testament book for which a female author (possibly Priscilla) has been posited with any seriousness, though Origen's sceptical 'God only knows' should be restated.[11] The use of the authorial 'we' through much of the letter could indicate that more than one author was involved in its composition (perhaps Priscilla and her husband Aquila), but yet again, 'God only knows'.

A key theme of the 'Sermon to the Hebrews' is the risk of apostasy, the preacher being concerned that there are those who had fallen away from, or were in danger of falling away from, the newly adopted faith. Concern surrounding this is found in 2:3, 3:12, 6:4–6, 10:29 and, most notably, in 10:35–39. The preacher is conscious that the listeners had already suffered a significant loss of social standing as a result of their faith, and many had been persecuted. We should note the seriousness of the claim in Hebrews 10:33–34: 'Sometimes you were publicly exposed to insult and persecution; at other times you stood side by side with those who were so treated. You sympathised with those in prison and joyfully accepted the confiscation of property, because you knew that you yourselves had better and lasting possessions.' The original listeners had already paid a significant price for becoming Christians and had paid it happily, as they were convinced that something better lay ahead for them. For all that, there was the real risk that prolonged struggle and loss could see them abandon their faith. They needed the preacher's encouragement: 'So do not throw away your confidence; it will be richly rewarded. You need to persevere …' (Heb 10:35–36a).

When and to whom are these instructions given?

Clement of Rome makes use of Hebrews in 96 CE, which therefore makes it the absolute outer limit for the date of writing. A yet earlier date is made probable by the reference in Hebrews 10:2 to the ongoing nature of the sacrifices in the Jewish Temple, which implies a date prior to the temple's destruction in 70 CE (or why else would this event not have been referred to?) Admittedly, arguments from silence are not without risk, but DeSilva's conclusion that 'Hebrews reads more naturally in a pre-70 setting' holds merit.[12]

Much of the letter (and certainly chapters 7–10) presupposes a clear understanding of Judaism, the Hebrew Scriptures and (especially) the temple sacrificial system, which DeSilva notes has led 'almost inevitably' to 'the suggestion that the problem addressed by Hebrews is a potential reversion to Judaism on the part of Jewish Christians who seek to avoid ongoing tension with their non-Christian Jewish families and neighbours'.[13] While DeSilva is not convinced by this view, and argues that Gentile converts would gain a comparable familiarity in a relatively short space of time, this chapter follows the conventional wisdom on this topic.[14]

The sample sermon towards the end of this essay therefore assumes that Hebrews is a pre–70 CE sermon, addressed primarily to Jewish converts to Christianity, who faced increasing opposition and who were consequently at risk of abandoning their faith. From a preaching perspective, if any of these assumptions is false it is unlikely that the sermon would be dramatically compromised, though the risk is greater if potential abandonment of Christian faith is not a key concern of the letter.

James

Although not uncontested, the authorship of James is usually ascribed to James, the brother of Jesus, who led the Jerusalem church from around 44 CE to 61 CE – or, if not James himself, at least to a close associate of James. While the quality of the Greek makes it improbable that James personally wrote the letter, he may well have done so with an amanuensis, who would have had significant freedom in shaping the final form of the document, though it would have reflected the thinking of James. Alternatively, if the letter is simply attributed to James to allow it a weight it would otherwise have lacked, it is nevertheless likely to bear sufficient resemblance to his thought to make the claim of his authorship credible. Though a detailed discussion of likely authorship is well beyond our scope here, for preaching purposes it is enough to note that the concerns raised in James are likely to reflect insights and sayings from the sermons of James – and that if James was not the actual author, then it was probably written shortly after his martyrdom in 62 CE.[15]

While Robert Wall originally sounds a little dismissive of James when he describes it as an 'apparent clipboard of moral exhortations', he more respectfully entitles his commentary on James *The Community of the Wise*.[16] In his commentary, Chris Morgan sets out to develop a coherent theology of James, and indeed calls his book *A Theology of James: Wisdom for God's People*, which is noteworthy if only to counter the assumption that James is essentially a collection of practical hints and tips on living out the Christian life.[17] That it is a letter with great wisdom (or a sermon with many wise insights) thus seems to be a reasonable conclusion.

It is impossible to preach from James without at some point addressing the question of the compatibility of James with the theology of Paul. Does James undermine the notion of salvation by grace through faith alone by injecting an insistent emphasis on the practical outworking of true faith, and his willingness to reject forms of faith that do not have an obvious impact on lifestyle. To cite James, 'Faith by itself, if it is not accompanied by action, is dead' (Jas 2:17). The controversial part of James is undoubtedly James 2:14–26, and certainly verse 24, if removed from its wider context, is provocative: 'You see that a person is considered righteous by what they do and not by faith alone.'

Is James, then, a genuine threat to the Reformation, causing us to doubt some of its key rallying cries? Only if we are foolish enough to examine the verse outside of the broader context of the sermon (and let's remember this is probably a summary of a sermon or a few sermons preached by James, with the passion and intensity of the original sermon often leaking through). James is horrified to think that anyone would embrace 'cheap grace' – to cite the description of barren faith given by German theologian Dietrich Bonhoeffer many centuries later.[18] In this, Paul is in full agreement with James. Consider Paul's own question and answer in Romans 6:1–2: 'What shall we say, then? Shall we go on sinning so that grace may increase? By no means! We died to sin; how can we live in it any longer?'

Both Paul and James argue against the trivialisation of grace, and are both insistent that grace, when genuinely received, impacts and transforms the lifestyle of the recipient. It is grace itself that is transformative, and James is concerned that the recipients of his sermon have been willing to settle for 'faith without deeds', as though the two can be separated. If they are, it can only be because the original faith was dead.[19]

While the letter identifies the recipients of the letter as 'the twelve tribes scattered among the nations', this is remarkably vague.[20] As Alec Motyer comments,

> If James were to post this letter today it would be marked 'Return to sender' on the ground of being insufficiently addressed. He names no names and specifies no place as destination: *twelve tribes* contains a lot of people and *the Dispersion*, in its special sense of the scattered people of God, was in principle world-wide.[21]

While the twelve tribes in dispersion were usually understood to mean the 'the totality of the Jewish community scattered outside Palestine', McKnight and Church suggest that here, 'the Diaspora refers to a far-flung Jewish-Christian community still comfortable with metaphors drawn from its Jewish roots and pressured by the wider Greco-Roman society whose values were antithetical to its own'.[22]

From a preaching perspective, then, this is likely to be a letter reflecting the thinking and preaching of James, a brother of Jesus, written in the early stages of the church (about 62 CE), written to a far-flung group of converts, probably most of whom were from a Jewish background, and who needed guidance as they attempted to live out their faith in a society with very different values to their own.

Jude

Warning as it does against false teaching, it is understandable that a negative tone runs through Jude (as through 2 Peter, which has significant similarities to Jude).[23] This can make preaching from it challenging, as popular preaching is usually optimistic and hopeful rather than cautionary and fearful. Not that people don't like the occasional creation of an enemy to be opposed, but often such preaching plays to people's lesser selves – the human tendency to feel we hold the moral high ground when we can denounce someone else as evil. However, this is not the case here, for the stakes behind Jude's letter (sermon) are high, as Jude challenges a libertine understanding of the gospel, where the grace of God is changed 'into a license for immorality' (v.4). Like James, Jude is concerned that 'cheap grace' could become the order of the day.[24]

This writing is usually ascribed to Jude, the brother of James and Jesus (of whom Jude simply says he is a servant rather than a brother).[25] Is this likely to be accurate? As Davids notes, 'The real issue with Jude, then, in terms of authorship, is not the date of Jude's life or the self-designation of the author, but the style of the work.'[26] Davids' point is that the Greek of the letter is too advanced for a family member of Jesus, especially as in Jude we 'have a work that is full of wordplays, alliteration, and other skilful rhetorical devices, all in Greek and none of which would work in Hebrew and Aramaic'.[27] Of course, the letter could have been written with the assistance of an amanuensis. This is a real possibility, especially as it is less likely that the letter is attributed to Jude to give it extra weight; Jude was not an especially influential leader in the church, and thus there was relatively little to be gained by attributing something to him. We will therefore assume that Jude was at least closely involved in the authorship of this letter.

While the context of the letter is clear, and we know that it was written because 'certain men whose condemnation was written about long ago have secretly slipped in among you', we know very little more than that.[28] These people may have taught an early form of Gnosticism, and the fact that they changed 'the grace of our God into a license for immorality' could indicate antinomianism, but we must be cautious in being too sure that we fully understand what the false teaching consisted of.[29] For preaching purposes, it is probably enough to know that false teaching is always a danger to the church, and that we to might need 'to contend for the faith that was once for all entrusted to God's holy people' (Jude 3). There are risks in this, for it can be too easy to dismiss those who disagree with us as 'godless' without the situation being anywhere near as serious as that faced by Jude.[30] It involves a thoughtful exercise of weighing up differences and making an informed decision as to when an alternative view is simply that – an alternative that can deepen and enrich our understanding – as opposed to when it genuinely undermines that which is of fundamental importance.

The Contextualisation Task

How, then, do we preach from Hebrews, James and Jude in an Australian context?

James is probably the easiest, for its insights quickly resonate with an Australian audience. An egalitarian tone runs through the letter, with the reprimand for showing favouritism to the rich likely to strike a chord with the average Aussie congregation.[31] However, the assumption that the reprimand would apply to anyone but ourselves is misleading. Paradoxically, we are often most guilty of that which we assume does not impact us. Australians might be egalitarian, but let any popular member of the British royal family visit and another face is quickly assumed.[32] While the backing of the welfare state helps to place a limit on how poor any one individual can be, it can also be seen to remove the need for private citizens to show kindness. It is easy to assume that compassion and looking after the needs of the vulnerable are the responsibility of the government, not individuals. Indeed, many Australians assume that anyone in Australia who faces actual financial hardship does so because of their own incompetence or misuse of the funds available through the welfare system.[33] There is the danger of blindness to the actual needs of others, and where the needs are spotted, it is easy to lapse into judgement, which dampens the conscience and absolves us from the responsibility of diving into the complexity of people's lives. James urges an open-heartedness to the other, a willingness to notice the other and to treat them with utmost seriousness.

At heart, James is an invitation to marry the three important 'orthos' behind genuine Christian faith: orthodoxy, orthopraxy and orthopathy.[34] Orthodoxy is about correct belief, orthopraxy, correct practice and orthopathy, correct feeling. It is the third we often overlook, but its absence is frequently an underlying problem, and in many instances it is the reason why those who reject the Christian faith are resentful towards those who believe. You see it in the older brother in the parable of the prodigal son.[35] Without faulting his beliefs or practice, his moral deficit becomes obvious when we spot the absence of empathy for either the plight of his younger brother or the feelings of his father.

To judge another without any empathy for their plight or understanding of the triggers that led to their actions is always an ugly thing, and James will not allow us to walk in this territory unchallenged. He has many remedies for the failure to integrate the different dimensions of faith holistically. James 1:19 instructs us to 'be quick to listen, slow to speak and slow to become angry'. Verse 22 adds that we must not merely 'listen to the word' but must 'do what it says'. James 2:13 reminds us that 'Mercy triumphs over judgement!' – and so it continues.

While some of this teaching can be appropriately applied in the context of the local church, in preaching from James it is as well to remind congregants that faith is lived out in the marketplace, which for most people is their workplace. At a time when a growing number of Australians are angry with and frustrated by the church, those who represent Jesus at their place of work are well advised to drink deeply from James 1:19. In being quick to listen and slow to speak we will, with time, master the art of conversation with people with whom we disagree, and sometimes even strongly disagree, partaking in conversation that is in the first instance shaped by genuine curiosity ('I'm intrigued that you see things in this way. Tell me why ... ') rather than judgement ('That's rubbish, and this is why ... '). The rules of conversation will, with time, see our curiosity reciprocated by those we have listened to.

If listening will, paradoxically, win us a hearing, so too will acts of genuine compassion and kindness. Nothing impresses Australians more than sermons without words – faith in action. In an era where most media reports on the church are strongly negative, an alternative story is sometimes told in local community newspapers, which report on the working bee from the local church that helped transform the garden of an elderly or unwell member of the community, or of the local churches involvement with homeless people, or of how the local church organised a fundraising drive to help enable medical treatment for a desperately unwell child. This is an aspect of faith in action, and it opens the hearts of those who observe its practice.

This is teaching that is easy to assent to, and few would challenge the insights; indeed, most Australians would cheer them on. It becomes more challenging when applied to some concrete and controversial situations. The original recipients of the letter are likely to have known exactly to what (and probably to whom) James was referring when he accused them of showing favouritism, and no doubt they bristled at the charge. Prophetic preaching often needs a clear focus (for example, our ruthless response to 'illegal' migrants), and the clearer the focus, the greater the likelihood of pushback. When preaching from James, it is wise to pray for what in 3:17 he calls 'the wisdom that comes from heaven', which he then describes as being 'first of all pure; then peace-loving, considerate, submissive, full of mercy and good fruit, impartial and sincere'. This does not mean we should lack courage when it comes to application. Indeed, James 4:4 holds no punches when James bursts out, 'You adulterous people, don't you know that friendship with the world is hatred towards God?'

While Jude has many beautiful features, and the doxology found in verses 24–25 is sung in many churches, its underlying message sits uneasily in current Australian culture, simply because it makes crisp, no-nonsense judgements and is not willing to consider alternative views. The enemy is the enemy, spoken about without mercy. They are 'godless men' (v.4); 'dreamers' (v.8); 'like unreasoning animals' (v.10); 'blemishes at your love feasts' (v.12); 'clouds without rain' (v.12); 'twice dead' (v.12); 'grumblers and faultfinders' (v.16) and for them 'the blackest darkness has been reserved forever' (v.13). You can imagine the average Australian hearing that and saying, 'Take a chill pill, mate. We're not sitting in parliament!'

Not that Australians don't relate to passionate outbursts. While outwardly, people appear to be relaxed and easy-going, deep emotion is never far from the surface. You see it in the mythology of the ever-popular song 'Waltzing Matilda'. Elsewhere I have written:

> Waltzing Matilda, which was almost declared the Australian national anthem in 1974, is a story of a tramp who camps by a creek and steals a sheep. When three policemen arrive, he commits suicide by diving in the creek rather than face arrest. No one denies that it is sloppily sentimental, yet a slow, soulful rendition leaves Australians dabbing tears from their eyes. It encapsulates so much of the Australian psyche, which though highly urbanized, likes to think of itself as being made up of ruggedly independent country folk who stand up against authority, and yet are forced to endure many injustices. It's the Crocodile Dundee imagery.[36]

The point is simple enough. Strong feelings are deemed appropriate if the cause is considered worthy. When preaching from Jude, the challenge is to demonstrate that this cause is worthy – and why orthodoxy matters. And orthodoxy does matter, for without it neither orthopraxy nor orthopathy are likely to be attainable. Preaching from Jude requires thoughtful translation from Jude's time to our own, as indeed does all preaching, though perhaps with Jude this might take a little more work, as the lines of correspondence are not as easily drawn.

It is as well to ask what are the particular heresies we must preach against in current Australian society. It is probably our worship of the unholy quadrilateral of money, sex, power and self. They are our contemporary idols, and they quickly lead us astray. None are inherently evil, but each has become an evil, because we have elevated its importance to godlike stature.

Materialism is a relatively new temptation in Australian society. Historically, we were more concerned that everyone had a fair go, and that we created a society where the vulnerable were protected. This is now slipping away. When politicians condemn 'lazy welfare bludgers', their political stakes usually rise, especially when they link it to a waste of taxpayers' money and suggest that we are paying for someone else's indolence. It plays to the worst part of our being, encouraging us to be indignant, fearful and selfish.

When it comes to sex, the church is as much in danger as the rest of society of paying so much attention to it that it starts to seem more important than God. It is sad that when most Australians think about the church, they most commonly think of paedophilia, the Royal Commission into Institutional Responses to Child Sexual Abuse and opposition to same sex marriage. All are seen to mark the church as hypocritical, and it is a significant stumbling block to many outside of the church, one which makes them refuse to engage with the message of the church. It requires us to rethink the way in which we speak about sex and human sexuality. At the very least, when we speak into such areas we should do so with humility, painting an invitational and aspirational portrait rather than one which quickly excludes and judges.

The idol of power is probably self-explanatory, but the idol of self is not. A genuine tension point between the Christian faith and the humanism of our time is that the wider society is opting for a lonely humanism, one where the rights of the individual trump all other concerns. Ironically, this leads to free but isolated individuals, fearful of trespassing across the boundaries of another but dramatically the poorer for having no significant part in the wider community. Jesus' insight that when we lose our life, we find it, needs to be unpacked over and over again. It is not that Christians are against humanism, it is rather that they are deeply convinced that we are only fully human when we are in right and deep relationship with God, others and the environment. Any other vision sells us short and ultimately dehumanises us.

If James is the easiest of the letters to preach from in an Australian context and Jude presents some challenges, Hebrews is probably the most difficult. This is simply because much of the imagery is linked to Judaism, and especially to the sacrificial system in place at the temple at the time of writing. One of the focal points of Hebrews is to show that Jesus has introduced a new and better way through which we can approach God, and that Jesus is superior to any prior revelation. What does this mean for a twenty-first-century Australian congregation? Perhaps the question is best answered by an example: a sermon I preached on the opening chapter of Hebrews.

Sample Sermon: Hebrews 1

This sermon was the opening message of a series on Hebrews with the series title, 'Something better … ' It was preached to a Perth congregation of around 250 adults. Though this book focuses on Aussie preaching, it should be noted that this congregation, like so many congregations in Australia, has more than its fair share of relatively recent immigrants to the country. Indeed, only about half the congregation would have been born in Australia – which doesn't mean that the other half are not Australian, simply that cultural backgrounds are usually rich and varied, and this is a normal feature of contemporary Australian life.

Here is the text of the message I preached, and I will discuss it afterwards. Within the sermon series this message covered all of Hebrews 1, though the focus was on Hebrew 1:1–4:

> In the past God spoke to our ancestors through the prophets at many times and in various ways, but in these last days he has spoken to us by his Son, whom he appointed heir of all things, and through whom also he made the universe. The Son is the radiance of God's glory and the exact representation of his being, sustaining all things by his powerful word. After he had provided purification for sins, he sat down at the right hand of the Majesty in heaven. So, he became as much superior to the angels as the name he has inherited is superior to theirs.

Sermon Text

Our house recently had its tenth birthday, and with that we decided a few changes and renovations were needed. Now let's be clear, neither my wife Rosemary nor I are great DIY people, and if Bunnings relied upon us for its business, it would have filed for bankruptcy years ago. Most things we got tradespeople to do, our wonderful daughter Amy served as a design and colour consultant (for as she noted, if we were left to ourselves, the house would turn out far worse than when we started) – and away we went.

I don't know what your experience of renovations is, but half way through, we lost heart. The house was busy being repainted, the painter had managed to include the blinds in his artwork (no extra charge for the paint he added to them), bills for the work were coming in steadily and the house looked like a dump. With nothing in the right place and dirt and dust everywhere, we asked the inevitable question, 'Is it actually worth it? After all, what was really wrong with the way it was before?'

True, now that it is finished, we are singing a different song and are pretty pleased with the finished product, but it sure didn't feel like that many times along the way. Often, our journeys turn out to be longer and tougher than anticipated, and when they do, our default tends to be to doubt the decision to make the trip.

That is what had happened to the people who received the letter to the Hebrews. Actually, it probably came in the form of a sermon preached to them, with the content written down and kept to refer back to. And the dominant message of the sermon was, 'Don't give up. When you chose to follow Jesus, you made an excellent decision. Jesus really is better than everything that has gone before.'

The original listeners needed to hear that. Most of them were converts from Judaism to Christianity. They faced rejection from their fellow Jews for their decision to follow Jesus, and now the Roman Empire had started to persecute them for their faith. Some had started to waver – actually, it was more than that. Some had given their new-found faith away.

We don't know who wrote the letter to the Hebrews (or preached it as a sermon to them), but we do know that they wanted to encourage the Hebrews in their faith by demonstrating why knowing Jesus was in every way better to what they had had before.

It went a step further.

This is a letter written to a Jewish audience. True, they were converts to Christianity, but these were tough times. They wondered if their Jewish past was not actually better – or, at the very least, if they should make sure that this new faith should continue to have a strong Jewish flavour. After all, it was starting to gather Gentile converts, and these Gentile converts had no background in Judaism. Wasn't there a risk that the really good things in Judaism would be forgotten and lost? They realised that some changes had to be made in the light of Jesus, but were reluctant to do anything too radical. Beneath their concern was the perpetual question, 'What are we to make of Jesus? Who exactly is Jesus?'

The writer of Hebrews has one simple aim in mind in writing this letter, and that is to make it abundantly clear that Jesus is superior to everything that Judaism ever offered and that in Jesus, a new and better era has begun. The subtext is simple. It's 'Jesus is amazing ... so stop wavering, stop hesitating ... dive right in and follow him without reserve'. Or more simply, 'Don't forget, Jesus is better. Better ...'

Hebrews chapter 1 starts with a then/now scenario.: Verse 1, 'In the past God spoke to our forefathers through the prophets …' That was then, but now, verse 2, 'In these last days he has spoken to us by his Son'.

A six-stage drama

The writer talks about us being 'in these last days' (v.2). What is meant? It reflects the biblical drama, which can be summarised in various ways, but perhaps it is best seen as a six-stage drama – or a book with six chapters or six main themes – with the 'last days' as one of the stages. The six stages are not of equal length, but all are significant. Let me quickly outline them by using each of these six chairs I have on the stage to represent a chapter. I'll sit on each of the chairs in turn.

Creation: Chair one represents creation. It's primarily spoken about in the first two chapters of the Bible, which answer the most fundamental of all questions, 'Do we live in an accidental universe, or has it been purposefully created?' The Bible's answer is crisp and clear. God is, and God has created the world. That simple proclamation changes everything. This is a world with a purpose. It has been intentionally made, and as created (rather than accidental) beings, we need to find out the purpose of our creation. Stage 1 in the Bible's story gives us some key clues as to the purpose of our creation. We won't unpack them today – but remember, this is what chair one in the biblical story covers.

Fall: Chair two represents the fall, that time when humanity shook the fist at God and did the one thing they had been forbidden to do – eat from the fruit of the tree of the knowledge of good and evil, thereby committing the original sin of wanting to be wise and self-sufficient apart from God, knowing good and evil outside of relationship with God and without having to refer to God. The consequences were devastating. The harmonious relationship between God, Adam and Eve and creation was broken. It was now a world where people hid from God, where childbirth was painful, and work was drudgery. It was an alienated world, far from the original purposes of creation.

Law and Prophets: Chair three represents God's response in the creation of a godly (though often not so godly) nation, Israel, and the giving of the law and commandments and the sending of the prophets. This essentially follows the biblical story from Genesis 11 to the end of the Old Testament. It was the stage the world was in when Jesus was born, and it is the stage that many of the readers of the letter to the Hebrews were starting to hanker for – the days when they had been thoroughly Jewish, trying to please God by keeping the law and the commandments.

Jesus: Chair four is the Jesus chair, reminding us of the birth, life and teaching of Jesus. It reminds us of his suffering, death and resurrection and of the forgiveness and new life we find because of his death on our behalf. It is the chair that changes everything. Because of Jesus, a new era is ushered in.

Church: Chair five is the chair we sit on now, and it is the same chair that those who first heard the letter to the Hebrews were sitting on. It's an exciting chair, for this stage has a clear mission – to spread the good news of Jesus far and wide and to live in anticipation of the coming kingdom God will bring. The writer calls this chair 'the last days' (Heb 1:2), because as we sit on this chair, there are no longer any major events we wait for other than the final coming of God's kingdom. It is the 'already but not yet' chair, where we already have forgiveness of our sins, the Spirit living within us, and the life of the community of the church to support and encourage us. But there are many 'not yet' parts as well. The reign of Jesus over all things has been promised, but we don't yet see it in its fullness. And at times we face struggle, even persecution, for living out our faith in Jesus. That was the problem the readers of Hebrews faced. Opposition to their new-found faith was growing. The pressure was mounting – and as it increased, they started to look back at chair three with nostalgia, and to think of the good old days when serving God meant doing your best to keep the 613 Jewish commandments, and hoping that one day God would return Israel to the glory days she had experienced under King David. In short, they had been called to live in chair five, but were hankering to sit on chair three again. And some had abandoned their new-found faith and had returned to chair three. It is this concern that drives much of the letter to the Hebrews.

All Things New: Chair six is the one we long for, where the story of God moves to a completely new level and where God's kingdom is ushered in, in all its fullness. It is the time when God will make all things new. We pray the prayer, '*Maranatha*', come Lord Jesus, as we long for the day when God will create a new heavens and a new earth. Because this is the next stage in the journey, as we sit in the fifth chair, we should live in the light of this sixth chair – and allow our ethics and living to be shaped by what will reign for eternity.

So, many of the largely Jewish audience who received this letter were hankering back to chair three, while the writer reminds them of the wonder of chair four (the Jesus chair) the responsibility of currently sitting in chair five (the church chair) and the hope of chair six. In light of this, the basic question behind Hebrews chapter 1 is, 'Why would you want to be stuck back and still sitting on chair three – chair five is so much better?'

Naturally, it revolves around understanding what happens when the Jesus chair is embraced and how it impacts how we now live as we sit on chair five.

Seven bold Jesus claims in Hebrews 1:2–4

The problem with staying on chair three is that it is a chair without Jesus. True, chair three had its moments. This was the era of the law and the prophets, the rise of Israel and its kings. At some lofty moments, angels even came and gave guidance and directed the nation on the path it should go. [Sermon note: sit on chair three and pontificate as if you are the person asking the questions.] You can imagine people sitting on seat three and asking, 'What are you getting so excited about? Yes, Jesus is great – but it's not as though we haven't had prophets before. And it isn't as though he was an angel. How do you top an era that has had angels? No human can do that, as there are three realms – God, angels then humans. And in scene three we had a fair few visits from angels – do you remember how the angel helped Deborah against the people of Meroz (Judg 5:22)? Called Gideon to fight the Midianites (Judg 6:11)? Announced the birth of Samson (Judg 13:3)? Ah – those were the days. Indeed, Hebrews 1:14 even gives us the helpful reminder that angels are ministering spirits sent to help those who will inherit salvation.' [Sermon note: Stand up from chair and walk away from it.]

So, what do you say to that? Why Jesus – when we had so much going for us?

The writer of Hebrews has no hesitation in swinging into action. The focus in Hebrews 1 is to show that Jesus is higher and more significant than the angels the Hebrew converts were pining after. (This is what the writer is speaking about in Heb 1:5–14). He makes the point with seven bold claims about Jesus:

1. God speaks to us though his Son (v.2)
2. Jesus is appointed heir of all things (v.2)
3. God made the universe through Jesus (v.2)
4. Jesus is the radiance of God's glory and the exact representation of God's being (v.3)
5. Jesus sustains all things by his powerful word (v.3)
6. Jesus provided purification for sins (v.3)
7. Jesus is seated at the right hand of the Majesty in heaven (v.3)

Add these seven together, and the conclusion is inevitable: Jesus is as much superior to the angels as the name he inherited (Son of God) is superior to theirs (angel) (v.4). In short, the writer says, 'Now think about it, which is more impressive … Son of God or angel?'

I remember, when our children were young, and we were living in Auckland, and a wonderful treat was to go to Rainbow's End – a theme and ride park. There was an almost good rollercoaster and a rather nice Gold Rush ride, some dodgem cars and a modest array of other activities. It made for a great day out. But some years later, we were able to go to Disneyland in Los Angeles. It was stunning! However, it did change our attitude to Rainbow's End.

As so often happens when people have never travelled or haven't been exposed to much, some of the locals said: 'Hmmm, what's the big deal about Disneyland? What does it have that Rainbow's End doesn't have?' Now, before we went to Disneyland we would quietly think, 'Probably a fair amount', but we didn't say anything. After we had been to

Disneyland, we knew how absurd such claims were. Sorry, Rainbow's End, you really aren't in the same league, and anyone who suggests that you are is profoundly ignorant.

That's the kind of line that the writer of Hebrews is taking here. Angels? Yeah, they're great – wonderful ministering spirits who serve those who will inherit salvation. But better than Jesus? Please. Who do you think you are fooling?

Let's dive into the claims ...

We don't have time to look at all seven claims about Jesus, each of which affirms that Jesus is better, but let's savour two of them.

Verse 2 tells us that 'in these last days God has spoken to us by his Son'. How do we know what God thinks or what God says? We listen to the words of Jesus. All the Bible is God-inspired, but some passages can be hard to follow and hard to understand. The key to interpreting everything in the Bible is Jesus. God speaks to us by his Son. If you are a theologian, you would know that we speak about reading the Bible christologically. In other words, we see and read everything in the light of Jesus. Do you want to know what God thinks? Well, ponder the parables of Jesus. Here is a person who has lost their way. Do you think God cares? Don't you remember that Jesus told the parable of a single lost sheep – and leaving ninety-nine behind to find it? Or the time when Jesus told a parable of a lost son – and of a father who kept lovingly waiting for him (Luke 15)? What is it saying? God speaks to us through Jesus, and the message is, 'God wants you home. God loves you. God cares for you.'

Or you may wonder if God really wants you to speak about the difference God has made in your life and how God has blessed you. You might worry that this might seem intrusive or insensitive. But then you remember the words of Jesus: 'Let your light shine for all to see' (Matt 5:15)

The Bible is a wonderful book of one 'God turned up' event after another. But in case there is any confusion over how we should interpret things, the writer of Hebrews makes it clear: in these last days, God speaks to us through his Son, and that is how we know with confidence.

Verse 3 claims, 'The Son is the exact representation of God's being'. For whatever reason we have sometimes become confused about what God the Father is like. Some people even say things like, 'The God of the Old Testament is harsh and hard to love ... but then we meet Jesus in the New Testament and that's okay – he is a lot more understanding'. The writer of Hebrews will have none of this. In Jesus we have an exact representation of God's being. If we think that God somehow changes between the Old and New Testament, it is because we haven't understood what God is like. When we see Jesus, we see God.

Now, you can imagine how hard it was for this Jewish readership to hear this. From their earliest years, they had grown up saying, 'Hear O Israel: The LORD our God, the LORD is one' (Deut 6:4). How then can Jesus be the exact representation of God's being, if God is one? But that is what the writer of Hebrews is saying: When we see Jesus, we see God. If you want to know what God is like, look at Jesus. Think of Jesus and the woman caught in adultery (John 8). You may ask, 'But is God as forgiving as that, averting his gaze and saying to the crowd, "If you are without sin, throw the first stone"? And as the crowd disperses, saying, "Neither do I condemn you. Go and sin no more". Is God like that?' Yes, yes and yes again, says the writer of Hebrews. The Son is the exact representation of God's being.

In all this, the message is very clear. Don't settle for a second-class Jesus. And don't follow Jesus half-heartedly.

The original readers of the letter to the Hebrews were Jewish converts to Christianity. But just enough time had gone by for them to be second-guessing their choice. Did following Jesus really represent a better way?

It is possible that in your own journey, you have landed at the same place. For whatever reason, your love for Jesus may be fading. You may be pushing back at the change that inevitably comes into life when you journey with Jesus, and you may be wondering if it is worth it. This passage says insistently, it is a wonderful privilege to live in scene five, the last days, the 'spread the word' days, the 'live in the light of Jesus' days.

And don't forget – scene six is on its way. We wait for all things to be made new. And we wait in hope because of Jesus. Because although he is currently seated, as Hebrews 1:3 says, 'At the right hand of the Majesty in heaven', one day he is coming for us – and all things will be made new.

So, wait in confident hope, because in these last days, God has spoken to us by his Son. And don't settle for a second-class Jesus, for Jesus really is bigger than anything you and I can imagine. Jesus is simply better.

Comments on the Sermon

Preaching an entire chapter in one sermon was challenging, and I therefore made the decision to focus on verses 1–4, while setting them within the broader argument (Jesus' superiority to the angels, a theme developed from Hebrews 1:5—2:18).

The thrust of the sermon was simple and summed up in one word, 'better', or for those who want something more expansive, why Jesus has introduced a better covenant and why we should continue to live in the light of the new covenant.

The sermon starts simply enough, with a story of our home renovation. I deliberately told it in a slightly self-effacing way (we're not much good at DIY), both in the interests of truthfulness, and because Australian audiences don't respond well if you imply that you are really good at something. The story had a clear intent, introducing the idea that sometimes when you are part-way through something, you second guess your decision. Most people can relate to wanting to give something up before completion, and I wanted the congregation to see such experiences as a link between our daily life and the dilemma faced by the recipients of Hebrews. There is a danger that homely illustrations trivialise the issue being spoken about, though I think we should credit our listeners with the ability to realise that the original situation faced was far more serious.

Because this was the opening sermon in a series, I took a little time to place this passage within the wider biblical narrative. Every few years I talk through the six scenes of Scripture, and I find it helpful to have six chairs on stage to illustrate each of them. It is a very simple visual clue, but each time I have used it, I have been surprised by how effective it has been. As a preacher, I tend to move around and to inject a fair amount of energy into the presentation, and being able to hop between chairs and point back to them encouraged a fluid and flowing presentation, with a substantial amount of content covered in a memorable manner (or at least, people said they found it memorable). The point about the original recipients of Hebrews being invited to live in scene five, but hankering to be back in scene three, was, I think, clearly made. I moved into narrative style a little later when I acted out one of the recipients nostalgically reminiscing about the good old days of scene three. It also gave me the opportunity of covering verses 5–14 of the chapter without obviously doing so.

While we communicate key ideas in preaching, we are constantly working to hold the attention of listeners, and varying the three P's of pace, pause and pitch are important. Both the use of the chairs and acting out the reflections of one of the letter's recipients, helped hold attention, while also making the point clearly.

Responsible preaching constantly points back to the text of Scripture, and though it wasn't possible to unpack the full richness of verses 2–4, by highlighting that it made seven claims about Jesus, and by intentionally numbering and naming each of the seven (numbering aids memory), the breadth of the argument was made clear.

I tried to read the verses out in such a way that the cumulative impact of the argument could be felt. ('So, Jesus is, one … and Jesus is, two … and Jesus is, three …'). I then tried to cement the impact with another home-grown illustration. I generally find that people relate better to actual illustrations from my life, so the comparison between Rainbow's End and Disneyland fell into that category. It drew a smile from listeners and helped regain attention.

I then chose two of the seven claims to focus on. Realistically I could have chosen differently. Preaching is a spiritual exercise, and I can only say that the two I highlighted were the two I felt led to highlight. If I preached from this passage on another occasion, it is perfectly conceivable that I could feel that others should be the focus. Certainly, the claim that Jesus has 'provided purification for sins' is a natural focal point, and another time I may well select it.

As it was, I selected the claim that God has spoken to us by his Son (v.2) and that the Son 'is the exact representation of his [God's] being' (v.3).

I chose the first because a regular question from this congregation has been about how to reconcile some of the more bloodthirsty passages of the Bible with the message of Jesus, and I have been trying to point them towards a christological reading of the Bible. While there was the risk of aiming too high here, my observation is that, provided there has been enough homely, grounded content, you can feed those who are looking for more by fairly quickly suggesting some ideas that stretch without losing those who are not at that place. This discussion fell into that category.

I'm not sure that the attempt to unpack the second claim about Jesus worked. There had already been a fair amount of content, and this perhaps pushed it a bit too far. It might have been better to simply unpack the first idea (God speaks definitively through Jesus) more fully. Certainly, the end felt a little hurried to me (the thirty minutes was up), and from a pastoral perspective I would have preferred to have taken more time to expand on what it means not to settle for a second-class Jesus and how we can keep trusting (and seeing) that Jesus is better.

I have included this sermon, not because I think it is without flaw, but because like most sermons, it has strengths and weaknesses – and hopefully something can be learnt from both. It held people's attention and provided much solid content. I am less confident that people kept thinking about it through the week, and it probably didn't provide enough of a bridge into everyday life. However, it did provide a reasonable introduction to some of the key themes of the letter to the Hebrews.

13

PREACHING REVELATION TO AUSTRALIANS

Ian Hussey

Introduction

The story is told of a group of students and a janitor in a US Bible college. The students were, for a season, playing basketball in a nearby high school gym. While they played, the janitor, who graciously allowed the seminarians to use the gym after hours, would borrow one of their Bibles and spend the hour reading it. One day, one of the young men asked the janitor, 'What have you been reading in the Bible?' 'Revelation', he replied. The seminarian chuckled, 'Yeah, right.' 'No, really', said the janitor. Having heard one of his professors say that no one really understands the strange book, the seminarian asked, 'Do you understand what you have been reading?' 'Oh, yes,' replied the now smiling janitor. Chuckling again, the seminarian asked, almost sarcastically, 'Well then, tell me what it means.' The janitor looked to his right and then to his left, leaned into the seminarian's ear and whispered, 'It means that Jesus is gonna win.'[1]

Perhaps no other book in the Bible strikes as much fear into the heart of the preacher than does the book of Revelation. 'Revelation 1 to 3? Oh sure, I've preached that.' But how about chapters 4 to 22? 'Oh, no, not really ...' I was recently speaking to a colleague who told me that when he was at Bible College, his homiletics lecturer had said that preaching Revelation should be reserved for only for experienced preachers. Certainly, in my tradition, Queensland Baptists, the dominance of a dispensationalist hermeneutic has meant that preaching Revelation would require exploring incredibly complicated end-time prophecies. In light of these complex interpretations, many preachers have felt inadequate to undertake this task, and perhaps even a little scared that their interpretation may not match some of the fiercely held views of some members of the congregation. As G. K. Chesterton wrote over one hundred years ago, 'Though St John the Evangelist saw many strange monsters in his vision, he saw no creature so wild as one of his own commentators.'[2] For this reason, Revelation has been off limits for many preachers.

However, my perception is that interest in preaching the book of Revelation has grown in recent years. There is an increasing awareness that this strange and mysterious book has much to say to Australian congregations.

The Hermeneutical Task

History of Interpretation

Interpreters of Revelation often identify four interpretive approaches. The historicist approach sees the events described in John's visions as occurring in the course of history between John's time and the return of Christ. In the thirteenth century, Joachim of Fiore located his generation near the end of the sequence and raised the expectations that the millennium would soon begin.[3] Luther also took a historicist approach to Revelation and used it to identify the papacy with the beast and the harlot.[4] The approach remained popular in the nineteenth and twentieth centuries in the Western Protestant church; however, it was always less common in Asia and Africa, except where introduced by Western missionaries.[5]

The second interpretive approach to Revelation can be called the futurist approach. This view identifies most of the visions as yet to be fulfilled. This approach was popularised in the West through the dispensational Scofield Study Bible and more recently by Tim LaHaye and Jerry Jenkins in their *Left Behind* books and movies. This approach is literalistic and predictive. As such, it renders Revelation largely irrelevant to Christian readers in every age except the present.[6] Readers who hold to a futurist approach may find the discussion in this chapter fairly frustrating, because I will not approach Revelation as primarily a predictive text. However, you will hopefully still find the discussion helpful to your preaching.

The third approach, the idealist interpretation, identifies Revelation as a book of symbolism. The symbolism is designed to help us understand God's interaction with the world in a general way, not to enable us to map out a course of events.

The fourth approach to Revelation can be called the preterist approach. This approach views most of the visions as predictive prophecies that have been fulfilled in the period before the reign of Constantine.[7] The symbols in the visions all refer to people, countries, and events in the world of that day, and John's purpose was to exhort his readers to remain faithful to Christ as they waited for God to deliver them into the eternal kingdom.[8] This approach is based on the assumption that the book of Revelation was written for the benefit of a group of people who were living at the time and was understandable by them.

This approach fits naturally with the grammatical-historical approach, which seeks to anchor interpretation in the original meaning of the text for the original recipients. The 'key' to understanding Revelation, then, is an understanding of the political, social, cultural and economic landscape of Asia Minor in the last part of the first century as the basis for application to this generation and context. This fourth approach will underpin the discussion that follows.

Genre

Along with many contemporary scholars, DeSilva recognises three genres within the book of Revelation, the recognition of which greatly aids in interpretation.[9] Firstly, John writes a letter to seven real communities of Christians in Asia Minor. The symbolic use of the number seven throughout Revelation suggests that the seven churches are in some way representative of a wider range of churches.

The book of Revelation also contains the genre of prophecy. Although Jewish prophecy could include a predictive element, more often it was a declaration of God's action in the present or God's perspective on the present actions of God's people. The oracles for the seven churches (2:1—3:22) are the clearest examples of this kind of prophecy in Revelation. The primary purpose of prophecy was not to give chronological predictions of the future, but to evoke a faithful response from God's people. For example, Jonah proclaimed that Nineveh would be overthrown in forty days (Jonah 3:4) yet when the people repented, God spared the city (3:10).

Finally, Revelation contains apocalypse. The book opens with the statement that it is a 'revelation (*apokalypsis*) of Jesus Christ'. By comparison with other first-century apocalyptic documents, a list of common features can be identified: insight through visions and pronouncements by divine or angelic mediators; journey into invisible regions surrounding the everyday world; narration of 'larger' historical perspectives than normal lived experience; a dualistic view of events and eschatological judgement. 'Apocalypses construct, and invite hearers into, the larger context, the "bigger picture" that provides an interpretive framework for lived experience.'[10]

These three genres need to be taken into account when interpreting the book of Revelation. As a letter, it is anchored in the historical context of the seven churches it addresses. As prophecy, it brings a message from the Lord to a specific group of people. As apocalypse, it opens up before the Christians of Asia Minor a vision of space and time that puts their mundane lives into proper perspective.

Interpreting the Imagery

Bauckham points out that Revelation's readers 'were constantly confronted with powerful images of the Roman vision of the world. Civic and religious architecture, iconography, statues, rituals and festivals, even the visual wonder of cleverly engineered "miracles" (cf. Rev 13:13–14) in the temples – all provided powerful visual impressions of Roman imperial power and of the splendour of pagan religion'.[11] Rome sought to capture the hearts and minds of people through media: processions, games, spectacles, standards carried by soldiers, even coins – all communicated Roman propaganda.[12] Revelation provides a set of Christian prophetic counter-images.

Along with their allusions to the Old Testament, the images of Revelation also echo images from the Graeco-Roman world. The dragon (12:3–9), for example, has biblical roots (Gen 3:14–15; Isa 27:1). However, the symbol would also have cultural resonance in the minds of non-Jewish readers, owing to its prominence in pagan mythology and religion. Another symbol, the invasion from the East (9:13–19; 16:12), would tap into a common concern of John's readers – an invasion from the Parthian Empire.[13] The interpreter needs to invest in research to identify the meaning of the various symbols.

It should also be noted that many scholars now recognise that the sequence of symbols and images in Revelation do not form a linear narrative.[14] As Marshall says, 'Rather than presenting one story in chronological order John takes us over the same ground several times, looking at the conflict from several different angles.'[15] The narrative units in Revelation overlap and reinforce certain underlying themes. As noted in the 'Describing Australians' chapter, Australians tend to prefer a chronological approach to life. However, we need to set aside this preference to engage with the non-chronological approach of Revelation. We also need to acknowledge that we will not always be able to fully understand the significance of the ancient symbols. We must be willing to 'just' experience the images without having to fully understand their Old Testament or contemporary background, although this should always be the goal. We can allow the images to flow over us without feeling the need to try and fit them into some logical and linear narrative.

Audience

The fact that John explicitly contextualises his message into the seven specific contexts of the seven churches means we should resist a common generalisation about Revelation: that it is a book written for the consolation and encouragement of Christians suffering persecution.[16] Not all of his readers were poor and persecuted by an oppressive system – some were affluent (see 2:17) and compromising with the system (18:4). The letter offers not only consolation and encouragement but severe warnings and calls to repentance.

For some of John's readers, the vividly described judgements should not be interpreted as judgements on their oppressors but as judgements they themselves were in danger of incurring.

Theological Purpose

As DeSilva observes, 'While Revelation may appear, then, to lift the veil from future events, Revelation's ultimate goal is to lift the veil from contemporary actors, events, and options.'[17] This 'lifting of the veil' means John sees the world from the heavenly perspective. He is also transported into the final future of the world, so that he can see the present from the perspective of what its final outcome will be. 'The effect of John's visions is to expand his readers' world, both spatially (into heaven) and temporally (into the eschatological future).'[18]

However, the 'power, the profusion and the consistency of the symbols have a literary-theological purpose. They create a symbolic world which readers can enter so fully that it affects them and changes their perception of the world'.[19] Truth conveyed in imagery can transform our vision more powerfully than truth conveyed in propositional language.[20]

Worship, Christology, judgement, witness and eschatology are well-known theological emphases of Revelation.[21] However, Bauckham identifies Revelation's distinctive doctrine of God as its greatest contribution to New Testament theology.[22] The image of the throne is also crucial. The throne room is the place from which God exercises his rule over the world. On earth, Rome challenges God's role and even presents itself as the ultimate power, even claiming divinity. 'But heaven is the sphere of ultimate reality and what is true in heaven must become true on earth.'[23]

Without mentioning the cross, John's theology of atonement is dominated by the Lamb that was slain. This substitutionary view of Jesus's death is not the main focus of the book of Revelation, however. In John's vision, Jesus confronts the powers of evil, absorbs them by his love and triumphs over them through the resurrection. This is a *Christus Victor* (Christ triumphant) view of salvation, through which the followers of Jesus receive power and transformed lives.[24] The Lamb refuses to adopt the methods and rules of evil, and in doing so bears its full force. As such, he is a model for believers facing the harsh realities and pressure to conform to the expectations of Graeco-Roman society.

Hence, Revelation is a *theopolitical* text.[25] It makes claims about who is truly God and about the right and wrong connections between God and the sociopolitical order. It challenges the political theology of empire and reveals that the Lamb alone, who exercises non-violent and non-coercive power, is the true sovereign one and the proper object of worship. 'The book is about the incompatibility of the exclusive monotheistic worship portrayed in chapter 4 with every kind of idolatry – the political, social and economic idolatries from which more narrowly religious idolatry is inseparable.'[26]

The Contextualisation Task

Most preachers who preach regularly will have preached through Revelation 1 to 3. Who can resist reaching for passages where Jesus says to our congregation exactly the things we would like to say to them?! Others who have preached chapters 4 to 22 have likely built those sermons on the clear theological themes of worship, Christology, judgement and eschatology. However, the aim of this volume is to guide preachers towards more nuanced applications that are especially appropriate for Australian congregations. Hence, in the following section I will discuss some particular dimensions of the theology of Revelation and make some suggestions regarding the implications of this theology for Australian congregations.

Recognising the Power of Images

In 2017 only fifteen percent of Australians attended church on a monthly basis.[27] This reality means that the people in our congregations are a 'minority' living in a world that has values increasingly contrary to theirs. Christian minorities in many parts of the world have been living in this scenario for centuries, but it is a new phenomenon for Christians in Australia.

A dominant culture, with its images and ideals, constructs the world for its occupants, and pushes them to perceive and respond to the world on its terms. The images we are exposed to through media and advertising are one powerful influence on Australian believers. There is also an accompanying narrative that the goal of life is self-fulfilment through career, experiences and possessions. Given the large amount of screen time that Australian subject themselves to, it is little wonder that we struggle to resist this narrative.

Bauckham says that 'one of the functions of Revelation was to purge and to refurbish the Christian imagination.'[28] It seeks to shape people's imaginative response to the world, because imagination is at least as deep and influential as intellectual conviction. Moreover, Revelation unmasks the dominant construction of the world as an attempt of the powerful to maintain their power. In its place, John's visions offer 'a different way of perceiving the world which leads people to resist and to challenge the dominant ideology'.

And so, while the Psalms appeal to our emotions and the epistles appeal to our intellect, Revelation appeals primarily to our imagination. Revelation 'contains a series of word pictures, as though a number of slides were being shown upon a great screen. As we watch we allow ourselves to be carried along by impressions created by these pictures'.[29] With its rapidly changing kaleidoscope of imagery, Revelation's fast-moving visual format is appropriate for today's society in which advertising, political discourse and personal communication often take place with quick images and sound bites.[30] Australia is becoming less literary and more visual as the digital revolution continues. Advertising agencies, politicians and other communicators use symbols to express what cannot be expressed in ordinary words.

James K. A. Smith would argue that systems of thought and doctrines are not the things that really motivate us.[31] We are motivated by the heart (our loves, longings and affections), which is the core of who we are. We are not what we think but what we love. Unfortunately, says Smith, our hearts have been hijacked by our culture. Because we have lost this awareness, we have failed to recognise the degree and extent to which *secular* liturgies influence us towards consumerism, nationalism and various other non-Christian paradigms. 'The devil has had all the best liturgies.'[32]

However, transformation is possible through reforming our loves. This requires re-habituation, because love is a habit. We acquire habits through exemplars, practices and narratives. Since we are storied creatures we behave in certain ways, because our hearts have been captured by certain stories. Smith quotes *The Little Prince*, by Antoine de Saint-Exupéry, to explain: 'If you want to build a ship, don't drum up people to gather wood. Teach them to long for the endless immensity of the sea.'[33] We preachers, then, should be trying to restore and 're-story' our congregations. In this way we reach the imaginations and perceptions of our congregations and make possible deep transformation.

The focus, then, should be on narratives. Stories are the means of 'emotional pre-focusing' that shape our 'take' on the world.[34] 'The heart has reasons of which reason knows nothing ... The heart drinks up narrative like its mother's milk.'[35] So, our congregations need to find themselves in the metanarrative of God's faithfulness to creation and to his people, like that revealed in Revelation.[36] All-pervading media means that contemporary Australians, just like their brothers and sisters in the first century, are confronted by a powerful force that distorts our perception of reality. Like the original readers of Revelation, we are in need of an alternative set of images to those provided by advertisers and our social media networks. The particular challenge of the preacher standing before Australian congregations in the twenty-first century is to undermine and replace the vision/narrative powerfully presented by the media and other powers with the real metanarrative that John unveils in Revelation. The preacher has in Revelation the ideal source of alternative images and stories to those of secular Australian society. The images of the beast, the prostitute and Babylon can open the eyes of our congregations to the systemic and structural evil that exists in our world. In contrast, pointing to the alternative narrative symbols of Revelation can help formulate alternative habits of the heart. Passionate and evocative presentations of these alternative narratives have the potential to have a profound effect on the lives of our congregations. As their hearts are 're-storied' so will their actions be transformed as they escape the habits of the world.

It's All Okay – The Lamb Is on His Throne

As we saw in the 'Describing Australians' chapter, Australians are an anxious lot. One of the reasons for this is the stream of bad news coming through the media. For whatever reason, bad news sells.[37] Hugh MacKay identifies that a 'major contributor to our present level of anxiety is the growing rumble of three big threats – climate change, international terrorism and the threat of a major global economic disruption. These things threaten us on a large scale and seem beyond our control. In the face of threats like these, many Australians feel powerless and vulnerable'.[38]

As I write this chapter, the images of global danger are prevalent. Russia seizes ships from the Ukraine and state-sponsored cyber attackers interfere in national elections. In Syria the dictator uses chemical weapons on his own people. The Chinese Navy confronts Australian ships in the South China Sea. North Korea taunts the world with threats of nuclear weapons and intercontinental ballistic missiles. Donald Trump is within reach of the red button. The Australian preacher should have no trouble in heightening the already present awareness of the dangerous world in which Australia, though somewhat on the edge, is still enmeshed.

In contrast, John shows us an alternative image. The Lamb is on his throne. As the janitor in the story in the introduction says, 'Jesus is gonna win.' If our congregations can grasp an understanding of the true reality, they will find peace instead of anxiety. There is a well-worn analogy that illustrates this principle well: the sports fan who enjoys the game more when he or she is relieved of the tension of not knowing how the game will end. Once they know their team will win, they can sit back and relax and endure, even enjoy, the ups and downs of the game, knowing that in the end they will win.

For the Australian church, there is the particular anxiety that comes from growing secularism and pluralism. But pluralism is nothing new, nor is persecution of Christian minorities. The preacher can use the book of Revelation to highlight that the contemporary experience of Australian Christians – that of living in a secular society that does not privilege the Christian perspective and in fact may even seem to persecute it – is not new. We stand in the long and noble tradition of those who have continued to worship the Lamb upon his throne rather than the dominant ethos of the day.

Resisting the Beast, the Prostitute and Babylon

In recent years, scholars have begun to read John's Revelation as a critique, if not a parody, of the Roman Empire.[39] John uses several metaphors for Rome to unveil what was invisible to his readers. Firstly, Rome is a monstrous and violent beast (13:1–10). Yes, there is a *Pax Romana*, but it comes at a great cost. The so-called 'peace' is enforced by intimidation. A second metaphor, the prostitute, with her sumptuous clothing and seductiveness (17:4), draws attention to the seductive power of the empire on the imaginations of the people, including the 'kings of the earth' (17:2).

In a similar way, the third metaphor, Babylon, draws attention to the exploitative and excessive consumption of the Roman Empire. John's list of goods in 18:12–13 highlights the prodigious economic activity that sustained the excessive lifestyle of the wealthy Romans. Seneca, tutor and advisor to Nero, lamented the extreme consumption of Rome: 'Did nature give us bellies so insatiable, when she gave us these puny bodies, that we should outdo the hugest and most voracious animals in greed?'[40] Nero apparently never made a journey with less than 1000 carriages.[41] Rome needed thousands of merchants to maintain its standard of living and was willing to offer tax and other concessions and incentives to those who cooperated.[42] A mutually beneficial relationship developed between Rome and entrepreneurs throughout the empire. The mark of the beast (13:11–17) can be seen as a sign of surrender to the Roman commercial system, which demanded allegiance to the emperor rather than just a willingness to trade.

However, central to John's critique of Rome was the cult of emperor worship. It was difficult to avoid such idolatry, since the imperial cult pervaded all sectors of society, including the economy. Ports and trade guilds were filled with temples to various gods, including the emperor.[43] In addition to buying allegiance through trade, the propaganda of the Roman Empire reinforced the notion that the emperors were in control of the world. A coin from 81–96 CE features an image of the infant Domitian seated upon the globe, surrounded by the seven astronomical bodies known to the ancient world.[44] The coins were a medium of the day, powerfully communicating an image and accompanying narrative.

John identifies that the first beast, whether the emperor or the empire, receives its power from Satan (13:2–4). Hence, Rome rules illegitimately by demonic mandate, and so believers should have nothing to do with the imperial system.[45] In Revelation, John names the beast an 'evil empire' and calls it out for what it is. 'Come out of her, my people!' cries a voice from heaven (18:4). To participate in the Roman economic order, they must take the mark of the beast (13:16–17). So, the faithful should resist involvement in the economic system.

However, John could not have been calling them to withdraw into a self-sufficient community, as the churches he addresses were in urban settings.[46] Awareness of the evil system, its impact on us and its contrast to true reality must bring a more subtle response from the listener than just withdrawal. Instead, it would seem that John was promoting a purified vision of the transcendence of God as the only way to effectively resist the human tendency to idolatry, which consists in absolutising aspects of this world.[47] The worship of the true God gives us the power to resist seduction (the prostitute), military and political power (the beast) and economic prosperity (Babylon).

John also presents an alternative image to the evil empire in his description of Jerusalem in chapters 21 and 22. In contrast to the elitist Roman economy, the enormous wealth of the city of gold and precious stones (21:18–21) is shared by all. The city has no temples except the Lamb himself (21:22), yet all of its residents are priests (1:6, 5:10) and enjoy the personal presence of the king.[48] God is more powerful than the emperor. The new Jerusalem is wealthier than Babylon.

The book of Revelation focuses on structural evil – the networks of commerce, politics, greed, violence and idolatry – that were woven together in the ethos of the Roman Empire, which dominated the world in which they lived.[49] It unveils the spiritual realities involved when Australians end up serving and worshipping an empire with depraved political and economic structures. In response, 'the language of witness, whether it is related to Jesus Christ, John, or one of John's fellow believers, suggests active resistance to contemporary cultic and political expectations.'[50]

Australian Christians face the constant temptation to live for consumption and to affiliate themselves with power. We are not forced to do these things, but they feel good, and they work for us on some level. It is here that the book of Revelation proves so useful for us as preachers. Its message does not condemn the desire to feel good but highlights the seductive quality of the evil empire, helping us to recognise the seductive, whore-like nature of the beckoning smile on the face of the politician, on the TV screen or in the magazine ad.[51]

However, Revelation's purpose is not necessarily to mobilise its hearers and readers to overthrow the evil empire, which they are largely powerless to do. Rather, it challenges them to recognise reality, resist it and come out of Babylon to become citizens of the new Jerusalem. But it is no easy call to live 'in' but not 'of' the city, for where else can we go? An option for some would be to quit their job, move to a rural setting and live in a commune. But this would be too difficult for most Australians, and geographic withdrawal does not appear to be John's point. Although presenting that option as a possibility, for better or worse, the preacher needs to look at more nuanced responses to the challenge of Revelation.

The value of the images and symbols of Revelation, such as the beast, the prostitute and Babylon, is that they enable Australians to name and confront the evil empire we battle with. The empire operates at different levels, to which we can orient our congregations through the preaching of Revelation. I step with hesitation into some ideas that some may consider too political for the pulpit, but that I find worthy of consideration, nonetheless. David Korten suggests that free-market ideology, with its priesthood of economics professors, has been embraced with an almost fundamentalist religious fervour in some circles.[52] The dogma proclaimed by the priesthood includes the teaching that economic growth is the only path for human progress, unrestrained free trade is good for everyone, as is economic globalisation, and that privatisation improves efficiency while government social intervention does not. Such an ideology would seem uncannily similar to that of Rome. The only significant difference would seem to be that in the twenty-first-century evil empire, transnational corporations are actually more powerful than most national governments.[53]

The evil empire might also be discernible in transnational media organisations such as Google, Apple and the social media giants. As I write, the founder of Facebook, Mark Zuckerberg, is being questioned by a congressional committee about how much the private data of Facebook users have been accessed by third parties and for what purpose they are being used. As Zuckerberg apologised, again, for sacrificing the privacy of users for profit, the stock value of Facebook soared, and thousands of new customers signed on for the free service ... in exchange for the sharing of a few personal details. Perhaps Australian preachers would be more virulent in their condemnation of unrestrained economic growth and globalisation, and social media, if we were not so enmeshed with them ourselves.

At an individual level, we can challenge our congregations to live with simplicity. A theologically inspired budget can help individuals and families to control their spending and use their resources for godly purposes rather than personal consumption. Families can also pursue ethical shopping practices by supporting fair trade products and consulting resources such as 'The Ethical Fashion Guide'.[54] We can't manage the economy, but we can decide to be wiser and more generous with our money. We can't stop the rising tide of technology, but we can be its masters, not its servants.[55]

Still, coming out of Babylon is a difficult thing for us to do. However, the wild imagery John gives us sharpens the choices.[56] It gives us the language, a metanarrative and the images to help combat rampant consumerism.

Saving the Old Earth in Preparation for the New One

Jewish eschatological hope was not just for the resurrection of individuals but for the future of God's whole creation.[57] Similarly, many see that Revelation proclaims a 'new heaven and a new earth', but that does not mean that 'God gives us a replacement for this current earth if we damage it beyond recovery'.[58] The Greek word *kaine* used for the 'new' earth in Revelation 21:1 can mean either 'renewed' or 'new', but it does not mean a 'different' earth. Rather the earth becomes 'new' in the sense of resurrection or renewal – just as our bodies will be resurrected and brought to new life. Since the whole creation is longing for the redemption Paul writes about in Romans 8:19–23, the earth hopes to be redeemed, made new and healed.

While John may not be labelled a 'greenie', he was 'certainly a critic of the insatiable appetites of the Empire'.[59] Unjust exploitation of colonised lands, resources and peoples were familiar in the ancient Roman world, and they are part of what Revelation indicts in its sweeping anti-Roman imperial critique. Revelation's wondrous New Jerusalem vision is contrasted with the city of Babylon in Revelation 17–18 as a critique of the Roman Empire and its exploitive political economy.

Coming from their dispensational perspective, authors such as Hal Lindsey,[60] Tim LaHaye and Jerry Jenkins[61] see Revelation as pointing to the total destruction of planet earth. For Lindsey, Revelation's proclamation of a 'new heaven and a new earth' is necessary because of 2 Peter's prediction that God will destroy the planet by fire, probably through thermonuclear war. But a prophecy of planetary destruction invites a potentially selfish non-concern for the world.

Instead, the image and narrative of Revelation 21–22 is that humans are not raptured into heaven but that God comes to earth. The strong sense of the impending 'end' in the book is referring not to the end of the earth but to the end of imperial injustice, especially the Roman Empire. Interestingly, Revelation 11:18 makes the proclamation that 'the time has come ... for destroying the destroyers of Earth'. At least some parts of Judaism held that destroyers and misusers of humanity's stewardship of the earth reversed the mandate God had originally given humanity (Gen 1:26) and would be punished.[62]

Hence Revelation could well proclaim, not God's curse or 'woe' against the earth, but rather a divine *lament* on behalf of the earth. The Greek word *ouai* (Rev 8:13 and 12:12) could indicate a state of intense hardship or distress[63] and could be translated as 'alas' rather than as 'woe', so that the verse becomes God's cry of mourning or lamentation over Earth as a result of Rome's exploitation of the planet.

The destruction of rivers, burning of one third of the earth and trees (8:7) and other calamities in Revelation's trumpets and bowls sequences can give the impression that God is anti-Earth. But Revelation's plagues are modelled on the Exodus plagues. They should be read not as punishments but as 'ecological signs' of God's liberating action.[64]

As discussed earlier, Revelation 17–18 depicts the Roman Empire as a great prostitute that has 'seduced' and 'intoxicated' rulers and nations with its economic trafficking.[65] Babylon/Rome is a world of buying and selling, frenetic commerce and accumulation of wealth, and the cargo list of Revelation 18:12–13 implies the environmental consequences. Two of the items in the cargo list are forest products: 'all kinds of scented woods' (*xylon;* citrus hardwood imported from North Africa) and 'objects made of ivory and of expensive wood'. Other items on the list also reflect Rome's extractive economy and power that forcibly brought the natural resources of conquered territories to Rome. In our time, when global deforestation is an increasing problem,

Revelation's ecological critique of Rome, together with its critique of imperialism and injustice, is timely.

In contrast to Rome/Babylon, the New Jerusalem offers a vision for an alternative economy of justice and healing for creation. The New Jerusalem offers the promise of a totally renewed urban world, where God takes up residence on Earth, in our midst, along a beautiful river and tree of life. The evocative description and contrast of the two cities can empower our congregations to make a renewed commitment to the health of our cities, rivers, forests and oceans as a preparation for the 'new' Earth.[66]

As noted in the 'Describing Australians' chapter, Australians tend to have a 'mastery' relationship to the natural environment rather than one of 'harmony'. Part of the reason for this adversarial approach to the land may stem from our urban lifestyles, which can disconnect us from the land and so compromise our relationship with it. However, Australia is the land of the long weekend. Many Australians have a love for the 'great outdoors' and enjoy boating, camping and fishing, as the name of the popular retail chain suggests. Perhaps, then, our preaching should encourage our congregations to nuance their attitude to the environment in light of Revelation's rebuke of Rome's exploitive attitude. The land is not to be *exploited* for our enjoyment but to be *enjoyed*, with thanksgiving and respect, as we delight in God's creative genius. Topics such as littering, 'Clean-up Australia Day', driving over sand dunes, fish size limits and vehicle engine capacity now move squarely into the realm of theology and call for an appropriate response from our congregations.

The preacher of Revelation may need to again enter the political realm here.[67] Activities that leave our earth devastated should be opposed. Even those who doubt climate change, or the influence of human activity on climate change, can be challenged to value the utilisation of renewable resources in preference to approaches that totally deplete resources the earth does not have the capacity to replace. Our relationship to the earth should be one of stewardship, not rape. The earnest preacher will step into the issues of energy generation, mining, land clearing and pesticides.

The Australian attitude to the environment is in stark contrast to the Indigenous peoples, who have a much greater appreciation of our intimate connection to the land (Gen 2:7). My understanding is that the relationship is one of mutual care. Indigenous theologian Graeme Paulson writes, 'Rather than seeing the earth as an adversary to be subdued, or a reservoir of resources to be exploited, or a *terra nullius* to be divided up at whim … "Animistic" spirituality has shaped respectful attitudes to the created order, which can hardly be seen now as inferior to the abusive theologies of the colonisers'.[68] It would be ironic, but perfectly appropriate, if our First Nations peoples were to lead Australians to an understanding of what a healthy relationship with the environment looks like.

A Taste of Heaven – the Multicultural Nature of the Church

Stevens[69] argues that the 'New Humanity' (Ephesians 2:14–15) is a multiethnic community and is a crucial metaphor in understanding the nature of the church as Paul envisaged it. This New Humanity is described as gathered at the throne in Revelation 5:9–10:

> And they sang a new song, saying:
>
> 'You are worthy to take the scroll
> and to open its seals,
> because you were slain,
> and with your blood you purchased for God
> persons from every tribe and language and people and nation.
> You have made them to be a kingdom and priests to serve our God,
> and they will reign on the earth.' (Rev 5:9–10)

The diversity in unity that characterises the Trinity as well as the New Humanity will not be obliterated on the new earth. Note that in chapter 21 when describing the new heavens and earth the voice says, 'They will be his *peoples*' (21:3). The Greek is *laoi*, the plural of *laos*. 'Peoples', not just 'people', are present in the new city. All of God's chosen peoples. God brings into the city the full range of the world's ethnic diversity. 'The new vision not only maintains the planet, it also maintains ethnic diversity. No one ethnic grouping can bear or manifest the full image of God. It takes us all. And in the new city, we are all there as God's multi-ethnic race.'[70]

In the first century, the city of Rome was being flooded with people from all over the Roman Empire seeking wealth in its capital. Tacitus complained that Rome had become a 'cesspool' of people from every corner of the earth.[71] The book of Revelation acknowledges the variety of cultures and traditions in this context.[72] This Roman discomfort with immigration, and the cultural diversity it brought, is not dissimilar to what we find in Australia at times. In contrast, the book of Revelation recognises that the various peoples, nations and tribes are part of the single plan of God.

The church in Australia can be thankful, and celebrate, that it largely does not share the ethnic tensions that have troubled the church in many other parts of the world.[73] Most of the literature related to multicultural churches emanating from the United States, for example, pivots around their response to the segregated nature of church life. Progress since Martin Luther King Jnr's 'most segregated hour of the week' comment has been disappointingly slow. Although there are a number of monoethnic churches in Australia, largely composed of refugees, there are many churches in Australia that have a delightful mix of people of different ethnicities. Hopefully a large number of these monoethnic churches will also transition into multiethnic churches in the decades ahead.

Either way, many Australian churches are blessed with worshippers from different ethnicities. As such, they reflect the 'now but not yet' character of the kingdom of God. We are to incessantly pray, 'Thy kingdom come, thy will be done, on earth as it is in heaven.' Yet, we need to view God's description of the future as our model for the present.[74] We cannot understand who we are or what we are called to do apart from understanding what we will ultimately be. The key to healthy multiethnic churches is that they reflect the true nature of the New Humanity, as an understanding of their self-identity, as revealed in Revelation.

One of the purposes of the weekly gatherings of the church on earth (as in 1:3, 9–10) is to be reminded of its heavenly identity through modelling its worship on that of the angels' and heavenly church's worship of the exalted Lamb.[75] This is why scenes of heavenly liturgy are woven throughout Revelation. It is from these passages that the churches get a pattern and zeal for corporate worship.

Few, if any, Australian churches today would consciously reject a fellow believer from a different ethnicity. Few churches, however, are conscious of the status quo bias that keeps us more comfortable with believers from the same ethnic or cultural group. It consequently takes initiative to intentionally nurture meaningful acceptance of ethnic diversity in unity. To do so can be quite uncomfortable, demanding sacrifice on our part. It may require a shift in the tacit culture and organisational practices of our church. In addition, we need to consciously work against natural affinity being the primary criteria for building Christian community. Natural affinity is the comfortable and natural way to group ourselves. The New Humanity, however, is not natural; it is supernatural.

Some have suggested that one of the great idols of our time is nationalism.[76] Revelation calls us to rise above nationalism to be the multinational, transnational worshipping community pictured in Revelation. Disciples of Jesus Christ, the emperor of emperors, need to be challenged to rise above allegiance to their particular nation and realise their primary allegiance is to Christ and his disciples. This means that an Australian Christian has more in common with a Chinese Christian than they do with an unbelieving fellow Australian. This is the stunning reality presented in Revelation that needs to be proclaimed to Australians.

Apparently, many churches in the United States have two flags on display alongside each other: the national flag and a Christian flag. Such a blending of religion and nationalism would be uncomfortable for most Australians. Some have noted, however, that the Australian observance of Anzac Day has become a secular religious event.[77] The quasi-religious observation of Anzac Day by many Australians, including Christians, and even some churches, may be seen to be dangerously close to the unhealthy marriage of Roman military power, 'nationalism' and religion critiqued by the book of Revelation. 'Nationalistic allegiance or devotion, especially when dressed in religious garb, may not feel like idolatry, but Revelation makes us face the issue head on (13:4, 8, 12, 15; 14:9, 11; 16:2; 19:20).'[78] It is one thing to live with discernment in the shadow of the empire, another thing altogether to unconditionally endorse that empire or to sacralise it.

If our congregations could fully embrace a self-understanding of being an international eschatological community and find their primary source of identity in that understanding, it would be more difficult for them maintain an ethnocentricity and suspicion of different ethnicities.[79] National pride, though not to be dismissed totally, needs to be critical and cautious. Our congregation should never identify themselves as Australians first and disciples second.

Some Final Thoughts on Preaching Revelation

John Sweetman provides some excellent guidelines for preaching Revelation:[80]

1. *Paint with a broad brush.* Talk about the world and a sovereign God. Talk about the spiritual behind the physical. Help listeners see that everything has cosmic dimensions.
2. *Provide inside information.* This could be an insightful interpretation of the symbols, some historical background that pertains to the passage, or some contemporary cultural information that shows the relevance of the theme. Offer a sense of the secret being revealed.
3. *Develop contrasts between the seen and unseen.* Help listeners understand what is really happening in the spiritual realm. Speak of the pervasive power and infiltration of evil as well as the infinite authority and rule of God.
4. *Paint stark pictures.* Help listeners picture the events, not just understand them. Send your congregation away with a vivid vision.
5. *Build tension.* The original recipients were in a state of tension. Their question was, 'Where is God in this mess?' It may be necessary to work hard to build this tension for self-satisfied and blasé Westerners.
6. *Leave room for some questions.* Not everything in apocalyptic visions was clear. It doesn't matter if there are still some issues unclarified or unresolved, as long as the theme is clear.

Graves emphasises that 'the sermon needs to employ symbols with which the listeners are familiar. The apocalyptic symbols in Revelation were drawn largely from the Old Testament. Even those symbols may be unfamiliar in our biblically illiterate times, presenting us with a unique challenge'.[81] He also points out that the message cannot be separated from the form and that, surprisingly, apocalyptic forms have never been more popular, even among the highly educated. Mythology has resurfaced powerfully in Western culture through its fascination with science-fiction literature and movies. Movies such as the Star Wars series have a distinctive apocalyptic nature to them and may prove to be a fruitful point of connection between the ancient text and the modern world. He also points out that one aspect inherent in apocalyptic literature is repetition. The preacher needs to capitalise on the power of repetition. One contemporary story or image piled on top of another can be very effective, as it is in the book of Revelation.

So then, in the midst of their fierce struggle with the media-savvy evil empire, worship and the preaching of the word is the place where Australians can reorientate themselves towards reality. Living in an authentically Christian way makes little sense without a proper appreciation of spiritual reality. In hearing and preaching the imagery and narrative of Revelation, we reimagine the world as God intended it to be. And we receive a foretaste of the new creation as God's design for the future begins to take tangible form.[82]

Sample Sermon: Revelation 6–18

Comments on the Sermon

This sermon was preached at Kruger Parade Baptist church on Sunday, 5 August 2018. Although, at the request of the church, the sermon represents an introduction to chapters 6–18 of the book of Revelation, it does show how some of the ideas in the previous discussion can be applied in a local church context. In particular, it attempts to use the images of Revelation to unveil the reality of twenty-first-century Australian life and addresses two particular distinctives of Australians: anxiety and consumerism.

Sermon Text

Did you know that the 'Frightful Five' are well on the way to dominating the world?

You might have heard of Spider-Man's 'Sinister Six' – six vicious foes who Spider-Man has to overcome: Dr Octopus, Venom, Black Cat, Electro, Green Goblin and Kraven.

But did you know that there are a Frightful Five who are well on the way to dominating the world?[83]

Technology writer Farhad Manjoo coined the phrase 'Frightful Five'– a discount version of Spider-Man's Sinister Six. 'The Frightful Five' sounds like a group of cartoon supervillains, but Facebook, Apple, Microsoft, Google and Amazon are the world's five largest private companies, and they're utterly dominant. Just this week the stock market value of Facebook crashed through the trillion-dollar barrier, and the others aren't far behind it. That is more than the gross national product of most nations in the world.

But their plans for world domination are far more terrifying than the Sinister Six – and far more advanced.

They have developed incredible reach. They own many more businesses than the core business that got them started. You might think of Google as a search company. But it actually has seven separate products with more than a billion regular users each. Billions more communicate with their friends via Messenger, WhatsApp and Instagram – all owned by Facebook.

Even services that you think have nothing to do with the Frightful Five end up being dependent on them: much of the internet runs on Google, Amazon and Microsoft's servers.

In the advertising world, Google and Facebook are now so powerful that they are known simply as 'the duopoly', claiming almost half of worldwide digital ad spending last year. No Western rival had more than three percent of the market.

The Frightful Five are collecting huge amounts of data from us. Sometimes we offer it to them freely, but other times they collect it as they monitor our online activity. Each of the frightful five track our movements through the software and seek to offer us things that we might like to purchase based on our browsing history. In fact, Google has now developed a little device that will listen to your voice and do what you ask – and collect a little more data about you as it does so. So has Apple.

In his book *World Without Mind*, US journalist Franklin Foer argues that the big tech firms are so powerful, they're even changing the way we think. He claims that we've traded so much of our knowledge and information – and privacy – to these companies that they now effectively shape the choices we make and our worldview.[84] Think about it. When you search for something online, out of the millions of options out there, ten will appear to you in your browser. Now, the appearance of those options does not happen by chance. Who decides what those options are? Amazon, Apple or Google, or Facebook, or Microsoft – that's who. As Foer writes: 'Facebook would never put it this way, but algorithms are meant to erode free will, to relieve humans of the burden of choosing, to nudge them in the right direction.'

Recent events have also shown that the Frightful Five are not as careful with the personal information that many people have shared with them as they should have been. In April, an American company called Cambridge Analytica accessed the Facebook user profiles of eighty-seven million people and used the data for questionable purposes. There are also allegations that social media has been used to pervert the course of elections in countries all over the world.

The leaders of the Frightful Five don't think of themselves as the bad guys. Indeed, they like to talk about how they make the world better. But the truth is that the tech giants are becoming too big for their own good – and for ours. And as with all the best villainous plots, by the time we wake up to what is happening, it may already be too late.[85]

The original readers of the book of Revelation found themselves in much the same situation.

So, what was the context of the book of Revelation? That is a question you might not have often asked yourself or heard others ask. Some people see the book of Revelation as largely a predictive text of what will happen in the last days. Problem is that most people who have interpreted it that way have concluded that the events that they think Revelation is predicting are playing out in their generation. So, rather than repeating the mistakes of history, I would like to focus on what the book of Revelation meant to the original hearers and to draw out some principles for application in our lives as a result.

Incidentally, that is the way that we usually interpret New Testament texts. We don't assume that the issues that the Corinthian church were facing are the same issues that we are facing in twenty-first-century Australian churches. However, we take the principles from our study of, say, 1 Corinthians and apply them. In the same way, the book of Revelation is an epistle to seven real churches that existed in what is now modern-day Turkey. There is a real and relevant message for them. I want to focus on what that is rather than assuming that everything that's put in writing in the book of Revelation is largely irrelevant to the original hearers.

So, what was the context of Revelation?

The original readers were standing face-to-face with a powerful empire that was seeking to dominate their lives.

The Roman Empire was aggressively seeking to dominate every aspect of people's lives. They were seeking to bludgeon people into total allegiance to the values of the empire. You see, the Romans were committed to a thing called the Pax Romana: the peace of Rome. But they were not committed to it for the good of the citizens, but for the thing that motivates most powerful governments – greed. They knew that if peace reigned across the empire, they would have to spend less money fighting wars, and trade would flourish. And where there is trade, there is tax. And the Romans loved tax. But they knew that peace would only reign in the empire if they could convince everybody that resisting the Roman way of life was totally futile. They were seeking peace through uniformity and conformity to the Roman values.

And so, Revelation's readers were constantly confronted with powerful images of the Roman vision of the world. It was a propaganda onslaught. Rome sought to capture the hearts and minds of people through media: grand architecture, processions, games, spectacles, standards carried by soldiers and even coins. The 'media' of the day powerfully communicated the image and accompanying narrative that Rome was good and benevolent and powerful, that the best thing you could possibly do would be to give your allegiance to the empire and that resistance was futile.

But Rome was presenting a second challenge to the readers of Revelation.

There was also the growth of emperor worship. The propaganda of the Roman Empire reinforced the notion that the emperors were in control of the world. The Roman emperors were becoming more and more self-deluded, and Domitian had declared himself a God and was demanding that everyone in the empire pay him homage. A coin from 81–96 CE features an image of the infant Emperor Domitian seated upon the globe, surrounded by the seven astronomical bodies known to the ancient world.

And the pressure to submit was immense. Even though Rome had a long and honourable history of freedom of speech, by the time of the reign of Domitian, criticism of the empire was prohibited. Further, measures such as high taxation, confiscation of property and economic marginalisation were being utilised to subjugate dissident minorities.

And it was difficult for believers to avoid such pressure towards idolatry, since the imperial cult pervaded all sectors of society, including the economy. Ports and trade guilds were filled with temples to various gods, including the emperor. Christians knew they could not worship Caesar, but they also knew the consequences of that would be dire.

And so, Rome just seemed to be getting stronger and stronger and more intrusive on their lives than ever before. Although there was not fierce persecution, it was becoming more and more difficult to live a sincere Christian life. It is in response to Rome's growing dominance and the pressure to worship the emperor that the book of Revelation is written.

It challenged the propaganda of empire and revealed an alternative, and not as easily visible, view of reality. This 'lifting of the veil' means John sees the world from the heavenly perspective. He gives us a glimpse behind the scenes of history and our current lives so that we can see what is really going on in the events of his time and place.

Let's have a look at Revelation 12 as an example. [Sermon note: read 12:1-6]

Now, what kind of literature is that? Many of you will be tempted to say it is apocalyptic. Why? Well, because it is in the book of Revelation, so it must be apocalyptic. If so, it is a bit like the story of the Sunday School teacher who asked her class, 'What is small and cute and furry and eats eucalyptus leaves?' There was a stunned silence. She looked at one little boy who looked particularly agonised by the question. 'Come on, it is easy, what is the answer Johnny?' He replied hesitantly, 'Well, this is Sunday School, so I know that the answer to every question is Jesus, but that sounds an awful lot like a Koala.'

If we can set aside our presuppositions about the book of Revelation and just read the text for what it is, we will see that Revelation 12:1-9 is actually history. It is history from the other side of the curtain. It is the incarnation as witnessed by the angels. It is the birth of Jesus viewed from heaven. Who is the pregnant woman? Mary. Who is the child she gives birth to, who will rule the nations with an iron sceptre? That sounds an awful lot like a koala. Who is the red dragon – that's Herod, isn't it? He tried to kill the king of the Jews as soon as he was born, but the child was rescued from his grasp. Where was the wilderness that the woman fled to? Egypt, where the infant Jesus was kept safe until Herod died.

So, what the text of Revelation 12 is doing is to reveal to us what really happened at the incarnation. It is an unveiling of reality. Sure, we know from the Gospels that there was an attempt to kill the baby Jesus, but what was really happening was that Satan was trying to thwart God's plans. It looked like King Herod, but actually it was Satan wearing a vicious fat man with a crown. As it says in verse 9, 'The great dragon was hurled down – that ancient serpent called the devil, or Satan, who leads the whole world astray. He was hurled to the earth, and his angels with him.'

In the *Terminator* movies, there are these machines that are covered in human skin. They look for all the world like humans – until they are involved in some sort of accident, and the skin is peeled back, and it reveals that they are actually machines. Revelation is a bit like that: it peels back the skin of human characters and organisations and reveals the devil hiding underneath.

So, the book of Revelation is also a subversive book that unveils the reality of the world and gives us the symbols and language to understand and resist the evil forces at work in our world. It is like an underground newspaper that educates people about reality, so they know they are in a fight. The book of Revelation reveals what is really going on in the world, and that insight made the original readers more powerful in the resistance against the Roman Empire.

The images and the narrative for the book of Revelation communicated at least two big truths to its original readers.

The first major message of Revelation to the original readers was, 'It's okay – Jesus is on the throne.'

Rome and its emperor were dangerous, violent and powerful monsters that seem to be unstoppable. But Revelation reveals the end of the story. Rome and the emperor are described with various images, like the dragon and the various beasts, but in each case the end is the same: the beast attacks the church but is always defeated by the Lamb or the rider on the white horse.

The Roman Empire is exposed for what it is. The Roman Empire is revealed to be just a cloak for Satan himself. And although powerful and dangerous Revelation reveals that Satan is losing. The Lion, who is the Lamb, is seated upon his throne, and even though things might seem dangerous in this world at the moment, the reality is that Satan is beaten, and the Roman Empire also is beaten.

But the book of Revelation has a second message for its readers as well. That message is, 'Don't dance with the harlot'.

As I mentioned earlier, although there was some persecution against Christians, it was not terribly widespread. It would get worse, but at the time it was not a major issue for most of John's readers. In fact, the danger was not so much an *attack* from Rome but a *seduction* by Rome. Many of the Christians were enjoying the benefits that came from embracing the positive economic environment that Rome had created. For sure, the good roads and the violent subjugation of criminal behaviour were motivated by the personal desire of wealthy and powerful Roman elite to make themselves more wealthy and powerful, but it had a spin-off benefit for a whole range of middle-class merchant traders throughout the empire, including those who are in Asia Minor. And including those who were members of the church.

So, John reveals another key image in Revelation: the great harlot or prostitute, Babylon. In the Old Testament, Babylon was a great and wealthy city of power and domination but also a city of depravity and violence. John picks up the historical narrative of Babylon and applies it to Rome. Turn with me to Revelation 18:1–4 [Sermon note: read text].

The metaphor, the prostitute with her ornate clothing and luxurious seductiveness, draws attention to the seductive power of the empire over the imaginations of the people, including the 'kings of the earth' but also those who were benefiting from the wealth generated by the system: 'The merchants of the earth grew rich from her excessive luxuries.'

Nero, apparently, never made a journey with less than one thousand carriages. Rome needed millions of human slaves to sustain itself, but it also needed thousands of merchants to maintain its standard of living and was willing to offer tax and other concessions and incentives to those who cooperated. A mutually beneficial relationship developed between Rome and entrepreneurs throughout the empire. The famous mark of the beast (13:11–17) could well be a sign of surrender to the Roman commercial system, which demanded allegiance to the emperor rather than just a willingness to trade.

And it would seem that some of John's readers were wallowing in the economic success of the Roman Empire. The Laodicean church seemed to have succumbed to temptation to embrace the empire.

And so, John unveils the reality: the Roman economic system, which is bringing such prosperity to those who are willing to compromise to take part in it, is in fact a tool of Satan that he uses to seduce people into his dominion. Believers need not only fear that Rome will overpower them, but that it will seduce them with beautiful things that come from economic prosperity. But, as the voice cries in Revelation 18:4, 'Come out from her my people!' John warns his readers that those who dance with the harlot Rome will join in the destruction that awaits her.

So, what is the message of Revelation for twenty-first-century Australians?

'It's okay – Jesus is on the throne.'

Even if we don't feel threatened by the Frightful Five, there are plenty of other things to feel anxious about. When we hear of wars and rumours of wars, when we see Donald Trump breaking alliances with traditional allies and forming new relationships with North Korea and Russia, we can become anxious. When we see our privacy being eroded, when the government and transnational corporations seem to take control of our lives out of our hands, we can feel anxious. When we hear the long list of things that will give us cancer, and the increasing difficulty in finding permanent full-time work, it is easy to feel anxious.

When the world looks out of control, when it looks like we are being overwhelmed by the invasive powers of darkness, take a stroll through the gallery of images in Revelation. The Lion, who is the Lamb, has conquered the world through his love and is seated upon his throne. Satan is thrashing around, causing a bit of damage here and there, but he is a beaten foe. That is the reality. Not the lies of the deluded dictators or the mighty armies or the media or the Frightful Five.

And the more that we dwell upon the image of the Lamb upon the throne, and the host of other powerful images in Revelation that show Jesus is in perfect control and being worshipped by people from every nation, the more we will find peace, and the more we will be set free from anxiety about the powers that seem to rule the world but which actually do not. When we know the end of the story, it means that the threats we face along the way don't seem nearly so scary.

When I was younger, I was a fanatical supporter of the West Tigers. But I used to find watching their matches traumatic, because I just didn't know how the game was going to turn out. In the end I pre-recorded the games, which meant I could find out if they won ahead of time, and if they did, I would sit down with a drink and a packet of chips and enjoy the game. Even if they had bad spells during the game and were a long way behind on the score board, I knew we would be all right at the end – and so I could enjoy the game anyway.

And it is the same with us in the face of the troubling course of world events. It can be pretty scary seeing such powerful events occurring totally beyond our control. But the good news is, we know how the game ends. And so, to a greater or lesser extent, we can sit back and enjoy the ride.

But there is a second message as well. 'Stop dancing with the harlot.'

Just as the original audience were tempted to sell themselves out to the economic system because of the benefits it would bring to them, we struggle with the temptation to sell ourselves out to the economic system we live in as well. We too are in combat with a harlot who would seek to seduce us. And the name of the harlot is consumerism. And her pimps are the Frightful Five. Consumerism and her henchmen look soft and friendly on the outside, but they are ruthlessly committed to one thing – shifting our love from Jesus to possessions and experiences. And to do that, they want to take your private information and preferences so that they can influence your buying habits.

Take your pastor into a quiet corner and interrogate them about what is the biggest issue facing the church and individual Christians, and they will tell you it is not same-sex marriage or heresy or persecution; they will tell you that it is consumerism. It consumes people's lives and sucks the life out of Christian spirituality and leaves a shell. Consumerism can seem like such an enjoyable thing. So harmless. But it is powerfully addictive and ultimately fatal to our souls – and sometimes even our physical bodies.

We need to disengage from the consumerism of Babylon. It is the instrument of Satan.

Can I suggest there are two ways you can do this?

Firstly, reduce the amount of advertising you expose yourself to. Satan employs the best movie producers, actors, scriptwriters, musicians and graphic designers to make us want things – we don't stand a chance. If we allow ourselves to be bombarded by advertising, we will be corrupted.

You see, free-to-air TV does not exist for your entertainment. They don't pay millions of dollars for content just because they want you to have something nice to entertain you for hours at night. It exists to sell advertising. It is all about money. It is all about getting you to watch the ads so their sponsors make more money and pay more for their advertising.

Both my daughters and their husbands have decided not to have TVs in their homes. That's bold, isn't it? Their friends must come over and say, 'Hey guys, somebody's nicked your TV!' But I suspect that they have a healthier spirituality because of it.

Secondly, get out of the grasp of the Frightful Five. Stop giving them your allegiance and information. The more personal information we give them, the more of us they own. It may not mean we stop using social media, but it must mean that we stop it from using us. If you cannot go an hour without checking social media, you are hooked. The harlot has got you firmly in her grasp.

Revelation unveils reality.

It challenges the propaganda of empire and reveals an alternative, and not as easily visible, view of reality. This 'lifting of the veil' means we can see the world from the heavenly perspective. It is an unveiling of reality. Revelation gives us a glimpse behind the scenes of history and our current lives so that we can see what is really going on in the events of his time and place.

Remember: It's okay. Jesus is on the throne.

ENDNOTES

Introduction

1. Tim Foster, *The Suburban Captivity of the Church: Contextualising the Gospel for Post-Christian Australia* (Moreland: Acorn Press, 2014), 30.
2. Graeme Goldsworthy, *Christ-Centered Biblical Theology: Hermeneutical Foundations and Principles* (Downers Grove, IL: InterVarsity Press Academic, 2012).
3. Daniel J. Treier, *Introducing Theological Interpretation of Scripture: Recovering a Christian Practice* (Grand Rapids, MI: Baker Academic, 2008).
4. Brevard S. Childs, *Biblical Theology of the Old and New Testaments: Theological Reflection on the Christian Bible* (London: Xpress prints, 1992).
5. By 'introductory', we mean here the issues of authorship, dating, audience, reason and purpose. Most commentaries will deal with these matters; the focus in this volume will be on what the *exegetical consequences* of these issues are for the interpretive process.
6. Raymond Williams, *Keywords* (Oxford: Oxford University Press, 1985), 87.
7. 'Culture', *Oxford English Dictionary Online* (2007), https://en.oxforddictionaries.com/definition/culture.
8. Kevin J. Vanhoozer, Charles A. Anderson and Michael J. Sleasman, *Everyday Theology: How to Read Cultural Texts and Interpret Trends* (Grand Rapids, MI: Baker Academic, 2007), 54–57.
9. John Webster, quoted in John Swinton and Harriet Mowat, *Practical Theology and Qualitative Research* (London: SCM Press, 2006), 90.
10. Foster, *Suburban Captivity*, 43.
11. Vanhoozer et al., *Everyday Theology*, 251.
12. Foster, *Suburban Captivity*, 37–42.
13. Clifford Geertz, 'Thick Description: Toward an Interpretive Theory of Culture', in *The Interpretation of Cultures: Selected Essays* (New York: Basic Books, 1973).
14. Vanhoozer et al., *Everyday Theology*, 47.
15. Swinton and Mowat, *Practical Theology and Qualitative Research*, 73–84.
16. Thanks to David Benson for this insight.

Describing Australians

1. From an unpublished conference paper provided by David Benson.
2. Luciara Nardon and Richard M. Steers, 'The Culture Theory Jungle: Divergence and Convergence in Models of National Culture', *Vlerick Leuven Gent Working Paper Series* 2006/38 (2006): 17. See also 'The Culture Theory Jungle: Divergence and Convergence in Models of National Culture', in *Cambridge Handbook of Culture, Organisations, and Work*, ed. Rabi S. Bhagat and Richard M. Steers (Cambridge: Cambridge University Press, 2009).
3. Nardon and Steers, 'Culture Theory Jungle', 8.
4. The material in the tables is adapted directly from ibid., 35.
5. See Nick Dyrenfurth, *Mateship: A Very Australian History* (Melbourne: Scribe, 2015).
6. Nardon and Steers, 'Culture Theory Jungle', 17.
7. Ibid., 19.

8   Charles Taylor, *A Secular Age* (Cambridge: Harvard University Press, 2007).

9   Renae Barker, 'Is Australia a Secular Country? It Depends What You Mean', *The Conversation*, 14 May 2015.

10 Australian Bureau of Statistics, Religion in Australia 2071.0, 'Census of Population and Housing: Reflecting Australia – Stories from the Census', http://abs.gov.au/ausstats/abs@.nsf/Lookup/by%20Subject/2071.0~2016~Main%20Features~Religion%20Data%20Summary~70.

11 As reported by Matt Wade, 'Ipsos Global Poll: Two in Three Australians Think Religion Does More Harm Than Good in the World', *The Age*, 12 October 2017.

12 'Postmodernism', *Oxford English Dictionary Online* (2007), https://en.oxforddictionaries.com/definition/us/postmodernism.

13 'Pluralism', *Oxford English Dictionary Online* (2007), https://en.oxforddictionaries.com/definition/us/pluralism.

14 'Our Pluralist Society: Permission to Speak Freely', *The Canberra Times*, 14 January 2015.

15 Wade, 'Ipsos Global Poll'.

16 Steve Spurr, 'Trust Crisis in Australia', *Edelman Magazine*, 24 February 2017.

17 Philip J. Hughes, Lachlan Fraser and Association Christian Research, *Life, Ethics and Faith in Australian Society: Facts and Figures* (Nunawading: Christian Research Association, 2014), 116.

18 Roy Morgan Inc., 'Roy Morgan Image of Professions Survey 2017', 7 June 2017, http://www.roymorgan.com/findings/7244-roy-morgan-image-of-professions-may-2017-201706051543.

19 Roy Morgan Inc., 'Roy Morgan Image of Professions Survey 2011', 25 April 2011, http://www.roymorgan.com/findings/finding-4655-201302180109.

20 Australian Bureau of Statistics, 'Census of Population and Housing: Australia Revealed, 2016', http://www.abs.gov.au/AUSSTATS/abs@.nsf/SearchProduct?readform&catno=2024.0&issue=2016.

21 Katie Blair et al., 'Challenging Racism Project 2015–16 National Survey Report', (Sydney: Western Sydney University., 2017), 16.

22 Mirriam Pepper and Kathy Jacka Kerr, 'Cultural Diversity on the Increase in Australian Churches', *National Church Life Survey Fact Sheets* (2017), http://news.ncls.org.au/cultural-diversity-increase.

23 For a recent example, see Eunjoo Mary Kim and Mark R. Francis, *Christian Preaching and Worship in Multicultural Contexts: A Practical Theological Approach* (Collegeville, MN: Liturgical, 2017).

24 Selim Jahan, 'Human Development Report 2016', (United Nations Development Programme, 2016).

25 Credit Suisse Research Institute, 'Global Wealth Report 2017: Where Are We Ten Years after the Crisis?', 14 November 2017, https://www.credit-suisse.com/corporate/en/articles/news-and-expertise/global-wealth-report-2017-201711.html.

26 Organisation for Economic Co-Operation and Development, 'Obesity Update' (Paris: OECD Publishing, 2017),

27 Fiona Pepper, 'Australia's Obsession with New Clothes and Fast Fashion Hurting the Environment', *ABC Radio Melbourne*, 12 January 2017, http://www.abc.net.au/news/2017-01-12/australias-obsession-with-new-clothes-hurting-the-environment/8177624.

28 Clive Hamilton, Richard Denniss and David Baker, 'Wasteful Consumption in Australia' (The Australia Institute, 2005).

29 As repoted by James Adonis, 'The Frenzy of Consumerism', *The Sydney Morning Herald*, 7 December 2012.

30 As reported by Anne Lim, 'Confronting the Idol of Consumerism', *Eternity News*, 31 October 2017, https://www.eternitynews.com.au/australia/confronting-the-idol-of-consumerism/.

31   Australian Bureau of Statistics, 'National Health Survey: First Results, 2014–15', http://www.abs.gov.au/ausstats/abs@.nsf/Lookup/by%20Subject/4364.0.55.001~2014-15~Main%20Features~Mental%20and%20behavioural%20conditions~32.

32   Emma Reynolds, 'Australia's Deadly Workplace Crisis: Hidden Epidemic in Job World', *news.com.au*, 24 November 2017.

33   Matt Wade, 'More Australians Fear Nuclear Attacks and Health Epidemics Than Average: Ipsos', *The Sydney Morning Herald*, 24 November 2017.

34   Alex Oliver, 'The Lowy Institute Poll', *Lowy Institute*, 21 June 2017, https://www.lowyinstitute.org/publications/2017-lowy-institute-poll.

35   Australian Bureau of Statistics, 'General Social Survey: Summary Results, Australia, 2014 (Cat. 4159.0)', http://www.abs.gov.au/ausstats/abs@.nsf/mf/4159.0.

36   Organisation for Economic Co-Operation and Development, 'How's Life? 2015' (Paris: OECD Publishing, 2015), 79.

37   Rebecca Cassells, Cathy Gong and Alan Duncan, *Race against Time: How Australians Spend Their Time* (AMP Limited, 2011), 4.

38   Ibid., 34.

39   Ibid., 15.

40   Wendell Cox, 'Commuting in Australia', *Newgeography*, 24 March 2013, http://www.newgeography.com/content/003587-commuting-australia.

41   Roy Morgan Research, 'Australians Still Spend More Time Watching TV Than Using the Internet at Home', (2016), http://www.roymorgan.com/findings/7069-more-time-watching-television-than-using-internet-at-home-australia-september-2016-201611291605.

Preaching the Pentateuch to Australians

1   Craig G. Bartholomew and Michael W. Goheen, *The Drama of Scripture: Finding Our Place in the Biblical Story* (Grand Rapids, MI: Baker, 2014), 20–23.

2   M. J. Selman, 'Law', in *Dictionary of the Old Testament: Pentateuch*, ed. T. Desmond Alexander and David W. Baker (Leicester: Inter-Varsity Press, 2003), 499.

3   Tremper Longman III and Raymond B. Dillard, *An Introduction to the Old Testament*, Second ed. (Grand Rapids, MI: Zondervan, 2009), 41.

4   Gordon J. Wenham, *Genesis 1–15*, Word Biblical Commentary (Waco, Texas: Word Books, 1987), xxvi.

5   For an excellent summary of historical and source criticism, see Gerald A. Klingbeil, 'Historical Criticism', in *Dictionary of the Old Testament: Pentateuch*, ed. T. Desmond Alexander and David W. Baker (Downers Grove, IL: InterVarsity Press, 2003), 401–20. See also Longman III and Dillard, *Introduction to the Old Testament*, 42–45.

6   Sidney Greidanus, *Preaching Christ from Genesis: Foundations for Expository Sermons* (Grand Rapids, MI: Eerdmans, 2007), 11.

7   Duane A. Garrett, *Rethinking Genesis: The Sources and Authorship of the First Book of the Bible* (Fearn: Mentor, 2000), 11.

8   Longman III and Dillard, *Introduction to the Old Testament*, 50.

9   Ibid.

10   Ibid., 51.

11   Bruce K. Waltke, *Genesis: A Commentary* (Grand Rapids, MI: Zondervan, 2001), 21–22.

12   Longman III and Dillard, *Introduction to the Old Testament*, 51.

13 Waltke, *Genesis*, 22.

14 John H. Sailhamer, *The Pentateuch as Narrative: A Biblical-Theological Commentary* (Grand Rapids, MI: Zondervan, 1992), 6.

15 Greidanus, *Preaching Christ from Genesis*, 27.

16 Ibid., 31, quoting Sailhamer, *The Pentateuch as Narrative*, 16.

17 Greidanus, *Preaching Christ from Genesis*, 27.

18 Ibid.

19 Klingbeil, 'Historical Criticism', 420.

20 For a summary of this debate, see V. J. Steiner, 'Literary Structure of the Pentateuch', in *Dictionary of the Old Testament: Pentateuch*, ed. T. Desmond Alexander and David W. Baker (Downers Grove, IL: InterVarsity Press, 2003), 544–56.

21 Ibid., 549.

22 Selman, 'Law', 498.

23 Ibid., 500.

24 Narrative is estimated to comprise approximately thirty to forty percent of the Old Testament. See Steven D. Mathewson, *The Art of Preaching Old Testament Narrative* (Grand Rapids, MI: Carlisle, Cumbria: Baker Academic, Paternoster, 2002), 20.

25 Thomas G. Long, *Preaching and the Literary Forms of the Bible* (Philadelphia: Fortress, 1989), 66.

26 Sidney Greidanus, *The Modern Preacher and the Ancient Text: Intepreting and Preaching Biblical Literature* (Grand Rapids, MI: Eerdmans, 1988), 188.

27 See, Mathewson, *Art of Preaching Old Testament Narrative*, 44.

28 Jeffrey D. Arthurs, *Preaching with Variety: How to Re-Create the Dynamics of Biblical Genres* (Grand Rapids, MI: Kregel, 2007), 72–76.

29 See Greidanus, *The Modern Preacher and the Ancient Text*, 208–13.

30 Michael D. Williams, *Far as the Curse Is Found: The Covenant Story of Redemption* (Phillipsburg, NJ: P&R, 2005), x.

31 Bartholomew and Goheen, *Drama of Scripture*, 21.

32 See Williams, *Far as the Curse Is Found*, xi.

33 Christopher J. H. Wright, *How to Preach and Teach the Old Testament for All Its Worth* (Grand Rapids, MI: Zondervan, 2016), 34–36.

34 Bartholomew and Goheen, *Drama of Scripture*, 22.

35 Ibid., 52.

36 See Wright, *How to Preach and Teach the Old Testament*, 119–35.

37 For extensive treatment of redemptive-historical preaching see Dennis E. Johnson, *Him We Proclaim: Preaching Christ from All the Scriptures* (Phillipsburg, NJ: P&R, 2007).

38 Timothy Keller, *Preaching: Communicating Faith in an Age of Skepticism* (New York: Viking, 2015), 22.

39 Ibid., 66.

40 See Iain M. Duguid, *Living in the Gap between Promise and Reality: The Gospel According to Abraham* (Phillipsburg, NJ: P&R, 1999).

41 Wright, *How to Preach and Teach the Old Testament*, 29 (his italics).

42 The ten are, the account of the line of the heavens and the earth (2:4); of Adam's line (5:1); of Noah's line (6:9); of Noah's sons (10:1); of Shem's line (11:10); of Terah's line (11:27); of Ishmael's line (25:12); of Isaac's line (25:19); of Esau's line (36:1); and of Jacob's line (37:2).

43 Waltke, *Genesis*, 18.

ENDNOTES

44 Wenham notes that 'God's blessing is manifested most obviously in human prosperity and wellbeing; long life, wealth, peace, good harvests, and children are the items that figure most frequently in the lists of blessings ...' (*Genesis 1–15*, 275).

45 See Genesis 12:7; 13:14–17; 14:19; 15: 5, 13–14; 17:6–8, 19; 18:10, 14, 18–19; 21:1–7, 12–13; 22:16–18; 24:7, 27, 60; 25:23; 26:3–5, 24; 27:29, 39–40; 28:3–4, 13–14.

46 Tremper Longman III, *How to Read Genesis* (Downers Grove, IL: InterVarsity Press, 2005), 128.

47 Wright, *How to Preach and Teach the Old Testament*, 88–89.

48 Andrew Reid, *Genesis: Salvation Begins*, Reading the Bible Today (Sydney: Aquila Press, 2000), 94.

49 Dale Ralph Davis, *Faith of Our Father: Expositions of Genesis 12–25* (Fearn: Christian Focus, 2015), 146.

50 Ibid.

51 Ibid., 148. Sailhamer also regards it as appearing to be 'a hard bargain' (*The Pentateuch as Narrative*, 180). Wenham argues that it is impossible to gauge whether it was a fair price or not, and leans in favour of saying it was; see Gordon J. Wenham, *Genesis 16–50*, Word Biblical Commentary (Dallas: Word Books, 1994), 129.

52 Ruth Whippman, *The Pursuit of Happiness and Why It's Making Us Anxious* (London: Hutchinson, 2016).

53 Waltke, *Genesis*, 220.

54 Duguid, *Living in the Gap*, 32–33.

55 Ibid., 43.

56 Davis, *Faith of Our Father*, 146.

57 According to Waltke, Jacob is a pun on *acab*, 'to seize someone by the heel, go behind someone ... to betray' (*Genesis*, 358). In Genesis 32 there is a further word play when God wrestled, 'Jacobed' him. See Wenham, *Genesis 16–50*, 295.

58 Wenham notes that the author 'is interested in all the sons of Jacob, not simply Joseph' and adds, 'Throughout Gen 37–50 the author shows his interest in the history of the whole family of Jacob, not just Joseph' (*Genesis 16–50*, 345).

59 Duguid, *Living in the Gap*, xv–xix.

60 Keller, *Preaching*, 127.

61 Ibid., 131.

62 Mark Sayers, *Disappearing Church: From Cultural Relevance to Gospel Resilience* (Chicago: Moody, 2016), 11.

63 Ibid., 17.

64 Ibid.

65 Keller, *Preaching*, 136–37.

66 See Sayers, *Disappearing Church*, 125–26.

67 Ibid., 76.

68 Ibid.

69 A. A. Milne, *The House at Poo Corner*, (London: Eggmont, 1970), 28.

Preaching Old Testament Law to Australians

1 The word 'Deuteronomy' comes from the Greek words that mean 'second' and 'law'. While Deuteronomy is not a second law, but Moses' sermons on the law, the law is being expounded a second time over!

2   David Clines, in his famous study of the theme of the Pentateuch, understands the theme of blessing in this way: David J. Clines, *The Theme of the Pentateuch*, JSOT Supplementary Series, 2nd ed. (Sheffield: Sheffield Academic, 1997), 31–35, 46–47, 49–51.

3   Romans 3:19–20.

4   This more 'positive' aspect of the law (knowing God's will) is put forward by several authors including Douglas Stuart, 'Preaching from the Law' in *Preaching the Old Testament*, ed. S. Gibson (Grand Rapids, MI: Baker Books, 2006), 89–91; and Daniel I. Block, 'Preaching Old Testament Law to New Testament Christians', *Southeastern Theological Review* 3, no. 2 (2012): 216–19. Block's article explains well the different corpora of law in the Pentateuch (202–07); see also Graeme Goldsworthy, *Preaching the Whole Bible as Christian Scripture* (Grand Rapids, MI: Eerdmans, 2000), 158.

5   Daniel Hays argues that this traditional approach to the law is invalid: the approach is arbitrary and without any textual support, it ignores the narrative context of the laws, and it fails to reflect the change from old to new covenant, (in Daniel Hays, 'Applying the Old Testament Law today', *Bibliothecra Sacra* 158 (2001): 21–35). On page 28 in particular, he notes that Christians are no longer under the Old Testament Law (Gal 2:15–16, 3:25, Rom 7:4, Heb 8–9). The same point against this traditional threefold division of the law is also made by Block, 'Preaching the Old Testament Law to New Testament Christians', 215.

6   See Patrick Fairbairn, *The Typology of Scripture* (Grand Rapids, MI: Zondervan, 1963).

7   Gerhard von Rad, 'The Interpretation of the Old Testament: II. Typological Interpretation of the Old Testament', *Interpretation* 15, no. 2 (1961): 174–92.

8   So Gerhard von Rad, *Old Testament Theology*, vol. 2 (Edinburgh: Oliver & Boyd, 1965), 361. M. Jay Wells calls this 'figuration', and emphasises that it comes, not from the interpreter, but from the Old Testament texts themselves. M. J. Wells, 'Figural Representation and Canonical Unity', in *Biblical Theology: Retrospect and Prospect*, ed. S. J. Hafemann (Downers Grove, IL: InterVarsity Press, 2002), 111–25.

9   Rad, *Old Testament Theology*, 363.

10 Ibid., 384; so also Graeme Goldsworthy, *According to Plan* (Leicester: Inter-Varsity Press, 1991), 381–85.

11 Rad, 'Typological Interpretation', 190.

12 Childs, *Biblical Theology*, 724.

13 Greidanus, *Preaching Christ from the Old Testament*.

14 Ibid., 249.

15 For example, Robert Thomas, 'The New Testament Use of the Old Testament', *The Master's Seminary J* 13, no. 1 (2002): 79–98.

16 Greidanus, *Preaching Christ from the Old Testament*, 252.

17 I'm sure there are many more than three! I will just mention these three to give an idea of different approaches to understanding and applying an Old Testament text to Christians today.

18 It is a human document but is also the word of God. James Barr is a very clear exponent of the human-only document approach; see especially: James Barr, *The Concept of Biblical Theology: An Old Testament Perspective* (London: SCM Press, 1999). See Murray Capill's fuller explanation of critical scholarship on the Pentateuch in the previous chapter under the heading 'Authorship'.

19 These two books are must reads: Graeme Goldsworthy, *Gospel and Kingdom* (Exeter: Paternoster, 1981) and *According to Plan*. Also important is Goldsworthy's *Preaching the Whole Bible as Christian Scripture*.

A similar approach is advocated by Daniel Hays and called 'principlism' ('Applying the Old Testament Law today', 30f). His approach also involves first exegeting the passage to determine its original meaning, but then deriving principles from the text. Walter Kaiser also speaks of finding the 'normative principle' in Old Testament laws when preaching on the laws (Walter Kaiser,

Preaching and Teaching from the Old Testament (Grand Rapids, MI: Baker Academic, 2003), 144). Douglas Stuart speaks of biblical law being 'paradigmatic' and suggests that principles need to be derived from it ('Preaching from the Law', 94).

Goldsworthy's approach goes beyond identifying principles by rooting those principles firmly in the unfolding revelation of the Bible itself. However, Goldsworthy's approach, in my opinion, certainly doesn't exclude drawing out the general principles or universal truths that lie behind the Old Testament laws.

20 Or Psalm 95 is said to be authored by the Holy Spirit, God and David (Hebrews 3:7— 4:13).

21 Luke 24:27.

22 Luke 24:44.

23 2 Corinthians 5:19-20.

24 Diagram taken, with permission from Aquila Press, from Martin Pakula, *Numbers* (Sydney: Aquila Press, 2006), 8. Goldsworthy himself says: 'I know it will not always be a simple matter to show how every text in the Bible speaks of the Christ, but that does not alter the fact that he says it does' (Goldsworthy, *Preaching the Whole Bible as Christian Scripture*, 23). See also the discussion of 'metanarrative' and preaching Christ from the Pentateuch in the previous chapter by Murray Capill.

25 Timothy Keller addresses this problem well. He says: 'It is possible to "get to Christ" so quickly in preaching a text that we fail to be sensitive to the particularities of the text's message ... The result will be this: Because we have not spent time in the text itself, the way that Jesus is described will sound the same from week to week ... if you don't go deeply enough into the original historical context, you will have two or three stock ways of bringing in Jesus, and they will sound the same every time ... So, we have a balance to strike – not to preach Christ without preaching the text, and not to preach the text without preaching Christ'. (*Preaching*, 66-67). Thanks to Ian Hussey for pointing me to this reference.

26 Matthew 5:21-22, 27-28.

27 1 Timothy 6:4 speaks about not having evil suspicions about others.

28 Katherine Smith, 'Ordered Relationships in Leviticus', chapter 2, in *Marriage, Family and Relationships* (London: Apollos, 2017).

29 To see how this works throughout the book of Numbers, see my commentary in the Reading the Bible Today series: Martin Pakula, *Numbers* (Sydney: Aquila Press, 2006).

30 Gordon J. Wenham, *The Book of Leviticus* (NICOT; Grand Rapids, MI: Eerdmans, 1979), 57.

Preaching Old Testament Narrative to Australians

1 Brent A. Strawn, *The Old Testament Is Dying: A Diagnosis and Recommended Treatment* (Grand Rapids, MI: Baker Academic, 2017), 28.

2 A key figure in this endeavour is Robert Alter, see: Robert Alter, *The Art of Biblical Narrative* (London: Allen & Unwin, 1981).

3 Long, *Preaching and the Literary Forms of the Bible*, 52.

4 John C. Holbert, *Old Testament Proclamation and Narrative in the Hebrew Bible* (Nashville: Abingdon, 1991), 27.

5 Alter, *The Art of Biblical Narrative*; Jerome T. Walsh, *Old Testament Narrative: A Guide to Interpretation*, 1st ed. (Louisville, KY: Westminster John Knox, 2009).

6 John Goldingay, *Key Questions About Biblical Interpretation: Old Testament Answers* (Grand Rapids, MI: Baker Academic, 2011), 238.

7 Peter Enns, *Inspiration and Incarnation: Evangelicals and the Problem of the Old Testament* (Grand Rapids, MI: Baker Academic, 2005), 154.

8   Mathewson, *Art of Preaching Old Testament Narrative*, 44.

9   Trent C. Butler, *Judges*, Word Biblical Commentary (Dallas: Word Books, 2009), 299.

10   There are a variety of factors that come into play when choosing a sermonic structure: Sally A. Brown, 'Designing the Sermon's Form', in *Ways of the Word: Learning to Preach for Your Time and Place*, eds Sally A. Brown and Luke Powery (Minneapolis: Fortress, 2016), 157–9.

11   Walsh, *Old Testament Narrative*, 43.

12   James Davidson Martin, *The Book of Judges*, Cambridge Bible Commentary: New English Bible (Cambridge: Cambridge University Press, 1975), 145.

13   Mary J. Evans, *Judges and Ruth*, Tyndale Old Testament Commentaries (Downers Grove, IL: InterVarsity Press, 2017), 5–6.

14   Mark E. Biddle, *Reading Judges*, A Literary and Theological Commentary (Georgia: Smyth & Helwys, 2012), 122.

15   Judges 11:1.

16   Lee R. Martin, 'Power to Save!?: The Role of the Spirit of the Lord in the Book of Judges', *Journal of Pentecostal Theology* 16, no. 2 (2008): 38.

17   Evans, *Judges and Ruth*, 128.

18   Hamlin concurs, this military victory is personal, E. John Hamlin, *At Risk in the Promised Land: A Commentary on the Book of Judges* (Grand Rapids, MI: Eerdmans, 1990), 118.

19   Evans, *Judges and Ruth*, 130.

20   Daniel Block, *Judges, Ruth* (Nashville: B & H, 1999). 362. Cundall describes Jephthah as 'confused', a person who makes mistakes in Arthur Ernest Cundall and Leon Morris, *Judges: An Introduction and Commentary* (Downers Grove, IL: Inter-Varsity, 1968), 144.

21   Leviticus 22:18, 27:9, Numbers 30:2.

22   Numbers 30:2, Deuteronomy 23:21.

23   Leviticus 27.

24   David Janzen, 'Why the Deuteronomist Told About the Sacrifice of Jephthah's Daughter', *JSOT* 29, no. 3 (2005): 345.

25   Ryan, who argues for a positive portrayal of Jephthah, believes that the word is closely connected with the burning of animals and that Jephthah would not have imagined the possibility of human sacrifice, see: Roger J. Ryan, *Judges* (Sheffield: Sheffield Phoenix Press, 2007), 86.

26   Barry G. Webb, *The Book of Judges*, The New International Commentary on the Old Testament (Grand Rapids, MI: Eerdmans, 2012), 329.

27   Evans, *Judges and Ruth*, 134. Other scholars also read the vow as having human sacrifice in mind, Martin, *Book of Judges*, 145., Cundall and Morris, *Judges: An Introduction*, 146., Michael Wilcock, *The Message of Judges: Grace Abounding* (Leicester: Inter-Varsity, 1992), 116., Dale Ralph Davis, *Judges: Such a Great Salvation*, Expositor's Guide to the Historical Books (Grand Rapids, MI: Baker, 1999), 147., Robert B. Chisholm Jr., *A Commentary on Judges and Ruth* (Grand Rapids, MI: Kregel Academic, 2013), 354.

28   Leviticus 20:1–3.

29   Chisholm, *Commentary on Judges*, 352.

30   John C. Yoder, *Power and Politics in the Book of Judges: Men and Women of Valor* (Minneapolis: Fortress, 2015), 107.

31   Walsh, *Old Testament Narrative*, 25.

32   Biddle, *Reading Judges*, 121.

33   Ryan, *Judges*, 89.

ENDNOTES

34 Pamela Tamarkin Reis, *Reading the Lines: A Fresh Look at the Hebrew Bible* (Massachusetts: Hendrickson Publishers, 2002), 117.

35 Yoder, *Power and Politics*, 154., Cundall along similar lines describes her actions as 'submissive nobility', Cundall and Morris, *Judges: An Introduction*, 149.

36 Ryan, *Judges*, 89.

37 Janzen, 'Why the Deuteronomist Told', 347.

38 Hamlin, *At Risk in the Promised Land*, 111.

39 Biddle, *Reading Judges*, 118.

40 Ibid., 117.

41 Terence E. Fretheim, *The Suffering of God: An Old Testament Perspective* (Philadelphia: Fortress, 1984), 36.

42 Walter Brueggemann, *Theology of the Old Testament: Testimony, Dispute, Advocacy* (Minneapolis: Fortress, 1997), 410.

43 Janzen, 'Why the Deuteronomist Told', 345-47. Younger concurs with Janzen that God is exasperated, see: K. Lawson Younger Jr., *Judges and Ruth*, NIV Application Commentary (Grand Rapids, MI: Zondervan, 2002), 244; Wilcock, *Message of Judges*, 109; or grieved: Davis, *Judges*, 136; or worn down by the suffering and moved to action: Biddle, *Reading Judges*, 118.

44 Younger, *Judges and Ruth*, 244.

45 Ibid., 245.

46 J. Clinton McCann, *Judges* (Louisville, KY: Westminster John Knox, 2002), 79., Also: Fretheim, *Suffering of God*, 129.

47 Samuel E. Balentine, *The Hidden God: The Hiding of the Face of God in the Old Testament*, Oxford Theological Monographs (Oxford: Oxford University Press, 1983), 155.

48 Judges 3:10, 6:34

49 Martin, *Book of Judges*, 38.

50 Biddle, *Reading Judges*, 126.

51 Martin, *Book of Judges*, 40.

52 Wilf Hildebrandt, *An Old Testament Theology of the Spirit of God* (Peabody, Massachusetts: Hendrickson Press, 1995), 113.

53 Martin, *Book of Judges*, 41.

54 Hamlin notes this is unlike Saul's vow that negatively impacts Jonathan in 1 Samuel 14:43-45 (*At Risk in the Promised Land*, 119).

55 McCann, *Judges*, 86., Also see: Joel S. Burnett, *Where Is God? : Divine Absence in the Hebrew Bible* (Minneapolis: Fortress, 2010), 176.

56 McCann, *Judges*, 87.

57 Mark McCrindle, 'Australia: The Digital Media Nation', (McCrindle Research, 2013).

58 Brown, 'Designing the Sermon's Form', 160.

59 Hugh MacKay, *Australia Reimagined: Towards a More Compassionate, Less Anxious Society* (Sydney: MacMillian, 2018), 10.

60 Ibid., 5-10.

61 Jill Stark, 'How Our Happiness Pursuit Is Making Us More Anxious Than Ever', *Sunday Life Magazine*, 26 July 2018.

62 MacKay, *Australia Reimagined*, 13.

63 Daniel 4:33.

64. Robert B. Chisholm, *Interpreting the Historical Books: An Exegetical Handbook* (Grand Rapids, MI: Kregel Publications, 2006), 89.
65. Walter Brueggemann, *The Land : Place as Gift, Promise, and Challenge in Biblical Faith* (Philadelphia: Fortress, 1977), 5.
66. Meredith Lake, *The Bible in Australia: A Cultural History* (Sydney: NewSouth Publishing, 2018), 86.
67. Ibid., 88.
68. Ibid., 99.
69. Peter Adam, 'Australia – Whose Land? A Call for Recompense', in *John Saunders Lecture* (Morling College 2009).
70. Gary M. Burge, *Whose Land? Whose Promise?: What Christians Are Not Being Told About Israel and the Palestinians* (Cleveland, OH: Pilgrim, 2003), 110–11.
71. Leviticus 18:25.
72. MacKay, *Australia Reimagined*, 22.
73. John Goldingay, *Israel's Life*, Old Testament Theology (Downers Grove, IL: InterVarsity Press, 2009), 383.
74. Andrew E. Hill and John H. Walton, *A Survey of the Old Testament* (Grand Rapids, MI: Zondervan, 2000), 190.
75. Randolph E. Richards and Brandon J. O'Brien, *Misreading Scripture with Western Eyes: Removing Cultural Blinders to Better Understand the Bible* (Downers Grove, IL: InterVarsity Press, 2012), 97.
76. Chisholm, *Interpreting the Historical Books*, 93.
77. Mary E. Mills, *Historical Israel, Biblical Israel: Studying Joshua to 2 Kings* (London: Cassell Biblical Studies, 1999), 82.
78. Richards and O'Brien, *Misreading Scripture with Western Eyes* 99.
79. 'Australian Coalition to End Loneliness', https://www.endloneliness.com.au/.
80. Lake, *Bible in Australia*, 301.
81. Tara Moss, *The Fictional Woman* (Sydney: HarperCollins, 2014), 1–4.
82. Lake, *Bible in Australia*, 348.
83. Ibid.
84. Phyllis Trible, *Texts of Terror: Literary-Feminist Readings of Biblical Narratives* (Philadelphia: Fortress, 1984), 108.
85. Julia Baird, 'Domestic Violence in the Church: When Women Are Believed, Change Will Happen.', *ABC News*, 23 May 2018.
86. Cundall and Morris, *Judges: An Introduction*, 149.
87. Mark McCrindle, 'Faith and Belief in Australia', (Sydney: McCrindle Research, 2017), 8.
88. Tom Frame, *Losing My Religion: Unbelief in Australia* (Sydney: UNSW Press, 2009), 173.
89. Ibid., 174.
90. Ibid., 187.
91. James K. A. Smith, *How (Not) to Be Secular: Reading Charles Taylor* (Grand Rapids, MI: Eerdmans, 2014), 62–63.
92. Ibid., 61.
93. Joseph R. Jeter and Ronald J. Allen, *One Gospel, Many Ears: Preaching for Different Listeners in the Congregation* (St Louis: Chalice, 2002), 59–60.
94. Biddle, *Reading Judges*, 128.

Preaching Wisdom to Australians

1. To the statement that 'there is a time for everything' Aussie culture responds with a resounding 'Yes! And that time is *now*!' Instead of pursuing the wisdom to choose between the good and the best, we pursue balance.
2. There are several features of Song of Songs that suggests it is wisdom literature (even though framed as love poetry). In particular, the importance of timing in this most powerful of human experiences: sexuality.
3. Donald, E. Gowan, *Reclaiming the Old Testament for the Christian Pulpit* (Edinburgh: John Knox, 1980), 100, 102.
4. Long, *Preaching*, 53.
5. Alyce M. McKenzie, *Preaching Proverbs: Wisdom for the Pulpit* (Louisville, KY: Westminster John Knox, 1996), xi.
6. Ibid.
7. Ibid, xiii.
8. The majority of these were broadcast on the Australian Christian Channel in early 2019 and are available on the Gymea Baptist Church website (www.gymeabaptist.org.au).
9. Alyce M. McKenzie, *Preaching Biblical Wisdom in a Self-Help Society* (Nashville: Abingdon, 2002), 27.
10. www.biblehub.com
11. Bruce K. Waltke, *The Book of Proverbs: Chapter 16–31* (Grand Rapids, MI.: Eerdmans, 2005), 11.
12. Roland Murphy, *Proverbs*, Word Bible Commentary, vol. 22 (Grand Rapids, MI: Eerdmans, 1998), 83.
13. R. N. Whybray, *Proverbs*, New Century Bible Commentary (Grand Rapids, MI: Eerdmans, 1994), 185.
14. Derek Kidner, *Proverbs*, Tyndale Old Testament Commentary (Leicester: Inter-Varsity Press, 1964), 93.
15. Paul Koptak, *Proverbs*, NIV Application Commentary (Grand Rapids, MI: Zondervan, 2003), 323.
16. McKenzie, *Preaching Biblical Wisdom*, 93.
17. Bruce K. Waltke, *The Book of Proverbs: Chapters 1–15* (Grand Rapids, MI: Eerdmans, 2004), 76.
18. Gordon D. Fee and Douglas Stuart, *How to Read the Bible for All Its Worth*, 4th edition (Grand Rapids, MI: Zondervan, 2014), 233.
19. Tremper Longman III, 'Preaching Wisdom' in *He Began with Moses ... Preaching the Old Testament Today*, ed. Grenville J. R. Kent et al (Nottingham: Inter-Varsity Press, 2010), 56.
20. Long, *Preaching and the Literary Forms of the Bible*, 56.
21. Geoff Aigner and Liz Skelton, *The Australian Leadership Paradox*, Sydney: Allen & Unwin, 2013.
22. Richard M. Steers, Luciara Nardon, and C. J. Sanchez-Runde, *Management across Cultures: Developing Global Competencies* (Cambridge: Cambridge University Press, 2013), 82.
23. Wright, *How to Preach and Teach the Old Testament*, 264. Wright also contrasts wisdom literature with the prophetic literature. Wisdom, he says, states what should be (especially in relationship to the monarchy) while the prophets tend to criticise the kings (265).
24. Wright, *How to Preach and Teach the Old Testament*, 264.
25. Ibid., 271.
26. Ibid., 268.

Preaching Psalms to Australians

1. John Donne, *The Showing Forth of Christ: Sermons of John Donne*, ed. Emand Fuller (New York: Harper and Row, 1964), 125. The lack of gender neutrality in this older material, and in other quotations throughout this chapter, is noted and lamented. However, out of respect for quoting the material as is, the original language is maintained.
2. J. Clinton McCann Jr. and James C. Howell, *Preaching the Psalms* (Nashville: Abingdon, 2001), 32.
3. Bernhard W. Anderson and Steven Bishop, *Out of the Depths: The Psalms Speak for Us Today* (Louisville, KY: Westminster John Knox, 2000), 203. Anderson also notes that it was during this period that the Psalter's formation was completed. This suggests that the formation was directly related to, and perhaps given impetus by, usage rather than that it was formed and *then* used.
4. Robert C. Gregg, trans., *The Life of Antony and the Letter to Marcellinus* (New York: Paulist Press, 1980), 109.
5. Jean Calvin, Arthur Golding and T. H. L. Parker, *A Commentary on the Psalms* (London: James Clarke, 1965), 16.
6. Patrick Jordan, 'An Appetite for God: Dorothy Day at 100. (Cover Story)', *Commonweal* 124, no. 18 (October 24, 1997): 14.
7. J. Clinton McCann, *Shape and Shaping of the Psalter*, JSOT Supplement Series 159 (JSOT Press, 1993). Another example of this kind of exercise is the more recent work by Nancy L. DeClaissé-Walford, ed., *The Shape and Shaping of the Book of Psalms: The Current State of Scholarship* (Atlanta: SBL Press, 2014) which highlights the ongoing discussion around this important issue.
8. An interesting example of this is Psalm 121. Although well-known to those familiar with the Psalter, it may be surprising to some that the psalm is one of the ascent psalms from 120–135, which were traditionally sung as worshippers ascended the temple mount.
9. Psalm 51, which is attributed to David following his encounter with Bathsheba and its consequences, has become a more universalised example of a prayer of repentance.
10. Hermann Gunkel, *Introduction to Psalms: The Genres of the Religious Lyric of Israel* (Macon: Mercer University Press, 1998).
11. Psalms 1, 19 and 119 are often considered to be Torah/wisdom psalms, Psalm 137 is a clear example of an imprecatory psalm while Psalm 45 is an example of a wedding song.
12. Lament psalms appear very early in the Psalter, beginning with Psalm 3, which is an individual lament. Psalm 44, while classic in its form as lament, expresses the distress of the community rather than an individual.
13. Claus Westermann, *Praise and Lament in the Psalms*, trans. Keith R Crim and Richard N Soulen (Atlanta, Ga.: J. Knox Press, 1981), 116ff. Westermann discusses the connections between declarative and descriptive praise along with their distinctive qualities.
14. Tremper Longman III, *Psalms: An Introduction and Commentary* (InterVarsity Press, 2014), xxxvii.
15. David J. Cohen, 'At the Edge of the Precipice: Psalm 89 as Liturgical Memory', *Paradosis* 2, no. 1 (2015): 134, 136.
16. Two of the most helpful books on Hebrew poetry are Alter's *The Art of Biblical Poetry* and Adele Berlin, Lida Knorina, and David Noel Freedman. *The Dynamics of Biblical Parallelism*. (Grand Rapids, MI: Eerdmans, 2008).
17. E.g. Hebrew poetry uses imagery in the form of similies, metaphors, personifications, anthropomorphism and also rhetorical devices such as alliteration, acrostics, word plays etc. All of which we find in a variety of poetry created within diverse cultural contexts.
18. Aelred Baker, 'Parallelism: England's Contribution to Biblical Studies', *The Catholic Biblical Quarterly* 35, no. 4 (October 1973): 429–40.

ENDNOTES

19   E.g. Psalm 30 is attributed to David at the dedication of the Temple. Psalm 46 is identified as being from the Korahites to be sung to Alamoth which seems to have been a known melody of some kind.

20   John T Willis, 'Song of Hannah and Psalm 113', *The Catholic Biblical Quarterly* 35, no. 2 (April 1973): 139–54.

21   Westermann, *Praise and Lament*, 257.

22   Walter Brueggemann, *The Message of the Psalms: A Theological Commentary* (Minneapolis: Augsburg, 1984).

23   It is interesting to note that Psalm 1 begins with the assertion, 'Happy are those who do not follow the advice of the wicked … ' with the final affirmation of Psalm 2 offering a kind of inclusion, but stating, 'Happy are those who take refuge in him'. (NRSV-A).

24   Catherine Brown Tkacz, 'Jesus, Esther and Psalm 22', *Catholic Biblical Quarterly* 70, no. 4 (2008): 710.

25   https://www.scimex.org/newsfeed/who-estimates-say-australian-is-the-most-depressed-country-in-the-western-pacific-region

26   https://www.beyondblue.org.au/

27   https://www.ncbi.nlm.nih.gov/pmc/articles/PMC486942/

28   https://mentalhealthdaily.com/2014/09/09/physical-symptoms-of-anxiety-and-stress/

29   Spurgeon, *Treasury of David*, 1:324.

30   Henry Ward Beecher, *Life Thoughts,* (Boston: Phillips Sampson, 1858), 8–10.

31   William Holladay, *The Psalms through Three Thousand Years: Prayerbook of a Cloud of Witnesses* (Minneapolis: Fortress, 1993), 359.

32   Australian Bureau of Statistics, 2071.0, 'Census of Population and Housing: Reflecting Australia – Stories from the Census, 2016', http://abs.gov.au/ausstats/abs@.nsf/Lookup/by%20Subject/2071.0~2016~Main%20Features~Snapshot%20of%20Australia,%202016~2 .

33   Natalie Skinner and Barbara Pocock, 'The Persistent Challenge: Living, Working and Caring in Australia', *Australian Work and Life Index 2014,* (Adelaide: Centre for Work + Life, 2014).

34   Ibid.

35   Ibid.

36   Karl Barth, *Call for God,* trans. A. T. Mackay (New York: Harper and Row, 1967), 40.

37   Russell A. Butkus, 'The Stewardship of Creation', *The Center for Christian Ethics at Baylor University* (2002): 20.

38   Walter Brueggemann, 'The Loss and Recovery of Creation in Old Testament Theology', *Theology Today* 53 (1996): 188.

39   Karl-Erik Sveiby and Tex Skuthorpe, *Treading Lightly: The Hidden Wisdom of the World's Oldest People* (Crows Nest: Allen & Unwin, 2006), xviii.

40   Richard Lischer, *The Preacher King: Martin Luther King, Jr. and the Word That Moved America* (New York: Oxford University Press, 1995), 219.

41   Brooke Prentis and Sandra Crowden, 'Learning to be Guests of Ancient Hosts in Ancient Lands' in *Thought Matters* 7 (The Journal of the Salvation Army Tri-Territorial Theological Forum, 2017).

42   And let us not forget that God makes 'wine that gladdens human hearts.'

43   McCann and Howell, *Preaching the Psalms,* 57.

44   Walter Brueggemann, *Finally Comes the Poet: Daring Speech for Proclamation* (Minneapolis: Fortress, 1989), viii.

45   McCann and Howell, *Preaching the Psalms,* 16.

46   Walter Brueggemann, *Spirituality of the Psalms* (Minneapolis: Augsburg, 2002).

47 John Goldingay, *Psalms Volume 1: Psalms 1–41* (Grand Rapids, MI: Baker Academic, 2006), 346. He summarises the theme of verses 1–2 as 'steady provision/shepherding'.

48 Robert Alter, *The Book of Psalms: A Translation with Commentary* (New York: W.W. Norton, 2007), 79. Alter explains the ambiguity of the Hebrew at this point arguing that he wants to retain the ideas of both shadow and death which seem implicit in the original language.

49 Roger E. Van Harn and Brent A. Strawn, eds, *Psalms for Preaching and Worship: A Lectionary Commentary* (Grand Rapids, MI: Eerdmans, 2009), 102.

50 Matthew 10:39.

51 Alter, *The Book of Psalms*, 80.

52 Erhard S. Gerstenberger, *Psalms: With an Introduction to Cultic Poetry Part 1* (Grand Rapids, MI: Eerdmans, 1988), 117.

53 David J. Cohen, 'Possession Is Nine-Tenths of the Law: Psalm 24, the Environment and Human Responsibility', Torch Trinity Journal 14, no. 1 (May 2011): 23–37, 27.

54 This seems to clearly be the case in Genesis 1 and 2 where God announces that various aspect of creation are 'good' and that humankind is 'very good.'

55 C. J. A. Vos, *Theopoetry of the Psalms* (Pretoria: Protea, 2005), 144.

56 Brueggemann, *The Message of the Psalms*, 42.

57 J. Clinton McCann, *A Theological Introduction to the Book of Psalms: The Psalms as Torah* (Nashville: Abingdon, 1993), 71.

58 This is a more literal translation of the Hebrew in this verse.

59 Genesis 1:28.

60 Revelation 21 also adds to the creation accounts to enhance our understanding of God's intentions for creation.

61 Cohen, 'Possession Is Nine-Tenths of the Law', 32.

62 Vos, *Theopoetry of the Psalms*, 144.

63 John 1:14 (MSG).

64 Cohen, 'Possession Is Nine-Tenths of the Law', 32.

65 'The Legacy: An Elder's Vision for Our Sustainable Future', *Mornings with Margaret Throsby* (ABC Classic FM, December 15, 2010), http://www.abc.net.au/classic//throsby/stories/s3090417.htm.

66 Nick Spencer, *Christianity, Climate Change and Sustainable Living*, illustrated edition (London: SPCK, 2007), 94. Italics ours.

Preaching the Prophets to Australians

1 In this chapter I will discuss the so-called Latter Prophets of Isaiah, Jeremiah, Ezekiel and The Twelve (sometimes called the Minor Prophets). I assume that Lamentations and Daniel raise different hermeneutical and homiletical concerns.

2 For example, Goldsworthy, *According to Plan*; C. H. H. Scobie, *The Ways of Our God: An Approach to Biblical Theology*. (Grand Rapids, MI: Eerdmans, 2003); Vaughan Roberts, *God's Big Picture: Tracing the Story-Line of the Bible* (Leicester: Inter-Varsity Press, 2003).

3 See https://thebibleproject.com

4 Kirk R. Patston, *Isaiah: Surprising Salvation*, Reading the Bible Today (Sydney: Aquila Press, 2010), 232.

5 Joel Rosenberg, 'Jeremiah and Ezekiel', in *The Literary Guide to the Bible*, ed. Robert Alter and Frank Kermod (London: Fontana, 1989), 193.

6   Anonymous, 'Plot Parallel', https://tvtropes.org/pmwiki/pmwiki.php/Main/PlotParallel. Although dated, I have used episodes of the Australian drama SeaChange to illustrate this. Some congregations might appreciate that it is also a Shakespearean device.

7   Dan Barker, *God: The Most Unpleasant Character in All Fiction* (New York: Sterling, 2016).

8   Andrew Sloane, 'Aberrant Textuality?: The Case of Ezekiel the (Porno) Prophet', *Tyndale Bulletin* 59 (2008): 53–76.

9   Walter Brueggemann, 'The Recovering God of Hosea', *Horizons in Biblical Theology* 30 (2008): 5–20.

10 Walter Brueggemann, *Theology of the Old Testament*, 503.

11 For example, Andrew West, 'Restoring Ethics and Faith in Politics', http://www.abc.net.au/radionational/programs/religionandethicsreport/restoring-ethics-and-faith-in-religion/10281626

12 von Rad, *Old Testament Theology*, 273–7.

Preaching New Testament Narrative to Australians

1   Paul Ricoeur, *Hermeneutics and the Human Sciences* (Cambridge: Cambridge University Press, 1981), 278–9; Fee and Stuart, *How to Read the Bible for All Its Worth*, 79–80.

2   For a fuller discussion of the importance of preaching through biblical books in their entirely, and an exploration of strategies for doing so, see Tim Patrick and Andrew Reid, *The Whole Counsel of God: Why and How to Preach the Entire Bible* (Wheaton: Crossway, 2020).

3   See Kevin J. Vanhoozer, *Is There a Meaning in this Text?* (Leicester: Apollos, 1998), 336; and 'The Semantics of Biblical Literature: Truth and Scripture's Diverse Literary Forms', in *Hermeneutics, Authority and Canon,* eds D. A. Carson and J. D. Woodbridge (Leicester: Inter-Varsity Press, 1986), 81.

4   D. N. Fewell, 'The Work of Biblical Narrative' in *The Oxford Handbook of Biblical Narrative,* ed. Fewell, D.N. (Oxford: Oxford University Press, 2016), 4.

5   See Vanhoozer, *Meaning*, 341–3.

6   Ibid., 340.

7   Ibid., 338.

8   Ibid., 348.

9   Ibid., 340, 343.

10 Ibid., 341.

11 Jerome Bruner, 'The Narrative Construction of Reality', *Critical Inquiry* 18, no. 1 (1991), 6–7, 13; Fee and Stuart, *How to Read the Bible for All Its Worth*, 82.

12 Grant R. Osborne, *The Hermeneutical Spiral: A Comprehensive Introduction to Biblical Interpretation* (Downers Grove, IL: InterVarsity Press, 1991), 159; Fee and Stuart, *How to Read the Bible for All Its Worth*, 82–83.

13 See Vanhoozer, *Meaning*, 341.

14 Susan Sniader Lanser, *The Narrative Act: Point of View in Prose Fiction* (Princeton: Princeton University Press, 1981), 92–97.

15 Osborne, *Hermeneutical Spiral*, 156–7; Tremper Longman III, *Literary Approaches to Biblical Interpretation* (Grand Rapids, MI: Acadamie Books, 1987), 85–88.

16 Osborne, *Hermeneutical Spiral*, 162–3; Bruner, *Narrative Construction*, 9–10.

17 See Vanhoozer, *Meaning*, 348.

18 Fewell, *Biblical Narrative*, 6, 10; Vanhoozer, 'Semantics', 81.

19 Longman, *Literary Approaches*, 86.

20 Vanhoozer, 'Semantics', 79–80.

21 Osborne, *Hermeneutical Spiral*, 172.

22 Fewell, *Biblical Narrative*, 18.

23 See N. T. Wright, *The Resurrection of the Son of God* (London: SPCK, 2003), 415–29, for a fuller discussion of this passage.

Preaching Paul's Epistles to Australians

1   See the excellent introduction to these challenges in William Arp, 'Preaching the Epistles', *Journal of Ministry and Theology* 17 (2013).

2   Ben Witherington III in Dallas Theological Seminary, 'Jesus, Canon, and Theology', http://www.dts.edu/media/play/jesus-canon-and-theology-darrell-l-bock-daniel-b-wallace-and-ben-witherington/.

3   Quicke observes, 'Scripture not only says things but also does things', and that the task of preaching is 'designing a sermon that says *and does* the same things the biblical text says *and does*'. Michael J. Quicke, *360-Degree Preaching: Hearing, Speaking, and Living the Word* (Grand Rapids, MI: Baker Academic, 2003), 53, 131.

4   Scot McKnight, *The Blue Parakeet: Rethinking How You Read the Bible* (Grand Rapids, MI: Zondervan, 2008), 49–52.

5   Note the warning of Haddon Robinson: 'Even in what is billed as 'expository preaching' the verses can become launching pads for the preacher's own opinions'. Haddon W. Robinson, *Biblical Preaching: The Development and Delivery of Expository Messages*, 2nd ed. (Grand Rapids, MI: Baker Academic, 2001), 25.

6   With apologies to Pentecostal readers, but you know how conservatives can be sometimes.

7   In speech-act terms, broadly speaking they communicate the 'locution', or meaning of the biblical text, but ignore or minimise the 'illocution', or force of the text. See Sam Chan, *Preaching as the Word of God: Answering an Old Question with Speech-Act Theory* (Eugene, OR: Pickwick, 2016), especially chapter 10, for an introduction to speech-act theory as it pertains to preaching.

8   I present this argument more fully in Tim MacBride, *Catching the Wave: Preaching the New Testament as Rhetoric* (Nottingham: Inter-Varsity Press, 2016), xi–xiii.

9   'The question, 'What is the passage trying to do?' may well mark the beginning of homiletical obedience.' David Buttrick, 'Interpretation and Preaching', *Interpretation* 25 (1981): 58.

10 Fred B. Craddock, *Preaching* (Nashville: Abingdon, 1985), 28. See also Thomas G. Long, *The Witness of Preaching*, 2nd ed. (Louisville, KY: Westminster John Knox, 2005), 189–90.

11 Chan helpfully puts this in the language of speech act theory: 'The preacher's speech act is the same as the speech act – locution and illocution – of the Scripture passage that is being "expounded"'. Chan, *Preaching as the Word of God*, 217.

12 Lloyd Bitzer, 'The Rhetorical Situation', *Philosophy and Rhetoric* 1 (1968): 6–8.

13 'He would much rather persuade so that the person being persuaded has a chance to embrace the vision on his own.' Ben Witherington, *The Letters to Philemon, the Colossians, and the Ephesians: A Socio-Rhetorical Commentary on the Captivity Epistles* (Grand Rapids, MI: Eerdmans, 2007), 94; see also 59.

14 Fee and Stuart, *How to Read the Bible for All Its Worth*, 31, encourage this practice: 'The answer to this question is usually to be found – when it can be found – within the book itself. But one needs to learn to read with their eyes open for such matters. If you want to corroborate your own findings on these questions, you might consult ... the introduction to a good commentary on the book'.

15 For an introduction to New Testament rhetoric in general, see Ben Witherington, *New Testament Rhetoric: An Introductory Guide to the Art of Persuasion in and of the New Testament* (Eugene, OR:

16. Donald W. Engels, *Roman Corinth: An Alternative Model for the Classical City* (Chicago: University of Chicago, 1990), 43–65.

17. Gordon D. Fee, *The First Epistle to the Corinthians* (Grand Rapids, MI: Eerdmans, 1987), 1–3.; Richard B. Hays, *First Corinthians*, Interpretation (Louisville, KY: Westminister John Knox, 2011), 3.

18. Ben Witherington, *Conflict and Community in Corinth: A Socio-Rhetorical Commentary on 1 and 2 Corinthians* (Grand Rapids, MI: Eerdmans, 1995), 23–24.

19. Roy E. Ciampa and Brian S. Rosner, *The First Letter to the Corinthians*, The Pillar New Testament Commentary (Grand Rapids, MI: Eerdmans, 2010), 3.

20. Lucian, *Merc. Cond.* 25, noted that a wealthy man would want to be associated with the best orators because 'it will make people think him … a person of taste in literary matters'.

21. Dio Chrysostom, 8.9. See also Sen., *Controv.* 10.15; Suetonius, *Tib.* 11.3; Philostr., *V.S.* 1.8.490.

22. Witherington, *New Testament Rhetoric*, 11; Bruce W. Winter, 'Is Paul among the Sophists?', *Reformed Theological Review* 53 (1994).

23. Witherington, *Conflict and Community in Corinth*, 41–42.

24. This is no longer restricted to the 'tabloid' sensationalism of news and current affairs programs, but has extended to programs set up to be informative and persuasive as well as humorous and satirical: for example, *The Project* and *The Weekly*, reflecting US trends such as *The Daily Show* and *Last Week Tonight*.

25. The part of a discourse in which the speaker narrated the facts that have occasioned the address.

26. So Margaret M. Mitchell, *Paul and the Rhetoric of Reconciliation* (Louisville, KY: Westminster John Knox, 1993), passim.; Stephen M. Pogoloff, *Logos and Sophia: The Rhetorical Situation of 1 Corinthians*, Dissertation Series / Sbl (Atlanta: Scholars Press, 1992), 102–03.; Witherington, *Conflict and Community in Corinth*, 74.; Larry L. Welborn, *Politics and Rhetoric in the Corinthian Epistles* (Macon: Mercer University Press, 1997), 6.

27. Pogoloff, 100–02.

28. Ibid., 273–74.

29. Ibid., 195–96.

30. For the majority view, see Witherington, *Conflict and Community in Corinth*, 24.; for the minority, see ibid., 196.

31. Duane A. Litfin, *St. Paul's Theology of Proclamation: 1 Corinthians 1–4 and Greco-Roman Rhetoric*, Snts Monograph Series (Cambridge: Cambridge University Press, 1994), 86., notes the pervasive culture of critique surrounding public oratory in Corinth.

32. Gordon D. Fee, *Paul's Letter to the Philippians* (Grand Rapids, MI: Eerdmans, 1995), 25–26.; Daniel L. Migliore, *Philippians and Philemon* (Louisville, KY: Westminster John Knox, 2014), 9–10.; Ben Witherington, *Paul's Letter to the Philippians: A Socio-Rhetorical Commentary* (Grand Rapids, MI: Eerdmans, 2011), 5.

33. 'Paul is trying to get his audience to raise their sights to a higher and prior kind of citizenship which includes all of them, not just an elite few. They are all to live as citizens worthy of the gospel', Witherington, *Paul's Letter to the Philippians*, 100.

34. *The Letters to Philemon, the Colossians, and the Ephesians: A Socio-Rhetorical Commentary on the Captivity Epistles*, 110–11.

35. Michael F. Bird, *Colossians & Philemon: A New Covenant Commentary* (Cambridge : Lutterworth Press, 2009), 73–74, 85.; Witherington, *Philemon, the Colossians, and the Ephesians*, 129–30.

36. Key ancient sources include Aristotle, *Ars Rhetorica*; Cicero, *de Oratore*; and Quintilian, *Institutio Oratoria*.

37 The possible exception is 2 Timothy, which is the only truly personal letter. Note how Paul mentions this practice of reading his letters aloud in Col 4:16.

38 See my overview of how to apply the principles of rhetorical criticism to preaching, in MacBride, *Catching the Wave*. For a defence of the appropriateness of applying this to Paul's letters, see my more technical discussion in *Preaching the New Testament as Rhetoric: The Promise of Rhetorical Criticism for Expository Preaching*, Act Monograph (Eugene, OR: Wipf & Stock, 2014), 22–35. See also Frank Hughes, 'The Rhetoric of Letters', in *The Thessalonian Debate: Methodological Discord or Methodological Synthesis?*, ed. Karl P. Donfried and Johannes Beutler (Grand Rapids, MI: Eerdmans, 2000). For an analysis of Paul's letters according to rhetorical conventions, Ben Witherington's commentaries as well as the *Paideia* series are a good starting point.

39 Mitchell, *Rhetoric of Reconciliation*, 9, warns us that 'one should not expect a deliberative or epideictic argument to follow the exact same arrangement as the forensic models from the handbooks'.

40 Witherington, *New Testament Rhetoric*, 16.

41 Long, *Preaching and the Literary Forms of the Bible*, 122–4, arrives at this approach as an example of preaching the text within its rhetorical situation.

42 This is the typical function of one of the three genres of rhetoric known as *epideictic*: the praising of a person or subject in order to inspire emulation. 1 Corinthians 13 is an epideictic interlude in a deliberative speech appealing for unity.

43 MacBride, *Preaching the New Testament as Rhetoric*, 116.

44 Scott Nash, *1 Corinthians*, Smyth & Helwys Bible Commentary (Macon: Smyth & Helwys, 2009), 92.

45 Witherington, *Conflict and Community in Corinth*, 113.

46 This contrasts with the many leaders in US folklore like Patton, Lee, Grant, MacArthur, etc. See, for example, Paul Keating's 'Eulogy for the Unknown Soldier', 11 November 1993: 'On all sides they were the heroes of that war: not the generals and the politicians, but the soldiers and sailors and nurses – those who taught us to endure hardship, show courage, to be bold as well as resilient, to believe in ourselves, to stick together'. Cited in Sally Warhaft, *Well May We Say … : The Speeches That Made Australia*, rev. ed. (Melbourne: Text, 2014), 138. A notable exception is Peter Fitzsimons' *Monash's Masterpiece*, a recent attempt to bring General Sir John Monash greater public acknowledgement.

47 See e.g., Epic. *Diss.*, 2.5.35; Sen. *Ep.*, 2.31.7; and especially Livy, 2.32.12.

48 Robinson, *Biblical Preaching*, 157., famously argued that 'the most powerful illustrations are those where your personal experience overlaps your listener's personal experience … [but the] least effective illustrations speak from the speaker's learned experience and into the audience's learned experience … [since] the audience may *understand* the illustration, but listeners will not *experience* it' (italics mine).

49 One important source is cinema, if Australian film maker George Miller is correct in his observation that the multiplex has become the new 'cathedral' and that film makers have become the 'new priests' who provide society with its shared stories. George Miller, cited in Michael Frost, *Eyes Wide Open: Seeing God in the Ordinary* (Sutherland: Albatross, 1998), 100.

50 Much of the material here is from David Starling, 'Preaching on Sex in a Post-Christendom World', in *Morling College Preaching Conference* (Morling College, 2018).

51 Nash, *1 Corinthians*, 147. Although one of the specifics is beyond even pagan tolerance (5:1), the general practices listed (5:9–11) and especially the visiting of prostitutes (6:15–16) were common in the surrounding culture. Further, see Kyle Harper, *From Shame to Sin: The Christian Transformation of Sexual Morality in Late Antiquity* (Cambridge, MA: Harvard University Press, 2013), 44–47, 52–60.

52 Will Deming, *Paul on Marriage and Celibacy: The Hellenistic Background of 1 Corinthians 7*, 2nd ed. (Grand Rapids, MI: Eerdmans, 2004), 48–57.; see also Antipater of Tarsus, *On Marriage* (*Stoicorum Vetica Fragmenta* 3.254–57), and Diogenes Laertius, *Lives* 6.51; 10.119.

53 Hervé Carrier, *The Sociology of Religious Belonging* (New York: Herder and Herder, 1965), 218.

ENDNOTES

54 This insight comes firstly from discussions with Chinese and Korean Bible college students, although there are, of course, many other cultures in which practices around idol worship and food need to be negotiated. For the scholarly discussion, see Khiok-Khng Yeo, 'The Rhetorical Hermeneutic of 1 Corinthians 8 and Chinese Ancestor Worship', *Biblical Interpretation* 2 (1994); Oh-Young Kwon, *1 Corinthians 1–4: Reconstructing Its Social and Rhetorical Situation and Re-Reading It Cross-Culturally for Korean-Confucian Christians Today* (Eugene, OR: Wipf & Stock, 2010), 209–28.; Greg Jao, 'Honor and Obey', in *Following Jesus without Dishonoring Your Parents: Asian American Discipleship*, ed. Jeanette Yep and Peter Cha (Downers Grove, IL: InterVarsity Press, 1998).

55 Mitchell, *Rhetoric of Reconciliation*, 31–32.; Kei Eun Chang, *The Community, the Individual and the Common Good*: Τὸ Ἴδιον *and* Τὸ Συμφέρον *in the Greco-Roman World and Paul* (London: Bloomsbury T&T Clark, 2013).

56 See the 'Describing Australians' chapter.

57 Witherington, *Conflict and Community in Corinth*, 306–07.

58 See, as but one example, the blog of the atheist Sam Harris: 'People of faith tend to ignore the coming resurrection of the dead – perhaps because the idea is so obviously preposterous. And yet this is precisely the form of afterlife one must expect if one is to be a serious Jew, Christian or Muslim' ('Will the Dead Walk Again?', 31 March 2011, <http://www.samharris.org/blog/item/the-coming-resurrection-of-the-dead/2011>).

59 Peter L. Berger, *A Rumor of Angels: Modern Society and the Rediscovery of the Supernatural* (Garden City, NY: Doubleday, 1969), 49–75, esp. 52ff.

60 'These Fellowing Men', in Dame Mary Gilmore, *The Passionate Heart* (Sydney: Angus & Robertson, 1918), 1.

61 In preaching Galatians 4:8–20 we would, of course, bring out the emotion-rich *pathos* Paul uses. Likewise, we would arouse our audience's indignation towards those who would seek to impose cultural practices on others for their own selfish reasons, when preaching Galatians 6:11–18. See MacBride, *Catching the Wave*, chapter 10.; Steven J. Kraftchik, 'Πάθη in Paul: The Emotional Logic of "Original Argument"', in *Paul and Pathos*, ed. Thomas H. Olbricht and Jerry L. Sumney (Atlanta: SBL Press, 2001).

62 See Gal 4:17; 6:12–13.

63 B. C. Lategan, 'The Argumentative Situation of Galatians', in *The Galatians Debate: Contemporary Issues in Rhetorical and Historical Interpretation*, ed. Mark D. Nanos (Peabody, MA: Hendrickson, 2002), 395. Mark D. Nanos, 'The Inter- and Intra-Jewish Political Context of Paul's Letter to the Galatians', ibid., 397–8, adds the possibility that the attraction was also the promise of fitting in with Jewish believers, since their following of Jesus would have pushed them to the margins of civic life as a result of their non-participation in the imperial cult, among other things.

64 Stanley Kent Stowers, 'Paul and Self-Mastery', in *Paul in the Greco-Roman World: A Handbook*, ed. J. Paul Sampley (London: Bloomsbury T&T Clark, 2016), 531–3; Craig S. Keener, *Galatians*, New Cambridge Bible Commentary (Cambridge: Cambridge University Press, 2018), 20; Josephus *Ag. Ap.* 2.282.

65 Phil Rothfield, 'Blake Ferguson Converts to Islam', *Sunday Telegraph*, 9 November 2013, https://www.dailytelegraph.com.au/news/nsw/news-story/f0b816041ab90b16c79d66be709189a0.

66 Richard N. Longenecker, *Galatians*, Word Biblical Commentary (Dallas: Word, 1990), 89; Douglas J. Moo, *Galatians*, Baker Exegetical Commentary on the New Testament (Grand Rapids, MI: Baker Academic, 2013), 165.

67 Henry Cloud, 'Action Steps for Monday', in *Willow Creek Global Leadership Summit*, DVD, 2005.

68 John Ortberg, *The Life You've Always Wanted* (Grand Rapids, MI: Zondervan, 2002), chapter 3.

69 With apologies to Louie Giglio, *How Great is Our God*.

Preaching the Petrine Epistles to Australians

1. Seamus O'Hanlon, *City Life: The New Urban Australia* (Sydney: UNSW Press, 2018), 8.
2. Ibid, 12.
3. Alan Kreider, *The Patient Ferment of the Early Church* (Grand Rapids, MI: Baker, 2016). Kindle Edition. While scholars differ on the structure of 1 Peter, I have followed the basic structure accepted by most commentators.
4. David Scutt, 'Here are the Professions Australians Trust the Most – and those we Think Are Dodgy', *Business Insider Australia*, 12 May 2016, https://www.businessinsider.com.au/here-are-the-professions-australians-trust-the-most-and-those-we-think-are-dodgy-2016-5.
5. Stuart Piggin, *Evangelical Christianity in Australia*. Oxford: University Press, 1996, 10.
6. Baird, 'Domestic Violence in the Church'.
7. See the sensitive treatment of this passage by Mary Willson, 'Following Jesus Far from Home (1 Peter 2:11–3:12)', in *Resurrection Life in a World of Suffering: 1 Peter*, eds. D. A. Carson and Kathleen Neilson (Wheaton: Crossway, 2018). Kindle Edition.
8. Ernst Käsemann, 'An Apologia for Primitive Christian Eschatology', in *Essays on New Testament Themes* (Studies in Biblical Theology, 1964), 169.
9. Nancy Guthrie and John Piper, 'Help me Teach 1 Peter', in *Resurrection Life in a World of Suffering: 1 Peter*, eds D. A. Carson and Kathleen Neilson (Wheaton: Crossway, 2018). Kindle Edition
10. William Wilberforce, *A Practical View of the Prevailing Religious System of Professed Christians: In the Higher and Middle Classes in This Country Contrasted with Real Christianity* (Glasgow: William Collins, 1833), 106.
11. For example, Sam Allbery, *Is God Anti-Gay?* London: Good Book Company, 2013, and Ed Shaw, *The Plausibility Problem: The Church and Same-Sex Attraction*. (Nottingham: Inter-Varsity Press, 2015).
12. There are three main views on interpreting 1 Peter 3:19–20: 1) The spirits are the fallen angels who are now in prison because of their sin in the days of Noah (Genesis 6:1–4). 2) After his resurrection, Jesus went and preached judgment to the spirits in prison, who are the wicked of Noah's day. 3) The Spirit of Jesus was preaching through Noah to the wicked of his day, who are now captives in prison.

Preaching the Johannine Letters to Australians

1. The source is Jerome and a translation can be found in R. A. Culpepper, *John. The son of Zebedee; the Life of a Legend.* (Edinburgh: T&T Clark, 2000), 165.
2. Constantine Campbell, *1,2 and 3 John.* (Grand Rapids, MI: Zondervan, 2017), 7, briefly surveys the different options suggested.
3. Jason L. Merritt, *Devils and Deviants. Religious Schism in 1 and 2 John* (Eugene, OR: Pickwick, 2017), 1; Colin Kruse, *The Letters of John* (Grand Rapids, MI: Eerdmans, 2000), 27, gives one account of the 'secessionists' and their teaching.
4. Daniel L. Akin, *1, 2, 3 John* (Nashville: Holman Reference, 2001), 29–30.
5. Daniel Streett, *They Went Out from Us: The Identity of the Opponents in First John* (Berlin: De Gruyter, 2011) comprehensively outlines the various options that have been proposed.
6. The classical expression of this threefold test is found in R. Law, *Tests of Life. A Study of the First Epistle of St John*. 3rd ed. (Grand Rapids, MI: Baker, 1968).
7. Judith M. Lieu, 'Authority to Become Children of God: A Study of 1 John' *Novum Testamentum* 23 (1981): 210–28; H-J. Schmid, 'How to Read the First Epistle of John Non-Polemically', *Biblica* 85 (2004): 21–41; Terry Griffiths, *Keep Yourselves from Idols: A New Look at 1 John*. JSNT Supplementary Series 233 (Sheffield: Sheffield Academic Press, 2004).

ENDNOTES

8 Merritt, *Devils and Deviants*.

9 For succinct and helpful overviews of the positions taken by commentators see Akin *1,2,3 John*, 37–48; Martin. M. Culy, *I, II, II John: A Handbook on the Greek Text*. (Waco, TX: Baylor University Press, 2004), xii–xx; Matthew D. Jensen, 'The Structure and Argument of 1 John: A Survey of Proposals', *Currents in Biblical Research* 12, no. 2 (2014), 194–215.

10 Ibid., 207.

11 Matthew D. Jensen, 'The Structure and Argument of 1 John', *JSNT* 35, no. 1 (2012): 54–73.

12 Jensen, 'Survey of Proposals', 57.

13 Ibid., 60–61.

14 For a comment on this see Culy, *Handbook*, xx.

15 Andrew Cameron, *Joined Up Life* (Leicester: Inter-Varsity Press, 2011), 52–53.

16 Cameron, *Joined Up Life*, 52.

17 See also the title of Craig Bartholomew and Thorsten Moritz, *Christ and Consumerism: Reflections on the Spirit of our Age* (Carlisle: Paternoster, 2000).

18 Gordon McConville, 'The Old Testament and the Enjoyment of Wealth', in Bartholomew and Moritz, *Christ and Consumerism*, 34–53, esp. 50.

19 See the other essays in Bartholomew and Moritz, *Christ and Consumerism* for details.

20 Jackman helpfully comments that the errors of John's day 'were really an accommodation to the prevailing ideas of the secular culture', in David Jackman, *The Message of John's Letters: Living in the Love of God* (Leicester: Inter-Varsity Press, 1988), 17.

21 Marianne Meye Thompson, *1–3 John* (Downers Grove, IL: InterVarsity Press, 1992), 28.

22 Thompson, *John*, 28.

23 See Matthew D. Jensen, *Affirming the Resurrection of the Incarnate Christ: A Reading of 1 John*. (Cambridge: Cambridge University Press, 2012) for an exposition suggesting the opening verses of 1 John extend to the resurrection of Jesus and not just the incarnation.

24 James A. Holstein and Jaber F. Gubrium, *The Self We Live By: Narrative Identity in a Postmodern World* (Oxford: Oxford University Press, 2012); Walter Truett Anderson, *The Future of the Self; Inventing the Postmodern Person* (New York: Putnam, 1997).

25 Robert Yarbrough, *1–3 John*. (Grand Rapids, MI: Baker Academic, 2008), 26.

26 See for example Mark Manson, 'The Virtue of Doubt', *The Observer*, 6 July 2016, https://observer.com/2016/06/the-virtue-of-doubt/.

27 Gabrielle Carey, 'On Being Australian', *Griffith Review* 51 (January 2016), accessed online at https://griffithreview.com/articles/on-being-australian-carey/.

28 Yarbrough, *1–3 John*, 27.

Preaching Hebrews, James and Jude to Australians

1 Hebrews 1:3. All biblical references in this chapter are taken from the NIV unless otherwise stated.

2 For an interesting discussion on the wider context of Luther's claim, and the attitude of the Reformers to James, see Timothy George, '"A Right Strawy Epistle": Reformation Perspectives on James', *Southern Baptist Journal of Theology* 4, no. 3 (2000).

3 Jude 22.

4 Ben Witherington III, *Letter and Homilies for Jewish Christians: A Socio-Rhetorical Commentary on Hebrews, James and Jude* (Grand Rapids, MI: InterVarsity Press, 2010), 11.

5 Ibid., 7–10.

6	His claim that these three letters are primarily sermons seems to have weight. For example, Alec Motyer opens his commentary on James with the words: 'As soon as we read through the letter of James we say to ourselves, "This man was a preacher before he was a writer"'. A little later he writes, 'We cannot help asking ourselves, therefore, if a spoken original lies behind the letter as we have it …' Alec Motyer, *The Message of James*, The Bible Speaks Today (Leicester: Inter-Varsity Press, 1985), 11. Douglas Moo, in his commentary on Jude, approvingly notes that 'F. Duane Watson has made a convincing case that the letter of Jude follows typical ancient rhetorical procedures'. Douglas J. Moo, *2 Peter and Jude*, The NIV Application Commentary Series (Grand Rapids, MI: Zondervan, 1996), 232.
7	For more on this, see my book Brian Harris, *When Faith Turns Ugly: Understanding Toxic Faith and How to Avoid It* (Milton Keynes: Paternoster, 2016).
8	The 2016 census showed that 52.1 percent of Australians were happy to be classified as Christian (no matter how nominally so), down from the 61.1% who claimed this title in 2011 – a drop of 9% in only five years. In 1991 it was 74%. http://abs.gov.au/ausstats/abs@.nsf/Lookup/by%20Subject/2071.0~2016~Main%20Features~Religion%20Data%20Summary~70
9	Kenneth Schenck, *Understanding the Book of Hebrews: The Story Behind the Sermon* (Louisville, KY: Westminster John Knox, 2003), 1.
10	Quoted in Eusebius, 'Ecclesiastical History', (325).
11	See Mary Ann Beavis and HyeRan Kim-Cragg, *Hebrews*, ed. Barbara E. Reid, vol. 54, Wisdom Commentary (Collegeville: Liturgical Press, 2015), lviii–lxii.
12	David DeSilva, *Perseverance in Gratitude: A Socio-Rhetorical Commentary on the Epistle 'to the Hebrews'* (Grand Rapids, MI: Eerdmans, 2000), 21.
13	Ibid., 2.
14	For the argument against an essentially Jewish readership, see ibid., 2–7. As a result of his argument, DeSilva concludes that the letter is 'unfortunately named'. Ibid., 6.
15	For a rationale for this, see the argument of Peter H. Davids. Peter H. Davids, *A Theology of James, Peter and Jude*, ed. Andreas J. Köstenberger, Biblical Theology of the New Testament (Grand Rapids, MI: Zondervan, 2014), 36–41.
16	Robert W. Wall, *Community of the Wise: The Letter of James*, ed. Howard Clark Kee and J. Andrew Overman, The New Testament in Context (Valley Forge: Trinity Press, 1997), 40.
17	Christopher W. Morgan, *A Theology of James: Wisdom for God's People*, ed. Robert A. Peterson, Explorations in Biblical Theology (Phillipsburg, NJ: P&R, 2010).
18	Dietrich Bonhoeffer, *The Cost of Discipleship*, 6th ed. (London: SCM, 1959), 35.
19	Thus James 2:17, 'faith by itself, if it is not accompanied by action, is dead.'
20	James 1:1
21	Motyer, *Message of James*, 23.
22	Edgar V. McKnight and Christopher Church, *Hebrews-James*, Smyth & Helwys Bible Commentary (Macon: Smyth & Helwys, 2004), 335.
23	Davids argues over one third of 2Peter is based on Jude. Davids, 251.
24	Bonhoeffer, 35.
25	Jude 1.
26	Davids, 255.
27	Ibid., 256.
28	Jude 4.
29	Jude 4.
30	Jude 4.

31 James 2:1–14.

32 Writing of Australians, Frank Fletcher says: 'With dead-pan flatness we mock the pretentiousness of the gentry … but still long for their approval'. Frank Fletcher, 'Drink from the Wells of Oz', in *Discovering an Australian Theology*, ed. Peter Malone (Homebush: St Paul, 1988), 65–66.

33 People often dismissively make comments like: 'Probably drinks it all away'.

34 For an elaboration on this, see Harris, *When Faith Turns Ugly*, 134–48.

35 Luke 15:11–32.

36 Brian Harris, 'Of Tall Poppies, Mateship and Pragmatism: Spirituality in the Australasian Context', *Stimulus* 16, no. 3 (2008): 18.

Preaching Revelation to Australians

1 Darrell W. Johnson, *Discipleship on the Edge: An Expository Journey through the Book of Revelation* (Vancouver: Regent College Publishing, 2004), 20.

2 Gilbert K. Chesterton, *Orthodoxy* (London: Bodley Head, 1909), 13.

3 Arthur William Wainwright, *Mysterious Apocalypse: Interpreting the Book of Revelation* (Eugene, OR: Wipf and Stock, 1993), 49–52.

4 Craig R. Koester, *Revelation and the End of All Things* (Grand Rapids, MI: Eerdmans, 2001), 11–12.

5 Steve Gregg, *Revelation, Four Views: A Parallel Commentary* (Nashville: Thomas Nelson, 1997), 34–35.

6 Ibid., 42.

7 Wainwright, *Mysterious Apocalypse*, 33–48.

8 Donald A. Carson and Douglas J. Moo, *An Introduction to the New Testament* (Grand Rapids, MI: Zondervan, 2005), 719–20.

9 David Arthur DeSilva, *Seeing Things John's Way: The Rhetoric of the Book of Revelation* (Louisville, KY: Westminster John Knox, 2009), 9–14.

10 Ibid., 13.

11 Richard Bauckham, *The Theology of the Book of Revelation*, New Testament Theology (Cambridge: CUP, 1993), 17.

12 Michael J. Gorman, *Reading Revelation Responsibly: Uncivil Worship and Witness: Following the Lamb into the New Creation* (Eugene, OR: Cascade, 2011), 42.

13 R. James Ferguson, 'Rome and Parthia: Power Politics and Diplomacy across Cultural Frontiers', *Centre for East-West Cultural and Economic Studies Research Papers* (2005).

14 Gorman, *Reading Revelation Responsibly*, 58.

15 I. Howard Marshall, *New Testament Theology: Many Witnesses, One Gospel* (Downers Grove, IL: InterVarsity Press, 2004), 548.

16 Bauckham, *Theology of the Book of Revelation*, 16.

17 DeSilva, *Seeing Things John's Way*, 14.

18 Ibid.

19 Ibid., 10.

20 Johnson, *Discipleship on the Edge*, 35.

21 For a good summary of the theology of Revelation see Carson and Moo, *Introduction to the New Testament*, 721–22.

22 Bauckham, *Theology of the Book of Revelation*, 23.

23 Ibid., 35.

24 J. Nelson Kraybill, *Apocalypse and Allegiance: Worship, Politics, and Devotion in the Book of Revelation* (Grand Rapids, MI: Brazos Press, 2010), 101.

25 Gorman, *Reading Revelation Responsibly*, 43.

26 Bauckham, *Theology of the Book of Revelation*, 35.

27 Mark McCrindle, 'Faith and Belief in Australia', (Sydney: McCrindle Research, 2017), 8.

28 Bauckham, *Theology of the Book of Revelation*, 159.

29 Mike Graves, *The Sermon as Symphony: Preaching the Literary Forms of the New Testament* (Valley Forge, PA.: Judson Press, 1997), 239.

30 Kraybill, *Apocalypse and Allegiance*, 33–36.

31 James K. A. Smith, *You Are What You Love: The Spiritual Power of Habit* (Grand Rapids, MI: Brazos Press, 2016), 1–25.

32 James K. A. Smith, *Imagining the Kingdom:* (Grand Rapids, MI: Baker Academic, 2013), 40.

33 Smith, *You Are What You Love*, 11.

34 Smith, *Imagining the Kingdom*, 38–41.

35 Ibid., 38.

36 James K. A. Smith, *Desiring the Kingdom: Worship, Worldview, and Cultural Formation* (Grand Rapids, MI: Baker Academic, 2009), 92.

37 Tom Stafford, 'Psychology: Why Bad News Dominates the Headlines', *Future*, 29 July 2014, http://www.bbc.com/future/story/20140728-why-is-all-the-news-bad.

38 Hugh Mackay, 'The State of the Nation Starts in Your Street', *Gandhi Oration*, 2 February 2017, https://theconversation.com/hugh-mackay-the-state-of-the-nation-starts-in-your-street-72264.

39 David L. Barr, 'John's Ironic Empire', *Interpretation* 63, no. 1 (2009): 20.

40 Moral letters to Lucilius/Letter 60.3. https://en.wikisource.org/wiki/Moral_letters_to_Lucilius/Letter_60.

41 Kraybill, *Apocalypse and Allegiance*, 63.

42 Ibid., 148.

43 Ibid., 147.

44 Ibid., 37.

45 Ibid., 147.

46 Justo L. Gonzalez, 'Revelation: Clarity and Ambivalence, a Hispanic/Cuban American Perspective', in *From Every People and Nation: The Book of Revelation in Intercultural Perspective*, ed. David M. Rhoads (Minneapolis: Fortress, 2005), 57.

47 Bauckham, *Theology of the Book of Revelation*, 160.

48 Kraybill, *Apocalypse and Allegiance*, 177.

49 Ibid., 154.

50 Brian K. Blount, 'Reading Revelation Today: Witness as Active Resistance', *Interpretation* 54, no. 4 (2000): 408.

51 Wes Howard-Brook and Anthony Gwyther, *Unveiling Empire: Reading Revelation Then and Now* (Maryknoll: Orbis Books, 1999), 255.

52 David C. Korten, *When Corporations Rule the World* (San Francisco: Berrett-Koehler Publishers, 1995), 69–70.

53 Howard-Brook and Gwyther, *Unveiling Empire*, 238–42.

54 https://baptistworldaid.org.au/resources/2019-ethical-fashion-guide/.

55 Mackay, 'State of the Nation'.

56 Johnson, *Discipleship on the Edge*, 304.

57 Bauckham, *Theology of the Book of Revelation*, 49.

58 Barbara R. Rossing, 'Rapture in Reverse: Reading Revelation Ecologically, for the Love of Creation', in *From Every People and Nation: Revelation in Intercultural Perspective*, ed. David Rhoads (Minneapolis: Fortress, 2005), 170.

59 Ibid., 166.

60 Hal Lindsey and C. C. Carlson, *The Late Great Planet Earth* (Grand Rapids, MI: Zondervan, 1970).

61 T. LaHaye and J. B. Jenkins, *Left Behind: A Novel of the Earth's Last Days* (Carol Stream: Tyndale, 2011).

62 Craig S. Keener, 'Revelation 11:18', in *The IVP Bible Background Commentary: New Testament* (Downers Grove, IL: InterVarsity Press, 1993).

63 William F. Arndt, Frederick W. Danker and Walter Bauer, *A Greek-English Lexicon of the New Testament and Other Early Christian Literature*, 3rd ed. (Chicago: University of Chicago Press, 2000), 734.

64 Rossing, 'Rapture in Reverse', 175.

65 Ibid., 177.

66 Ibid., 178.

67 I hope I have convinced you that Revelation is a strongly political document, even though it does not advocate outright rebellion. Preachers may be reluctant to enter the political dialogue for fear of offending some of the congregation. But is this really a legitimate excuse for not preaching what Revelation seems to critique about exploitation?

68 Graham Paulson, 'Towards an Aboriginal Theology', *Pacifica* 19, no. 3 (2006): 311.

69 David Stevens, *God's New Humanity: Biblical Theology of Multiethnicity for the Church* (Eugene, OR: Wipf & Stock, 2012), 95–119.

70 Johnson, *Discipleship on the Edge*, 374.

71 Tacitus, *Annals*, 13.32

72 Gonzalez, 'Revelation: Clarity and Ambivalence', 58.

73 Although the painful experiences of Australia's First Nations people during colonisation should be frankly acknowledged at this point.

74 Stevens, *God's New Humanity*, 220.

75 G. K. Beale, 'Revelation (Book)', in *New Dictionary of Biblical Theology*, ed. T. Desmond Alexander and Brian S. Rosner (Downers Grove, IL: InterVarsity Press, 2000), 361.

76 Johnson, *Discipleship on the Edge*, 237.

77 Adam Brereton, 'Anzac Day as Australian Religion: Can a Bloody Defeat Every Really be Sacred?' 25 April 2015, https://www.theguardian.com/news/2015/apr/25/anzac-day-as-australian-religion-can-a-bloody-defeat-ever-really-be-sacred. For a discussion of how Anzac Day has historically been interpreted by Australians see: Carolyn Holbrook, 'Anzac Day: How it Came to Occupy a Sacred Place in Australians' Hearts', 25 April 2017,

http://www.abc.net.au/news/2017-04-25/how-anzac-day-came-to-occupy-sacred-place-in-australias-heart/8470002.

78 Gorman, *Reading Revelation Responsibly*, 180.

79 Ibid., 134.

80 From John's Malyon College lecture notes on Contemporary Preaching.

81 Graves, *Sermon as Symphony*, 243–45.

82 Kraybill, *Apocalypse and Allegiance*, 186.

83 Robert Colville, 'Facebook, Apple, Microsoft, Alphabet and Hammers on Have Taken over the World and It's Time We Stood up to Them', *The Sun*, 27 October 2017, https://www.thesun.co.uk/news/4708220/facebook-apple-microsoft-alphabet-and-amazon-have-taken-over-the-world-and-its-time-we-stood-up-to-them/.

84 Ibid.

85 Ibid.

www.ingramcontent.com/pod-product-compliance
Lightning Source LLC
Chambersburg PA
CBHW060418010526
44118CB00017B/2266